GEORGETOWN UNIVERSITY ROUND TABLE ON LANGUAGES AND LINGUISTICS 1999

Language in Our Time: Bilingual Education and Official English, Ebonics and Standard English, Immigration and the Unz Initiative

James E. Alatis and Ai-Hui Tan, *Editors*

Georgetown University Press/Washington, D.C.

Georgetown University Press, Washington, D.C.
© 2001 by Georgetown University Press. All rights reserved.
Printed in the United States of America

10   9   8   7   6   5   4   3   2   1   2001

This volume is printed on acid-free offset book paper.

Library of Congress Catalog Number
ISBN 0-87840-132-6
ISSN 0186-7207

IN MEMORY OF
REVEREND RICHARD J. O'BRIEN, S.J.
1922–1999

Contents

James E. Alatis, *Georgetown University*
Introduction to the volume   1

David L. Red, *Foreign Service Institute, U.S. Department of State*
Adults learning to read in a second script: What we've learned   2

Margaret E. Malone, *Peace Corps—Washington, D.C.*
Trends in Peace Corps volunteer language proficiency   19

Pardee Lowe, Jr., *National Cryptologic School*
Evidence for the greater ease of use of the ILR language skill level
descriptions for speaking   24

Madeline Ehrman, *Foreign Service Institute, U.S. Department of State*
Bringing learning strategies to the student: The FSI language learning
consultation service   41

Beth A. Mackey, *Department of Defense*
Can you beat guessing in multiple-choice testing?   59

Frederick H. Jackson and Marsha A. Kaplan,
Foreign Service Institute, U.S. Department of State
Lessons learned from fifty years of theory and practice in government
language teaching   71

James R. Child, *National Security Agency, Department of Defense*
Analysis of texts and critique of judgment   88

Roger W. Shuy, *Georgetown University*
Paved with good intentions: Words of advice for the rocky road of
bureaucratic language   98

Stephen D. Krashen, *University of Southern California*
Bilingual education: Arguments for and (bogus) arguments against   111

Rosalie Pedalino Porter, *Institute for Research in English
Acquisition and Development (READ)*
Educating English language learners in U.S. schools: Agenda for a new
millennium   128

Eric J. Stone, *U.S. ENGLISH Foundation*
The Official English movement and bilingual education reform 139

Anna Uhl Chamot, *The George Washington University*
Literacy development in high school English language learners 149

Bernard Spolsky, *Bar-Ilan University*
Languages in Israel: Policy, practice, and ideology 164

Donna Christian, *Center for Applied Linguistics*
Language and policy issues in the education of immigrant students 175

Colleen Cotter, *Georgetown University*
The pragmatic implications of "boilerplate" in news coverage of
California ballot initiative controversies 187

Leanne Hinton, *University of California at Berkeley*
Involuntary language loss among immigrants: Asian-American
linguistic autobiographies 203

Salikoko S. Mufwene, *University of Chicago*
Ebonics and standard English in the classroom: Some issues 253

Ralph W. Fasold, *Georgetown University*
Ebonic need not be English 262

Denise E. Murray, *Macquarie University*
Whose "standard"? What the Ebonics debate tells us about language,
power, and pedagogy 281

Walt Wolfram, *North Carolina State University*
From definition to policy: The ideological struggle of
African-American English 292

Shaligram Shukla, *Georgetown University*
South Asian bilingualism: Hindi and Bhojpuri 314

John A. Rassias, *Dartmouth College*
Gods, demi-gods, heroes, anti-heroes, fallen angels, and fallen arches 323

G. Richard Tucker, *Carnegie Mellon University*
A global perspective on bilingualism and bilingual education 332

Anne Pakir, *National University of Singapore*
Bilingual education with English as an official language:
Sociocultural implications 341

Reinhold Freudenstein, *Philipps-Universität, Marburg*
Bilingualism, language policy, and the European Union 350

Wendy D. Bokhorst-Heng, *American University*
Bilingual education and the dialectics of national integration 356

Edwin Thumboo, *National University of Singapore*
The sweet breath of words: Language as nuance in Diaspora creativity 371

Roger Bowers, *The World of Language, London*
What in the world is the World of Language? 389

Tom McArthur, *English Today, Cambridge University Press*
World or International or Global English—and what is it anyway? 396

Ronald Scollon, *Georgetown University*
Multilingualism and intellectual property: Visual holophrastic discourse
and the commodity/sign 404

Roger W. Shuy, *Georgetown University*
The removal of Arturo: An immigration case nightmare 418

Introduction to the volume

James E. Alatis
Chair, GURT '99

This volume contains the published versions of papers from the 1999 Georgetown University Round Table on Languages and Linguistics, also known as the Round Table, or GURT, for short. The theme of the 1999 conference was "Language in Our Time: Bilingual Education and Official English, Ebonics and Standard English, Immigration and the Unz Initiative."

The year 1999 marked the return of the Round Table after a two-year hiatus, in time for its fiftieth anniversary celebration. Sponsored by Georgetown University's Center for International Language Programs and Research, GURT '99 followed tradition by bringing together college and university professors, program administrators, researchers, government professional staff, elementary- and secondary-school teachers, authors, and students of languages and linguistics. Scholars and students from the United States and other countries—among them, Germany, Israel, Singapore, and the United Kingdom—met for days of listening, discussing, and learning from each other.

The conference was opened by the chair, Dr. James E. Alatis, the evening of Thursday, May 6, 1999, with a plenary panel featuring Stephen Krashen of the University of Southern California, Delia Pompa of the U.S. Department of Education, Rosalie Pedalino Porter of the Institute for Research in English Acquisition and Development, and Eric Stone of the U.S. English Foundation.

The rest of the conference featured twenty-four speakers over a two-day period. Preconference events included a full-day program by members of the federal Interagency Language Roundtable (ILR) and the Society of Federal Linguists on the following themes: "Lessons learned from a half-century of language learning, teaching, and testing in the U.S. government" and "The present cutting edge in U.S. government language programs." There were also two concurrent tutorial sessions. One by John Rassias of Dartmouth College introduced the methodology of the Dartmouth Method to second-language learning and teaching. The other, by Stephen Krashen, presented an overview of Dr. Krashen's GURT presentations since 1989.

Selected papers from Round Table 1999 are presented in this volume.

Adults learning to read in a second script: What we've learned

David L. Red
Foreign Service Institute, U.S. Department of State

Introduction. What happens when people learn a new language written in a new script? What can educators do to make the process more efficient and rewarding for students? Why does anecdotal evidence suggest that learning to read a language written in a new script is such a hard process? Research in reading both first and second languages (L1 and L2) has concentrated on other areas, such as comprehension and strategy instruction, and has not addressed the basic issues of acquiring new scripts. As a result, the field lacks solid information on which to base pedagogy.

At the Foreign Service Institute, we have been teaching languages in non-Roman writing systems to native English speakers for many years. Recently, we have been making concerted efforts to investigate the process by which adults learn to read languages written in these scripts and how students continue to make progress in reading these languages. This paper summarizes research literature pertinent to the acquisition of new writing systems, and presents findings from action research that I have conducted at the Foreign Service Institute. I address the pedagogical implications of the research and make suggestions for future research.

I am referring only to learning to read in alphabetic writing systems in this paper. I do not discuss reading in logographic writing systems such as Japanese Kanji or Chinese, except when reviewing published literature that refers to these writing systems.

The reading process. We know that reading is a complex process involving a number of components (Adams 1994; Juel 1991; Perfetti and Marron 1995). Grabe (1991) identified six major components as (1) automatic recognition skills, (2) vocabulary and structure knowledge, (3) formal discourse structure knowledge, (4) content and world background knowledge, (5) synthesis and evaluation skills and strategies, and (6) metacognitive knowledge and skills monitoring. These components are interactive; that is, they are thought to occur simultaneously and to support each other. The first two, automatic recognition skills and vocabulary and structure knowledge, are generally considered bottom-up, data-driven processes that are dependent on the text for activation. The other four are top-down, context-driven processes inherent in the reader and applied to comprehension of the text.

Automatic recognition skills refer particularly to feature, letter, and word level recognition (Samuels 1994; Stanovich 1991). At these levels, "automaticity may be defined as occurring when the reader is unaware of the process, not consciously controlling the process, and using little processing capacity" (Grabe 1991: 379–380). The automaticity of the process results in freeing of processing capacity in the working memory, and the freed processing capacity that is then applied to global comprehension is essential for fluent reading (Daneman 1991).

Children achieve automatic recognition skills by learning to identify words in stages (Ehri 1994). The first is the logographic stage, in which children can identify letters and words that occur in the environment, such as "McDonald's" or "Coca-Cola," or the "m" in the word "camel" because it resembles a hump. At this stage, they base their recognition on only a small portion of the visual array. They then progress to the alphabetic stage, where they gradually become able to phonologically recode, that is, to convert the visually based representation into its corresponding phonological code (Daneman 1991). After converting the visual representation into the phonological code, the children can then determine the meaning of the word based on their knowledge of the spoken language. Children achieve full automaticity in the orthographic stage, which is characterized by the ability to instantly analyze words into orthographic units without converting the words phonologically. The phonological information is accessed along with the visual representation and is available to the reader; but fluent readers normally access the word in its holistic form and not in its constituent, phonological parts (Samuels 1994). This instant analysis of the word is referred to as word recognition, in which readers encode the visual pattern of a printed word and access its meaning in their mental dictionary or lexicon (Daneman 1991). Stanovich (1991) suggested that word recognition in fluent readers is an automatic skill occurring as a modular process. Modular processes are encapsulated; that is, they occur rapidly and without attention and are not influenced by prior knowledge structures stored in long-term memory. In short, encapsulation allows readers to know a word independent of context. Indeed, when readers need to use context to comprehend a word, they are using a compensatory mechanism that necessarily results in more attention being focused on the word and not on determining the global meaning of the text (Stanovich 1980, 1991).

Kintsch (1994) proposed a model of fluent reading, the construction–integration model, which includes automatic recognition skills as a critical component. After initial automatic word recognition, several other processes come into play. At the sentence level, readers must extract the underlying propositions, the basic units of meaning that describe a state or action, and the participants of that state or action (Kintsch 1994; Daneman 1991). From the knowledge acquired from the merging of the extracted information and the general knowledge of the reader, readers then construct a text base. This text base is tentative, fragile, and subject to change, based upon further integrating the information into a coherent whole (Kintsch 1994). That is, readers constantly weigh the locally extracted information in light of their general comprehension of the text as a whole, and integrate the new information they have constructed into a more confident and solid rendering of the text. Working memory, where information is temporarily stored, is where this construction and integration takes place (Daneman 1991). Less skilled readers demonstrate smaller working memory capacities because they are presumably devoting so much attention to word and proposition-level reading that they are not easily able to integrate that information with previously read text. Furthermore, they often are not aware of inconsistencies in their representation of the text because of this inability to devote attention to this higher-level text integration (Daneman 1991). Poor readers "have problems interrelating successive topics and integrating information to derive the overall gist or main theme of a passage" (Daneman 1991: 526–527). Skilled readers, on the other hand, have larger functional memory capacities, most likely because of their encapsulated automatic word recognition skills. They are able to concentrate their attention on integrating the easily constructed basic units, and subsequently are able to achieve an overall interpretation of a text (Kintsch 1994).

Reading in a second language. Reading in a second language involves both language and reading skills. Two hypotheses have been advanced to explain the interaction of these two skills (Bernhardt and Kamil 1995: 17). The *linguistic threshold hypothesis* suggests that "in order to read a second language, a level of second language linguistic ability must first be achieved." The *linguistic interdependence hypothesis* states that "reading performance in a second language is largely shared with reading ability in a first language."

Both of these hypotheses are appealing as explanations for understanding reading ability in an L2, but neither is completely explanatory. Indeed, Bernhardt and Kamil (1995) found that even after combining both explanations for reading skill, 35 to 50 percent of the variance in L2 reading was left unexplained. Second language reading is ultimately "a process that requires some unique reading capacities and lexical and grammatical flexibility" (Bernhard and Kamil 1995: 31). The unique reading capacities clearly would encompass the skills necessary for reading in non-Roman scripts.

Research findings in L2 reading. Second language readers bring several types of knowledge to the reading process. As adults, they often have extensive background knowledge, or schemata, for comprehending the text, and well-developed strategies for processing text (Carrell and Eisterhold 1988; Wenden and Rubin 1987). What the new readers lack is knowledge of the language. And this deficiency in language obviously affects the lower-level processes of reading, which are so closely tied to language comprehension abilities (Eskey 1988).

Automatic word recognition processes are very difficult for new readers in an L2 to achieve. Indeed, researchers have found that inefficient word recognition processes can hamper the reading of even advanced readers of an L2 (Segalowitz, Poulsen, and Komoda 1991). For example, French-English bilinguals demonstrated comparatively slow reading skills when reading in their less dominant language. Another study found that native English readers could read a social science text in English in twenty minutes, but native Hebrew students in the same college class took from one to two hours to complete the same text (Cohen et al. 1988). Although the researchers did not draw the conclusion that script differences may have been responsible for the differences in processing in this study, it seems reasonable to suspect that they could have been a factor.

A reader's awareness of the form class of a word has been shown to be a predictor of reading abilities in English as an L2 (Guarino and Perkins 1986). Readers who demonstrate an awareness of the root meanings of words encountered and sensitivity to the grammatical function of morphemes and the placement of the word within the phrase or sentence read more accurately than readers who lack this awareness.

Beyond words and phrases, L2 readers also differ in overall comprehension. In one study, college nonnative and native readers of the same English text recalled equal numbers of high-level or macrostructure ideas of a text but differed significantly in their ability to recall subordinate propositions (Connor 1984). The native English speakers recalled a larger number of these subordinate propositions and included elaborative details in their recall. The nonnative readers mentioned the main ideas but supplied minimal elaboration.

Readers of different scripts. Only a very few studies of L2 reading have focused on issues of script differences, although several studies have included subjects whose native language was not written in Roman script and who were reading English as an L2. Recently, studies have been conducted that take differences in scripts as a point of departure.

One of the first studies to focus on readers of different scripts investigated two college levels of native readers of Chinese reading English (Haynes and Carr 1990). The study found that even though the Chinese were students who had read many of their texts in English, their mastery of the English writing system was not complete. The problems the students demonstrated were not at the letter level, however. At the grapheme level they read with the same facility as native readers of English. The Chinese readers differed from native readers at the word level. For example, they were unable to profit from predictable sequencing of letters. The problems they had at the word level affected their reading speed, their overall comprehension, and their ability to learn new words from context. The more experienced Chinese readers were superior in new word learning from reading, suggesting that reading more in the L2 does ultimately have its rewards.

The researchers concluded that speed of reading eluded the Chinese readers more than either comprehension or skill at inferring word meanings from context. They added that word learning may depend on both accuracy and speed of reading. These researchers also observed a relationship between the subjects' general knowledge of English as a spoken medium of communication and their skill in reading English. One of the significant conclusions from this work is that "writing-system knowledge continues to exert an impact on reading outcomes beyond the early stages of language learning in general and beyond the early stages of exposure to any given text, particularly in situations like that of new word learning in which effective discrimination among potentially confusable word forms is essential" (Haynes and Carr 1990: 413).

Other studies have looked at the transfer of reading skills across orthographies (Chikamatsu 1996; Horiba 1996; Koda 1990, 1992). Using a construct of a continuum from shallow to deep orthographies, these researchers have compared native readers of different orthographies reading different scripts. Shallow orthographies are those that are highly recodable, having a high correspondence between sound and symbol. Examples are Serbo-Croatian, Japanese Kana (syllabaries), and Hindi and Nepali. Deep orthographies are those like Chinese or Japanese Kanji, where the relationship of sound to symbol is not easily discerned. English and several other languages, such as Arabic, Hebrew, and Thai, lie between the two extremes. Japanese and Chinese readers are assumed to rely more on visual access to process words because in reading their native language they first access meaning visually, then phonologically. These readers employ these visual processing strategies when reading English. Conversely, native readers of English reading Chinese and Japanese Kanji demonstrate a reliance on the phonological recoding inherent to English even when an initial visual strategy would have been more appropriate (Chikamatsu 1996; Koda 1990, 1992).

In think-aloud protocols of Japanese and American students reading stories in their nonnative languages, subjects made comments more frequently on lower-level processes and less frequently on higher-level processes, whereas while reading in their native language the subjects did the reverse (Horiba 1996). Specifically, the L2 readers commented on grapheme, word, and sentence phenomena, while L1 readers elaborated on the basic factual information in the text that they had clearly understood. On rereading the same texts, the L2 readers paid more attention to larger linguistic units and elaborated more. Overall, "L2 readers were not sensitive to how the ideas in the sentence were related to the prior text; they did not generate backward inferences according to the causal structure of the text" (Horiba 1996: 449–450).

Evidence from interviews with nonnative readers of Nepali supports the results of the empirical studies cited above (Abadzi 1994). These readers of Nepali as an L2 suggested that their reading got off to a brisk start, but soon reached a plateau beyond which they could not progress. They also said they had limited ability to recognize patterns of spelling and letter combinations in words. They read at a low speed and had difficulty consolidating the material they were reading. These readers had high error rates in what they read, and were overly dependent on context to make sense of words. They also found they had to sound words in order to read them. They frequently segmented words incorrectly across morphemes. Likewise, they had difficulty recognizing letters they knew when they encountered nonstandard writing or printing styles. In short, these readers found themselves in a perpetual beginning stage, even though they were advanced speakers of Nepali.

Investigations at FSI. For several years, I have been conducting informal observations and action-research projects with students of Hindi and Nepali. Both languages are written in the same script, Devanagari, which has close sound to symbol correspondence. My formal efforts have been as a teacher of Hindi to beginning (Red 1995) and intermediate students (Red 1997), and as a teacher of Hindi and Nepali to intermediate students as described in an unpublished study. As a teacher of new students, I taught two adult students two hours a day for four days a week. One student took class for sixteen weeks, and the other for twenty-three. I kept notes on my teaching and conducted interviews with the students on several occasions. I compiled the observations from this class into a report (Red 1995).

On another occasion, I worked with two students of Hindi reading authentic texts once a week for one to two hours (Red 1997), using the following methodology:

(1) Student read passage aloud in Hindi.
(2) Student gave meaning of entire passage in English, with no comment from me.
(3) Student read passage silently as long as needed.
(4) Student added to initial report in English, again with no comment from me.
(5) I provided student with vocabulary gloss and had him or her read passage silently as long as he or she felt necessary.
(6) Student read sentence by sentence aloud in Hindi and gave meaning in English. I explicated the grammar, vocabulary, syntax, and morphology as much as needed to help the student to understand the text. I also helped with pronunciation and phrasing, if necessary.
(7) Student read entire passage aloud in Hindi.

I chose this methodology because I wanted to determine how efficiently the students would read new text material, and what they would understand with several readings. The first reading of the text aloud gave me an understanding of their general comprehension as demonstrated by their control of the letters, words, phrases, and sentences. The second reading of the text indicated to me whether the students were able to understand more with a second, silent reading. The third reading with a vocabulary list allowed me to learn how much of their comprehension difficulty was based on vocabulary and how much was based on lack of understanding of syntax and other linguistic features.

I had the students read sentence by sentence aloud for two reasons. First, I wanted to determine if after interacting with the text several times, they would demonstrate a greater understanding of the grouping of letters, syllables, and words in their oral reading. Second, I wanted to determine if they were able to understand the microstructure, or lower-level ideas, of the text.

The final oral reading was to determine whether, after several interactions with the text and discussion about meaning, syntax, and word forms, the students would demonstrate their better understanding by reading aloud more expressively.

An unpublished study I conducted with Hindi and Nepali students investigated the types of interactions I had to perform as a teacher to help the students read a text. By tape-recording the sessions, I was able to analyze the frequency with which I performed different types of interactions. Overwhelmingly my comments to the students were focused on vocabulary and correct assignment of meaning, including identifying letters correctly, correcting misreading of words, and correcting misunderstandings about the part of speech of a word. Approximately half of my interventions were at the word level. My next most common intervention was helping them to understand the grammatical form of a sentence and to provide them with a translation when they were unable to fully comprehend the manner in which the elements combined to convey meaning.

Observations about learning new scripts. Based on my review of the research literature and my own research efforts, I have formed ideas and hypotheses about learning to read in new writing systems. These observations are in the categories of general issues, word-related issues, reading-aloud issues, and overall-comprehension issues.

General issues. I propose five general issues for new readers of different scripts. They are:

(1) The issue is not the script itself; instead, it is the automatized recognition of letters and words. Learning to read a new alphabetic system is a task that most learners can accomplish quickly. The problems arise after the recognition of new letters has been accomplished, because the recognition of the letters takes a long time to become automatized (if it occurs at

all). Also, combining the letter recognition into word recognition is a laborious task because most words encountered are new to the students.

(2) Training in reading should take place with actual reading texts, and interventions should be appropriate for the student. Strategy instruction in general will not be effective if the students are not applying the strategies to the actual texts they are required to read. Intervention should be based on the need of the student at the time to ensure that they learn the most from the intervention. I have observed that students can become quite proficient in reading nonauthentic texts—those created for classroom use—but then can have immense difficulty with authentic texts—for example, newspaper articles from a given country. The language and forms are so different in authentic texts that students must learn appropriate strategies for comprehending those texts, even when they have developed sophisticated strategies for comprehending the nonauthentic classroom-generated texts. This observation does not negate the need for practice with nonauthentic texts. I believe such texts are necessary for building skills. But in order to process authentic texts, students must receive explicit instruction in how to read them.

(3) Students improve over months of training, but remain at a low level of reading proficiency compared to their native language ability. Reading in a second script remains laborious throughout the initial year of training (and likely beyond). The skills that students have in skimming and scanning their native language are rarely achieved in the new writing system. The difficulty of reading encourages them to make guesses about the overall content of text, but they lack the skills to easily check for the accuracy of their guesses.

(4) Students exhibit small working memory capacity, having to reread text multiple times to form a complete idea of the text. The demands of reading in a second script take their toll on the working memory. In order to construct a text base and integrate it as one reads along, the reader must make multiple attempts to read the same text.

(5) People do not benefit from shallow orthographies, that is, from predictable sound-symbol correspondences. The shallowness of Hindi and Nepali orthography has not proven to be of great help to students because they still do not attend to each letter and the especially important endings on words. Even though with appropriate time they should be able to sound out letters and thus pronounce words, observation suggests that they do not always manage to do this.

Word-related issues. Students appear to have the most trouble reading at the word level. Among their problems with words are the following:

(1) In writing systems that lack capital letters, students sometimes misidentify proper nouns and other word forms. Students lack the knowledge of the meaning of words and must use context and other clues to learn the meaning. Their incomplete knowledge of syntax and vocabulary on one level, and lack of cultural background knowledge on the other combine to make word identification very difficult. Their random guessing of the meaning of words, or admittance that they have no idea about the word illustrates the difficulties they face in trying to become fluent readers of the language. Students are very sensitive to typeface changes, often misreading words and numbers they know in other typefaces. With increasing use of computer typefaces, students face numerous stylistic differences in presentation of letters and numbers. Their incomplete knowledge of the writing system is revealed in their inability to recognize all forms of letters and numbers, and their consequential lack of automaticity at even the feature and letter level.

(2) Lack of vocabulary knowledge hampers students throughout their training period. Students certainly acquire vocabulary during their training periods of up to ten months at FSI. The preponderance of vocabulary used in the press, however, continues to stymie students, resulting in reading being difficult throughout training. One of the features of most languages written in non-Roman scripts is that they are very foreign to English, and practically every word in the language must be learned. Almost no cognates and only a few English borrowings combine to make learning vocabulary a major part of learning the new language.

(3) Students find it very hard to learn vocabulary from reading and need to receive glosses primarily in English. Students encounter several new words in each sentence or paragraph of authentic texts. The number of new words requiring attention does not allow students to use other clues in the text to understand the words. Even presenting the students with simple definitions in the target language has proven to be of limited use. Translating words into English has been the most effective means to provide students with enough knowledge to continue reading texts.

(4) Throughout their training time, students read word-by-word upon their first contact with text. The act of reading aloud has shown me that students still struggle with text when they first encounter it. They are dealing with the individual words and their elements and are not able to read in word groups using natural phrasing. This reading style is evidence that they are not yet able to comprehend text easily on the first encounter.

(5) Students often misread longer, unfamiliar words. They appear to access the first letters of a word and for the sake of utility neglect to read the full word. Evidence of this comes from their misidentification of a number

of words when reading aloud. This phenomenon suggests that students' working memories are overtaxed and they are compensating by reading a minimum of text to gain understanding.

(6) Students have trouble with affixes and syllabification due to lack of knowledge of word formation. They certainly appear to lack information about word formation in the two languages I have studied. From their reading aloud, I have learned that they have trouble recognizing prefixes or suffixes appended to roots, and thus do not break words down into their constituent parts. As a result, students complicate the process of learning words by trying to remember each word they encounter as a discrete unit, rather than as a member of a family of words.

Reading aloud. The practice of reading aloud is not currently advocated in teaching reading to adults, yet I have observed benefits of this practice. Having students read has alerted me to their understanding of grammatical constructions, affixes, and syllabification. As mentioned in the previous section, students often misread word endings and parse words incorrectly in their first encounter with text. They also indicate by reading word by word that they are not able to group words together in natural phrasing. By correcting them as they read, I have been able to alert them to problems and provide them with knowledge they can apply to subsequent readings. I want to caution here that I am endorsing reading aloud once the students have some fundamental knowledge of the writing system and the language. In addition, the texts they read aloud have to be at least partially accessible to them. Otherwise the practice is merely testing decoding without achieving any meaningful purpose. Obviously, in logographic scripts where sound-symbol correspondence is minimal at best the time for reading aloud by students will be at a much more advanced stage.

Students benefit from being read aloud to by a teacher because it informs them of natural phrasing and pausing and forces their eyes to move across the page at natural speed. Understanding of texts appears to be aided by the teacher reading aloud. Because at the Foreign Service Institute students are learning the spoken language in separate classes, and their spoken language is superior to their reading, hearing texts read aloud enhances their understanding.

Overall comprehension. Students demonstrate an increasing ability to give an overall gist of a text in the latter stages of their training, but not without large gaps due to lack of vocabulary knowledge and lack of understanding of grammatical constructions. When asked to give a summary of a text that they had read once, students have been able to give a more accurate summary of such texts as the training progressed. Frequently, however, they leave out major portions of the text in their reporting. They also misinterpret sections of the text they thought they had understood. In the latter case, the reports the students have given indicate that they were using their background knowledge to interpret the text and were not relying on every aspect of the actual text on the page for their information.

Relation between L1 and L2 reading theory and implications for instruction. In many instances, L1 reading theory is helpful in explaining L2 reading. Differences exist in some areas, primarily because L1 reading theory is based on initial acquisition of literacy by children, whereas those learning foreign languages at FSI are adults who are already fluent readers of their native language. Comparing similarities and differences between L1 and L2 reading acquisition can at least guide us in designing appropriate training for L2 readers.

Differences between L1 and L2 reading acquisition. A primary area of difference between L1 and L2 reading acquisition is in the area of emergent literacy (Purcell-Gates 1995). Emergent literacy is the term that describes a child's growing awareness of the meaning of print in the environment. Clearly, literate adults have gone through this stage and enter the learning of reading in an L2 already fully aware of the significance and use of print. Similarly, children go through a logographic phase of reading development. In this stage they recognize letters and words as much because of their shape and environment as the letters and words themselves. Adults do not demonstrate this stage much in the classroom other than mentioning early in training that they remember a letter because of its shape or distinguishing characteristics. Because adults already have developed the alphabetic principle from reading English, they enter into the alphabetic stage almost simultaneously to learning the letters. They differ substantially from children, however, in not reaching the orthographic stage that fluent readers acquire (at least not within the first year of training, and likely not after that). Thus interventions for new L2 readers should focus on building automatic recognition skills very early in their training and continue throughout.

Similarities between L1 and L2 reading acquisition. Similarities between L1 and L2 reading acquisition appear to exist, suggesting that interventions used for L1 readers also can be appropriate for L2 readers. Stanovich (1980) hypothesized that readers compensate for deficiencies in one part of the reading system by relying upon others, and the adult readers I have encountered display behaviors that suggest they were compensating. Specifically, they compensate for the lack of vocabulary and word recognition skills by over-relying on their background knowledge and other higher-level skills. The adult readers bring with them sophisticated cognitive and metacognitive skills and strategies and appear to rely upon these to compensate for their inability to decode the text. Another example of a compensatory strategy is when students neglect to read endings of words because in reading their L1 they access the word so quickly and completely that they do not need to devote attention to its parts. This strategy fails them in reading Hindi or Nepali because the strategy is dependent upon automatic word recognition. Focusing on this problem area should help students to recognize the necessity of paying attention to all the elements of a word.

At a more global comprehension level, the readers in my studies and in others have consistently assumed they have full knowledge of the content of the text, even when their reports suggest otherwise. In terms of Kintsch's model of reading, they were performing integration without having adequately constructed the more basic elements of text. In schema-theoretical terms, they were relying on their initial interpretation of the text and not heeding (or not understanding) information that contradicted their interpretation (Anderson et al. 1977). Focusing their attention on the linguistic elements in texts should help students rely less on top-down strategies and more on essential bottom-up ones.

When students read a text more than one time, especially after intervention by the teacher to aid comprehension, they demonstrate far more accurate comprehension. This phenomenon suggests that on their first reading the local context comprehension process overtaxes their working memory, and they are unable to direct their attention to overall comprehension. Only by successive rereading are they able to free their working memory to create a coherent representation of the text. This is the same process poor readers demonstrate in their L1. Encouraging rereading is an easy and effective intervention that students can practice throughout their training period.

In addition, students demonstrate little knowledge of syllable juncture and derivational knowledge, presumably because of their unfamiliarity with the language in general and word formation in particular. Native English readers show this same problem in early stages of reading for the same reasons. American students in school require four to five years of education to demonstrate a sufficient knowledge of syllable juncture and derivational knowledge. Students reading at the Foreign Service Institute usually cannot make significant progress toward acquiring this bank of knowledge in their less than one year of study. I know of no research that indicates how long it would take native readers of English to acquire this knowledge in languages written in non-Roman scripts. Teaching students explicitly about word formation throughout training could help them in this area.

In general, the problems that students face when reading languages written in non-Roman scripts appear to be located more at the construction phase, or lower-level processing phase of reading. Integration does not easily occur, but one can presume that if the students attained a sufficient knowledge of the language and vocabulary, they could use their sophisticated background knowledge and well-developed reading strategies to full advantage. Thus, Kintsch's reading model is especially appealing as a model for those working with students learning to read languages written in non-Roman scripts because it focuses on the necessity of word recognition and basic syntax connection to ensure integration of the text elements into a cohesive whole.

General pedagogical implications. Teachers should continue to foster solid reading practices in their students that focus on higher-level skills, such as predicting, schema activation, and monitoring of reading. Yet they should also give more attention to developing their students' lower-level skills. Exercises that focus students on letter, word, and basic syntax areas would greatly benefit their progress in overall reading.

At a very basic level, students should be provided with a print-rich environment. All the objects in a room can be labeled, so students are constantly associating written symbols with items in a meaningful context. Similarly, from the very beginning teachers should teach the writing system. They should also write all new words on the board, even before students can easily read them. Constant bombardment with print can help the students to become familiar with the written language more quickly.

Similarly, students should be encouraged to write from the very beginning of their training. At first, they should be encouraged to write down all their words in the script, rather than in transliteration as they often prefer to do. Later, they should begin writing lists, sentences, and notes in the language. As in L1 literacy acquisition, journal writing would be very helpful for new students to become immersed in the literate form of the language. Teachers could also encourage the students to create dialogue journals, in which teacher and student carry on conversations in writing.

Whatever exercises or activities are created for enhancing reading skills, they should be directly linked to actual reading material. Isolated exercises are often ineffective for preparing students to read texts. Ideally, the student would have a teacher who would work with the student on specific texts and when problems or examples arose, the teacher could address them at that moment. The intervention would be most memorable because it would be timely and necessary. The teacher could elaborate on points, draw comparisons with previously taught material, or encourage the student to use appropriate strategies. If the teacher is not able to provide the student with this kind of intervention because of class size, then the solution can be well-designed activities and exercises.

A special set of exercises should be developed to enforce automaticity as much as possible. One way to build this automaticity is to create readings that are simple and repetitive enough to free the working memory to work on overall comprehension. Creating written exercises that use only vocabulary and grammar that the student has encountered is one good way to ensure easy reading. Adults studying languages written in non-Roman scripts appreciate reading materials that are not peppered with new words, so creating simple texts can also boost their feeling of accomplishment. As the students increase in sophistication in the language, the teachers can create extensive exercises that prepare the students for reading authentic texts themselves.

Every writing system and language has specific features that students need to learn to recognize and utilize. Generic reading strategy instruction is useful, but cannot address each specific language. Consequently, special care must be given to providing the student with practice in attending to the special forms to which native readers attend while reading. Teachers should, therefore, create exercises that focus the students on the specific strategies that are helpful for reading the language. An example from Hindi would be to create exercises that forced the students to pay attention to word endings that indicate the relationship of the nouns to the verb. The verb in many types of Hindi sentences falls at the end of the sentence and indicates gender; it will usually agree with a noun in the sentence, whether the subject or the object, depending on the construction of the sentence. Frequently students ignore this crucial information because it is of little importance in English, and therefore do not recognize visual signals about the agent or patient of a sentence, thus missing the essential meaning of a sentence.

Furthermore, exercises should be developed that focus the reader on improving the speed at which they read. Here, too, specially created texts can be combined with appropriate exercises that force students to read with increasing speed. In the absence of special exercises, rereading can be a simple approach to building reading speed.

Further research. The need for further research on the question of how students learn to read languages written in non-Roman scripts is obvious. Perhaps the most pressing need is to disentangle the effects of orthography from the effects of language structure, that is, to separate word recognition from syntax and other linguistic knowledge. It may be that it is impossible to separate the two, but without research we can only guess. This research could help us better design materials that will strengthen students' abilities in both areas of knowledge.

At another level, it would be helpful to know how native readers of non-Roman script languages read their languages. This information would guide us in developing strategy training for our students because we could help them to attend to those features that native readers do.

The current trend toward more research on the brain and its functions could be potentially useful to our field. For example, we could learn if there are indeed patterns established in the brain for reading in different languages. We could also learn if biliterates are accessing different parts of the brain to accomplish the reading task. Brain research could help us to learn what we might change and enhance by intervention, and what would not benefit from intervention.

A pressing need is to find whether adults can achieve automaticity in reading in non-Roman scripts at all. Much language acquisition research has suggested that language learning that occurs after puberty does not result in native-like proficiency. It is not unreasonable to expect parallels for script acquisition; people may well attain a level of proficiency but may not be neurologically able to mimic native-like reading proficiency. Thus, more research on the process of adults acquiring a new writing system could help us learn the limits and possibilities for our students and guide our instruction. In a similar vein, conducting research on literacy acquisition of adults who have never attained literacy could provide insights into the process of adult script acquisition. Comparing the results of this research with research on literate adults acquiring a second writing system could inform us of basic issues in script acquisition.

Conclusion. The process by which students learn to read in a non-Roman script is becoming clearer to us. We know that students can quickly learn the script itself but have most problems at the word level. This difficulty at the word level appears to be a major factor in preventing students from attaining fluent reading in the new L2. For native English students, the large amount of new vocabulary encountered in languages written in non-Roman scripts means that many words encountered in reading are encountered relatively infrequently. Since frequency of exposure to a word is a determining factor in efficient word recognition, then we know that our students have a difficult task before them.

The research I have conducted is qualitative and limited to a very special population. I cannot predict how much of what I observed will be found in other populations. I therefore call upon members of the profession to conduct research and share their insights, so we can have a better picture of the reading acquisition process in languages written in non-Roman scripts. Research I have reviewed and conducted along with practice I have implemented in the classroom have suggested what types of intervention are effective in helping students to learn. We need to know much more. I hope that other practitioners and researchers will begin to work in this fascinating, but neglected area of reading.

REFERENCES

Abadzi, Helen. 1994. *What we know about acquisition of adult literacy: Is there hope?* World Bank Discussion Papers no. 245. World Bank: Washington, DC.

Adams, Marilyn Jager. 1994. Modeling the connections between word recognition and reading. In Robert B. Ruddell, Martha Rapp Ruddell, and Harry Singer (eds.), *Theoretical models and processes of reading,* 4th edition. Newark, DE: International Reading Association. 838–863.

Anderson, Richard C., Ralph E. Reynolds, Diane Lemonnier Schallert, and Ernest T. Goetz. 1977. Frameworks for comprehending discourse. *American Educational Research Journal* 14(4): 367–381.

Bernhardt, Elizabeth B., and Michael L. Kamil. 1995. Interpreting relationships between L1 and L2 reading: Consolidating the Linguistic Threshold and the Linguistic Interdependence hypotheses. *Applied Linguistics* 16(1): 15–34.

Carrell, Patricia L., and Joan C. Eisterhold. 1988. Schema theory and ESL reading pedagogy. In Patricia L. Carrell, Joanne Devine, and David E. Eskey (eds.), *Interactive approaches to second language reading*. Cambridge, UK: Cambridge University Press. 73–92.

Chikamatsu, Nobuko. 1996. The effects of L1 orthography on L2 word recognition. *Studies in Second Language Acquisition* 18(4): 403–432.

Cohen, Andrew, Hilary Glasman, Phyllis R. Rosenbaum-Cohen, Jonathon Ferrara, and Jonathon Fine. 1988. Reading English for specialized purposes: Discourse analysis and the use of student informants. In Patricia L. Carrell, Joanne Devine, and David E. Eskey (eds.), *Interactive approaches to second language reading*. Cambridge, UK: Cambridge University Press. 152–167.

Connor, Ulla. 1984. Recall of text: Differences between first and second language readers. *TESOL Quarterly* 18(2): 239–256.

Daneman, Meredyth. 1991. Individual differences in reading skills. In Rebecca Barr, Michael Kamil, Peter Mosenthal, and P. David Pearson (eds.), *Handbook of reading research*, vol. 2. New York: Longman. 512–538.

Ehri, Linnea C. 1994. Development of the ability to read words: Update. In Robert B. Ruddell, Martha Rapp Ruddell, and Harry Singer (eds.), *Theoretical models and processes of reading*, 4th edition. Newark, DE: International Reading Association. 323–358.

Eskey, David E. 1988. Holding in the bottom: An interactive approach to the language problems of second language readers. In Patricia L. Carrell, Joanne Devine, and David E. Eskey (eds.), *Interactive approaches to second language reading*. Cambridge, UK: Cambridge University Press. 93–100.

Grabe, William. 1991. Current developments in second language reading research. *TESOL Quarterly* 25(3): 375–406.

Guarino, Regina, and Kyle Perkins. 1986. Awareness of form class as a factor in ESL reading comprehension. *Language Learning* 36(1): 77–82.

Haynes, Margot, and Thomas H. Carr. 1990. Writing system background and second language reading: A component skills analysis of English reading by native speaker-readers of Chinese. In Thomas H. Carr and Betty Ann Levy (eds.), *Reading and its development: Component skills approaches*. San Diego: Academic Press. 375–421.

Horiba, Yukie. 1996. Comprehension processes in L2 reading. *Studies in Second Language Acquisition* 18(4): 433–473.

Juel, Connie. 1991. Beginning reading. In Rebecca Barr, Michael Kamil, Peter Mosenthal, and P. David Pearson (eds.), *Handbook of reading research*, vol. 2. White Plains: Longman. 759–788.

Kintsch, Walter. 1994. The role of knowledge in discourse comprehension: A construction–integration model. In Robert B. Ruddell, Martha Rapp Ruddell, and Harry Singer (eds.), *Theoretical models and processes of reading*, 4th edition. Newark, DE: International Reading Association. 951–995.

Koda, Keiko. 1990. The use of L1 reading strategies in L2 reading: Effects of orthographic structures on L2 phonological recoding strategies. *Studies in Second Language Acquisition* 12(4): 393–410.

Koda, Keiko. 1992. The effects of lower-level processing skills on FL reading performance: Implications for instruction. *The Modern Language Journal*, 76(4): 502–512.

Perfetti, Charles A., and Maureen A. Marron. 1995. *Learning to read: Literacy acquisition by children and adults*. Technical Report No. TR95-07. Philadelphia: National Center on Adult Literacy.

Purcell-Gates, Victoria. 1995. *Other people's words: The cycle of low literacy*. Cambridge: Harvard University Press.

Red, David L. 1995. Learning to read Hindi. In Vijay Gambhir (ed.), *The teaching and acquisition of South Asian languages*. Philadelphia: University of Pennsylvania Press. 97–107.

Red, David L. 1997. Entry into a new world: New readers in new scripts. Paper presented at TESOL convention, Orlando.

Samuels, S. Jay. 1994. Word recognition. In Robert B. Ruddell, Martha Rapp Ruddell, and Harry

Singer (eds.), *Theoretical models and processes of reading,* 4th edition. Newark, DE: International Reading Association. 359–380.

Segalowitz, Norman, Catherine Poulsen, and Melvin Komoda. 1991. Lower level components of reading skill in higher level bilinguals: Implications for reading instruction. *AILA Review* 8: 15–30.

Stanovich, Keith E. 1980. Toward an interactive-compensatory model of individual differences in the development of reading fluency. *Reading Research Quarterly* 16(1): 32–71.

Stanovich, Keith E. 1991. Word recognition: Changing perspectives. In Rebecca Barr, Michael Kamil, Peter Mosenthal, and P. David Pearson (eds.), *Handbook of reading research,* vol. 2. White Plains: Longman. 418–452.

Wenden, Anita, and Joan Rubin. 1987. *Learner strategies in language learning.* Englewood Cliffs, NJ: Prentice-Hall.

Trends in Peace Corps volunteer language proficiency

Margaret E. Malone
Peace Corps—Washington, D.C.

Background. The Peace Corps Act of 1981 stipulates that "[n]o person shall be assigned to duty as a Volunteer under this act in any foreign country unless at the time of such assignment the person possesses such reasonable proficiency as the assignment requires in speaking the language of the country or area to which the person is assigned" (Section 24). This paper investigates how "reasonable proficiency" in Peace Corps languages is measured via oral proficiency testing by examining trends in Peace Corps volunteer oral proficiency scores after preservice training and at the end of the two-year Peace Corps service.

The Peace Corps Language Testing Program supports language testing and training of language testers at Peace Corps posts worldwide. Each year, the program trains or retrains 80 to 120 language professionals (language teachers, language coordinators, and Peace Corps staff) to conduct the Peace Corps Language Proficiency Interview (PC LPI). The results of this interview demonstrate the oral proficiency attained by Peace Corps trainees and volunteers in more than sixty countries.

Program Description. From 1961 until 1969, the oral proficiency of Peace Corps trainees and volunteers was tested at close of preservice training by Foreign Service staff (or U.S.-based trainers), using the Language Proficiency Interview and rating according to the Interagency Language Roundtable (ILR) scale (Lowe 1988). During the 1960s, most language training took place in the United States. As the number of volunteers increased, and as training moved from sites in the United States to sites overseas, the Peace Corps recognized the need to internalize language testing systems (Rice 1982). Therefore, in 1969, a contract was awarded to Educational Testing Service (ETS) to manage training of testers at Peace Corps Training Centers overseas. ETS-trained testers at overseas and US-based training facilities and maintained a database of volunteer language scores.

In 1982, the provisional American Council on the Teaching of Foreign Languages (ACTFL) Guidelines were released. Unlike the ILR scale, the ACTFL Guidelines focused primarily on the lower levels of speaking proficiency. By the late 1980s, the ACTFL Guidelines were in wide use in academia. Because trends showed that few Peace Corps volunteers achieved the highest levels on language proficiency on the ILR scale, and because of the focus on the lower ends of the scale, Peace Corps elected to shift from the ILR scale to the ACTFL scale (Anderson 1993). From 1989 to 1990, ACTFL tester trainers conducted sixty-one workshops to retrain previously certified testers and train new testers to use the ACTFL Guidelines in testing Peace Corps volunteers.

In 1996, Peace Corps–Washington instituted the position of language testing specialist at headquarters to integrate language testing into the language training program. In doing so, Peace Corps–Washington has emphasized the importance of testing in providing feedback on the efficacy of language training.

Timeline for Testing. Though each post approaches language testing slightly differently, testing usually occurs at specific points during training and service. All posts that test language proficiency do so at the end of the eight- to twelve-week preservice training that prepares volunteers for their Peace Corps service. At some posts, volunteers are also tested after one year of service and at close of service.

Trends in Peace Corps Testing. This part of the paper explores three types of trends in Peace Corps testing: reporting test scores from posts to Peace Corps–Washington, trends in proficiency attainment in major Peace Corps languages, and trends in proficiency attainment according to language difficulty.

Reporting trends. Because the language-testing program was incorporated into Peace Corps–headquarters fewer than three years ago, not all posts report proficiency scores regularly. Some trends are evident in score reporting, however. In the less commonly taught languages such as Bulgarian, Macedonian, Turkmen, and so on, posts were far more likely to report preservice training scores than mid- and close-of-service scores. Conversely, the commonly taught languages such as French, Russian, and Spanish had the highest rate of close of service scores reported.

These trends may reflect Peace Corps volunteers' perceptions of possible benefits of testing for their post-service careers. In the less commonly taught languages, emphasis is placed on language proficiency for Peace Corps service, perhaps because volunteers perceive little use for the language outside of the country of service. By contrast, post-service uses for the more commonly taught languages (French, Russian, and Spanish) are emphasized. This emphasis encourages volunteers to participate in oral proficiency testing at close of service. In addition to practical implications for individual returned volunteers, this emphasis allows Peace Corps–headquarters to track language gains during service.

Trends in proficiency attainment: Major languages. Trends in proficiency attainment were explored in French, Russian, and Spanish by investigating 465 pre- and post-service proficiency scores. All scores were entered into a Microsoft Excel database and means were computed. Table 1 shows the means for proficiency attainment in the three major languages.

The trends in Table 1 show that most volunteers are able to attain an ACTFL proficiency level of intermediate-low or better in the three most commonly taught languages by the end of preservice training. Since the intermediate-low level is considered characteristic of survival ability, this is considered adequate for most Peace Corps volunteers. Table 1 also indicates that volunteers achieve even higher levels of proficiency during their two years of service and leave Peace Corps with an intermediate-high or advanced level of proficiency. Since the advanced level is considered necessary for "most workplace interactions" (ACTFL Guidelines 1986), these data demonstrate that most volunteers are able to communicate in workplace settings in French and Spanish. Volunteers show slightly lower mean scores in Russian.

The slight difference in mean scores between Russian and the two Romance languages suggests that it may be more difficult to acquire higher levels of Russian language proficiency than French and Spanish. The next part of the data analysis investigates global differences between language proficiency scores at different levels of language proficiency.

Trends in proficiency attainment: Language difficulty categories. In addition to examining the data by major language categories, proficiency scores were also grouped by language difficulty categories. The Defense Language Institute has classified a number of languages according to relative difficulty of acquisition of a specific language by native speakers of English. Each language is classified according to four categories, with category 1 languages considered the least difficult

Table 1. Mean Scores: Major Languages

Language	Preservice ACTFL Score	End of Service ACTFL Score
Spanish	Intermediate-low/mid	Advanced
French	N/a	Advanced
Russian	Intermediate-low	Intermediate-high

Note: Countries included for Spanish are Chile, Costa Rica, Dominican Republic, Ecuador, Paraguay, Uruguay; for French, Benin, Burkina Faso, and Niger; and for Russian, Moldova, Russia, and Ukraine.

for native speakers of English to learn and category 4, the most difficult. Table 2 shows the results of an analysis of mean proficiency scores by the DLI's language difficulty classifications.

Table 2 shows the differences in proficiency levels at the end of preservice training and at close of service represented by the four language difficulty categories. Predictably, the highest scores are achieved in category 1 languages. One interesting difference can be found between close of service scores in category 2 and 3 languages. Volunteers showed scores approximately one ACTFL sublevel lower in category 2 languages than in category 3 languages, when the reverse would be predicted.

There are two possible explanations for the discrepancy. One is that most volunteers being tested in category 2 languages were teaching English as a foreign language in their host countries. It is possible that, because the primary work assignment of these volunteers involved speaking English, they had less opportunity to achieve higher levels of proficiency in the local language. In addition,

Table 2. Proficiency Scores by Language Difficulty Category

Language Category	Preservice ACTFL Proficiency Score	End of Service ACTFL Proficiency Score
Grade 1 (French, Spanish) (N= 359)	Intermediate low/mid	Advanced
Grade 2 (Estonian, Bulgarian, Romanian) (N= 84)	Intermediate low	Intermediate mid
Grade 3 (Latvian, Lithuanian, Berber, Nepali, Polish, Russian) N= 363	Novice-high/ intermediate-low	Intermediate high
Grade 4 (Arabic) N= 64	Intermediate low/mid	Intermediate high

Note: Countries included for Spanish are Chile, Costa Rica, Dominican Republic, Ecuador, Paraguay, Uruguay; for French, Benin, Burkina Faso, and Niger; for Latvian, Latvia; Lithuanian, Lithuania; Berber, Morocco; Nepali, Nepal; Polish, Poland; Russian, Moldova, Russia, and Ukraine; Arabic, Morocco.

based on recent experience in testing trends at the Foreign Service Institute, some language specialists at the Department of State have suggested that Estonian and Bulgarian should be reclassified as category 3 languages.

Future directions. This paper has examined trends in oral proficiency attained by Peace Corps volunteers at the end of eight to twelve weeks of preservice language training and gains made by the close of service two years later. The data show that, by end of preservice training, volunteers are able to attain at least a survival level of language proficiency, even in languages categorized as most difficult for native speakers. The data also show that most volunteers are able to achieve higher levels of proficiency, often increasing their score by two or more ACTFL sublevels, by close of service. The data also suggest that additional encouragement should be given to posts to promote oral proficiency testing in all languages at close of service.

These data are the first to examine trends in oral proficiency attainment by Peace Corps volunteers. Future studies will examine more closely the relationship between volunteers' assignments, age, and previous language background in attainment of oral proficiency.

REFERENCES

American Council on the Teaching of Foreign Languages. 1982, 1986. *ACTFL proficiency guidelines.* Hastings-on-Hudson, NY: ACTFL.

Anderson, Neil. 1993. *Manual for classroom testing in Peace Corps second language courses.* Washington, DC: Peace Corps.

Lowe, P. 1988. The unassimilated history. In P. Lowe and C. W. Stansfield (eds)., *Second language proficiency assessment.* Engelwood Cliffs, NJ: Prentice-Hall Regents.

Rice, G. 1982. *Twenty years of Peace Corps.* Washington, DC: Government Printing Office.

Evidence for the greater ease of use of the ILR language skill level descriptions for speaking

Pardee Lowe, Jr.
National Cryptologic School[1]

Introduction. In this article I address possible reasons that the *U.S. Government's Interagency Language Roundtable's (ILR's) Language Skill Level Descriptions for Speaking* may be more readily usable than those for the other ILR skill modalities: Writing, Listening, and Reading. Three types of reasons are cited: historical, anecdotal, and empirical. The speaking descriptions,[2] both with and without its example sections, are compared to those for the other three ILR skill modalities; and the conclusion is drawn that strong reasons exist in support of the greater ease of use of the speaking descriptions. A similar study should be conducted for the related ACTFL/ETS guidelines, but that must await another article in part because the ACTFL/ETS descriptions are currently under revision for all four skill modalities.[3]

Why do the U.S. Government's Interagency Language Roundtable (ILR) Skill Level Descriptions for speaking seem more readily usable than those for the other ILR skill modalities? Besides greater frequency of use, there are historical, anecdotal, and empirical reasons that can be marshaled in explanation.

Historical reasons. In the mid-1950s, when the Foreign Service Institute (FSI) of the U.S. Department of State first devised what are now referred to as the *U.S. Government's ILR Language Skill Level Descriptions,* Speaking was the skill modality most in need of description and assessment. Academia lacked suitable approaches for describing and assessing Speaking, so it was the skill modality undertaken first and to which the most effort was devoted. The Speaking descriptions have probably been used more often than any of the others. They also have been revised more frequently and more completely than the other descriptions.

Anecdotal reasons. Anecdotally, users of the ILR skill level descriptions in more than one skill modality have often remarked to the author that Speaking is more readily usable. To pursue such comments more systematically we devised a questionnaire and administered it to thirty major users of the ILR descriptions (see figure 1 for the questionnaire and list 1 for the list of those surveyed).[4] Of the thirty persons responding, one did not compare any set to Speaking, marking Reading easiest to use, and three ranked writing easiest to use; twenty-three ranked Speaking easiest to use. Furthermore, two tied Speaking and Reading in ease of use, and one tied Speaking and Listening. To summarize, a majority of respondents, 77%, ranked Speaking easiest to use.

There appears to be a strong relationship between frequency of use and ease of use for any given set of ILR descriptions. Several respondents remarked that their rankings were influenced by the frequency with which they used the various sets and that greater frequency led to greater familiarity and usually to greater ease of use. Five made no comment on frequency of use at all. For the most used category, one listed Listening as the skill most used, while another cited Reading. Seventeen of the thirty respondents to the questionnaire reported Speaking as the set most used. Another five tied Speaking with another skill: three tied Speaking and Listening; one tied Speaking and Reading, and another Speaking and Writing. Finally, two tied Listening and Reading. Coupling the number who found Speaking most frequently used outright with the number who tied Speaking as the most frequently used with another skill amounted to twenty-two out of thirty, or 73%, which approaches the percentage cited for easiest to use, which is 77%. But it should be noted that those who marked Speaking as "easiest to use" were not always those who identified the Speaking definitions as the "most frequently used." Thus, for some respondents, Speaking's ease of use did not always result from frequency of use. From the questionnaire's answers we can see that it is possible to be more specific about the anecdotal reasons.[5] It would, however, be helpful to adduce evidence beyond the anecdotal and historical as to why the Speaking definitions might be easier to use.

Empirical evidence. Answers of an empirical nature to the question of why the Speaking definitions are more useful than the others grew in part out of research begun and described in the author's "Keeping the Optic Constant: A Framework of Principles for Writing & Specifying the AEI Definitions of Language Abilities" (Lowe 1998). That article presented the results of an empirical study of the statements in the Speaking definitions. To understand the results to be reported in this article on the comparison of the Speaking definitions to those of the other ILR skill modalities, certain features of that earlier article are recapitulated here. (For fuller details and a broader context, see the article itself.)

Some years ago, my colleagues and I noted that the definitions could be crafted from several different perspectives. Moreover, the perspectives could shift between and even within levels. Three perspectives emerged: a best case (BC), an average case (AC), and a worst case scenario (WC).[6] Level 0 in Speaking, for example, contains a worst case scenario—*Unable to function in the spoken language* (WC)—while Level 5 contains a best case example—*The individual uses*

Figure 1. Survey on the ease of use of the ILR language skill level descriptions.

NAME: _____   Date: _____

Take this survey if you use any two of the ILR Skill Level Descriptions, say Speaking & Reading. If you use other descriptions than those for Speaking, tell us how easy they are to use comparatively speaking.

SECTION A: EXAMPLES

4 = Most Easy to use down to
1 = Least Easy to use

Pardee Lowe, Jr.'s Rankings

SKILL	RANKING	COMMENTS ON FREQUENCY OF USE	POSSIBLE RESPONSES
Speaking	4	Used to use constantly	
Listening	1.5	Use sporadically	
Reading	3	Use constantly	4 = Most Easy to Use
Writing	1.5	Use rarely	

James R. Child's Rankings

SKILL	RANKING	COMMENTS ON FREQUENCY OF USE	POSSIBLE RESPONSES
Speaking	NA		3
Listening			2
Reading		3 Essential for our work	
Writing	UNDECIDED	4 Essential for our work	1 = Least Easy to Use

POSSIBLE RESPONSES:
Tied = -.5
Undecided
NA = Don't Use

SECTION B: YOUR RANKING:

Now mark the four skill modalities according to your own experience: Using 4 for most easy to use down to 1 for least easy to use, NA for descriptions not used at all, or if undecided, write UNDECIDED next to the skill modality to which that applies. If you find two sets of descriptions equally useful you may give them the same rating.

You rank the skills as:
4 = Most Easy to use down to
1 = Least Easy to use

SKILL	RANKING	COMMENTS ON FREQUENCY OF USE
Speaking		
Listening		
Reading		
Writing		

While my results will remain anonymous, I will allow my name to be printed as having participated in this survey: YES NO (Circle One)

YOUR TITLE: _____   INSTITUTION: _____

List of those surveyed

Sabine Atwell	OPI Trainer at DLI
Abdelfattaq Boussalhi	OPI Trainer, Arabic OPI Tester at DLI
Maria Brau	OPI Trainer at the FBI
Christine Campbell	Test Project Director at DLI
James R. Child	Senior Language Research Analyst DOD
John L.D. Clark	Former Dean of Program Evaluation, Research & Testing at DLI
Ray T. Clifford	Provost, Defense Language Institute Foreign Language Center DLI
Pat Dage	Tester Trainer DLI
Katrin Gardiner	Former Chief of Testing LTD
Helen Hamlyn	Administrator of all ACTFL OPI Tests
Martha Herzog	Dean, Evaluation and Standards DLI
Dariush Hooshmand	Former Director of Test & Standards Division at DLI
Monika Ihlenfeld	OPI Trainer & German OPI Tester at DLI
Frederick Jackson	Director of Research, Evaluation & Development FSI
Gordon Jackson	Tester Trainer & Researcher into Oral Proficiency Testing DLI
Steve Koppany	Coordinator of the DLI/NSA Diagnostic Project DLI
Pardee Lowe, Jr.	Chair, ILR Testing Committee, Former Chief of Testing LTD
Thomas Parry	Dean, Asian School 2, Former Chief of Testing LTD
Danielle Reulen	French OPI Tester ACTFL
Donald Smith	English and Russian OPI Trainer DLI
Andy Soh	DLPT Developer, Korean OPI Tester DLI
Stephen Soudakoff	English and Russian OPI Trainer DLI
Elvira Swender	Director of Professional Programs (includes OPI Testing & Training) ACTFL
John Thain	English OPI Tester DLI

Marijke Van Der Heide	OPI Trainer FBI
Phil White	English OPI Tester DLI
Protase Woodford	OPI Trainer for Peace Corps at ETS, Spanish OPI Tester ETS

Key:

ACTFL = American Council on the Teaching of Foreign Languages: Yonkers, NY

DLI = Defense Language Institute's Foreign Language Center: Monterey, CA

DOD = Department of Defense: Washington, DC

ETS = Educational Testing Service: Princeton, NJ

FBI = Federal Bureau of Investigation: Washington, DC

FSI = Foreign Service Institute of the Department of State: Arlington, VA

ILR = U.S. Government's Interagency Language Roundtable: Washington, DC

LTD = Language Training Division of the Central Intelligence Agency: Washington, DC

OPI = Oral Proficiency Interview

Note: Three respondents preferred anonymity. Their responses were most informative, however, and their data were included in the survey. Any person connected with ACTFL was queried only on the ease of use of the *ILR Language Skill Level Descriptions.*

the language with complete flexibility and intuition, so that speech on all levels is fully accepted by well-educated native speakers in all of its features, including the breadth of vocabulary and idiom, colloquialisms, and pertinent cultural references* (BC).

Level 0 also illustrates how more than one perspective can be contained in the description at the same level: *unable to function in the spoken language* (WC); *oral production is limited to occasional isolated words* (AC); *has essentially no communicative ability* (AC).

What, then, do these perspectives contribute to the utility of the definitions? The answer is that the non-AC statements furnish boundaries. When a BC statement abuts on the next higher range or a WC statement touches the range just below it, a boundary is created. This renders the definitions more readily usable, because there is now a clear delimitation of why range X differs from range Y. In the previous study it was shown in Speaking that boundaries are present at all but the level 3/3+ border (see table 1). We call this feature of the ILR skill level descriptions *boundedness*; that is, the extent to which one range is delimited from another.

Other skill modalities. In this study we looked at the distribution of BC, AC, and WC statements in each of the other ILR skill modalities—Writing, Listening, and Reading—and then compared the results to speaking in order to determine the extent of boundedness for each ILR skill modality. In order to

Table 1. ILR Speaking

ILR Level	Best Case	Average Case	Worst Case	Total Statements
5	1	2		3
4+		2	1	3
4	1	6	1	8
3+		1		1
3		7	1	8
2+		4	1	5
2		5	2	7
1+		7	1	8
1		6	1	7
0+		3	2	5
0		2	1	3
Average number of statements/level	0.18	4.09	1.00	5.27

Note: This tabulation of best case, average case, and worst case statements includes only the definition proper and excludes both the interactive Listening component and the examples section within the *ILR Skill Level Descriptions for Speaking.* Levels with no statements have been left blank.

accomplish this most directly, the examples sections in speaking were initially excluded from consideration (see table 1). After making the initial comparison between Speaking without examples to the other ILR skill modalities, I factored the Speaking examples section in. Those results are described at the end of this section.

Writing. As another production skill modality, one might expect Writing to parallel Speaking in the number of boundaries present. And, in fact, they were very close (see table 2). In Writing the evidence uncovers two missing boundaries: one between 4+/5 and one between 4/4+. It is our experience that these boundaries fall precisely at those levels where there is not much government writing.

Table 2. ILR writing

ILR Level	Best Case	Average Case	Worst Case	Total Statements
5	1	5		6
4+		3		3
4		6	1	7
3+		4	1	5
3	1	8	1	10
2+		8	2	10
2		7	2	9
1+		11	1	12
1		7	1	9
0+		4	1	5
0			1	1
Average number of statements/level	0.18	5.91	1.00	6.91

Note: Levels with no statements have been left blank.

Listening. One might expect some difference between the reception skills—Reading and Listening—and the production skills—Speaking and Writing. This was not, however, the case, at least for Listening, where one boundary was missing when compared to writing, and two boundaries when compared to speaking, for a total of three: 4+/5, 4/4+, and 3+/4 (see table 3). Note again that these boundaries also mainly fall above where most government listening is done. It has been the experience of my colleagues and me that the Listening skill level descriptions are not as easy to use as the Speaking. Besides being less bounded, Listening skill descriptions lack description of text types, and, to date, no attempt has been made to deal with text types in the Listening skill level descriptions. Indicating the type of text is also a problem with the Reading skill level descriptions, but for Reading a text typology has been proposed (see next section).

Table 3. ILR listening

ILR Level	Best Case	Average Case	Worst Case	Total Statements
5	1	2		3
4+		4		4
4		7		7
3+		7	1	8
3	1	7	1	9
2+	2	5		7
2	1	7		8
1+		9	2	11
1		6	4	10
0+		6	2	8
0		2	1	3
Average Number of Statements/Level	0.45	5.64	1.00	7.09

Note: Levels with no statements have been left blank.

Reading. This skill modality proved to be very different from the others. In Reading, six boundaries were missing: 4+/5, 4/4+, 3+/4, 3/3+, 2+/3, 2/2+ (see table 4). Note that these missing boundaries occurred at the middle and upper ranges. If one hazards a guess as to why they remain unspecified, one might point out that the *ILR Skill Level Descriptions for Reading* are concerned more with describing abilities and less with the specification of text difficulty at these levels, although this is also true for Listening, where the gaps are fewer. Many of the missing gaps for Reading are provided by James R. Child's work on text typology (1987). The fact that so many boundaries are missing in Reading may, however, help to explain why the Reading definitions prove harder to apply.

Table 4. ILR reading

ILR Level	Best Case	Average Case	Worst Case	Total Statements
5	1	6		7
4+		5		5
4		10		10
3+		6		6
3		7		7
2+		7		7
2		10		10
1+		7	1	8
1		6	2	8
0+		4	1	5
0				0
Average Number of Statements/Level	0.09	6.18	0.36	6.64

Note: Levels with no statements have been left blank.

Comparing skill modalities. Table 5 summarizes for each ILR skill modality the number of boundaries missing, the levels at which they are missing, and the number of statements per level. Eighteen out of the twenty-five respondents to our questionnaire remarked that Speaking proved to be the most usable of the ILR skill level descriptions. One could hypothesize that this might be the case because of the number of statements per level. But of the average number of statements per level (excluding the examples sections in Speaking, which may influence the outcome), Speaking has the lowest average with 5.27, Reading is next with 6.64, Writing with 6.91, and Listening with 7.09 statements per level each (see Table 5). I will return to this aspect later. What may contribute to the greater utility of Speaking is the number of boundaries: Speaking has only one boundary missing, while Writing has two, Listening three, and Reading six. Having used the Reading definitions for passage rating, item design, and rating of Reading ability, we can personally attest that they are harder to apply than Speaking. It may also be the case that the reception skill modalities are harder to characterize than production skill modalities due in part to the need for describing text types as well, which the current descriptions do not do. The comparisons in table 5 were possible because we excluded the example sections contained only in Speaking.

Table 6 shows what the examples add to each level in Speaking (levels 0 and 5 lack example sections). In all likelihood this further exemplification also helps to render the Speaking definitions more usable compared to those for the other ILR skill modalities. The example sections contain 69 statements in total, which when divided by the 11 possible levels add an average of 6.27 statements per level, a significant increase. When the number of statements for the examples section are added to the Speaking section, the average comes to 11.72, by far the greatest average for any of the skill modalities (see table 5). While this makes the Speaking definitions more usable overall, *it does not solve the boundary problem at 3/3+ border,* as the added statements are either AC or WC, but not the required WC for 3+ or the required BC for 3! It should be noted that the majority of additions in the examples sections for Speaking are AC, not BC or WC statements. Moreover, the non-AC statements tend to be WC, not BC (see table 6).

Conclusion. The goal of this article was to ascertain possible reasons as to why the *U.S. Government's ILR Language Skill Level Description for Speaking*

Table 5. Average number of statements per level

Listening	Writing	Reading	Speaking with no examples	Speaking examples only	Speaking with examples
7.09	6.91	6.64	5.27	6.27	11.55

Table 6. ILR speaking examples only

ILR Level	Best Case	Average Case	Worst Case	Total Statements
5				0
4+		6		6
4		7		7
3+	1	5		6
3	2	5		7
2+	1	6		7
2		6		6
1+	1	9		10
1	1	7	7	15
0+		4	1	5
0				0
Average Number of Statements/Level	0.55	5.00	0.73	6.27

Note. Levels with no statements have been left blank.

might prove more readily usable than the ILR descriptions for the other skill modalities. To that end I compared the boundedness of each of the skill modalities to Speaking. The results reveal that Speaking is most bounded (one boundary missing even when one includes the examples section in the Speaking definitions); Writing is less bounded (with two boundaries missing); Listening still less (three boundaries missing); and finally, Reading is the least bounded (with six boundaries missing). One possible reason for the difficulty some have found in applying the Reading definitions may lie in the fact that so many boundaries are missing at the mid and upper ranges.

Conversely, the greater utility of the speaking descriptions may lie in their almost maximal boundedness.[7] Another possible reason may lie in the examples sections, which increase the number of best case, average case, and worst case statements available at each level. In addition to historical and anecdotal evidence, it is therefore possible to adduce empirical bases for the varying levels of utility of each of the ILR skill level descriptions, particularly for the greater ease of use for Speaking. As one of the users of the descriptions in all four ILR skill modalities, we can say that our experience in actually applying the descriptions generally matches the data produced for the greater utility of Speaking. Of course, research similar to that carried out for the ILR descriptions remains to be undertaken for the ACTFL guidelines. The author proposes to do this in a follow-on investigation.

REFERENCES

American Council on the Teaching of Foreign Languages (ACTFL). 1986. *ACTFL provisional proficiency guidelines.* Hastings-on-Hudson: ACTFL.

Child, James R. 1987. Language Levels and the Typology of Texts. In Heidi Byrnes and Michael Canale (eds.), *Defining and developing proficiency: Guidelines, implementations, and concepts.* Lincolnwood, IL: National Textbook. 97–106.

Lowe, Pardee, Jr. 1998. Keeping the optic constant: A framework of principles for writing and specifying the AEI definitions of language abilities. *Foreign Language Annals* 31(3): 358–80.

Lowe, Pardee, Jr., and Charles W. Stansfield. 1988. Introduction. In Pardee Lowe, Jr., and Chalres W. Stansfield (eds.), *Second Language Proficiency Assessment: Current Issues.* Englewood Cliffs, NJ: Prentice Hall Regents. 1–10.

U.S. Government Interagency Language Roundtable (ILR). 1985. *Interagency Language Roundtable Skill Level Descriptions.* Washington, DC: Government Printing office.

APPENDIX A. WRITING: BEST CASE (BC)/WORST CASE (WC)

Level 0 (No Proficiency): *No functional writing ability* (WC).

Level 0+ (Memorized Proficiency): *Ability to write is limited to simple lists of common items such as a few short sentences* (WC).

Level 1 (Elementary Proficiency): *Making continual errors in spelling, grammar, and punctuation* (WC).

Level 1+ (Elementary Proficiency, Plus): *Can produce some past verb forms but not always accurately or with correct usage* (WC).

Level 2 (Limited Working Proficiency): *Can write simply about a very limited number of current events or daily situations* (WC).
Still makes common errors in spelling and punctuation (WC).

Level 2+ (Limited Working Proficiency, Plus): *Shows a limited ability to use circumlocutions (WC), though style is still obviously foreign* (WC).

Level 3 (General Professional Proficiency): *Employs a full range of structures (BC), but style may be obviously foreign* (WC).

Level 3+ (General Professional Proficiency, Plus): *Organization may suffer due to lack of variety in organizational patterns or in variety of cohesive devices* (WC).

Level 4 (Advanced Professional Proficiency): *Writing adequate to express all his/her experiences* (WC).

Level 4+ (Advanced Professional Proficiency, Plus): none.

Level 5 (Functionally Native Proficiency): *Has writing proficiency equal to that of a well-educated native* (BC).

APPENDIX B. LISTENING: BEST CASE (BC)/WORST CASE (WC)

Level 0: *Essentially no ability to comprehend communication* (WC).

Level 0+: *Sufficient comprehension to understand a number of memorized utterances in areas of immediate needs* (WC).
Slight increase in utterance length understood but requires frequent long pauses between understood phrases and repeated requests on the listener's part for repetition (WC).
Understands with reasonable accuracy only when this involves short memorized utterances or formulae (WC).
Can understand only with difficulty even such people as teachers who are used to speaking with non-native speakers (WC).

Level 1: *These (simple questions, answers, and simple statements) must often be delivered more clearly than normal at a rate slower than normal with frequent repetitions or paraphrase (that is, by a native used to dealing with foreigners).*

In the majority of utterances, misunderstandings arise due to overlooked or misunderstood syntax and other grammatical clues (WC).

Comprehension vocabulary inadequate to understand anything but the most elementary needs (WC).

Strong interference from the candidate's native language occurs (WC).

Level 1+: Cannot sustain understanding of coherent structures in longer utterances or in unfamiliar situations (WC).

Understanding of descriptions and the giving of precise information limited (WC).

Level 2: Can follow essential points of discussion or speech at an elementary level on topics in his/her special professional field (BC).

Level 2+: Can sometimes detect emotional overtones (BC).

Some ability to understand implications (BC).

Level 3: Does not understand native speakers if they speak very quickly or use some slang or dialect (WC).

Can understand without difficulty all forms of standard speech concerning a special professional field (BC).

Level 3+: Increased ability to understand native speakers talking quickly, using nonstandard dialect or slang, however comprehension not complete (WC).

Level 4: none.

Level 4+: none.

Level 5: Able to understand fully all forms and styles of speech intelligible to the well-educated native listener, including a number of regional and illiterate dialects, highly colloquial speech and conversations and discourse distorted by marked interference from other noise (BC).

APPENDIX C: READING: BEST CASE (BC)/WORST CASE (WC)

Level 0: Consistently misunderstands or cannot comprehend at all (WC).

Level 0+: none.

Level 1: In commonly taught languages, an R-1 may not control the structure well (WC).

Level 1+: Characteristically, however, the R-2 is quite slow in performing such a process (WC).

Level 2: none.

Level 2+: none.

Level 3: none.

Level 3+: none.

Level 4: none.

Level 4+: none.

Level 5: Can read extremely difficult and abstract prose (BC).

Appendix D: Speaking without examples: Best case (BC)/worst case (WC)

Level 0 (No Proficiency): *Unable to function in the spoken language* (WC).

Level 0+ (Memorized Proficiency): *Shows little real autonomy of expression, flexibility, or spontaneity* (WC).
Attempts at creating speech are usually unsuccessful (WC).

Level 1 (Elementary Proficiency) *The individual is unable to produce continuous discourse except with rehearsed material* (WC).

Level 1+ (Elementary Proficiency, Plus): *Range and control of the language are limited* (WC).

Level 2 (Limited Working Proficiency) *Errors are frequent* (WC).

Level 2+ (Limited Working Proficiency, Plus): *When under tension or pressure, the ability to use the language effectively may deteriorate* (WC).

Level 3 (General Professional Proficiency): *Pronunciation may be obviously foreign* (WC).

Level 3+ (General Professional Proficiency, Plus): no BC or WC statement.

Level 4 (Advanced Professional Proficiency): *The individual's language usage and ability to function are fully successful* (BC).
The individual would seldom be perceived as a native (WC).

Level 4+ (Advanced Professional Proficiency, Plus): *The individual would not necessarily be perceived as culturally native* (WC).

Level 5 (Functionally Native Proficiency): *The individual uses the language with complete flexibility and intuition, so that speech on all levels is fully accepted by well-educated native speakers in all of its features, including breadth of vocabulary and idiom, colloquialisms, and pertinent cultural references* (BC).

Appendix E: Speaking examples: Best case (BC)/worst case (WC)

Level 0: none.

Level 0+: *Even with repetition, communication is severely limited even with people used to dealing with foreigners* (WC).

Level 1: *Structural accuracy is likely to be random or severely limited* (WC).
Vocabulary is inaccurate (WC).
The individual often speaks with great difficulty (WC).
By repeating, such speakers can make themselves understood to native speakers who are in regular contact with foreigners (WC).
Almost every utterance may be characterized by structure errors and errors in basic grammatical relations (WC).
Vocabulary is extremely limited (WC).

Use of structure and vocabulary is highly imprecise (WC).

He/she might give information about business hours, explain routine procedures in a limited way, and state in a simple manner what actions will be taken (BC).

Level 1+: *Speaking ability may extend beyond immediate survival needs* (BC).

Accuracy in basic grammatical relations is evident, although not consistent (WC).

But may make frequent errors in formation and selection [of more common verb tenses] (WC).

Ability to describe and give precise information is limited (WC).

Pronunciation is understandable to natives used to dealing with foreigners (WC).

Has difficulty in producing certain sounds in certain positions or in certain combinations (WC).

Speech will usually be labored (WC).

Frequently has to repeat utterances to be understood by general public (WC).

Level 2: none.

Level 2+: *Discourse is often incohesive* (WC).

Level 3: *Can reliably elicit information and informed opinion from native speakers* (BC).

Use of structural devices is flexible and elaborate (BC).

Level 3+: *Discourse competence in a wide range of contexts and tasks, often matching a native's strategic and organizational abilities and expectations* (BC).

Level 4: none.

Level 4+: none.

Level 5: none.

NOTES

1. The thoughts expressed herein are those of the author and in no way reflect those of the Department of Defense. I wish to thank James R. Child and Beth Mackey for critiquing an earlier version of this article. Naturally, any errors are the responsibility of the author.

2. At times the terms "description(s)" and "definition(s)" are employed as a short hand for the longer ILR Language Skill Level Descriptions.

3. One way to show the relatedness of the ILR Language Skill Level Descriptions and the ACTFL/ETS Guidelines is to encompass them by the acronym AEI. In the acronym AEI, the A refers to ACTFL (American Council on the Teaching of Foreign Languages), the E to the ETS (Educational Testing Service), and the I to the ILR (The U.S. Government's Interagency Language Roundtable), respectively. These organizations (in an order reverse to that of the acronym) have contributed historically to the development and elaboration of definitions of foreign language proficiency—defined in this context as "the functional use of language," be it Speaking, Listening, Reading, or Writing. The reason to use the cover term AEI comes from the fact that the ACTFL Guidelines are derived from the ILR Skill Level Descriptions and the resulting ACTFL/ETS scale is basically commensurate with the ILR's. For a discussion of the differences between the two scales, see Lowe and Stansfield (1988). While the AEI scales have been used for several purposes, the focus in what follows is on testing.

4. Originally designed as a single page paper-and-pencil questionnaire, the author was forced on one occasion early on to administer it by phone and found that the procedure permitted him to answer any questions not covered in the relatively short instructions and examples of the paper-and-pencil version. Therefore, with three exceptions, he standardized on the phone approach.

5. The author is loath to draw further conclusions from the survey. The reason lies in the almost universal comment on the part of those surveyed that for them strong differences in frequency of use existed among the ILR skill modality descriptions. Very few responded with equal or almost equal use of any two, let alone three or four skill modality descriptions. By and large, the majority of answers made it clear that respondents found ILR Speaking descriptions more usable, but, in general, it was harder to describe their responses in the aggregate in relation to the other skill modalities.

6. The heuristic used to determine best case and worst case statements was, "Is this the best or worst that could be said of a language user and still rate her or him in this range?" The BC and WC statements for each of the four skill modalities may be found in the appendixes to this article. Statements not cited there are assumed to be AC and were excluded to save space.

7. In an earlier article (Lowe 1998), I suggested approaches to finding those features that would aid in delimiting the missing boundaries. While the distinction made there between "constructs" and "findings" still holds for this current research, it may be necessary to delimit the borders sooner than the availability of suitable "findings." As a result of this more expedient approach, revisers may have to employ "constructs" as an intermediate step and test their applicability by using them in an interim revised set of descriptions (see Lowe 1998: 366f.)

Bringing learning strategies to the student: The FSI language learning consultation service

Madeline Ehrman
Foreign Service Institute, U.S. Department of State[1]

Introduction. The Foreign Service Institute (FSI) provides full-time intensive training in some sixty languages to adult members of the U.S. foreign affairs community. Students at FSI are about forty years of age on average, and about two-thirds are between thirty and fifty. They come from a variety of agencies, ranging from the Department of State and the U.S. Information Agency to the Department of Defense and the Department of Commerce. Training generally includes five to six hours of daily contact time and homework; courses are twenty-four to eighty-eight weeks in duration, depending on the difficulty of the language for English speakers.

In the 1970s and early 1980s, FSI language students tended to be relatively field independent and analytic in style (Chapelle 1995; Chapelle and Green 1992; Ehrman 1996b, 1997; Witkin and Goodenough 1981); that is, they could quickly pick out what was important to learn, reconceptualize easily, and work well with material out of context. They were often accomplished language learners who had a good control of learning strategies needed for their classroom training. They were able to pick out quickly what they needed to focus their learning on and concentrate, without becoming distracted. They worked well with grammar and vocabulary with minimal context.

In recent years, however, the student body at FSI has become increasingly heterogeneous in terms of language learning aptitude and learning style. Many more students than before are field dependent (i.e., have difficulty working with material out of context and in setting learning priorities). Such students often learn material in context well, however, especially if they have some "scaffolding" support from the training program in the form of direct explanations, drill and practice, and the like. A substantial number of other students are both field dependent and not very adept at making use of language in context and authentic material (created by native speakers and readers for native speakers and readers). Many entering language students at FSI are more naïve than their predecessors about how to learn languages. Thus, there is now a greater need to help students develop effective learning strategies.

History of the Learning Consultation Service. Like other institutions, FSI initially attempted to offer group workshops in learning strategies. As in other cases, this approach was found to be ineffective: students had widely differing needs, and the learning strategies and suggestions introduced at the beginning of language training were not necessarily available later when they really needed it (Chamot and Rubin 1994; Rees-Miller 1993, 1994; Wenden 1995). A new way to help students with learning strategies was required. A number of institutions, many of them outside the United States, have tried training students to achieve autonomy as learners and then work with a variety of materials and programs partially on their own (Benson and Voller 1997; Dickinson 1995; Fitzgerald, Morrall, and Morrison 1996; Wenden 1991). This approach would have required more curriculum revision and teacher development than FSI could support at the time. Instead, FSI needed a way to provide learning strategies assistance within the existing full-time intensive training structure. Ideally, the teachers would be the source of strategy intervention, on a "just-in-time" basis. However, FSI has more than 200 language teachers, and it was unrealistic to attempt to bring all of them to the point where they could make sophisticated learning strategies interventions in a short time.

Instead, based on Ehrman's experience working with other government institutions (box 1) and on the results of research conducted at FSI on learning styles (Ehrman 1993, 1994a, 1994b, 1996a, 1997, 1998a, 1998b; Ehrman and Leaver unpublished), we chose to work through learning style diagnosis and a small group of carefully trained specialists who would work with students and teachers to help meet students' needs. Over time, it is planned that increasing numbers of classroom teachers will become familiar with the learning style models and the concepts in use, as well as the learning strategies associated with the various styles. This is an evolutionary process, and not every teacher is equally adept at using styles and strategies to advise students. The role of the specialists will therefore continue to be critical.

There are four separate roles in this program, which has been formalized recently as the Language Learning Consultation Service (LCS). Staff in all of the roles work together to make the LCS succeed. The first is, of course, the classroom teacher, who focuses on daily instruction and the immediate learning of the students. Second, the language-training supervisor oversees the work of the teachers, provides general structure to the curriculum, serves as section administrator, and may work with students who have special needs. Third, there is a small corps of "counselors" working in the central administration who administer and interpret the learning style questionnaires when students arrive. Finally, in many sections there are specialists called learning consultants who advise and advocate on behalf of students. Most of these are experienced teachers who have been trained to provide follow-through for the diagnostic learning style information gathered when students arrive. They also use information about learning styles to advise students on effective learning strategies for various kinds of learning tasks.

Box 1. History of the learning consultation initiative

1988–1989	Ehrman worked with DLI on design of a pilot consultation service (Lett and O'Mara 1990).
Early 1990s	CIA Language School experimented with a similar initiative and still provides advisory services (Lea Christensen 1998, personal communication).
1991	FSI's School of Language Studies began its Language Learning Profiles Project, which consisted of research into individual differences that affect language learning. This research continues at a low level.
1993–1995	FSI attempted to provide group training to students in learning strategies with variable success, limited by the wide variation of student needs that made workshops impractical.
1994–1995	Occasional requests for assistance emerged from the Language Learning Profiles Project; training supervisors began to refer "problem" students.
1994–1995	The French Pilot Project was the outcome of a re-evaluation of how FSI designs and implements language courses. As part of the Pilot Project, Ehrman designed the role of learning consultant and trained the first two learning consultants.
1995–present	The French Pilot Project was expanded to other languages and renamed Accelerated Personalized Training (APT). The formal learning style diagnostics that proved most useful in the Language Learning Profiles Project were integrated into the APT initiative, as was the Learning Consultant role.
August 1995	A formal invitation to participate in the Learning Consultation Program was extended to all entering students for the first time. Those not in "APT" languages were encouraged to work with one of the "counselors" whether or not they were having difficulties, in order to enhance their learning.
May 1999	The program has two "counselors" (and two in training) who interpret results of the diagnostic questionnaires in individual consultations. (Ehrman still does the group sessions and the special cases.) Between forty and ninety students from every input group go through the entire process.
	The Learning Consultation Service is now available to U.S. government employees who are not in FSI language training and is listed in the FSI annual schedule of courses.

Because they provide much of the follow-up advice on learning strategies, the learning consultants are the key to the success of this program. A summary of their role is provided in box 2. The remainder of this paper focuses on the "counselor" and learning consultant roles.

All incoming students are introduced to the Learning Consultation Service and are invited to participate in it, whether or not they are having trouble with their language learning. They are urged to use the service to find out how to make better use of their time at FSI. They are offered confidentiality, and participation is voluntary. Some participate in the LCS program as part of their initial training, but they are free to decline to participate. Others take the initiative to request the service; still others are referred to the LCS by their teachers, language training supervisors, or learning consultants. Box 3 displays the learning consultation process. Box 4 shows the number of consultations and the languages that used the Learning Consultation Service in 1998.

Box 2. About the Learning Consultant

- Most learning consultants are teachers. A few are training supervisors.
- Each learning consultant serves a high-enrollment language section, for example, Spanish or Russian, or a group of low-enrollment languages, such as the languages of the Baltic region.
- The work of learning consultants complements that of the two general "counselors" who provide the individual feedback and special consultations in Research, Evaluation, and Development.
- Learning consultants are familiar with the diagnostic scales; they usually receive special training to understand them.
- Learning consultation is a standard feature in accelerated personalized training (APT) programs.
- A learning consultant's group has formed to share ideas and tips on dealing with challenges and to discuss special cases. This is so successful that some training supervisors are requesting that non-consultant teachers attend for the staff development value of the experience.

Learning Consultant responsibilities:
- Sits in on the individual feedback session with the student and participates in discussion with the counselor and the student about how to use the information gained from the questionnaires.
- Conveys relevant information to the student's teachers (with student permission).
- Consults periodically with the student to enable the student and the teaching staff to use the information gained through the diagnostic process for the student's benefit.

Box 3. The Learning Consultation Process

1. *Making the Consultation Service available.* Students are invited on input day to participate in the Consultation Service. They are assured that
   * it is voluntary; and
   * it is for people who are not having trouble as well as to help those who are.
2. *Completing the diagnostic questionnaires:*
   * If in languages participating in the accelerated personalized training (APT) initiative, students complete the questionnaires on their first day of training.
   * Others may "walk in" to the Research, Evaluation, and Development Division at any time and are given the questionnaires at that time.
   * Language sections sometimes refer students who are having difficulties.
3. *Group sessions:*
   * After scoring, general information about the questionnaires is provided in large-group sessions to students who complete them at the beginning of training.
4. Other students receive the general information in individual sessions with 'counselors.' *Individual sessions:*
   * Students in APT programs may sign up for individual feedback sessions. They usually have a section representative present.
   * "Walk-in" students always have individual sessions at which they receive the general information about the questionnaires.
5. *Follow-up:*
   * in the language section: the system works best if the student's designated Learning Consultant takes responsibility for ensuring that information is used to the student's benefit by other teachers and by the student (e.g., advice on preparation and classroom strategies).
   * Individual students: Students may choose to return for follow-up consultations on special learning strategies or management of anxiety, for instance.

The Learning Consultation Service is a key component of accelerated personalized training (APT), another FSI initiative to enhance the quality of the training students receive. APT has four strands: individualization, flexibility, multiple ways of delivering training (including educational technology), and attention to specific professional language use needs. Individualization begins with comprehensive analysis of student learning styles that is exploited throughout training by students and teachers to maximize learning efficiency. Students are empowered to make

---

Box 4. Learning Consultation Use in 1998

Total number of participants	388 students
Participation as a regular part of training program	16 languages

      Albanian
      Dutch
      Finnish
      French
      German
      Greek
      Hebrew
      Italian
      Polish
      Portuguese
      Romanian
      Russian
      Spanish
      Swedish
      Ukrainian
      Turkish

Self-referrals and referrals from language section	13 languages

      Amharic
      Arabic
      Armenian
      Azerbaijani
      Bengali
      Cambodian
      Chinese
      Czech
      Japanese
      Korean
      Serbian
      Thai
      Urdu

effective learning choices and make sure that their ongoing needs are met. Programs participating in APT provide choices and options in the curriculum; the self-knowledge that students achieve through the LCS and the appropriate support provided by counselors and learning consultants promote greater learner autonomy. It is believed that this kind of individualization and opportunity for making choices will help develop employees who can continue to learn in much less structured settings overseas.

Procedures. In almost all cases, students complete a set of questionnaires (see Box 5 and Ehrman 1996b) that evaluate learning styles and highlight the individual's preferred learning strategies in the classroom and on their own. All students read and hear explanations of the questionnaires, and they can then request an individual feedback session that focuses on what the questionnaire results mean for them. In language programs with learning consultants, the consultant attends that session, so that the counselor, the student, and the learning consultant can discuss what the questionnaire results mean for the student. The learning consultant is then expected to continue communicating with the student throughout his or her training, ensuring that individual needs are met and providing on-the-spot strategy suggestions. Some students return to the counselors for additional expert strategy consultation on such topics as managing anxiety.

Learning strategies. The general learning strategy model in use in this program is from Schmeck (1988): the LCS calls student attention to the distinction between surface, achievement, and deep strategies. Surface strategies are those that are needed to get a job done and no more. Achievement strategies are those that result in a good grade or build relationships with teachers or other students. Deep strategies make associations between what is new and what is known and among concepts and experiences. Deep strategies are the ones that most directly result in long-term retention, although achievement strategies can make use of deep strategies possible. For example, a discussion with one's teacher (achievement strategy) might result in suggestions for effective "deep" learning techniques.

Diagnostic instruments for styles and strategies. The LCS uses a biographical data questionnaire to learn about the student's educational and language-learning history. This simple questionnaire serves as the base for finding out a great deal about how the student has gone about learning languages, what has worked well and what has been difficult, and the student's feelings about language learning. The other instruments currently used are the Modern Language Aptitude Test (MLAT), Motivation and Strategies Questionnaire (MSQ), the Ehrman and Leaver Learning Style Questionnaire (E&L), the Myers-Briggs Type Indicator (MBTI), and the Hartmann Boundary Questionnaire (HBQ).

The Modern Language Aptitude Test. The MLAT (Carroll and Sapon 1959) has proved useful for addressing learning strategies in individual conferences with students. It has five subscales ("parts") that are used for examination of styles and preferred strategies. The parts are listed in the appendix to this paper.

Learning strategies are of particular importance in part V of the MLAT. The interviewer calls the students' attention to strategies when discussing this paired associates exercise in which the test taker must learn twenty-four foreign language words in a short time. Because it is a complete task, it can be interpreted as

Box 5. Diagnostic dimensions and instruments currently used

Dimension	Instrument(s)
Biographic background	Biographic Background Questionnaire
age	
education (level, subjects, GPA)	
previous language learning experiences	
special problems (e.g., vision, learning disability)	
Personality factors	
Extraversion-Introversion	Myers-Briggs Type Indicator
Sensing-Intuition	Myers-Briggs Type Indicator
Thinking-Feeling	Myers-Briggs Type Indicator
Judging-Perceiving	Myers-Briggs Type Indicator
Tolerance of ambiguity	Hartmann Boundary Questionnaire (HBQ)
Field sensitivity	Ehrman and Leaver Style Questionnaire, HBQ
Perceptual and cognitive styles	Some examples:
visual-auditory-kinesthetic	Motivation and Strategy Questionnaire
field independent-dependent	Ehrman and Leaver Style Questionnaire
field sensitive-insensitive	Modern Language Aptitude Test subscales
impulsive-reflective	Ehrman and Leaver Style Questionnaire
random-sequential	Ehrman and Leaver Style Questionnaire
polyactivity	Motivation and Strategy Questionnaire
Language learning aptitude (cognitive factors)	Modern Language Aptitude Test
Motivation, anxiety, and self-efficacy	Motivation and Strategies Questionnaire
motivation	
self-efficacy as a language learner	
anxiety	
perfectionism	
Learning strategies	Motivation and Strategies Questionnaire
open-ended vs. closed-ended activities	
preferred specific learning activities (in and out of the classroom)	

providing some information about (a) student word-learning strategies and (b) certain metacognitive strategies of planning a task, keeping an appropriate pace of learning, and evaluating one's progress. (The metacognitive activities are done so rapidly that most students are unaware that they are doing them.)

MLAT part III (spelling clues) is a highly speeded exercise that can also provide useful information about how students manage a task. In this part, students must decode an English word in unusual spelling and select the closest synonym from a list of four possibilities. One of the most interesting findings to come out of part III is the tendency of some students to perseverate in an approach that is not paying off for them, instead of shifting to a more productive one. This kind of information emerges when the counselor asks students what they did on each MLAT part on which they received a low score.

The MLAT also provides information about learning styles that affect student learning strategy choices. The most important feature of the MLAT for learning consultants and others involved in the consultation process is that it examines field independence using verbal stimuli rather than the visual-spatial ones that are usually employed. For example, high scores on MLAT parts III (spelling clues) and IV (words in sentences) suggest the ability to make use of field independent strategies, that is, seeing what is important, setting immediate processing priorities, and reconceptualizing what is presented (Ehrman 1996b, 1997, 1998b). Students who have a field independent approach usually need relatively little help with strategies for analysis and direct learning, though some may not learn well through material in context. Students who respond well to material in context often do considerably better on MLAT part II (phonetic script) than on parts III and IV. Such students, if they do not have field independent skills, may need assistance with extracting selected material from the context or dealing with decontextualized material. Some students, usually the best classroom language learners, do well across the board on MLAT parts II, III, and IV, and show both field independence and the ability to learn successfully from rich contexts. (See Ehrman 1998b for more information use of the MLAT in language counseling.)

Motivation and Strategy Questionnaire. Additional strategy information comes from the motivation and strategies questionnaire (see Ehrman 1996b). This questionnaire has a section in which respondents can endorse or reject a set of fairly common classroom activities. In another section, they indicate how much they use a variety of study approaches, such as jumping right in to a task. This information is used to corroborate other information from other instruments specifically aimed at learning styles, but it is also used to address learning strategies directly.

Ehrman and Leaver Learning Style Questionnaire. A self-report instrument that focuses on learning style, the E&L (Ehrman and Leaver unpublished) is an experimental instrument that explores cognitive styles, specifically those that relate to the dimension commonly called "global-analytic." Ehrman and Leaver (unpublished) have reconceptualized this dimension, renaming it "synoptic-ectenic" to avoid using terms already in use with other meanings. ("Synopsis" refers to processes done almost unconsciously so that the knowledge or insights come to awareness with relatively little effort; "ectasis," the Greek opposite of synopsis, refers to processes that take either considerable conscious control or rely on outside structure.) The base construct is represented by ten subscales such as synthetic-analytic, random-sequential, and leveling-sharpening (box 6 and table 1). During the interview, this questionnaire sometimes evokes discussion of learning strategies. For example, an interviewer may suggest building sentences to a student who self-reports a strong preference for analyzing but who needs to develop more "synthetic" skills.

Table 1. E & L learning style questionnaire, v.2: Descriptive statistics for subscales and general score (N = 375)

Scale	Mean	SD	Median	Mode	Range
Analog-digital	13.6	3.8	14	14	3-27
Concrete-abstract	12.0	4.1	12	12	3-26
Field independent-field dependent	13.6	4.2	13	12	3-24
Field sensitive-field insensitive	12.7	4.6	12	12	3-26
Global-particular	14.1	4.3	14	12	3-26
Impulsive-reflective	14.7	4.9	15	12	4-25
Inductive-deductive	16.6	4.7	17	17	3-27
Leveling-sharpening	13.8	4.0	14	12	3-25
Random-sequential	16.4	4.8	16	16	3-27
Synthetic-analytic	13.9	5.2	14	12	3-27
E&L General Score	35.8	12.6	32	32	11-90

From Ehrman and Leaver 2000. Note: lower scores indicate synopsis.

Box 6. E&L Learning Style Questionnaire: Subscale Definitions

Field sensitivity *as learning style*: prefers to address material as part of context and often picks up material by "osmosis." It relates to wholes that cannot be disassembled. It can be compared to illumination by a floodlight that shows the whole scene.

Field insensitivity: makes little or no use of the whole context and often excludes "incidental" learning.

Field independence: *as learning style*: prefers to separate material from context. It can be compared to a spotlight that focuses sharply on one thing, in contrast to field sensitivity.

Field dependence: relies on context and does not select out what is important for focus.

Random (nonlinear): follow internally developed order of processing.

Sequential (linear): follows externally provided order of processing.

Global processing: attends to gestalts and "big picture"; is aware of "forests" (vs. trees), oriented toward processing from the "top down."

Particular processing: attends to discrete items and details, is aware of "trees" (vs. forests), oriented towards processing from "bottom up."

Inductive: goes from specific to the general, generalizes from experience.

Deductive: goes from the general to specific, applies generalizations to experience.

Synthesis: comprehends through assembly of components into a constructed whole.

Analysis: comprehends through disassembly into components.

Analogue: qualitative or metaphoric approach to interpreting experience.

Digital: quantitative or literal approach to interpreting experience.

Concrete: interacts with the world directly, learns through application, often physical, of knowledge. Experiential.

Abstract: interacts with the world through cognitive constructs, learns from formal rendition of knowledge. Theoretical.

Leveling: often does not notice disparities and may seek to reduce them; looks for similarities. Tends not to notice articulations within composites.

Sharpening: notices disparities and seeks to explore and account for them. Tends to be aware of componential structure.

Impulsivity: reacts quickly in acting or speaking with little or no conscious "thinking it through"; acts on "gut"; thought may follow action.

Reflectivity: "thinks it through" before action; often does not trust "gut reaction"; action usually follows thought.

The E&L addresses field independence and a related concept, "field sensitivity." Field independence is often contrasted with field dependence, which can mean either lack of field independence or a responsiveness to picking up material in the environment in a broad, almost osmotic way. In order to avoid this ambiguity, Ehrman (1996b, 1997) contrasts field independence with its absence (field dependence), and on a different scale, contrasts field sensitivity, that is, responsiveness to the surrounding environment, with its absence (field insensitivity). A student can be both field independent and field sensitive, one or the other, or neither. (The best language learners are often both field independent and field sensitive; that is, they can work with material that is not embedded in context or can see what is most important, and they can also pick up language in a relatively global way from being exposed to it.) Field sensitivity is closely allied to the constructs measured by MLAT part II and the Hartmann Boundary Questionnaire. The E&L adopts Ehrman's (1996b, 1997) model of field independence versus field dependence and field sensitivity versus field insensitivity.

Myers-Briggs Type Indicator and Hartmann Boundary Questionnaire. The MBTI (Myers and McCaulley 1985) and the HBQ (Hartmann 1991) are personality instruments. Although they do not directly address learning strategies, they reflect learning styles and have substantial implications for strategy choices. The MBTI, used for second language acquisition research since 1989 (Ehrman and Oxford 1989, 1990), has scales that address extraversion and introversion, sensing (concrete and practical) and intuition (symbol- and meaning-oriented), thinking (logic-based decisions) and feeling (values-based decisions), and judging (closure-orientation) and perceiving (open-ended). All of these have classroom implications; specific relations between MBTI scales and learning strategies are outlined in Ehrman (1989).

The HBQ addresses the distinction between thick and thin ego boundaries. This scale is operationally defined as the relative need to compartmentalize one's experience. Thick boundaries reflect a need to keep aspects of personal experience separated and compartmentalized; they are often associated with intolerance of ambiguity. Thin ego boundaries are usually associated with receptivity (including languages and foreign cultures), but people with thin ego boundaries may encounter learning difficulties if they cannot set priorities in what to learn or impose cognitive structure on input. (MLAT parts III and IV provide some information about this ability.) In terms of strategies, thick boundary learners tend to rely most on drilling and conscious control of material, whereas thin boundary learners may respond well to language presented in rich, even naturalistic contexts. (Findings for the HBQ and second language learning are treated in Ehrman 1993, 1996b, 1998b.)

Two students. The following two contrasting cases illustrate the concepts used in the Learning Consultation Service. Jennifer and Geoffrey learn very differently and present widely varying challenges to their teachers.

Jennifer. Jennifer is an "extroverted sensing thinking judging" type (ESTJ) on the MBTI, which means that she prefers to learn in concrete ways and to focus on practical topics. She does not like open-ended activities, and she likes clear ground-rules. She works hard and completes her assignments on time. Her overall MLAT score is in the FSI mid-range; her highest part scores were on parts I (number learning) and V (paired associates), suggesting relative skill in oral comprehension, mnemonic strategies, and possibly metacognitive strategies. She reports "thick" boundaries on the HBQ, consistent with her MBTI type (thick boundaries on the HBQ tend to correlate with MBTI sensing, thinking, and judging). In her individual interview, she confirms considerable intolerance of ambiguity. She says that she feels frustrated when she deals with language she does not fully understand and cannot find correspondences between the target language and English. On other questionnaires and in her interview, she adds that she wants to be prepared ahead of time, likes repetition and a clear outline of the curriculum that the program follows. Jennifer prefers to learn one thing at a time and not move on until mastering a point. She has a tendency to be a perfectionist. She does not like unclear or ambiguous assignments, such as reading unfamiliar material, or "read this story." These characteristics are consistent with a largely "ectenic" learner, and indeed, she reports preferences for deductive, sequential, and "digital" (literal) learning approaches. Jennifer's English vocabulary and general knowledge fall somewhat below the FSI average. She says, "Without a classroom ritual set down, I sometimes get confused. And I want to know what to do when I walk out of class."

Geoffrey. Geoffrey contrasts with Jennifer in a number of ways. He is essentially a "synoptic" learner, in particular liking holistic and "analog" approaches to learning (through metaphors and stories, rather than literal). However, he is not extreme in this respect. An "introverted intuitive feeling judging" type (INFJ) on the MBTI, he likes a certain amount of "creativity" in his classroom activities. He enjoys interacting with others and tends to be motivated by getting to know the people of the target culture better, interacting with them informally as well as formally. Although he likes global learning strategies (beginning with the "forest" then proceeding to the "trees"), he does not much want to design his own program, as might a more extreme "synoptic" learner who scores high on induction and nonlinear learning.

Geoffrey, like Jennifer, scored in the mid-range on the MLAT. His peaks were in parts I (number learning) and II (phonetic transcription), which support his context-oriented learning style. His lower scores on parts III (spelling clues) and IV (words in sentences) suggest a field sensitive but field dependent learner; this is confirmed by his self-report on the E&L. Geoffrey thus wants some external structure, but he can manage with considerably less than Jennifer, and he is much more comfortable with ambiguous, naturalistic input than she. His average total score on the HBQ suggests a moderate tolerance for ambiguity. "Thin" scores on items indicating tolerance for lack of neatness and preference for soft edges tend to predict tolerance for linguistic ambiguity, at least among FSI students. His control of English vocabulary and general knowledge are well above FSI average.

A relatively concrete (experiential) learner, Geoffrey likes to demonstrate knowledge by doing something "real" rather than through paper-and-pencil activities. In the same vein, he likes field trips and simulations. In general, he is comfortable with such open-ended learning activities as finding and reporting on news articles. He favors learning strategies that involve making associations between what is known and what is not, and he rejects mechanical drilling and rote memorization.

Geoffrey appreciates a well-designed syllabus but can manage reasonably well when the teacher deviates from it. He summarizes his approach by saying, "Give me a lot of language, in stories, in conversation, and in role plays. But I want review and help making sense of it all, too." Jennifer and Geoffrey can be placed in the same class, but teachers will have difficulty giving both of them what they need. Both of them may need to accept that they cannot have everything exactly as they want it, and the teachers can meet their individual needs much of the time. In addition, the teachers can work with them to tailor homework and self-study activities to make use of their strengths and to "stretch" their styles to less comfortable domains. For example, both learners may need work on coping with the kinds of unstructured situations that they will meet daily after leaving the classroom and arriving at their overseas posts. (This will be something less of a stretch for Geoffrey than for Jennifer.) The teachers are helped in dealing with these two students by the fact that Geoffrey will tolerate and even appreciate a considerable amount of the external structure that Jennifer depends on, whereas a more extreme "synoptic" learner might chafe with the drilling and following of the syllabus that both of these students like.

The information about Jennifer and Geoffrey presented above, and more, would come out during the individual feedback session that includes the counselor, the student, and the learning consultant. The learning consultant would then provide some of the information to take the information to Jennifer's and Geoffrey's teachers, with their permission, and continue to work with them to help them learn as effectively as possible. The learning consultant would begin with Jennifer by finding ways for her to study in ways she finds comfortable, but during the training program, the learning consultant would work with her on coping more effectively with ambiguous input and with working out ways to learn when there is no clear syllabus. The learning consultant would find ways to get a rich context to Geoffrey so that he could begin his learning in a way he finds effective and then work with him to help him in the areas he finds less comfortable so that he can increase his flexibility as a learner.

Conclusion. There is much yet to be done to allow the FSI program to reach its full potential. The LCS program needs to make training of learning consultants more systematic, and more quality control is needed. Some students receive more follow-up from their learning consultants than others, so some standardization of learning consultant functions is needed. The teaching staff as a whole should become more knowledgeable about the styles and strategies models, so that they can help their students at appropriate moments in the classroom, rather than waiting until a learning consultant or a central counselor can intervene. We continue to seek ways to make the learning styles and strategies models more accessible to the teachers and their supervisors through formal workshops, training of individuals, and application to work with students having difficulty.

The Learning Consultation Service was designed to meet the specific needs of FSI's intensive, high-stakes language training for foreign affairs personnel. Other programs, such as the usual non-intensive teaching done in university language programs, would probably address individual needs in other ways, such as self-access centers. Even in programs in which learner autonomy is the center of the learner training, however, well trained advisory staff can help with the necessary "scaffolding" that precedes full autonomy, and various learning style models can prove useful to different students. Some of what we are learning at FSI may thus be of use to other programs, no matter what their structure and mission.

REFERENCES

Benson, Phil, and Peter Voller (eds.). 1997. *Autonomy and independence in language learning.* Harlow, England: Longman.

Carroll, John, and Stanley M Sapon. 1959. *Modern Language Aptitude Test.* New York: Psychological Corporation.

Chamot, Anna Uhl, and Joan Rubin. 1994. Comments on Janie Rees-Miller's "A Critical Appraisal of Learner Training: Theoretical Bases and Teaching Implications." *TESOL Quarterly* 28(4): 771–776.

Chapelle, Carol A. 1995. Field-dependence/field-independence in the L2 classroom. In Joy M. Reid (ed.), *Learning styles in the ESL/EFL classroom.* Boston: Heinle & Heinle: 158–168.

Chapelle, Carol, and Pat Green. 1992. Field independence/dependence in second language acquisition research. *Language Learning* 42: 47–83.

Dickinson, Leslie. 1995. Autonomy and motivation: A literature review. *System* 23(2): 165–174.

Ehrman, Madeline E. 1989. Ants and grasshoppers, badgers and butterflies: Qualitative and quantitative investigation of adult language learning styles and strategies. Unpublished Ph.D. dissertation. The Union Institute. (Dissertation Abstracts International, 50(12):5876B. (University Microfilms No. 9005257)).

Ehrman, Madeline E. 1993. Ego boundaries revisited: Toward a model of personality and learning. In James E. Alatis (ed.), *Strategic interaction and language acquisition: Theory, practice, and research.* Washington, DC: Georgetown University: 331–362.

Ehrman, Madeline E. 1994a. The *Type Differentiation Indicator* and language learning success. *Journal of Psychological Type* 30: 10–29.

Ehrman, Madeline E. 1994b. Weakest and strongest learners in intensive language training: A study of extremes. In Carol Klee (ed.), *Faces in a crowd: Individual learners in multisection programs.* Boston: Heinle & Heinle: 81–118.

Ehrman, Madeline E. 1996a. Psychological type and extremes of training outcomes in foreign language reading proficiency. In Alice Horning and Ronald Sudol (eds.), *Understanding literacy: Personality preferences in rhetorical and psycholinguistic contexts.* Cresskill, NJ: Hampton Press: 231–273.

Ehrman, Madeline E. 1996b. *Understanding second language learning difficulties.* Thousand Oaks, CA: Sage.

Ehrman, Madeline E. 1997. Field independence, field dependence, and field sensitivity. In Joy M. Reid (ed.), *Understanding Learning styles in the second language classroom.* Englewood Cliffs, NJ: Regents Prentice Hall: 62–70.

Ehrman, Madeline E. 1998a. Ego boundaries and tolerance of ambiguity in second language learning. In Jane Arnold (ed.), *Affect in language learning.* New York: Cambridge. 68–86.

Ehrman, Madeline E. 1998b. The Modern Language Aptitude Test for predicting learning success and advising students. *Applied Language Learning* 9(1&2): 31–70.

Ehrman, Madeline E., and Betty L. Leaver. Development of a profile approach to learning style diagnosis. Unpublished manuscript.

Ehrman, Madeline E., and Rebecca L. Oxford. 1989. Effects of sex differences, career choice, and psychological type on adult language learning strategies. *The Modern Language Journal,* 72: 1–13.

Ehrman, Madeline E., and Rebecca. L. Oxford. 1990. Adult language learning styles and strategies in an intensive training setting. *The Modern Language Journal* 74: 311–327.

Fitzgerald, Sue, Andy Morrall, and Bruce Morrison. 1996. Catering for individual learning styles: Experiences of orienting students in an Asian self-access centre. In Leslie Dickinson (ed.), *Autonomy 2000: The development of learning independence in language learning.* Bangkok, Thailand: King Mongkut's Institute of Technology Thonburi: 55–69.

Hartmann, Ernest. 1991. *Boundaries in the mind: A new psychology of personality.* New York: Basic.

Lett, John A., and Francis E. O'Mara. 1990. Predictors of success in an intensive foreign language learning context: Correlates of language learning at the Defense Language Institute Foreign Language Center. In Thomas Parry and Charles W. Stansfield (eds.), *Language aptitude reconsidered.* Englewood Cliffs, NJ: Prentice Hall. 222–260.

Myers, Isabel Briggs, and Mary McCaulley. 1985. *Manual: A guide to the development and use of the Myers-Briggs Type Indicator.* Palo Alto: Consulting Psychologists.

Rees-Miller, Janie 1993. A critical appraisal of learner training: Theoretical bases and teaching implications. *TESOL Quarterly* 27(4): 679–689.

Rees-Miller, Janie. 1994. The author responds [response to Chamot and Rubin 1994]. *TESOL Quarterly* 28(4): 776–781.

Schmeck, Ronald. R. 1988. *Learning strategies and learning styles.* New York: Plenum.

Wenden, Anita L. 1991. *Learner strategies for learner autonomy.* Englewood Cliffs, NJ: Prentice-Hall.

Wenden, Anita L. 1995. Learner training in context: A knowledge-based approach. *System* 23(2): 183–194.

Witkin, Herman A., and Donald R. Goodenough. 1981. *Cognitive styles: Essence and origins: Field dependence and field independence.* New York: International Universities.

APPENDIX. MODERN LANGUAGE APTITUDE TEST PARTS

Part	Name of Part	Description (from the MLAT Manual; Carroll and Sapon 1959)
I	Number Learning	This subtest requires the examinee to learn four morphemes and interpret them in combinations that form numbers; it is entirely orally delivered. The manual describes it as measuring part of memory and "auditory alertness."
II	Phonetic Script	Examinee selects a written equivalent (in phonemic transcription) for an orally delivered stimulus. The MLAT manual describes the sub-test as dealing with the ability to associate a sound with a particular symbol, memory for speech sounds, and mimicry of foreign language speech sounds and sound combinations.
III	Spelling Clues	In this entirely written subtest, an English word is presented in a very nonstandard spelling. The examinee must select the correct synonym. Vocabulary items are progressively more difficult. According to the manual, scores on this part depend largely on a student's English vocabulary and to some degree on ability to make sound-symbol.
IV	Words in Sentences	The stimulus is a sentence with an error. The examinee indicates which part of another sentence matches the designated part. The subtest is entirely in writing. It is described as dealing with the examinee's sensitivity to grammatical structure. No grammatical terminology is used, so scores do not depend on knowledge of grammatical terms.
V	Paired Associates	The examinee learns twenty-four foreign words with their English equivalents. This subtest is said to measure the examinee's ability to memorize by rote.

NOTE

1. The content of this article does not represent official policy of the U.S. Department of State; the observations and opinions are those of the author.

Can you beat guessing in multiple-choice testing?

Beth A. Mackey[1]
Department of Defense

Introduction. The National Security Agency (NSA) tests applicants to ensure that their language levels are appropriate for the government's work. The Language Performance Test (LPT) is used to assess reading comprehension at the Interagency Language Roundtable (ILR) level 2/level 2+. Due to the volume of tests administered each year, many of the tests are in a multiple-choice format to allow for machine scoring. This paper is a result of our desire to better understand how our agency's Language Performance Tests work. Many of the LPTs are formatted to produce an effective, machine-scorable language test.

The machine-scorable LPT is made up of two distinct sections: the keyed completion section and the information identification section. A major goal in designing the keyed completion section was to attempt to overcome the effect of guessing, a main drawback of traditional multiple-choice testing. The potential exists that a testee would be able to improve his or her score by guessing the answer. The possible effects of guessing vary by the number of choices given to the test taker. With five options per item, the chance of getting the right answer is 20%, with four options 25%; and with three options 33.3%. The keyed completion model attempts to reduce the effect of guessing by increasing the number of available choices for each item from the often used four options to twenty.

The other component of the LPT is the information identification section, which is designed to determine how well the testee, given a full text, comprehends the semantic structure or content of texts. It uses a more traditional, four-choice response bank, which is exploited in a novel way to minimize guessing.

Developing the LPT. The Language Performance Test has been in use at NSA for the past twenty years, and in that period James R. Child, the agency's senior language testing researcher, has developed an effective process for test design. The test requires at least two complete text passages: one for the keyed completion section and one for the information identification section. It is often more practical to choose two passages for either or both sections to increase the variety of keyed items. The first stage in the design process is to select the appropriate texts. They should be from authentic, in-country graphic material,[2] generated by a native writer for a native audience. Using Child's text typology (1987) as a guide, passages should be in the instructive mode.

The keyed completion section. As mentioned previously, the first part of the LPT is the keyed completion section, which tests knowledge of grammar in the context of communication; that is, the items are designed to test meaning first and form second. Once the passages have been selected, the test designer creates a one-to-one gloss for the keyed completion section before translating it in full. Many might regard this as an extra step, but it has proven useful for test design, in that it furnishes clues as to possible items that might prove difficult for the English reader.

The keyed completion section is based on the cloze format first introduced by Taylor (1953) in which every n-th word is chosen for deletion and the examinees are asked to predict the best word to fill in the blank. In the keyed completion model, the test designer selects the items to be tested, the "keys," by considering both the meanings as well as the forms (i.e., consideration of the text from the perspectives of subject matter and grammar).

In contrast to the original cloze format in which the examinee produced the answer based on his knowledge, the keyed completion model supplies the test taker with a list of options. The next step in the design process, therefore, is to build the lists of possible responses: the "keyed" answers and the "intended" distractors.[3] "Intended" distractors are those possibilities that the test designer believes will be attractive to the test taker whose language skills are not sufficiently internalized,

---

Box 1. Instructive Mode

Language texts in the instructive mode are those that can be tied ultimately to the external world but are not dependent on immediate visual and auditory stimuli for their full interpretation. They are the products of speakers or writers who are conveying facts or exchanging information about situations and occurrences but are not analyzing or expressing personal involvement in the material conveyed. Texts at this level may be rationalized to include a variety of forms (other than news-item), such as extended instructions on how to assemble objects or direction to remote places, recounting of incidents in one's past, narration of historical events, or certain kinds of material where a supposedly factual treatment is strongly influenced by political theory. The content should neither be offensive or repugnant, nor should it contain information that could make it dated. The material should be at the high 2/2+ level of difficulty according to the Interagency Language Roundtable skill level descriptions for reading, and should yield approximately fifty items per section.

Box 2. Interagency Language Roundtable Skill Level Descriptions for Reading

---

Reading 2 (Limited Working Proficiency). Sufficient comprehension to read simple, authentic written material in a form equivalent to usual printing or typescript on subjects within a familiar context. Able to read with some misunderstandings straightforward, familiar, factual material, but in general insufficiently experienced with the language to draw inferences directly from the linguistic aspects of the text. Can locate and understand the main ideas and details in material written for the general reader. However, persons who have professional knowledge of a subject may be able to summarize or perform sorting and locating tasks with written texts that are well beyond their general proficiency level. The individual can read uncomplicated but authentic prose on familiar subjects that are normally presented in a predictable sequence which aids the reader in understanding. Texts may include descriptions and narrations in contexts such as news items describing frequently occurring events, simple biographical information, social notices, formulaic business letters, and simple technical material written for the general reader. Generally the prose that can be read by the individual is predominantly in straightforward or high-frequency sentence patterns. The individual does not have a broad active vocabulary (that is, which he or she recognizes immediately on sight) but is able to use contextual and real-world cues to understand the text. Characteristically, however, the individual is quite slow in performing such a process. He or she is typically able to answer factual questions about authentic texts of the types described above.

Reading 2+ (Limited Working Proficiency, Plus). Sufficient comprehension to understand most factual material in nontechnical prose as well as some discussions on concrete topics related to special professional interests. Is markedly more proficient at reading materials on a familiar topic. Is able to separate the main ideas and details from lesser ones and uses that distinction to advance understanding. The individual is able to use linguistic context and real-world knowledge to make sensible guesses about unfamiliar material. Has a broad active reading vocabulary. The individual is able to get the gist of main and subsidiary ideas in texts that could only be read thoroughly by persons with much higher proficiencies. Weaknesses include slowness, uncertainty, inability to discern nuance or intentionally disguised meaning.

whether in meaning or in form. These "intended" distractors and correct responses are then arranged in four or five columns. Items involving nominal, verbal, or other categorical entity are grouped with like entities. This is probably the most difficult stage in the design, as the "intended" distractors must be valid in some context, but must not be correct answers for the item or any other keys in the text.

Simultaneously, the designer completes an English rendition of the passage(s). She can manipulate the English to clue or mask any item, depending on the degree of difficulty needed at any point of the test. Clueing gives a hint through the English rendition and makes an item easier, masking on the other hand renders meaning more indirectly through the English and, therefore, increases its difficulty.

As the test designer builds the Keyed Completion test, three components emerge: (a) the skeleton text, (b) the columns of distractors, and (c) an English rendition. The test designer builds in only one or two "intended" distractors into the columns of possible responses, suggesting that the keyed completion test will function as a traditional multiple choice test. As we will see, however, the columnar arrangement generates more responses than the designer projects. Weaker test takers, in particular, will be attracted not only to the "intended" distractors but to other responses in the column.

The information identification section. The second part of the LPT is the information identification section, which attempts to determine how well the testee, given a full text, comprehends the semantic structure or content of texts. The information identification section uses a traditional multiple choice format with a four-choice item bank, thus increasing the possibility that students could improve their scores by guessing. Students are permitted dictionaries on this section as it is a performance test, which "relates to a person's skill in performing a language task typical of or similar to one required in the workplace" (Child, Clifford, and Lowe 1993: 20). Child has found that "the solution to the problem (of guessing) lies in the skillful linguistic design of the exercise, for example, avoidance of 'code matching' responses (such as matching the syntax of the original language) or development of plausible 'counter plots' across a set of items" (Child 1995). A counterplot suggests an alternate, but incomplete, scenario. It is yet another means of generating attractive distractors.

I have outlined the nature of the information identification section for the purposes of contrasting its use of four multiple-choice options with the twenty options in the keyed completion section. We will return to the information identification model for this purpose shortly, but first we must focus on the results of our research question in the keyed completion model.

Does the Keyed Completion model reduce the effect of guessing? Compared to the information identification section, the keyed completion section is not easy to develop. It takes considerable skill to select the key items, determine

Box 3. Sample Keyed Completion in German

This sample in German, although illustrative of the general principles of the keyed completion format, represents an earlier model of the test. Newer tests have a more sophisticated arrangement of possible answers, wherein like entities such as nominals or verbals are grouped together.

Skeleton text

_____ _____ Regierungsrates _____ Nikaragua, Daniel Ortega, _____ die
　1*　　2Δ　　　　　　　　3•　　　　　　　　　　　　　　　　4

USA _____ Wochenende erneut _____ einer _____ Intervention gewarnt.
　　　5•　　　　　　　　　　6•　　　　　7Δ

_____ Fernsehansprache _____ _____ das Ausmaß der von _____ gesteuerten
　8*　　　　　　　　　　9Δ　　10　　　　　　　　　　11*

und unterstützten _____, _____ die Nikaragua gegenwärtig _____ Souveran-
　　　　　　　　　12Δ　13•　　　　　　　　　　　　　　14

ität und _____ Integrität ernsthaft bedroht _____. _____ Gefahr _____ sich für
　　　　15　　　　　　　　　　　　　　　16*　17*　　　　18

Nikaragua _____ Beginn der gemeinsamen Kriegsmanöver der USA _____
　　　　　19*　　　　　　　　　　　　　　　　　　　　　　　20Δ

Honduras. Weiter informierte Ortega _____ zunehmende Sabotageakte auf
　　　　　　　　　　　　　　　　　21Δ

Industrieanlagen, _____ er _____ Bestandteil der Destabilisierungspläne der
　　　　　　　　22*　　23

USA bezeichnete.

English rendition. Daniel Ortega, the coordinator of Nicaragua's ruling council, renewed his warning to the U.S. over the weekend against military intervention. In a television address he pointed to the dimensions of the provocations directed and supported by the U.S., by which Nicaragua currently sees its sovereignty and territorial integrity seriously threatened. Nicaragua sees a particularly dangerous development in the start of joint U.S.-Honduran war maneuvers. Ortega went on to announce increasing acts of sabotage against industrial installations, which he characterized as part of the U.S. destabilization plans.

Box 3. (*Continued*)			
Possible Responses			
	*	Δ	•
A	An	Aber	am	als
B	Befinden	Als	Bei	auf
C	Den Koordinator	Auf	Dafür	aus
D	Den USA	Das	Damit	entwickele
E	Der Koordinator	Des	Daß	entwickeln
F	Der USA	Dich	den Flugzeugen	entwickelte
G	die	Ein	Dessen	haben
H	Eine besondere	Errichtung	durch	hat
I	Einem	Er sah	für	hatte
J	Einer	Er verwies	Seiner	hatten
K	Eines	Es	Seines	hätte
L	Eins	militärische	Sich	ihre
M	in deren	militärischen	sie	sandisten
N	Indessen	Provokation	So	sandinistische
O	in einem	Provokationen	Über das	seine
P	In einer	Sah	von	sollen
Q	mit	Sah er	von Flugzeugen	territoriale
R	sah	über	vor	zu
S	sehe	und	Wurden	zum
T	sind	verwies er	Würden	zur

plausible distractors, arrange the choices into columns, and translate the passage(s) into English. The keyed completion section also has some face validity problems. Test takers who are unfamiliar with this model are often frustrated by the hand-eye coordination it requires to match their responses with the correct block on the machine-scorable form. It is also difficult for some testees to follow the three

Box 4. Sample Information Identification

Der Damm des bösen Geistes Asi Abo <u>Aus der südwestchinesischen Provinz</u>
1

Yunnan <u>ist eine Sage überliefert</u>, die die Herkunft eines der schönsten Natur-
2

denkmäler Chinas <u>bezeugen soll</u>. <u>Vor langer Zeit</u>, <u>so heißt es dort</u>, lebte in
3   4   5

dieser Gegend <u>der böse Geist Asi Abo</u>, <u>der alle Menschen vertreiben wollte</u>.
6   7

Als sich die Jäger und Bauern <u>des Stammes der Sani und Axi</u> <u>weigerten ihr
8

<u>Land zu verlassen</u>, <u>beschloß er</u>, <u>sie zu vernichten</u>. <u>Von weit her</u> schleppte der
9   10   11   12

Geist gewaltige Felsbrocken heran, <u>um einen Damm am Nanppanjiang- Fluß
13

<u>zu errichten</u>. Städte und Dörfer und <u>die fruchtbaren Felder</u> sollten <u>in den
14

<u>Wassermassen versinken</u>.
15

Response sheet
A. from China's southwestern province
B. south of China's western province
C. except for China's southwestern province
D. from the Chinese provincial southwest

A. an old proverb has it
B. a certain sage has handed down
C. a saga has been transferred
D. there is a traditional tale

A. is intended to explain
B. should testify to
C. should convince
D. will convince

A. too long a time
B. for a longer time
C. for a long time
D. a long time ago

Box 4. (*Continued*)

A. as hot as it was there
B. as it says there
C. as it is called there
D. as he calls it there

A. of the wicked ghost Asi Abo
B. the wicked spirit Asi Abo
C. of the friendly spirit Asi Abo
D. the chief spirit Asi Abo

A. who wanted to chase all the people out
B. who would have chased out all men
C. who would drive all men
D. whom everyone wanted to drive out

A. of the stem of the Sani and Axi
B. the Sani and Axi system
C. stemming the Sani and Axi
D. of the Sani and Axi tribe

A. refused to leave their land
B. refused to allow her land
C. refused to rely on their land
D. refused to trust their land

A. did he complete
B. he decided
C. he completed
D. did he decide

A. to destroy it
B. to anihilate her
C. to anihilate them
D. to deny them

A. from far away
B. from right here
C. far from here
D. long ago

Box 4. (*Continued*)

A. to reach the Nanppanjiang dam
B. to put a curse on the Nanppanjiang
C. to build a dam on the Nanppanjiang
D. to reach the Nanppanjiang river

A. the barren fronts
B. the fertile fields
C. which were fertile fields
D. the barren fields

A. sink in the backed up waters
B. sink the watery mass
C. deep in the waters
D. sink the masses of water

---

separate, but related, components of the test. We have tried to overcome these difficulties by allowing examinees to write in their test booklets and by using page layout to keep the three components of the section aligned at any one point in the test. In the future, computer-assisted testing may address these face validity issues.

As mentioned previously, the test designer builds in a few "intended" distractors; so does it really prove to be any different from a traditional multiple-choice test? In other words, does the Keyed Completion model reduce the effect of guessing?

Box 5. Page layout (facing pages throughout the selection)

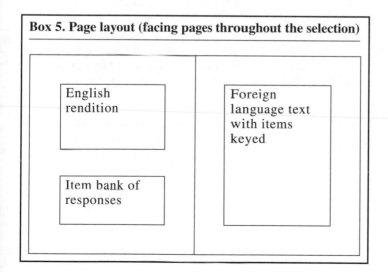

Research Methodology. In order to conduct the necessary research, answer sheets from 1997 and 1998 Language Performance Tests were evaluated. Each of the three tests had been previously validated under contract by the Educational Testing Service in Princeton, New Jersey. For this study the data was rescanned into our local system and manipulated in Excel 97 and SPSS 7.0. The research goal was to investigate whether or not the keyed completion format had any effect on the number of answers chosen for each item when compared to the four-choice response bank in the information identification section.

Results. There are at least two ways to reduce the effect of guessing. The first is by increasing the number of choices given to the test taker. The keyed completion model does this by providing the test taker a twenty-item bank of possible responses. As explained previously, however, the designer only builds in two or three "intended" distractors. As table 1 shows, on average, test takers are attracted to almost double that number of possible responses, including the correct response.

One aspect of reducing guessing is the number of times weaker test takers are attracted to less correct or totally incorrect answers. Our study has shown that this can be done by increasing the number of possible distractors on the keyed completion section from four distractors to twenty. But it can also be accomplished by making the distractors more attractive. The test data were used to study the attractiveness of wrong answers. An attractive distractor was defined as one that was selected by at least 10% of the test population. The Russian test produced, by far, the most attractive distractors, but the results were mixed and further research is indicated (see table 2).

Future Research. Another research question connected with the concept of attractiveness is a study of whether the test designer's "intended" distractors proved to be truly attractive, how often, and for what types of words. This is not the only possible area of future investigation. Although preliminary research confirms that the keyed completion test effectively discriminates between test takers,[4] a more thorough analysis of the relationship between the number of

Table 1. Average number of responses

Language	Average number of answers, Keyed completion	Average number of answers, Information identification
Arabic	5.7	2.8
Russian	6.9	3.5
Chinese	6	3

Table 2. Attractiveness of responses

Language	At least two attractive distractors	At least one attractive distractor
Arabic	5 out of 53 questions	34 out of 53 questions
Russian	13 out of 53 questions	40 out of 53 questions
Chinese	6 out of 54 questions	20 out of 54 questions

Note: I define "attractive" as a response by 10% or more of the testing population.

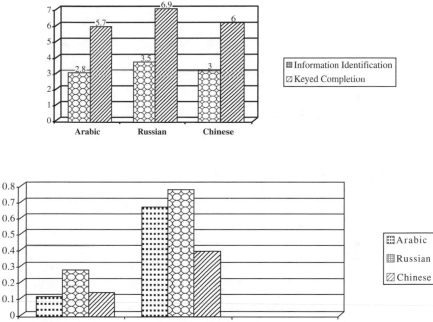

responses chosen and item discrimination would be beneficial. Other research issues include how the language being tested impacts on the results, how the "key" items are selected, what makes the intended distractors attractive, and how this format can be adapted to computer-based testing. We hope that continued research will continue to improve on the Language Performance Test design.

Conclusions. It appears then, from this initial study, that the keyed completion model does reduce the effect of guessing by increasing the number of available responses and, to a certain extent, by including attractive distractors. An unanticipated research result is that the more traditional, four-item multiple choice information identification section of the test is so strong, especially on the Russian LPT, and the causes of this should be investigated further.

REFERENCES

Child, James R. 1987. Language Proficiency Levels and the Typology of Texts. In Heidi Byrnes and Michael Canale (eds.), *Defining and Developing Proficiency: Guidelines, Implementations and Concepts.* Lincolnwood, IL: National Textbook. 97–106.
Child, James. 1995. "Description of graphic level 2 testing system." Unpublished manuscript available from author.
Child, James, Ray Clifford, and Pardee Lowe, Jr. 1993. Proficiency and Performance in Language Testing. *Applied Language Learning* 4(1 and 2): 19–54.
McIntyre, Sandra S. 1986. Paper presented at the Eighth Annual Language Testing Research Colloquium, February.
Taylor, W. L. 1953. Cloze Procedure: A New Tool for Measuring Readability. *Journalism Quarterly* 30: 414–438.

NOTES

1. The thoughts expressed herein are the author's own and in no way reflect those of the Department of Defense. I would like to express my gratitude to four colleagues, Mr. James R. Child, my mentor and advisor; Mr. Pardee Lowe, Jr., for his encouragement to pursue this paper and for his considerable feedback on the draft versions; Mr. Reginald Lee Heefner, for helpful suggestions and comments; and Mr. Christopher Bean, for his patience with statistics.
2. In U.S. government work, graphic material is defined as any written format, which would include news items, literary materials, handwritten correspondence, etc.
3. The quotation marks around "intended" distractor(s) reflect the fact that these options are the test designer's estimation that these distractors will prove "attractive" prior to any pilot testing. Further research should investigate the "attractiveness" of the "intended" distractors.
4. A study by the Defense Language Institute concludes that "[O]n the positive side, the keyed completion format seems almost unique in its ability to discriminate with a very high reliability and power across a wide range of reading proficiency levels" (McIntyre 1986).

Lessons learned from fifty years of theory and practice in government language teaching

Frederick H. Jackson
Foreign Service Institute, U.S. Department of State
Marsha A. Kaplan
Foreign Service Institute, U.S. Department of State

Introduction. This paper is about the interface among theory, practice, purpose, and result during the fifty years of existence of the Foreign Service Institute (FSI), and the lessons that have been learned from that interface. We will present our view of what has been learned from FSI's half century of practical experience preparing thousands of adult learners to carry out complex, professional tasks in foreign languages. The core of the paper will be ten pragmatic lessons about adult language learning and instruction at FSI. Although most of these lessons will be seen to be congruent with recent thinking in the field of Second Language Acquisition, some of them present a different perspective.[1]

The Foreign Service Institute is the training arm of the State Department. It was established in 1946 to train members of the U.S. diplomatic community to undertake assignments in U.S. embassies, consulates, and other posts overseas. It delivers close to one million hours of training each year to nearly 2,000 language students in more than sixty languages. Its clientele are all adults who will use the foreign language in their government service jobs abroad or their adult dependents. Although FSI's School of Language Studies was established to provide training for State Department employees, in recent years one-third of its students typically come from other government agencies. The school is not authorized to train nongovernment personnel.

From FSI's earliest days, when its staff included the linguists Henry Lee Smith, Charles Ferguson, Carleton Hodge, and Albert Valdman, and the anthropologists Edward Hall and Ray Birdwhistel, its language training has been influenced by the findings of research and the theoretical insights that derive from them. But the test for FSI of all such insights has consistently been whether or not they actually improve the ability of the learners to use the language. The FSI Language Proficiency Test has been one consistent means of measuring our success in training, but the most important measurements have been reports from the embassies and other posts where our graduates serve about what they can and cannot do with the language in the field. These reports have had the most important influences on FSI's training approaches. That is, when the application of a theoretical principle has failed to result in better learning, as indicated by such reports, either the application or the principle has had to be modified.

The term "language proficiency" was first used in the late 1950s by FSI staff. For us, it refers to *the ability to use language as a tool to get things done.* Language-training programs at FSI are accountable for developing prespecified proficiency levels in students in as short a period of time as possible. The accountability goes far beyond test scores and end-of-training student evaluations. It goes to whether graduates of our programs can use the language to carry out the important and complex work for which they are responsible. If their language limitations cause them not to be able to do that work, the FSI program heads will hear about it in no uncertain terms. Language educators at FSI get direct evaluative feedback from our clients and stakeholders. When a dissatisfied cable comes to us from post, it receives our immediate attention.

Almost all FSI language courses would be characterized as *foreign-language training* (FLT), rather than *second-language training* (SLT), in that the training takes place in the United States and there are few if any native speakers of most of the languages easily available outside of the classroom (Nayar 1997). This means that the FSI programs are themselves responsible for providing learners with the very great preponderance of the experiences with the language from which the students must learn. Sridhar (1994) has pointed out that FLT may be the most typical language-learning situation in the world today. Our programs are not given a lengthy period in which to prepare learners to do their work. For example, students in the Russian program are expected to progress in ten months of intensive training from no functional ability in the language to the ability to read almost any professionally relevant text and discuss in detail with a Russian-speaker any and all implications of that text for Russian-American relations. Ten months of intensive language study may seem like a long time, but, in fact, it is very short when the scope of the goal is considered. There is no time to waste with nonproductive activities.[2]

The proficiency levels that FSI language programs are required to achieve among the learners are based on the *Interagency Language Roundtable* (ILR) *Language Skill Level Descriptions,* which are summarized in table 1. The ILR descriptions characterize six *base levels* of language proficiency (levels 0–5). Intermediate gradations on the scale are indicated by a plus mark; for example, a rating of S-2+ describes a proficiency that is substantially stronger than S-2 but still falls short of the criteria required for a rating of S-3. The six *base levels*, together with the five *plus-levels,* encompass a full range of proficiency from *no proficiency* to *functionally native proficiency.*

The sixty-odd FSI language programs, then, are for us the proving grounds for the usefulness of any theory about language learning and teaching. The crucial

Table 1. U.S. Government Proficiency Ratings

Rating	Description
S/R-0	No functional proficiency
S/R-1	*Elementary proficiency*: Able to satisfy routine courtesy and travel needs and to read common signs and simple sentences and phrases.
S/R-2	*Limited working proficiency*: Able to satisfy routine social and limited office needs and to read short typewritten or printed straightforward texts.
S/R-3	*General professional proficiency*: Able to speak accurately and with enough vocabulary to handle social representation and professional discussions within special fields of knowledge; able to read most materials found in daily newspapers.
S/R-4	*Advanced professional proficiency*: Able to speak and read the language fluently and accurately on all levels pertinent to professional needs.
S/R-5	Functionally equivalent to an educated native speaker.

question has been and will continue to be whether an innovation, in fact, improves the speed with which our learners can meet the proficiency standards or enhances in some way the quality of the language skill that they do achieve. Working within this system of accountability, we at FSI have learned some things that we believe matter in helping adult learners to develop a high level of proficiency in languages in a short specified period of time. In this paper, we present ten of the lessons we have learned.

Lesson 1. Mature adults can learn a foreign language well enough through intensive language study to do things in the language (almost) as well as native speakers. The goal of language training for FSI students is typically general professional proficiency (S-3/R-3) in reading and speaking the language, including interactive listening comprehension. This level is approximately equivalent to "superior" on the scale used by the American Council for the Teaching of Foreign Languages. The mean age of language students at FSI is forty-one. Although many of our students know more than one foreign language—in recent years, the average FSI student begins class knowing 2.3 non-English languages—most of them enroll as absolute beginners in the language they are assigned to study. Despite this obstacle, approximately two-thirds of FSI's full-time students achieve or exceed their proficiency goals, and almost all of the others nearly meet the goals. This is due both to the characteristics of the programs and to the abilities of the learners.

Research on aging has shown us repeatedly that short-term memory declines with age, but in FSI's students this is compensated for by increased experience, which actually helps in the language learning process (see Kulick 1988; Schleppegrell 1987). The result is that skilled adults learn some aspects of languages better and faster than children (Harley 1986). Diane Larsen-Freeman (1991) has quoted Patsy Lightbown as estimating that young children spend 12,000 to 15,000 hours learning their native languages. At FSI, adult students in a forty-four-week language program spend 1,100 hours in training to achieve a highly significant proficiency level in a new language. They can do this because they have learned how to learn.[3]

Most adults are not good at eliminating accents and developing a native-like pronunciation, but, for FSI, as stated earlier, proficiency refers to the ability to use language as a tool to get things done. Native accent is typically not a practical criterion for success in this ability (although intelligibility is). But as Kachru (1994), Sridhar (1994), and others have pointed out, mainstream second-language acquisition (SLA) researchers have the "fundamental misconception"—the term is Kachru's—that the target of foreign language learning is "the idealized native speaker's competence" (Sridhar 1994:801) or "to use [the language] in the same way as monolingual native speakers" (Kachru 1994:797). Once we identify a more pragmatic goal than "native-like" accent or competence, we can perhaps clarify what we mean by adult language learning—and make it appear more like the learning of other complex skills (McLaughlin 1987).

Lesson 2. "Language-learning aptitude" varies among individuals and affects their classroom learning success (but at least some aspects of aptitude can be learned). Any language teacher anywhere in the world knows that some people are simply much better classroom language learners than others. In intensive language programs such as FSI's, differences among learners can easily become magnified. By "aptitude" we are not referring to any theoretical construct. We mean the observable fact that some people know how to learn a language very efficiently in a classroom and others do not, regardless of the effort they put in.

Language-learning aptitude is not a single unitary trait, but a constellation of them (Oxford and Ehrman 1992). Some aspects of aptitude can be measured (Harley and Hart 1997; Skehan 1991). Although it was designed more than forty years ago, John Carroll's Modern Language Aptitude Test (MLAT) is still the best single predictor of learning success at FSI, especially at the extremes of the MLAT scale (Ehrman 1998b; see also Spolsky 1995:132–133).

Although the research is somewhat equivocal on the question of whether language aptitude is innate or potentially subject to change (Harley and Hart 1997), it appears to us that at least some of the skills and awareness that underlie aptitude can be learned. As adults learn more about languages and how to learn them, they can get better at it. We have observed clear instances of this. It is also possible for a flexible language program to adapt to learner traits so as to minimize weaknesses and maximize learning strengths *for particular learners.* That is, we might say that some learners, in a sense, demonstrate higher "aptitudes" in one style of language program than in another.

Finally, from our experience, motivation, self-discipline, and power of concentration may be equally or more important than cognitive aptitude in helping learners achieve language learning success—or in contributing to their failure to succeed.

Lesson 3. There is no "one right way" to teach (or learn) languages, nor is there a single "right" syllabus. Students at FSI and in other government language training programs have learned and still do learn languages successfully from syllabi based on audio-lingual practice of grammatical patterns, linguistic functions, social situations, task-based learning, community language learning, the silent way, and combinations of these and other approaches. Spolsky (1989: 383) writes, "Any intelligent and disinterested observer knows that there are many ways to learn languages and many ways to teach them, and that some ways work with some students in some circumstances and fail with others." This matches our experience precisely.

It is also clear, as many have reported, that learners' needs change over time—sometimes rapidly. Types of activities that worked very well for certain learners at an early stage in a course may be almost completely useless a couple of weeks later for those same learners (Larsen-Freeman 1991: 336–37). At the same time, the lesson plan that works beautifully for "Class B" on Monday morning may not work at all for a "Class C" that is at exactly the same stage in a course. Learning is more efficient when the focus is on providing each learner with what he or she needs in order to learn right now, not on teaching a preset curriculum.[4]

One generalization that *can* be made here is the need for changes of pace in long-term language training. This is why immersions and excursions are so valuable for learners—they afford the learners opportunity to try out their language skills. Especially in long-term training where learners typically encounter the frustrations of extended learning "plateaus," breaks in the routine can re-energize and refocus them.

Another generalization is that some kind of explicit grammar instruction helps most people to learn efficiently. Some focus on an overview of the grammatical system early in a course also appears to make language learning more efficient for FSI's students by creating awareness of form(s) so that learners can attend to them when they are ready. If there is insufficient early focus on form, we have learned that learners may, indeed, risk automatizing ingrained errors (see Higgs and Clifford 1982).

Lesson 4. Time on task and the intensity of the learning experience appear crucial. Language learning is not an effortless endeavor for adults (or for children, for that matter). For the great majority of adult learners, learning a language rapidly to a high level requires a great deal of memorization, analysis, practice to build automaticity, and, of course, functional and meaningful language use. Learning as quickly as possible to speak and understand a language automatically and effectively in a variety of situations and for a range of purposes requires intensive exposure to and interaction with that language. At FSI, we have found that it requires at least four class hours a day—usually more—for five days a week, plus three or more additional hours a day of independent study.

Learning a language also cannot be done in a short time. The length of time it takes to learn a language well depends to a great extent on similarities between the new language and other languages that the learner may know well. The time necessary for a beginning learner to develop professional proficiency in each language—proven again and again over a half century of language teaching—cannot be shortened appreciably. FSI has tried to shorten programs, and it has not worked (see also lesson 5).

Class size makes a difference. For rapid learning, basic classroom groupings of six students at lower proficiency in cognate languages like French or Spanish are the maximum. For other languages and at advanced levels, a class size of four or fewer is the most efficient. Occasional one-on-one language learning is highly beneficial for almost all learners—it intensifies time on task, increases interaction opportunities with a native speaker, and provides security for learners to try out aspects of the language they are not confident about—but strictly tutorial training alone is not the best solution for the majority of learners, who benefit from collaborating and interacting with classmates.[5]

Focused practice of some kind, including "drills," appears necessary for almost all language learners to develop confidence and automatic language use (see also lesson 7).

Immersion experiences, where only the language is used, have great pay-offs in morale, motivation, perception of skill, and stamina in using the language. They appear to have the greatest payoff above the S-2 level. Despite what some published research has indicated, for example Brecht, Davidson, and Ginsberg (1993), our experience is that in-country immersion is most effective where the learner is at higher levels of proficiency.

There is no substitute for simply spending time using the language. Segalowitz and his colleagues have pointed out how crucial to reading ability is the simple fact of doing a lot of reading (e.g., Favreau and Segalowitz 1982). Our experience at FSI indicates unequivocally that the amount of time spent in reading, listening to, and interacting in the language has a close relationship to the learner's ability to use that language professionally.

Lesson 5. Learners' existing knowledge about *language* affects their learning. All else being equal, the more that learners already know that they can use in learning a new language, the faster and better they will learn. The less they know that they can use, the harder learning will be.

Government language educators are all familiar with the language categories that FSI and DLI have developed. The categories indicate gross differences in how hard it is for native speakers of American English to learn different languages. For example, FSI's three categories indicate that Spanish—a category I language—is among the easier languages for English speakers to learn; Japanese is among the hardest; and Russian, Hungarian, and Thai are among those in the middle. Table 2 summarizes these differences.

Two things need to be understood about these categories. First, they are based solely on FSI's experience of the time it takes our learners to learn these languages. (FSI recently had to start teaching several languages that had not been taught before in government language schools. We estimated that these would prove to be category II languages, and for the most part we were right. But at least two of them—Georgian and Mongolian—have proven to be harder than that.) Second, the categories reflect various parameters of linguistic distance (see Child 2000). Stated simply, the more commonalties a language shares with English—whether due to a genetic relationship or otherwise—the easier and faster it is for a native English speaker to learn that language.

The length of time it takes to learn a language well also depends to a great extent on similarities between that language and any other languages that the learner knows well. The more dissimilar a new language is—in structure, sounds, orthography, implicit world view, and so on—the longer learning takes. For knowledge of one language to be a real advantage in learning another, however, it needs to be at a significant level. Thain and Jackson (n.d.) and an interagency group determined recently that this kind of advantage takes effect at a three-level proficiency or better. Below that level, knowledge of a second language does not appear to make any useful difference in acquisition of a related third language.[6]

Table 2. Approximate learning expectations at the Foreign Service Institute

Language Categories	Weeks to achieve goal	Class hours to achieve goal
Category I: Languages closely cognate with English: French, German, Italian, Portuguese, Romanian, Spanish, Swedish, Dutch, Norwegian, Afrikaans, etc.	23–24	575–600
Category II: Languages with significant linguistic and/or cultural differences from English: Albanian, Amharic, Azerbaijani, Bulgarian, Finnish, Greek, Hebrew, Hindi, Hungarian, Icelandic, Khmer, Latvian, Nepali, Polish, Russian, Serbian, Tagalog, Thai, Turkish, Urdu, Vietnamese, Zulu, etc.	44	1100
Category III: Languages that are exceptionally difficult for native English speakers to learn to speak and read: Arabic, Chinese, Japanese, and Korean	88 (2nd year is in the country)	2200

Note: All estimates in this figure assume that the student is a native speaker of English with no prior knowledge of the language to be learned. It is also assumed that the student has very good or better aptitude for classroom learning of foreign languages. Less skilled language learners typically take longer. Although languages are grouped into general "categories" of difficulty for native English speakers, within each category some languages are more difficult than others. In the cases of Indonesian, Malaysian, and Swahili, learning expectations are halfway between category I languages and category II languages.

It seems to us that such observations lead inevitably to the conclusion that *language transfer* relationships, involving learners' native languages but also other languages that they may know, play complex and highly significant roles in the learning of new languages. As recognized in Pica (1994), Larsen-Freeman (1991), and, especially, Odlin (1989), SLA researchers can no longer reasonably claim that knowledge of other languages has no significant effect on learning a new one.

In addition to the often unconscious effects of transfer-based phenomena, language learning may also be affected by whether the learners possess an overt declarative knowledge of salient linguistic and grammatical concepts. It appears increasingly clear at FSI that such knowledge helps many learners to be able to progress faster and more surely, and that lack of that knowledge can slow them down. Such concepts may include basic ideas like *subject, predicate, preposition, or sentence,* but also more language-specific concepts like *tone, aspect, palatalization, declension, topicalization,* and so on. Knowing such concepts increases the accessibility of such resources as reference grammars, textbooks, and dictionaries, and also serves an important purpose in making adult learners aware of types of language phenomena to watch for. Because of this, several FSI language programs have recently put together short written guides to grammatical terminology and concepts in order to help learners to tune in to the new language.

Lesson 6. A learner's prior experience with learning (languages or other skills) also affects classroom learning. If learners already have learned a foreign language to a high level, that is a great advantage in learning another language, regardless of whether or not it is related to the first, but if they do not know how to learn a language in a classroom, that is a disadvantage. Prior formal language study makes a difference, no matter how remote it was. Knowing how to learn a language in a formal setting helps the learner, both cognitively and affectively. In contrast, *bilingualism acquired naturally as a child does not, in and of itself, appear to aid in learning a third language in a classroom.*

We see individuals on a regular basis who know exactly what they have to do in order to learn a new language. Some of them are so good that they are truly astonishing, and they are each different. Earl Stevick emphasized this point in his 1989 book, *Success with Foreign Languages,* by describing seven such superb learners— each with different learning approaches. Programs at FSI need to be flexible enough to make it possible for each learner to progress as rapidly as he or she is able. We have found the following adult learning axiom to be revealing: "If an adult tells you that he needs something in order to learn, the chances are very good that he's right."

Richness of background knowledge and experience appear to have a marked influence on how well and how quickly many adults can learn a new language. Part of this may be a matter of having things to talk about. A wonderful teacher whom one of us met when first arriving at FSI, now retired, used to say seriously, "This [teaching at FSI] is the greatest job in the world. All I do is spend every day teaching a bunch of very smart and interesting people how to tell me everything that they know!" In contrast, both of us have also had experience with suffering learners who complain that they "do not know what to talk about!"

FSI's language teachers are all native speakers of the language they teach and were brought up and educated within a culture where that language was used. But FSI has also found that there is considerable value in having at least one member of the program team who learned the language as an adult and who can therefore serve as a kind of object model for the new learners and can discuss with them the issues that they are wrestling with. For most of FSI's fifty years, such a human resource has been a crucial component of our training model.[7]

Lesson 7. The importance of "automaticity" in building learner skill and confidence in speaking and reading a language is more important than has been recognized by the SLA field over the last two decades. Successful language learning requires "stretching" learners some of the time through "i +1"-type tasks. Yet it is also important to build up processing skills by varying the pace and giving learners some tasks that they can perform easily. This is particularly important in intensive programs, where students are constantly confronted with new structures and vocabulary to learn. Although techniques associated with audiolingual methodology have been in disrepute since the 1960s and early 1970s, the fact remains that many of our students desire occasional pattern practice. Pattern practice—drill—is a technique that continues to be useful for FSI learners, when used in concert with the various communicative, experiential, and task-based approaches. It is valued not only at the early stages of our students' learning, but at the more advanced as well, as review. In training programs with time-specified outcomes, such as at FSI, the automatization of basic grammatical structures and communicative routines is essential for efficient learning. McLaughlin argued this point nearly twenty years ago. As he explains in a more recent work, "[t]he acquisition of a cognitive skill [results] from the automatization of routines or units of activity. Initially, the execution of these routines requires the allocation of large amounts of mental effort (controlled processing), but repeated performance of the activity leads to the availability of automatized routines in long term memory. The result of this process is that less and less effort is required for automated routines and the learner can devote more effort to acquiring other sub-skills that are not yet automated" (McLaughlin 1987:149). In order to perform higher order communicative skills—such as participating in social conversations (see lesson 10) and other such job-related uses of the target language—our students must produce spontaneously and accurately the relevant grammatical structures and routines of the language.

The importance of promoting automaticity is true for reading as well as speaking. Adults need to read considerable amounts of "easy" material in order to build up stamina and to automatize processing skills. Segalowitz and his collaborators have shown us that iteration of relatively easy processing tasks is crucial to developing reading skill. Red (this volume) has also shown that, for an adult, learning to process a completely foreign writing system automatically enough to focus on comprehension appears to take much more time and effort than many reading researchers had once thought (see also Everson, Harada, and Bernhardt 1988 and Bernhardt 1991). Without some degree of automatic processing capability, reading becomes a painful decoding process, leaving the reader with little cognitive energy available for understanding and interpretation.

Lesson 8. Learners may not learn a linguistic form until they are "ready," but FSI's experience indicates that teachers and a well designed course can help learners become ready earlier. The research on natural sequences of acquisition by scholars in Europe, Japan, the United States, and Australia is striking and must be attended to by any serious person in the field of language education (e.g., Pienemann 1984). However, to conclude on the basis of such studies, as Craig Chaudron did in a conference with Southeast Asian language educators in January 1994, that "the structural syllabus is intellectually bankrupt" is not supported by the experience at FSI.

Diane Larsen-Freeman (1991: 337) has written, in this respect, "[i]t may not be reasonable for teachers to expect students to master aspects of the language which are too far beyond their current stage of development." This makes absolute sense to us, but our experience also is that it is possible for a teacher to increase learners' awareness and create in them what Nina Garrett has referred to as "concepts of grammaticality" for aspects of the language that they might not otherwise notice. Ellis (1993, 1998) has speculated, we believe convincingly, that explicit instruction of grammatical forms can help learners develop awareness of the forms before they might otherwise do so and thereby become "ready" to learn them sooner.

At FSI, we find more and more that *early* focus on form makes an important difference—not focus on form at the expense of use or meaning, but focus that helps learners to develop awareness of significant aspects of the language that they will need later to capture precise distinctions in meaning. For example, English-speaking learners of tonal languages like Thai and Chinese do not attend to phonemic tone distinctions readily unless a "focus on form" has made the distinctions salient. Similarly, in highly inflected languages, such as Russian or Finnish, significant meaning is encoded at the ends of words and must be attended to. Students learning Russian must literally choose from 144 possible endings for each noun, adjective, demonstrative, and pronoun they wish to utter. In both examples, it is not possible for the learner to not make a choice. To utter any word in Thai entails giving it a tone; to say a noun in Russian requires attaching a case marker. Failure to pay attention to such forms in speaking, reading, and listening will lead not just to a foreign accent, but to serious misunderstanding.

It is true that instructed input does not automatically become intake, but without explicit consciousness-raising of formal aspects of the language, they may be learned too slowly—or not at all. Because of FSI's specified time constraints, it just does not work to let structures "emerge" naturally when they want to. Celce-Murcia, Dornyei, and Thurrell (1997) quote Widdowson (1990) approvingly as follows: "the whole point of language pedagogy is that it is a way of short-circuiting the slow process of natural discovery and can make arrangements for learning to happen *more easily and more efficiently* than it does in 'natural surroundings'" (emphasis added).

Lesson 9. A supportive, collaborative, responsive learning environment, with a rich variety of authentic and teacher-made resources, is very important in fostering effective learning. Madeline Ehrman (1998a) has observed that end-of-training comments from students after six to ten months of intensive training at FSI typically mention their teachers as the factor that contributed most to their success in learning. The consistency of such comments is striking. Ehrman writes, "[a]lthough [students] often mention as positive forces well-designed textbooks and a suitable curriculum, their true enthusiasm is reserved for their teachers and the relationships the teachers establish with them." The ultimate goal of language training is to develop learner autonomy, so that individuals can use the language effectively outside and after the classroom. To accomplish this, Ehrman points out that even the very best adult learners need support, feedback, and mentoring at times from their teachers. The teachers' abilities to empathize, help the students manage their feelings and expectations, and tune interventions appropriately to the emotional and developmental state of the learners are key factors in many successful learning outcomes.

Effective language teachers find ways to provide learners with support and scaffolding when they need it, and to remove the scaffolding when the learners no longer need it. This is true in small ways as well as in large. One type of scaffolding that Ray Clifford of the Defense Language Institute believes to be crucial for adult learners is frequent and constructive formative feedback to the learners on the effectiveness of their language use (Clifford, personal communication). Such feedback might take the form of tacit assent to the truth (and intelligibility) of a learner's utterance, but it might also be explicit correction of a pattern of errors or even an extended consultation, depending on what is needed.

Freeman (1989) and other leaders in the field of language-teacher education describe language teaching as a series of complex decision-making processes based on the teacher's awareness and understanding of what is going on with the learners and the interplay of the teacher's own attitudes, knowledge, and repertoire of skills. In this most helpful model, teaching is not a "methodology" or a set of "behaviors," but rather the ability to make and carry out appropriate decisions (see also Jackson 1993).

The job of language teaching at FSI is to find ways to create environments in which each student is able to learn the language efficiently and successfully. If one kind of environment does not work with a particular group of students, then we have to find another one that does. The model that we try to implement at FSI is one in which students, instructors, and program managers take joint collaborative responsibility for the students' learning.[8]

Lesson 10. Conversation, which on the surface appears to be one of the most basic forms of communication, is actually one of the hardest to master. A seasoned Foreign Service officer, who had learned several languages to a high level, was overheard to remark that engaging in conversation—particularly in multiparty settings—was the ultimate test of someone's language ability.

For many of our graduates, a fundamental part of their work involves taking part in ordinary and informal conversations with host country officials and business, cultural, and community leaders on a variety of personal and professional topics. Yet of all the tasks graduates carry out at post in the foreign language—articulating policy, conducting interviews, managing offices and local staff—ordinary conversation is the one area of language use in which they unanimously claim to experience the most difficulty, noting specifically problems in *following* the threads of conversations in multigroup settings. Many officers report that they would much rather give a speech or conduct an interview than be the only nonnative surrounded by native speakers at a social engagement such as a dinner party or reception (Kaplan 1997).

Interestingly, such reports appear to fly in the face of some of the assumptions of the language proficiency level descriptions of the Interagency Language Roundtable and ACTFL, which relegate "extensive but casual social conversation" to a relatively low-level speaking skill while raising professional language use and certain institutionalized forms of talk to a higher level.

The properties of ordinary social conversation imply that language learners need to practice at least all of the following:

- following rapid and unpredictable turns in topic,
- displaying understanding and involvement,
- producing unplanned speech,
- coping with the speed of the turn-taking, and
- coping with background noise.

Participants in conversation must at once listen to what their interlocutor is saying, formulate their contribution, make their contribution relevant, and utter their contribution in a timely way, lest they lose the thread of the conversation. Unlike most other typical face-to-face interactions, no individual can successfully "control" a free-wheeling multi-party conversation.

In a sense, conversation is more about listening than about speaking, especially when the conversationalist is either trying to determine where the interlocutor might stand on certain important issues or is searching for an opportune moment to make a particular point. A former director of the Foreign Service Institute, Ambassador Lawrence Taylor, used to remark that Foreign Service officers need to be able to conduct what he called "educated assertive gossip"—*educated,* because the officer needs to be informed about (and able to discuss) anything of importance to that culture and time; *assertive,* because the officer must search for opportunities to make points that further the interests of the United States; and *gossip,* because the officer needs to be able to follow the interlocutors into any topic or turn of thought (or joke or tale) that may arise.[9]

FSI has developed a number of tasks and other kinds of activities to help learners develop skills and the "comfort level" that they will need to participate in these conversations (see, e.g., Kaplan 1997), but we recognize that there is still much for us to do.

Conclusions. We hope that the present paper will not be interpreted as yet another blow in some emotional battle between "researchers" and "practitioners" (viz. Clarke 1994). We at FSI value the results of research highly. Indeed, we wish often that we had more time and opportunity to investigate formally certain research questions among our programs.

What we do want to suggest, however, is that the practical day-to-day, week-to-week, year-to-year experiences of training institutions like the Foreign Service Institute offer data that are informative for anyone thinking seriously about language learning. In our half century of language education at FSI, we have moved from "teaching the textbook" to "helping the learner to learn," from a strict diet of sentence-based pattern drills to a range of "communicative activities," from using predominantly teacher-developed materials to a heavy emphasis on authentic or "found" materials and realia. Based on reports from overseas, we believe that we are doing a better job of preparing our students now than we ever did before. Yet, the interesting fact remains that Foreign Service officers used to learn their languages to high levels in the 1960s, just as they do today. For us at FSI, we see our task as one of continuing to tinker so as to try to help more learners to learn to use more languages better, and to listen carefully to what the posts overseas tell us about what we are doing well—and what not so well.

But for our colleagues and friends in the great research institutions, it seems to us that at least part of your tasks ought to be to seek answers to why some of the things we have described are the way they are. Why did learners learn almost as successfully in the early days of the long histories of FSI, the Defense Language Institute, Georgetown's English Language Institute, and other comparable institutions, as they do today, despite the clear increases in the field's understanding of teaching and learning? Do the curriculum and teaching techniques, in fact, not really matter? Why is a class size of more than four too inefficient when we try to teach learners at really high levels of proficiency? Why is an early grammatical overview so helpful to adult learners of languages like Russian or German? Why is, for example, Estonian so much harder for English speakers to learn well than, say, Swahili, even though neither of them is related to English? Why is it really so hard for an adult English reader to learn to read another writing system fluently? There are many more questions like these.

One research question of vital interest to government language educators concerns language maintenance and attrition. The kind of small-group intensive long-term language training that we have described in this paper is extremely expensive. Having made this investment, it is crucial to determine what can be done to maintain the language skills that the graduates have achieved or, preferably, to improve them. Language maintenance at post may not simply be a matter of giving the speakers a set of strategies to use there, but more one of attaining a "critical mass" of language proficiency. Informally, we have observed in the languages that we have worked with that an individual departing for post following training with a borderline professional proficiency (or lower) is very likely to experience attrition. An individual with a strong professional proficiency (S-3 or S-3+) will maintain or improve proficiency, and with advanced professional proficiency (S-3+ or S-4) will almost certainly continue to improve. Does this "critical mass" vary according to the language, post of assignment, length of tour, nature of job, or characteristics of the individual? Is there anything that language-training programs can do—either in the United States or in the country—to enable all learners to improve their language skills once they get to the country?

REFERENCES

Bernhardt, Elizabeth B. 1991. A psycholinguistic perspective on second language literacy. In Jan H. Hulstijn and Johan F. Matter (eds.), *Reading in two languages,* vol. 8 of the *AILA Review.* Amsterdam: Free University Press. 31–44.

Brecht, Richard D., and A. Ronald Walton. 1994. Toward a language learning framework for Southeast Asian languages. *Journal of Southeast Asian language teaching* 3.

Brecht, Richard D., Dan Davidson, and Ralph B. Ginsberg. 1993. *Predictors of foreign language gain during study abroad.* Washington, D.C.: National Foreign Language Center.

Celce-Murcia, Marianne, Zoltan Dornyei, and Sarah Thurrell. 1997. Direct approaches in L2 instruction: A turning point in communicative language teaching? *TESOL Quarterly* 31(1): 141–152.

Child, James. 2000. Factors affecting distances between languages. Paper presented at the ILR Preconference session at GURT, May 4.

Clarke, Mark A. 1994. The dysfunctions of the theory-practice discourse. *TESOL Quarterly* 28(1): 9–26.

Ehrman, Madeline. 1998a. The learning alliance: Conscious and unconscious aspects of the second language teacher's role. *System* 26(1): 93–106.

Ehrman, Madeline E. 1998b. The Modern Language Aptitude Test for predicting learning success and advising students. *Applied Language Learning* 9(1–2): 31–70.

Ellis, Rod. 1993. The structural syllabus and second language acquisition. *TESOL Quarterly* 27(1): 91–114.

Ellis, Rod. 1998. Teaching and research: Options in grammar teaching. *TESOL Quarterly* 32(1): 39–60.

Everson, Michael E., Fumiko Harada, and Elizabeth B. Bernhardt. 1988. Second language (L2) reading of German, Japanese and Chinese: An investigation into three eye-tracking studies. Paper presented at the annual meeting of the National Reading Conference, Tucson, Arizona. December 3.

Favreau, M., and Norman Segalowitz. 1982. Second language reading in fluent bilinguals. *Applied Psycholinguistics* 3: 329–341.

Freeman, Donald. 1989. Teacher training, development, and decision-making: A model of teaching and related strategies for language teacher education. *TESOL Quarterly* 23(1): 27–46.

Harley, Brigit. 1986. *Age in second language acquisition.* Clevedon, Avon, England: Multilingual Matters.

Harley, Brigit, and Doug Hart. 1997. Language aptitude and second language proficiency in classroom learners of different starting ages. *Studies in Second Language Acquisition* 19(3): 379–400.

Higgs, Theodore V., and Ray T. Clifford. 1982. The push toward communication. In Theodore V. Higgs (ed.), *Curriculum, competence and the foreign language teacher.* The ACTFL Foreign Language Education Series no. 13. Lincolnwood, IL: National Textbook.

Jackson, Frederick H. 1993. On the implementation of inservice teacher education in an institutional context. In James E. Alatis (ed.), *Georgetown University Round Table on Languages and Linguistics 1993.* Washington, DC: Georgetown University Press. 492–508.

Kachru, Yamuna. 1994. Sources of bias in SLA research: Monolingual bias in SLA research. *TESOL Quarterly* 28(4): 795–800.

Kaplan, Marsha A. 1997. Learning to converse in a foreign language: The reception game. *Simulation and Gaming* 28(2): 149–163.

Kulick, Katherine M. 1988. Considerations in teaching adult learners: Psychological, physiological and pedagogical. Presentation at a Department of Defense–ACTFL Symposium, Linthicum, MD, August.

Larsen-Freeman, Diane. 1990. On the need for a theory of language teaching. In James E. Alatis (ed.), *Proceedings of the Georgetown University Round Table on Languages and Linguistics 1990*. Washington, DC: Georgetown University Press. 261–270.

Larsen-Freeman, Diane. 1991. Second language acquisition research: Staking out the territory. *TESOL Quarterly* 25(2): 315–350.

McLaughlin, Barry. 1987. *Theories of second language learning*. Baltimore, MD: Edward Arnold.

Nayar, P. Bhaskaran. 1997. ESL/EFL dichotomy today: Language politics or pragmatics? *TESOL Quarterly* 31(1): 9–38.

Odlin, Terrence. 1989. *Language transfer: Cross-linguistic influence in language learning*. Cambridge: Cambridge University Press.

Oxford, Rebecca, and Madeline Ehrman. 1992. Second language research on individual differences. *Annual Review Of Applied Linguistics* 13: 188–205.

Pica, Teresa. 1994. Questions from the language classroom: Research perspectives. *TESOL Quarterly* 28(1): 49–80.

Pienemann, Manfred. 1984. Psychological constraints on the teachability of languages. *Studies In Second Language Acquisition* 6(2): 186–214.

Schleppegrell, Mary. 1987. The older language learner. *ERIC digest*. Washington, D.C.: Center for Applied Linguistics.

Skehan, Peter. 1991. Individual differences in second language learning. *Studies In Second Language Acquisition* 13: 275–298.

Spolsky, Bernard. 1989. *Conditions for second language learning*. Oxford: Oxford University Press.

Spolsky, Bernard. 1995. *Measured words*. Oxford: Oxford University Press.

Sridhar, S. N. 1994. Sources of bias in SLA research: A reality check for SLA theories. *TESOL Quarterly* 28(4): 800–805.

Stevick, Earl W. 1989. *Success with foreign language: Seven who achieved it and what worked for them*. New York: Prentice Hall International.

Thain, John, and Gordon Jackson. n.d. Conversion training in the US Government. Unpublished interagency report, available at Defense Language Institute, Monterey, CA.

Widdowson, Henry. 1990. *Aspects of language teaching*. Oxford: Oxford University Press.

NOTES

1. We wish to express our gratitude and appreciation to our FSI colleagues James Bernhardt, Doug Gilzow, and David Red for their very helpful comments and advice during the preparation of this paper and to David Argoff for his insightful comments on our final draft. We also would like to thank Emily Urevich, Bianka Adams, Jane Kamide, and Ray Clifford for their encouragement and helpful suggestions at the GURT Pre-Conference Session. All errors of fact or interpretation are, of course, the responsibility of the authors. The content of this paper does not reflect any official policy of the Foreign Service Institute or the U.S. Department of State; the observations and opinions expressed are solely those of the authors.

2. Students are assigned to training for specific periods, which are timed so that the students will be ready to take up jobs overseas at the same time that the incumbents of those jobs are rotated elsewhere. If a student is not yet ready linguistically (or otherwise) to fill a vacated position, it creates a "gap" at post. Because they impair an embassy's ability to represent U.S. interests effectively, such gaps cannot easily be tolerated.

3. It is important to note here that FSI's experience shows that not all languages are equally accessible to native speakers of English. For example, although there are many cases on record at FSI of exceptional students starting training as beginners in cognate European languages and achieving proficiencies in the classroom of as high as S-4/R-4 (advanced professional proficiency), similar very high achievements do not occur in such languages as Chinese, Korean, Thai, Finnish, or Arabic. FSI has determined that the achievement of advanced professional proficiency in what Brecht and Walton (1994) refer to as the "truly foreign languages" requires even the most gifted learners to be immersed for an extended time in a culture where the language is spoken.

4. It is sometimes said at FSI that we began forty to fifty years ago with a metaphor of "teaching the course," but that, as the years have passed and we have understood more, we have moved from that concept to "teaching the class," to "teaching the students," to "teaching each student," to the present metaphor of "helping each student find ways to learn."

5. Professor John Rassias of Dartmouth reminded everyone at his presentation at the GURT presession that he has long emphasized the need for small classes and intensive language learning sessions for effective language learning.

6. In fact, our experience at FSI—based on work with such related languages as Thai and Lao, German and Dutch, Russian and Ukrainian, French and Italian, and Spanish and Portuguese—is that a relatively weak knowledge of one language may be an actual hindrance in trying to learn a related third language.

7. This model is not unique to FSI, of course. Professor Eleanor Jorden of Cornell University and Bryn Mawr has long advocated and used an instructional model based on the closely coordinated instruction of professional native-speaking and non-native-speaking instructors.

8. The Dean of FSI's School of Language Studies, Dr. John Campbell, emphasized in his remarks in the plenary panel at GURT's Pre Conference session that FSI is committed in its program of Accelerated Personalized Training (APT) to four core principles:

    • Students are encouraged to take responsibility for their own learning, including researching the types of tasks they will be responsible for at post;
    • Students take an active role in their learning and have input into how they wish to structure their training schedule and their training day;
    • When available, educational technology is an integral part of the program, thereby enabling each individual learner to meet his or her own needs; and
    • Emphasis is placed on helping the learners to learn "how to learn" when they are on their own.

9. Officers assigned to Europe, especially, often report that if they are in a conversation at a social gathering and cannot keep up, their interlocutors will often switch abruptly to English, almost always with a shift in topic and in the tone of the interaction. That is, the officers' ability in the language needs to be at a high level, indeed, before they can successfully participate in such conversations.

Analysis of texts and critique of judgment

James R. Child[1]
National Security Agency
Department of Defense

Introduction. For several decades, the *Interagency Language Roundtable* (ILR) *Language Skill Level Descriptions* have provided language-learner profiles in the form of "can do" and "can't do" statements, including examples of kinds of texts these individuals can produce or understand. These descriptions, useful as they have been for a number of purposes, are not standards in themselves, although they imply standards.

Within the last ten to fifteen years attempts have been made to develop explicit standards. These have taken the form of a scale of *textual* levels of increasing complexity from the perspective of the native speaker/writer, rather than that of the learner, of a given language. They are derived from four modes of language realization (discussed later in this paper).

Finally, studies have been undertaken in the last five years to determine whether the explicit standards as currently drafted are useful in determining skill levels in the context of proficiency testing, hence, supportive of and complementary to the ILR descriptions. Such a determination is obviously a question of judgment as raters work to calibrate standards to the skill level statements and to apply the composite to persons tested (see table 1).

Language levels: degrees of skill attained by learner/users (L/U). These cover base levels 0 through 5, with "plus" levels from 0+ through 4+ for four skills: speaking, listening, reading, and writing (SLRW). They provide "can do" statements at the beginning of each base- and plus-level description and follow those with notations of inadequacies ("can't do"), for use in developing profiles for "learner/users"(L/U).

The concept of learner/user derives from the relatively recent practice of using natural texts both in connection with second-language curricula and test development. The progress of learners can then be evaluated in regard to developing communicative skills in their actual use of the language rather than their ability to internalize paradigms. (It should be noted that by the time a learner/user can perform at level 3 the "learner" descriptor can be dropped.)

Table 1. Model-copy matrix: Modes (horizontal axis), skill levels (vertical axis), exercise of judgment (on diagonal): Conversion of textual modes to standards in rating process.

Exercise of Judgment	Orientational		Instructive		Evaluative		Projective	
A. Mastery of Textual Levels	Pure Mode (L1 standard)	Mixed Mode (L2 standard)	Pure Mode (L2 standard)	Mixed Mode (L3 standard)	Pure Mode (L3 standard)	Mixed Mode (L3 standard)	Pure Mode (L4/5 standard)	Mixed Mode (L4 standard)
B. Applying Them as Standards in Rating Skills	Proficiency Rating/ Performance Rating	Proficiency Rating/ Performance Rating	Proficiency Rating/ Performance Rating	Proficiency Rating/ Performance Rating	Proficiency Rating/ Performance Rating	Proficiency Rating/ Performance Rating	Proficiency Rating/ Performance Rating	Proficiency Rating/ Performance Rating
L0								
L1								
L1+								
L2								
L2+								
L3								
L3+								
L4								
L4+								
L5								

Implicit standards in current descriptions. The skill-level statements imply standards in citing examples of texts L/Us produce or understand at the respective levels, for example, reading level 2: "news items describing frequently occurring events, . . . formulaic business letters and simple technical material written for the general reader." Such texts deal with topics that are likely to be familiar to most test takers and are quite accessible to learners with modest control of second language grammar and vocabulary.

These statements take as their point of departure the perspective content/ form (C/F) in which the nature and degree of complexity of subject matter is stressed; only later is mention made of form/content (F/C) questions, where syntax and vocabulary are treated in the context of the communication. Turning (again) to reading level 2, for an F/C example: "Generally, the prose that can be read by the individual is predominantly in straightforward/high frequency sentence patterns." While the communicative nature of textual processing takes precedence (i.e., the C/F direction), the F/C orientation is also very important, especially at the lower levels (level 0+ through level 2).

Citations of this sort are useful as far as they go, but they remain on so high a level of generalization that accurate assessment of a L/U's progress is difficult. To attempt to remedy the situation, James R. Child published a paper in the American Council on the Teaching of Foreign Languages' *Foreign Language Annals* (1998) relating skill levels, textual levels, and the rating process. The major points of this paper are covered later in this paper.

Language levels: Standards to be met by L/Us. The standards discussed here apply to all skills and levels.

C/F and F/C in the system of text modes. Child's 1998 paper was based on an earlier one, "Language Skill Levels and the Typology of Texts" (Child 1987), which posited four textual "types" (now referred to as *modes*), classifying these in ascending order of C/F complexity as orientational (O), instructive (I), evaluative (E), and projective (P). This classification was originally intended as a way to codify texts in each language *in that language's own cultural and formal terms* and to provide language-internal standards for native speakers. However, since the scheme is graduated, as well as roughly compatible with the ILR skill levels, it may also be used as a cross-language standard for L/Us. The basic C/F organization makes subject matter the primary consideration, and the F/C direction concerns the micro- and macrostructures of the L/U's second language: morphology and syntax, appropriateness of register, functional sentence perspective, discourse marking, and so on. Systems of grammar and lexicon are aligned with the purposes reflected in texts and classes of texts, mode by mode.

Obviously, as soon as F/C direction is introduced into the scheme of modes questions arise regarding the structure of the particular language of the text. To avoid generating a virtual infinity of standards—one for the relationship of every language of the world to English—it is possible to group individual languages historically or typologically in respect to major syntactic and lexical features, and to indicate what features are prominent in which textual modes. Given the compatibility of the language forms and the intentions of the speaker or writers, one should be able to plan curricula, test language learners, and carry out other operations involving text processing.

Review of modes in ascending order of complexity. The term *mode* as employed here is intended to express the ways in which language is realized according to the purposes of users. As such it is not necessarily intended as a hierarchical system. As a matter of convenience, however, it has been useful to present the modes as a scheme of increasing complexity and, in this context, to refer to them as textual levels corresponding roughly to the ILR skill levels. The modes have been discussed at length in other papers in terms of the purposes underlying them; therefore the emphasis here will be on their use as virtual standards.

ORIENTATIONAL (O) MODE. The purpose of texts covered by this mode is to make information immediately available in the form of simple spoken or written texts to those needing it. Examples of such texts are traffic signs, locations or addresses of business establishments, names and titles of persons, and other indications of identity. Events mainly in the present or immediate future are also included: arrivals and departures of carriers, times and places of meetings, orders to be carried out, and many other fact-centered transactions.

Texts in the O mode are almost always accessible to L/Us who have learned or acquired the rudiments of a second language, because of their brevity and grammatical simplicity. At the same time they are part of the real world, hence amenable to use as standards for skill levels 0+ and 1. The C/F direction has been suggested in the examples above, the F/C direction in the easily memorized words and phrases of the texts to be supplemented on occasion by high-frequency verb and noun forms in inflected languages, a textually modest requirement.

INSTRUCTIVE (I) MODE. Texts are as fact-centered as those in the O mode, but their variety and scope is much greater. Media accounts of domestic and international events are excellent examples, but to quote from the *Foreign Language Annals* paper, "obviously many other text types are equally citable: somewhat detailed instructions on the assembly of a piece of equipment; . . . a topographical description of a geographical area, or a technical description of the properties of a chemical compound."

Clearly, the extended description or narration characteristic of I texts demands much more formal control of grammar and vocabulary than is the case with O texts. An F/C description of these requires solid treatment of verb forms and their functions; particles, "function words" marking inter-clause and inter-sentence relationships; and high-frequency vocabulary, all of which inform extended texts. The C/F–F/C relationship here is also more complicated than in O texts, where form and content are generally isomorphic. Nonetheless, the topics considered are usually of a kind that are either intrinsically familiar or resolvable from context, and the formal aspects have few, if any, of the lexical nuancing frequent in evaluative and typical of projective texts. An L/U with some knowledge of national and international affairs and a general awareness of how the world works will be able to process most non-specialized texts if he or she has adequate F/C control of the language studied.

EVALUATIVE (E) MODE TEXTS. These require something like a "quantum leap" in the move from I texts. These compose the standard for skill level 3. To quote once again from the 1998 paper, that standard sets forth "a perspective in which facts are selected and pressed into service in order to develop points of view; explain or apologize for personal conduct; state and defend past or projected policies." It goes on to say that "the various text types under E have in common a teleology in which the selection process is informed by a social purpose of some kind, as with an editorial disapproving or advocating some action." It is evident that in these transactions the semantic component of the language has taken on special significance for textual processing. C/F considerations come to the fore, such as coherence on the level of discourse (beyond interclausal or even intersentential coherence) and the role of rhetoric in highlighting or embellishing given items at various points of the presentation. F/C elements by definition include finely tuned lexical collocations on phrase and clause levels and highly specific ordering of elements not normally found in lower level texts.

The L/U, in producing or internalizing the content of E texts, is operating at a quite demanding level. For one thing the sheer quantity of grammatical constructions and vocabulary has exponentially increased, a result, in part, of coming up against a cultural outlook unfamiliar to him or her. The individual, besides mastering a good deal of grammar and vocabulary, needs to have a feel for the cultural imperatives in the use of the language he or she is studying beyond the immediate comprehension of language employed in texts in the orientational, as well as a facility in dealing with most texts in the Instructive mode. The L/U should be able to "think" to some degree in the second language, which means to employ those elements of grammar and vocabulary the L/U has internalized to understand or produce second-language texts in much the same way as a native speaker.

TEXTS IN THE PROJECTIVE (P) MODE. These reflect "an innovative approach to whatever topic the speaker/writer addresses" in terms of C/F. Conception and expression are so intimately connected, however, that C/F–F/C distinctions are at times impossible to finally establish. It is certainly the case that such syntactic devices as functional sentence perspective, in which word order may be employed for various rhetorical effects, as well as the increasingly nuanced wording of E texts are both present in the P mode. Nevertheless, the blend of syntax and semantics is such that the shock of the elements as a whole takes precedence over effects produced in one place or another in the texts, a typical result of *individuation*. For the purposes of the treatment of textual modes generally, and this paper in particular, individuation is to be understood as the continuing process of differentiation of writers and speakers from the "faceless" producers of signs, announcements, and the like in the O mode to the unique voices associated with P mode texts. Examples of texts reflecting this very high form of verbal individuation are to be found in systematic philosophy, literary criticism, lyric poetry, and certain kinds of personal essay.

In the face of so demanding a complex of tasks the user (no longer a learner in the usual sense of the word) must have become highly acculturated to the society in which the language is spoken and written, and sensitive to the ways in which individual writers or speakers follow or diverge from assumed cultural norms of language use. In addition, the user must have a strong cognitive bent in producing or comprehending the kinds of abstract language frequent in P texts. Mastering these diverse requirements virtually demands the ability to handle allusion and metaphor in the target language almost as readily as in one's own, a truly difficult standard to meet.

Standards and judgment. The ILR level descriptions have been treated from time to time as though they were proper standards. In fact, they actually contain *implied standards* (from which explicit ones may be derived), both in respect to the generalizations they contain and the examples cited in support of these. The implicit standards of the ILR statements are inferred from the kinds of text cited at each skill level *learners of second languages* have shown (through formal testing or other means) that they can produce or understand. The explicit standards specify the C/F–F/C relationships, semantically and grammatically, from the perspective of the *native speakers* of target languages. The acts of judgment informing the ILR statements cover several decades of an evolving system of testing and description (from at least the late 1950s to the present). Those concerned with the explicit standards are the fruit of the deliberations of the ILR Testing Committee over the last fifteen years or so, plus papers by Child (1987, 1998) and Alison Edwards (1996). Boiled down, one might say that the contributors to the ILR skill level statements put themselves in the shoes of second language *learners,* while the drafters of the papers on textual modes were concentrating on the nature of the texts *any* user might confront: pedagogy versus textual linguistics.

Implied standards, ILR descriptions. The kind of judgment implied in the ILR descriptions is largely a matter of experience in testing and common sense.

Reading "very simple connected written material in a form equivalent to usual printing or typescript" means to almost anyone a minimum accomplishment in the learning of a second language; hence the person rated is an R1 in reading.

The level 2 reader is clearly at a higher level in that he or she has "sufficient comprehension to read simple, authentic written material in a form equivalent to usual printing or typescript on subjects within a familiar context." The judgment here presupposes that the reader is not restricted as the level 1 reader is, to (presumably) very short stretches of texts barely qualifying as "connected material" (and, in fact, often supplemented by visual clues); the person can read "with some misunderstandings straightforward familiar factual material . . . in an expanded temporal and spatial frame of reference." Considered from a top-down perspective this is a reasonable way of setting forth a qualitative difference.

At level 3 the ability "to read within a normal range of speed and with almost complete comprehension a variety of authentic prose material on unfamiliar subjects" suggests major attainments in several directions. For one thing the reader is no longer limited to reading material of a kind he or she is familiar with but can deal with a variety of texts with something approaching full understanding, and at a normal rate of speed. Finally, the reader is able to deal with texts "including hypothesis, argumentation and supported opinions" (encountered, for example, in many editorials from major newspapers), which speaks not only to variety as such but to a high level of language text.

These factors taken together contribute, again, to a language profile qualitatively superior to that of the next lower level, and the rationale supplied is, as far as it goes, sensible and practical.

The attainments of the relatively few readers at the highest level are great enough to warrant at least one qualitative distinction above level 3. Whether levels 4 and 5 are justifiable or practical has been the source of disagreement among the contributors to the skill level system; to avoid this difficulty level 4 and level 5 citations will be conflated in the following commentary.

The level 4 reader is "able to read fluently and accurately all styles and forms of the language pertinent to professional needs." In so doing, he or she can "relate inferences [drawn from] the text to real-world knowledge and understand almost all sociolinguistic and cultural references." These achievements reflect a degree of cultural awareness and sophistication in the use of the second language that certainly justifies the creation of a fourth level. In tandem with the level 5 "can read extremely abstract and difficult prose, for example, general legal and technical writings," a picture emerges of an extremely well-rounded (if not erudite) and imaginative reader steeped in the culture of the second language.

As with the other levels, the conceptualization of level 4 competence reflects a reasonable approach, especially in the recognition of "unpredictable turns of thought [encountered] in, for example, [certain] literary texts" and the ability to "read and understand the intent of the writer's use of nuance." Taken together with the level 5 "able to read . . . contemporary avant-garde prose, poetry and theatrical writing," a profile of high language competence emerges that merits the recognition of at least one distinct level.

The overview above of the kinds of judgment associated with the four (five) skill levels subsumes the so-called "plus" levels (level 0+ through level 4+). The reasoning behind plus statements is the same as that for the base levels, except that the persons rated do not consistently perform at the next higher level. Thus, an individual judged to be capable of performing at level 2+ can do, by and large, whatever a level 2 can do, as well as operate at level 3 in certain areas where he or she has considerable knowledge of the relevant subject matter but may be limited to those areas.

With all due respect to the reasoning behind the ILR statements (and their implied standards) as well as their practical value over the years, they need to be buttressed by standards in which C/F–F/C relationships are spelled out for as many types of texts and text levels as possible. The fact is that each of the four modes covers a variety of text types that, in turn, may occupy lower, middle, or upper range within particular modes.

Validity of text modes as explicit standards. In a previous section the system of modes was presented as a means of codifying textual levels in the semantic (C/F) terms of originator intent and as a set of standards for L/Us. How valid is this proposition? To answer this question (at least in part) it will be useful to review the work of the ILR Testing Committee in establishing a full range of textual levels over a period of roughly ten years, as well as extensive parallel studies conducted at the National Cryptologic School in connection with language test design at levels 2 and 3. Finally, in a paper published in the *Modern Language Journal* (vol. 80, no. 3, 1996), Alison Edwards reports findings from her research on Child's paper on text typology and its possible utility as an explicit set of standards for establishing skill levels through formal testing or other means. To quote at some length from her abstract: "The following question guided this research: Does the Child discourse-type hierarchy predict text difficulty for L2 [second language] readers? Test data were collected from 62 U.S. Government employees having some previously demonstrated French proficiency. Nine authentic French texts and a combination of testing methods were employed. The results suggested that the Child text hierarchy may indeed provide a sound basis for the development of FL reading tests when it is applied by trained raters and when such tests include an adequate sample of passages at each level to be tested" (Edwards 1996: 350).

Whether Edwards's findings or continuing research on textual questions in the ILR or elsewhere will be valid for all languages and skills remains to be seen. For the present, however, there is sufficient evidence that the system of text modes, and the C/F–F/C standards derived from them, sufficiently undergird the ILR statements. Thus, in any instance where users of these statements desire a text-oriented slant they can turn to Child's 1987 paper on text typology, at the same time using the skill level statements with a fair degree of confidence.

There are to be sure some questions regarding the "fit" of the four modes to the six base ranges on the skill level spectrum (0–5); textual standards required for plus levels (if separate standards are indicated); the general applicability of C/F standards to F/C production, especially at the lower levels of the ILR system; and mastery of specialized subject matter and the lexicon appropriate to it.

To help resolve the first question, the wording of the P mode readily covers the conflated levels 4 and 5, because these relate to such high levels of personal attainment that they are hard to justify—in the author's opinion—as qualitatively separate entities. As for the very low skill level ranges 0 and 1, the standard for the O (Orientation) mode accommodates.

As for plus-level standards (as distinct from those for base levels), these would have to be crafted as "mixed-mode" statements, for example, "instructive/evaluative" for level 2+. There would, however, be great variation among the mixed mode texts and differences among L/U skills would be daunting. The best course is to use "the next standard up the scale" (which for level 2+ would be the Evaluative mode) throughout the system.

Next, there is the complex relationship of C/F to F/C. Unfortunately the two have not always been kept clear, so that, for example, an instructive mode text may be viewed simply as a passage a level 2 L/U can process rather than one produced for a communicative purpose. At higher levels this difficulty does not obtrude to the same extent, since the L/Us have attained a degree of second-language control roughly comparable (though rarely equivalent) to that of the educated native. Nonetheless, it does remain a consideration in the use of high-level, low-frequency vocabulary.

Finally, mention must be made of subject matter and the register appropriate to it, for the L/U will on occasion have to read (or otherwise process) texts dealing with specialized subject matter he or she does not control. "Control" is certainly a question of degree: It can be a matter of understanding the main thrust of an article on ecology or archaeology or of complete mastery of some aspect of Buddhist philosophy. However, when the L/U has no grasp at all of a specialized subject he or she cannot deal with it in any language, whether foreign or native. That fact does not in itself mean that a given text of, say, a scientific nature is at a high level: many such are in the instructive (level 2) or evaluative (level 3) mode, or some mix of the two. The reader who knows the subject of the text very well, but with a modest control of the source language, may be able to give a decent accounting of it. Neither ILR skill level statements nor detailed presentation of the system of modes can provide reliable guidance or standards in cases where L/Us cannot function with texts by reason of total unfamiliarity with text material. For most cases, however, where general proficiency is at issue, the ILR guidelines and the standards derived from text modes should serve the purposes of language assessment.

REFERENCES

Child, James R. 1987. Language Proficiency Levels and the Typology of Texts. In Heidi Byrnes and Michael Canale (eds.), *Defining and developing proficiency: Guidelines, implementations and concepts.* Lincolnwood, IL: National Textbook. 97–106.

Child, James R. 1998. Language Skill Levels, Textual Modes and the Rating Process. *Foreign Language Annals* 3: 381–397.

Edwards, Alison L. 1996. Reading Proficiency Assessment and the ILR/American Council on the Teaching of Foreign Languages Text Typology: a Reevaluation. *Modern Language Journal* 80: 350–361.

NOTE

1. The thoughts expressed herein are those of the author and in no way reflect those of the Department of Defense. I am greatly indebted to Pardee Lowe, Jr., and Beth Mackey, both of the National Cryptologic School, for their contributions to this paper. Lowe typed the entire manuscript, making many valuable suggestions along the way. In proofing the text, Mackey not only caught some errors, but contributed greatly to the improvement of one section. I am, of course, personally responsible for the overall content.

Paved with good intentions: Words of advice for the rocky road of bureaucratic language

Roger W. Shuy
Georgetown University

Those who have lived inside the comfortable confines of the Washington, D.C. beltway often find it difficult to appreciate the degree of disdain with which bureaucracies are held by the rest of the country. When one has not had bureaucrats as neighbors, associates, and friends, it may be easy to think of them as purveyors of the sump hole into which unjust taxes are funneled. It may not be difficult to believe that their main purpose in life is to see to it that communications from the government are deliberately unclear, that their tasks are to withhold information from the public, or that they really want to prevent constituents from receiving what is due them. Perhaps because I recently moved two thousand miles from D.C., I have begun to realize the utter contempt that distant, unsympathetic, frustrated outsiders to Washington can have of the bureaucracies of the federal government.

Most businesses use printed language to convince consumers to buy their products, to instruct them about how to use these products, and, when mandated, to warn them about the potential dangers when the products are used. In contrast, much of a government's use of language has a more limited range, primarily to advise people about their rights and what to do about them. Unfortunately, this attempt to be advisory is frequently unclear, and it sometimes even appears to be unnecessarily negative, even threatening. Even worse, the effort can be interpreted as an attempt to disguise constituents' rights or to withhold information rather than to provide it.

This paper, based on research on legal disputes between various federal bureaucracies and constituents, points out some of the difficulties government employees have in communicating with recipients of their services. But it also tries to get beneath these assumptions of ill will and to identify the real points of difficulty in past misunderstandings about the actual intentions of federal bureaucracies. It is my belief that the intentions of most bureaucrats are honorable and that their problems in delivering messages to the public are the result of other factors, many of which can be resolved with the help of linguistic knowledge. Although this paper is addressed to the problems of federal bureaucrats, it also has salience for others who try to communicate helpful written messages of advice in nonbureaucratic settings.

It is only fair to point out that the federal government has not been insensitive to or unresponsive about the complaints of the public about bureaucratic language. During the administration of President Jimmy Carter, such problems were realized, resulting in the creation and initial funding of the Document Design Center, a branch of the American Institutes of Research. Its mandate was to assist government and business in their efforts to write clear prose.

In May 1978, the U.S. Office of Consumer Affairs sponsored a conference on insurance policy issues of concern to consumers, which include the language actually used in insurance contracts (Shuy 1998). It should be noted, in addition, that agencies such as the Social Security Administration (SSA) collected complaints about the lack of clarity of their notices and, as a result, developed a "clear writing" division in 1984 to address their problems (Shuy 1998). More recently, in January 1998, the Securities Exchange Commission capped a two-year effort to improve the readability and utility of certain disclosure documents by adopting final rules for its "plain English" initiative. Plain English, in this instance, was defined as short sentences, concrete everyday language, active voice, use of bullets whenever possible, no legal or business jargon, and no multiple negatives.

As promising as these examples of bureaucratic awareness of the problem may be, they tend to exist in a sociolinguistic vacuum. They are based on the assumption that by setting forth a set of rules, even good ones, change will inevitably follow. The fact that this issue surfaces about every ten years suggests that the "let's just do it" approach has not worked very well. This is not to say that the work of the Document Design Center was not useful, for it came up with some very useful guidelines for clear writing, even if, in the long run, it did not change the face of bureaucratic writing. Today, some insurance policies are a bit clearer than they were before the 1978 Consumer Affairs conference, but most are still bogged down with legal and business expressions and syntax that confuse and confound. The approach taken by the Social Security Administration is another matter and one that bears careful scrutiny, as its notices have improved greatly over the past fifteen years. In fact, the principles that I propose here have been largely fulfilled by SSA, a kind of success story amidst the hand-wringing efforts of most agencies (Shuy 1998).

For bureaucracies trying to write clearly, I offer the following eight areas of advice:

1. Accept the fact that you begin with two strikes against you. The fact that you are a federal bureaucracy puts you in the hole to begin with. You get little help from congresspeople who claim to their home state constituents that they are suffering hardships by just having to live in Washington. They love to hate the bureaucrats whose task it is to implement the laws they created. Often, in fact, their campaigning is based on an anti-Washington motif. Nor is industry much of an ally. Federal agencies, such as the Food and Drug Administration (FDA) and the Occupational Safety and Health Administration (OSHA), produce regulations governing the wording of warnings required for products that pose dangers to consumers. This causes manufacturers to have to say clearly and precisely what can go wrong with their products, a task that, for obvious reasons, they clearly do not favor.

Then there is the issue of taxes. Americans appear to want a government when they want it, usually to provide services that protect them and provide opportunities and comfort. But they do not seem to want to pay for different services needed by others.

Beginning with a downside such as this makes bureaucratic writing much more difficult than the everyday writing that most of us do. The audience is, by definition, skeptical, if not hostile, to start with. Bureaucratic writers must first recognize this disadvantage and produce prose that overcomes it. They do not begin in neutral. They begin with two strikes against them.

2. Keep a clear focus on why you are doing what you are doing. Bureaucrats write to the public to convey advice about the rights of recipients and how to achieve these rights. However self-evident this fact may be, it is clear that it gets forgotten easily. In order to communicate these rights and procedures, one must have a very clear picture of the recipients, what rhetoricians call recipient design. It is easy for bureaucratic writers to begin with the law or regulation that is to be communicated and then try to translate it into words that the recipient can understand. Wrong. Begin with a clear idea about what the recipient might need or want to know, then translate the law or regulation to suit the reader's goals, not those of the agency. To be sure, such an effort must not distort the intention of the law or regulation, but it has a quite different starting point.

The issue here is a simple one: Why are you here? You are here to serve the interests and needs of the public, not the interests and needs of the laws and regulations.

In our two years of working with the clear writing project of the Social Security Administration, Jana Staton and I addressed this problem in a sociolinguistic way. First, we had writers bring to class the current notices on which they were working. Then, noting that these efforts simply translated regulations, we devised a field trip to a local nursing home. Writers were to pick elderly patients, present the notice, and get feedback about what the patients thought it meant, whether or not they liked it, and what they thought they should do about it. The results of this field trip were enlightening. The patients, on the whole, had no idea what the notice meant or what they were supposed to do as a result of getting it. In short, they hated it. To a person, the writers found the visit invaluable. From that point on, we had them visualize the individual patient they visited each time they wrote a new notice. They established a real person as a reader of their message, not just an amorphous one. It became clear to the SSA writing staff that they were there to communicate with real recipients and that to do so, they had to start with the recipients' perspective, not SSA's.

3. Remember that not everything can get done at once. What seems to characterize the governmental approach to change is that the event of a decision means that compliance or change will follow immediately. Thus, President Carter's mandate for a service agency to be made available to bureaucracies was enacted with the assumption that things would be different from that point on. Likewise, the Office of Consumer Affairs's 1978 effort to hold a conference on insurance language was assumed to be the turning point after which clear writing would obviously flow. The Security Exchange Commission's (SEC's) 1998 listing of principles of clear writing, along with a mandate to follow them, is assumed to change traditional ways of formatting text and designing prospectuses, proxy statements, and annual reports.

The simple fact is that change of this type does not flow so smoothly. For one thing, institutional memory is almost nonexistent. The fact that the problem of clear writing keeps being rediscovered every ten years or so is evidence enough of this. In addition, the overlay of political appointments in bureaucracies itself causes rapid turnover of those charged with tasks such as clear writing. Of the hundred or so writers that Staton and I trained during the mid-1980s, only a couple are still connected with the project. Some were justifiably promoted to other positions; others left SSA for other opportunities; the head of the project has since retired; the acting director of SSA who shepherded the writing project at its inception was replaced when a new president was elected. Those outside of Washington bureaucracies seldom understand the fragility of life within an agency.

Again, SSA provides the best example of a more continuous effort to create clear and understandable prose. After Staton and I completed our two years of training SSA writers, I heard nothing more about the project. One can only hope, under such circumstances, that the seeds we sowed took hold and yielded good fruit. But we really didn't know for sure until I retired in 1998 and began to receive social security notices myself. I was pleased, as well as relieved, to learn that the current notices are a distinct improvement over those of the mid-1980s. Apparently our work endured the changes of staff, administration, laws and regulations, technology, and other contributing factors.

What differentiated the SSA approach from other awarenesses of the needs of clear language is that SSA recognized that immediate change was unlikely, if not impractical. More important, SSA went beyond a mandate or policy statement. It created an entity for carrying out the idea, brought in outsiders to help with it, and had the patience to wait for eventual improvement. It recognized that not everything would get done at once.

4. Realize that the harder you try, the worse it can get. Staton and I found that the context in which bureaucratic writing takes place is less than conducive for the task. Sitting at a desk in an office with other fellow employees around may work for some writers but it can be deadly for many others. Most people have certain routines that facilitate writing. Bertrand Russell, for example, always sharpened twelve pencils before he set out to write. Others find safe and effective writing spots, favorite chairs or pillows, or special windows to look out of for comfort and inspiration. We discovered that most offices at SSA were starkly governmental. Furniture was standard issue. Decoration was sparse. For the highly motivated or the type who can focus so completely that outside stimulus is unimportant, such a context can work. But for most of us, it can be deadly. Staton and I spent a couple hours wandering around the massive office complex of the agency and found some inspiration spots that we recommended to our writers. One was a little used eating area overlooking a pleasant patio. In warm weather there were many nicely landscaped areas immediately outside the buildings. We encouraged our writers to find a writing spot where they could go to visualize their reader and escape the cacophonous sounds of their assigned desks. Some thought the idea ludicrous but others found that their highly focused efforts to write at their desks was actually more a detriment than an asset.

We also discovered that some of our more highly motivated writers were trying so hard to find the right word that they became blocked. We suggested that they not start at the beginning but, rather, find a major idea they were trying to communicate and begin there, saving the introduction for later. This made sense to them, and obvious analogies are easy to find in life. For example, you can't introduce somebody until you've met them. We urged that the writers get to know their topic before they try to introduce it, a strategy that I have long advocated to struggling dissertation writers at Georgetown. Write what you know first; then worry about how to set it up with an introduction.

Other writers were victims of their most recent information, in this case the same type of list that the SEC has recently produced. They had in their minds a set of marginally useful rules, which in themselves are not wrong, but which focus on the more trivial aspects of writing. For example, short sentences are thought to be better than long ones. Readability formulas stress this rather simplistic notion. Yet short sentences containing unclear cohesion and unclear relationships can be more difficult than long sentences with clear cohesion and clear relationships. In our training program, we dealt with such issues as those noted in the SEC list of rules only after we had focused on the discourse concepts of topics, decision trees, and speech acts, all of which we considered more salient to the development of clear communication. We encouraged our writers to approach their own notices in the same order. Trying too hard to solve the little things tended to block their creation of the big things.

5. Try not to catch it from your colleagues. Bureaucracies are no different from other areas of life in the matter of language contagion. It is clear that first-year law students, if they are to be successful, must learn to write like lawyers. The same can be said for medical students, business people, and academics. This is not bad in itself, of course, because an internally used jargon can be quite useful. Socially, it tells other members of the group that you are one of them and therefore deserve their respect. Cognitively, it provides a shortcut for shared information that need not be made explicit every time the occasion arises. The problem comes when such jargon is used outside the in-group for which it bears these social and cognitive advantages.

There is little reason to identify the marks of in-group bureaucratic language. We all know about Washington's love of acronyms, for example. Nor is there any need to be reminded of the favorite expressions of a government that "shoots down" ideas, "mobilizes" opposition, encourages "zero-defect" systems, "touches base" with the public, or "puts a hard probability" on things. More recently, but already out of fad, are expressions like "pushes the envelope" and "that dog won't hunt."

We may all borrow such language fads, at least until we come to our senses. But in-group members have more at stake. This is their equivalent of a physician's black instrument bag or stethoscope around the neck. It is the lawyer's oversized brief case or the policeman's badge. It marks them as members. And that's okay. The problem comes when doctors, lawyers, policemen, or bureaucrats use this language to people who don't speak it. This, in fact, is what is basically wrong with bureaucratic language. It's not the structure or use within the bureaucracy. It's lack of recognition that outsiders also don't use it. The contagion of bureaucratic language is perfectly acceptable within the bureaucracy. It can be deadly when it is used as the medium for trying to communicate with constituents.

Learning and using bureaucratic language within an agency is not the only motivation for its common existence. Most outsiders are unaware of the competition among branches of the same agency or, for that matter, among agencies for a piece of the federal budget or, in some cases, for survival. Just as one might doubt the expertise of a physician who does not talk like a doctor or an attorney who does not speak like a lawyer, government bureaucracies face the same problem. Who would fund a branch of an agency that can't or won't speak in the expected fashion? Thus, bureaucratic language feeds on itself, not just at the level of individual bureaucrats, but also at the level of the bureaucracy itself.

This being the case, it is questionable whether the word "contagion" is actually appropriate. Perhaps a better term would be "survival." What is clear is that fellow bureaucrats cannot be expected to be allies in ridding the agency of bureaucratese. Simply wiping out bureaucratic language is clearly not the answer. It is not even feasible and it may not even been desirable. Those who would eradicate it are probably barking up the wrong tree.

6. Get help from language specialists. Bureaucracies that genuinely wish to do a better job of communicating with outsiders to their agencies often do a poor job when they try to go it alone. Proclamations that we will do a better job meet with blank looks. Conferences about the problem are amorphous and ineffective. Even setting up an outside vehicle, such as the Document Design Center, merely offers assistance only when and if such is thought to be necessary.

I can think of no better model of how to bring about improvements in communicating with the public than the one devised by the Social Security Administration during the early 1980s. It should be pointed out that the agency was not innately predisposed to improve its notices. To be sure, it recognized that complaints were pouring in, but the major impetus to change came about when Congress required that SSA send out a notice to all recipients of social security that they might also be entitled to supplementary security income.

Dutifully, SSA prepared a draft form of this new notice. After reviewing it, the National Senior Citizens Law Center (Gray Panthers), which had just won a prolonged judgment against Health and Human Services (of which SSA is a part), believed that SSA was trying to obscure the message to the extent that eligible recipients would not be able to take advantage of it. On the other hand, the Gray Panthers also feared that still another lengthy lawsuit might not be in the best interests of Medicare recipients. So instead of taking the matter to court, they asked me to review the offending notice and try to rewrite it so that the intent of Congress might be revealed clearly. I did so, and not only did the Gray Panthers like it, the Social Security Administration also thought it was an improvement. In fact, a few days after seeing it, the director of SSA called me and asked if I would help them with other writing issues.

In light of what I noted earlier about the good intentions of bureaucrats, this event is instructive. Note that once SSA saw how their notice could be made clear, the agency jumped at the chance to accept this new version, hardly evidence of any evil intentions or a desire to disguise the required information. What is more, SSA recognized the inefficiency in its current procedures and acted almost immediately to seize the opportunity to borrow the resources of the Gray Panthers, its adversary in much previous litigation.

The Social Security Administration knew, as other bureaucracies seem not to know, where to get help. To see how bad things were at SSA, it may be useful to assess, as Staton and I did, the state of SSA notice writing in the mid-1980, when we were asked to begin the training program for SSA writers. One of the early notices in our involvement can do this nicely. Appearing on SSA letterhead, the notice read in all caps exactly as shown in box 1.

Not only was the document design of this notice made ineffective by the use of all capital letters, it also suffered from an inept discourse structure, a failure to provide a road map decision tree for the beneficiary to follow, the presence of negative speech acts where it would be quite possible to provide positive ones, and the use of unfamiliar, if not confusing, terminology.

Box 1. Social Security Award Notice

Social Security
Award Notice
From Department of Health and Human Services
    Social Security Administration
RETIREMENT /84 $432.70
HOSPITAL 7/84
MEDICAL 7/84

BECAUSE OF A CHANGE IN THE LAW, YOUR REGULAR PAYMENT WILL
BE ROUNDED DOWN TO THE DOLLAR EVEN THOUGH YOUR MONTHLY
BENEFIT OF RECORD MAY BE IN DOLLARS AND CENTS.

A MONTHLY PREMIUM OF $14.60 IS REQUIRED TO KEEP YOUR MEDICAL
INSURANCE PROTECTION. YOU WILL BE BILLED FOR THESE PREMIUMS.
YOU WILL RECEIVE YOUR FIRST PREMIUM NOTICE BEFORE */84. AFTER
THAT NOTICES WILL BE SENT EVERY 3 MONTHS. THESE NOTICES WILL
SHOW THE MONTHS COVERED, TOTAL PREMIUM AMOUNT, AND THE
DATE PAYMENT IS DUE.

YOU CANNOT QUALIFY FOR MONTHLY BENEFITS BASED ON ANOTHER
PERSON'S SOCIAL SECURITY RECORD WHEN YOU ARE ENTITLED TO
AN EQUAL OR LARGER INSURANCE BENEFIT BASED ON YOUR OWN
EARNINGS RECORD.

BASED ON THE INFORMATION GIVEN TO US, YOU WERE BORN ON 7/27/19.

IF YOU NEED MEDICARE SERVICES BEFORE YOU RECEIVE YOUR HEALTH
INSURANCE CARD, YOU MAY USE THIS NOTICE AS PROOF OF COVERAGE.
YOU SHOULD RECEIVE YOUR CARD WITHIN 4 WEEKS.

IF YOU RETIRE FROM YOUR BUSINESS OR CORPORATION BEFORE THE
MONTH YOU ATTAIN AGE 70, YOU WILL BE REQUIRED TO PROVIDE
EVIDENCE OF YOUR RETIREMENT BEFORE YOUR BENEFITS CAN BE
PAID.

YOU ARE NOT ELIGIBLE FOR ANY TYPE OF BENEFIT OTHER THAN
STATED ON THIS CERTIFICATE. ENTITLEMENT TO ANOTHER BENEFIT ON
THIS OR ANY OTHER RECORD IN THE FUTURE REQUIRES A SEPARATE
APPLICATION.

IF YOU BELIEVE THIS DETERMINATION IS NOT CORRECT, YOU MAY RE-
QUEST THAT YOUR CASE BE REEXAMINED. IF YOU WANT THIS RECON-
SIDERATION, YOU MUST REQUEST IT NOT LATER THAN 60 DAYS FROM
THE DATE YOU RECEIVE THIS NOTICE. YOU MAY MAKE YOUR REQUEST
THROUGH ANY SOCIAL SECURITY OFFICE. IF ADDITIONAL EVIDENCE IS
AVAILABLE, YOU SHOULD SUBMIT IT WITH YOUR REQUEST.

This certifies that you (or other person(s) on whose   Martha A. McSteen
behalf you applied), became entitled under the   Acting Commissioner
Social Security Act to the benefits shown.   of Social Security

Remedies for these problems suggested themselves almost immediately. It was news to the SSA writers that all capital letters make for difficult reading. We had the writing team carry out a topic analysis of this notice to see the flow of ideas presented. They produced the following topic sequence:

1. Your payment will be rounded down
2. You'll be billed for monthly insurance premiums
3. You can't qualify on another person's SS record
4. You were born
5. Use this notice until you get your health insurance card
6. If you retire, provide us with evidence
7. You're not eligible for other benefits
8. What to do if you disagree with these facts

The ludicrous nature of this topic sequence became apparent once the topics were written down in this way. We discussed the fact that this was actually a "good news" notice, telling the recipient that he would be getting benefits. Yet somehow the good news part of the message was not even stated. The writers began to wonder why rounding down of the payment was placed at the most prominent part of the notice, why the bad news of insurance premiums was second, and a warning about using someone else's record was placed third. Gales of laughter accompanied the inclusion of the birth announcement as the fourth topic. It was also decided that the amount the recipient would be getting deserved prominence in the text of the notice rather than being relegated to the inconspicuous box in the top right hand corner.

The SSA writers agreed that a simple topic analysis could help them revise extant notices. It was a short step from this realization to get them to understand that topic analysis could also help them create a viable sequence of new notices that they were currently creating by, first of all, fronting the purpose of the notice then creating a logical sequence of information from the reader's perspective, not the agency's. We also explored different ways of marking the topics of a notice, including headings, question-answer formats, and performatives (such as, "This notice is to inform you that . . ." or "You will receive $435 a month . . .") rather than embedded or implied topics.

Nor did we feel that speech act theory was too complex and academic for the SSA notice writers to grasp. We introduced rudimentary speech act concepts to them, and they appeared to have no trouble grasping their significance. We pointed out that such analysis comes closer to the kind of intentionality that they needed to understand as they addressed their audience. They needed to figure out the intention of the documents they were trying to revise and to predict the reactions of their unseen recipients. We pointed out that some speech acts, such as offering, promising, thanking, congratulating, and advising, were more positive and polite than others, such as warning, complaining, giving directives, and threatening, which were more innately negative. The writers then marked each speech act in their notices and got a kind of picture of the effect they were likely to produce on their readers. Even much of the necessary negative information the writers had to provide could be couched in more positive terms, as in sentences like "Your case will not be reviewed unless you ask us to," which could just as easily be stated, "We will review your case if you ask us to."

The SSA writers discovered that many of the SSA notices contained warnings when advice would do nicely instead. They found many missed opportunities to offer and even promise. They even found threats in some of the notices. They discovered that they were often giving directives when they just as easily could be providing the advice of alternatives or options.

My point here is that the Social Security Administration, realizing that it was lacking in something, turned to linguistic analysis for help. It knew that it had a problem that was not being solved and did what linguists know to be the right thing but which we do not often experience.

7. Establish a powerful authority for how you use language. Even after numerous successful revisions were made in SSA notices, impetus to continue such revisions was eventually lost. It is the nature of bureaucracies to lose even a good impetus. New directions are decided, new personnel are hired, new administrations have new thrusts. SSA was not unique to this problem. After our two-year training program ended, we wondered whether or not the improvements in notice writing would endure. As noted earlier, I discovered the answer when I retired and began to get notices from SSA myself. I was delighted to discover that they were vastly improved over the notices we reviewed in the mid-1980s. Apparently some force managed to cause this new approach to notice writing in the agency to be preserved.

In retrospect, the reason for this may be that we also built into our training a method for justifying changes to superiors (who may not be sympathetic to altering old notices); and we provided procedures for writing new notices. The issue of authority is a big one in bureaucracies. It is also the case that bureaucracies commonly have competing authorities, such as the authority of law, the authority of leadership, the authority of precedence or policy, and the authority of politics. The SSA writers were subject to all of these authorities and, at least when we worked with them, had no particular authority of their own to combat the many authorities that influenced their work.

This situation produced a kind of hopelessness in many of the writers. It seemed to them that no matter what they wrote, somebody would insist that it be changed to conform to some other version of authority. Our early ethnographic work at SSA revealed such disillusionment to us. Some writers felt that they had to please the policy people. Others expressed concern that the systems people (computer center) forced formats on them that discouraged clear writing. Others blamed the general counsel's office for forcing them to write like lawyers.

As it turned out, none of those bugaboos actually existed at SSA. Representatives of general counsel, systems, and policy participated in our training sessions and, when faced with such accusations, denied them entirely. The general counsel's office made it clear to the writers that they were not expected to produce lawyer-like prose. Representatives from policy claimed that the regulations they had to follow were not etched in stone and that the writers should try to express them in terms that the beneficiaries could actually understand. The systems people, as it turns out, were delighted to hear our criticisms of the archaic computers, then printing all capital letters, for they wanted new equipment as much as the writers did. Fear of the various authorities of policy, systems, and general counsel were entirely unfounded.

Now realizing that these false fears of authority were not, indeed, true, the SSA writers were still without their own weapons of authority. Absent the authority that linguistic analysis could offer, the agency had sought out other authorities, notably the Flesch Readability Formula (1949). But even SSA had relatively little faith in readability formulas and was easily inclined to reject them once it was pointed out that the basic premises of such formulae are seriously flawed. Shortness of words or sentences does not indeed equate with clarity, which is more likely to occur when words and sentences are cohesive, syntactically clear, and presented in a reasonable discourse style.

Once the authority of readability formulas and simplistic lists of do's and don'ts, such as the one recently offered by the SEC, are discounted, what authority is left for the SSA writers? In order to justify their revisions of extant notices and the new text they produced, these writers needed to be able to convince skeptics, such as supervisors, that they were right in what they wrote. One of the aims of the training program was to create a competing authority, a credibility, a muscle for the SSA writers in order to give them footing in the decision-making process. Such an authority should contain a theory, terminology, and knowledge-based grounding for the language choices they made. Needless to say, these were borrowed from linguistics.

To objectify this authority, together with the SSA writers we constructed what they chose to label the Notice Review Guide, as shown in box 2.

The SSA writers used this review guide as a check on each notice they worked on, whether it was a revision or a totally new notice. When challenged about their choices, they could pull out this record and point out to skeptics exactly why they wrote what they did. It helped, of course, that the critics had little idea of the terms and concepts on the review guide. This gave the writers a technical authority that was not likely to be challenged. The writers, in this case, knew something that the critics did not. More important, of course, is that it provided a constant reminder to the writers themselves about the things that really mattered in the creation of their work.

Box 2. Notice Review Guide			
Categories	**No changes**	**Changes**	**Further changes**
Topics:			
Topics fronted:			
Topics marked:			
Headings:			
Question-answer:			
Embedded in first sentence:			
Topics sequenced appropriately:			
Explicitness:			
Ambiguities, inferences:			
presuppositions made explicit:			
Reader decision points clear:			
Reader actions specified:			
Speech Acts:			
Match speaker intentions:			
Made positive:			
Made explicit:			
Cohesion:			
Cohesive ties appropriate:			
Pronoun reference clear:			
Relationship markers clear:			
Lexical repetition effective:			
Comprehension:			
Concrete words for abstract:			
Active voice for passive:			
Relative pronouns used:			

8. Become bi-stylistic. Despite the difficult lessons learned from experiences such as the Oakland School Systems fiasco with Ebonics, there is a similar and very important lesson found in bureaucratic language: There is a time to use it and a time not to. Even though this principle should be self-apparent, those teaching writing often neglect it. College students are trained to write essays that get them through college, but it is seldom the case that they are also taught the wider, more commonly used, informal styles of writing. In law school the focus is only on writing like lawyers. Whether explicitly taught or not, medical students naturally focus on using the specialized language of doctors. Similarly, bureaucrats must learn the approved, internal style that will preserve and advance them in their work.

There is nothing wrong with learning any of these styles, and it would probably be disastrous not to. What seems to have been forgotten is that there is more than one audience that needs to be addressed. Most college graduates do not spend their lives writing academic essays. Most lawyers and doctors have to communicate outside the confines of law and medicine. Even bureaucrats have to talk and write to the world outside of their agencies. As we found at Social Security, beginning such communication with a clear notion of the audience, the participant perspective, is key to being bi-stylistic.

The need for such bi-stylism must be both recognized and promoted in bureaucratic agencies. Without it, the absurdities of unnecessary miscommunication are likely to continue.

Conclusions. It may be only passively or reactively helpful to be told that bureaucratic writers begin with two strikes against them, that they should keep a clear focus on their tasks, that they can't get everything done at once, that trying hard can actually make things worse, and that they can catch bureaucratese from their colleagues.

Many bureaucrats already know these things.

The more proactive words of advice involve getting help from specialists in language, establishing an authority to combat the other authorities of the bureaucracy, and learning to switch between the styles needed within the bureaucracy and those needed outside it. Nor can the lack of these things be placed solely on the shoulders of bureaucracies. Linguists, who can offer important help to bureaucrats, have been seldom willing or available. This paper is not only an analysis of the rocky road paved with good intentions of bureaucrats. It is also a plea for linguists to provide the services they need. Our field is uniquely equipped to help bureaucracies in the effort to communicate effectively to their constituents. Recent developments in discourse analysis, speech act theory, pragmatics, language policy, and sociolinguistics offer the core of our potential contributions to a smooth and effective use of language in government. Most linguists have this knowledge. Most bureaucrats do not. It is time for us to bridge this gap of knowledge and actively seek out opportunities to help bureaucracies do their important work more effectively.

REFERENCE

Shuy, Roger W. 1998. *Bureaucratic Language in Government and Business.* Georgetown University Press.

Bilingual education: Arguments for and (bogus) arguments against

Stephen D. Krashen
University of Southern California

Introduction. It is helpful to distinguish two goals of bilingual education. The first is the development of academic English and school success, and the second is the development of the heritage language. Good bilingual education programs achieve both goals, but my focus in this report is on the first.

Confusion about the first goal is understandable: How can children acquire English, their second language, while being taught in their first language? This occurs for two reasons: First, when we give a child good education in the primary language, we give the child knowledge, knowledge that makes English input more comprehensible. A child who understands history, thanks to good history instruction in the first language, will have a better chance of understanding history taught in English than a child without this background knowledge. And more comprehensible English input means more acquisition of English.

Second, there is strong evidence that literacy transfers across languages, that building literacy in the primary language is a short-cut to English literacy. The argument is straightforward: If we learn to read by understanding the messages on the page (Smith 1994; Goodman 1982), it is easier to learn to read if we understand the language. And once we can read, we can read: The ability transfers to other languages.

The empirical support for this claim comes from studies showing that the reading process is similar in different languages, studies showing that the reading development process is similar in different languages, and that correlations between literacy development in the first language and the second language are high when length of residence is controlled for. All the above is true even when the orthographies of the two languages are very different (Krashen 1996).

Thus, good bilingual programs have these characteristics:

1. They provide background knowledge through the first language via subject matter teaching in the first language. This should be done to the point that subsequent subject matter instruction in English is comprehensible.
2. They provide literacy in the first language.

3. Of course they provide comprehensible input in English, through English as a second language (ESL) and sheltered subject matter teaching. In sheltered classes, subject matter is taught to intermediate second language acquirers in a comprehensible way. (Sheltered classes are for intermediates; they are not for beginners and not for advanced acquirers or native speakers. It is extremely difficult to teach subject matter to those who have acquired none or little of the language. Beginners should be in regular ESL, where they are assured of comprehensible input. Including more advanced students in sheltered classes is problematic because their participation may encourage input that is incomprehensible to the other students. There is substantial evidence supporting the efficacy of sheltered subject matter teaching for intermediate-level, literate students [Krashen 1991]).

A sample program. The "gradual exit" model is one way of doing a bilingual program that utilizes these characteristics (table 1). In the early stage, non-English speaking students receive all core subject matter in the primary language. At the next stage, limited English-proficient children receive sheltered subject matter instruction in those subjects that are the easiest to make comprehensible in English, math, and science, which, at this level, do not demand a great deal of abstract use of language.

Putting sheltered subject matter classes at this stage ensures that they will be comprehensible. Students in sheltered math, for example, have had some ESL, giving them some competence in English, and have had math in the primary language, giving them subject matter knowledge. These two combine to help make sheltered math comprehensible. Those forced to do subject matter in the second

Table 1. A sample bilingual program

	Mainstream	**ESL/sheltered**	**First language**
Beginning	Art, music, PE	ESL	All core subjects
Intermediate	Art, music, PE	ESL, math, science	Social studies, language arts
Advanced	Art, music, PE, math, science	ESL, social studies	Language arts
Mainstream	All subjects		Heritage language development

language immediately, without any competence in second language, have neither of these advantages. The gradual exit program appears to be the fastest way of introducing comprehensible subject matter teaching in English. Note also that while the child is doing sheltered math, he or she is developing additional background knowledge and literacy through the first language in subjects that are more abstract, social studies and language arts. This will serve to make instruction in English at later stages more comprehensible.

In later stages, math and science are done in the mainstream, and other subjects, such as social studies, are taught in sheltered classes in English. Eventually, all subjects are done in the mainstream. In this way, sheltered classes function as a bridge between instruction in the first language and the mainstream.

Once full mainstreaming is complete, advanced first language development is available as an option. This kind of plan avoids problems associated with exiting children too early from first language instruction (before the English they encounter is comprehensible) and provides instruction in the first language where it is most needed. This plan also allows children to have the advantages of advanced first language development.

In the gradual exit program, the second language is not delayed. It is introduced as soon as it can be made comprehensible. Quite early on, students in these programs do a considerable amount of serious academic work in English, well before they reach the very high levels required for official reclassification. The gradual exit model is thus not subject to the criticism that bilingual education programs delay exposure to English for years.

The evidence for bilingual education. Evidence supporting bilingual education is of several kinds: (1) the results of program evaluations, (2) the effect of previous education on immigrant children's academic performance, and (3) the effect of measured first language ability on immigrant children's second language acquisition. This framework also helps explain the strong impact of socioeconomic status (SES) on school success for immigrant children and why some are successful without bilingual education.

Program evaluations. I would like to suggest a somewhat different approach in evaluating and reviewing research on bilingual education, relaxing one requirement that others adhere to strictly, but insisting on others. The one I insist on is the definition of bilingual education: A program can be considered a properly organized bilingual education program when it provides (a) subject matter teaching in the primary language without translation to the point that subject matter instruction in the second language is made comprehensible, (b) literacy development in the primary language, and (c) comprehensible input in the second language. My prediction is that full bilingual programs, with all three conditions met, will be superior to those in which fewer conditions met. I also insist that studies have adequate sample sizes and that the programs run for at least one year (which may be far too short to show an effect).

Other reviewers have required that there be some kind of control for experimental–comparison group differences that may have existed before the study began. Everyone agrees that randomization is the best way to do this. Lacking randomization, another technique is to statistically control for differences, in pretest scores and/or background differences. In this review, I relax this requirement and allow studies to enter the analysis where there is no compelling reason to suspect that the groups come from different populations. The logic behind this approach was presented in Krashen (1996): With a large number of post-test studies of this kind, randomization is present.

My conclusions are these: In all published studies in which these conditions are met, bilingual education is a winner. Children in bilingual programs acquire more of the second language than those in all-English programs (Mortensen 1984), even eventually doing as well as native speakers of English (de la Garza and Medina 1985; Burnham-Massey and Pina 1990). Results of studies in other countries are similar (Fitzpatrick 1987; Modiano 1968—literacy instruction in L1 only; Appel 1984; Verhoeven 1991—literacy only).

In addition, apparent counterexamples, cases in which bilingual education was thought to be inferior, do not meet the conditions outlined above. In these comparisons, bilingual education is not described or inaccurately described, sample sizes are small, and/or real comparisons are not made.

For example, Rossell and Baker (1996) present ten studies in which "immersion" is considered to be better than bilingual education. Six are actually comparisons of different versions of Canadian immersion, a program that satisfies all three of the characteristics given above: They are all bilingual education. In all versions of Canadian immersion, children obtain enough background knowledge and develop enough literacy through the first language, both in school and at home, to make subject matter taught in the second language comprehensible (Krashen 1996). Thus, those with more comprehensible input in the second language acquire more of it, because factors (a) and (b) are fully satisfied.

In several other cases, categorization is inaccurate. What Rossell and Baker consider to be "immersion" and "submersion" are actually bilingual education; comparisons that Rossell and Baker consider to be between bilingual education and submersion or immersion are really comparisons of different versions of bilingual education (e.g., El Paso and McAllen: see Krashen 1996).

In many reports we have no idea whether the experimental (bilingual) or comparison groups met any of these conditions, as descriptions are lacking. This eliminates many studies that others have allowed into their analyses, such as Gersten (1985)—which also suffers from a very small sample size—Moore and Parr (1978), and Rossell (1990). All of these studies are considered by Rossell and Baker (1996) to support immersion or submersion over bilingual education.

In other cases, results of studies are inaccurately reported: In Curiel, Stenning, and Cooper-Stenning (1980), which Rossell and Baker consider to be an example of the superiority of submersion, nonbilingual students were better in grade 6, but in grade 7 bilingual education students had higher GPAs, fewer had been retained, and there was no difference in English reading. In addition, Curiel and colleagues note that the bilingual program was used as a remedial program for some students who previously had been in the monolingual English program. Thus, a finding of no difference suggests that those placed in bilingual education were able to catch up to the others.

Natural experiments. Two natural experiments meet the criteria outlined above: Spanish-speaking children who had all their schooling in the United States were compared to those who had some of their education in Mexico. In one case, all children were in a bilingual program (Gonzales 1989); the study thus compared the impact of *some* first language instruction with *more* instruction. In the other study, education in the United States was all-English (Ferris and Politzer 1981). In the former case, sixth graders with some education in Mexico did better than all-U.S. educated comparisons in English reading, while in the latter there was no difference between the groups in English writing in junior high school, but the Mexican-educated children had higher grades in English, and, according to teacher reports, were more dedicated students. Ferris and Politzer also report that the socioeconomic status of those with schooling in Mexico was lower than that of the all-U.S. educated group.

Impact of education in L1. Also consistent with this theoretical stance are studies showing that those with more education in the primary language are more successful in English language acquisition, a result that confirms the powerful influence of subject matter knowledge and literacy gained through the first language. Here is just one example: Gardner, Polyzoi, and Rampaul (1966: 3) studied the impact of education in the first language on progress in intensive ESL classes for Kurdish and Bosnian adult immigrants to Canada who had "virtually no English" when they arrived. The subjects were classified into three groups: those with a great deal of formal education (mean = fifteen years), those with some (mean = seven years), and those with no formal education.

Table 2 presents the gains made by each group on tests of oral and written English after participation in intensive ESL (twenty hours per week, for one to one and a half years). For both measures, it is clear that the higher the level of literacy in the primary language, the greater the gains. This was true of both measures and extremely powerful in the written test, in which preliterates' posttest scores were lower than the high literates' pretest scores. The strong impact of first language education on English development has been confirmed in several other studies (Chiswick 1991; Chiswick and Miller 1995; Espanshade and Fu 1997).

Table 2. Gains after intensive ESL instruction

Oral test scores	Pre-	Post-
High literates	10	71
Semiliterates	7	58
Preliterates	1	43
Written test scores		
High literates	17	91
Semiliterates	0	48
Preliterates	1	10

Note: Perfect score = 100 for both tests.
Oral test: Personal questions, picture description, discussion of leisure activities, family.
Written test: write name, circle correct time, copy words, label pictures, answer personal questions, read text and write answers to questions, fill in blanks with correct prepositions, verb tenses, multiple choice vocabulary.
Source: Gardner, Polyzoi, and Rampaul 1966.

SES as de facto bilingual education. Our framework helps explain the consistent positive relationship between SES and English language development (Krashen 1996). Children from wealthier families have, most likely, more and better education in their primary language, caregivers who are better able to help them with schoolwork (in their primary language), and, in general, more access to print.

Immigrant success. The research presented here helps explain why some immigrants did well in school without bilingual education: They came with a good education in their own country, making instruction in English much more comprehensible (Krashen 1996; Tse 1997). Such cases are arguments for bilingual education, not against it.

Bogus arguments against bilingual education. Many of the arguments used to attack the effectiveness of bilingual education violate one or more of the principles presented here.

Is immersion successful? In several cases, the media has claimed success for "immersion" when no comparison was made at all with similar children under bilingual education.

Orange Unified School District. According to the *Los Angeles Times* (Orange County edition), "A controversial new English immersion program in the Orange Unified School District [in southern California] appears to help many students learn to speak the language faster than traditional bilingual programs" (April 18, 1998). The article, which appeared in the middle of the Proposition 227 campaign, announced that "almost a quarter of the district's 4,132 elementary students in the immersion program had advanced their fluency by at least one level in the first five months of study." Orange Unified, the *Times* reported, dropped bilingual education the year before and "went with English immersion."

A closer look shows that this did not occur at all: First, while Orange Unified claimed that it dropped bilingual education, its current English immersion program used at least some first language support, supplied by paraprofessionals. Even more serious, no comparison was made of the progress made by children in the current program and children in the older program. Finally, the progress was not remarkable. I concluded (Krashen 1999) that at the rate these children were progressing, for those starting with no English, fewer than half would be ready for sheltered subject matter instruction in English after one year, and fewer than 20% would be ready for the mainstream in one and a half years. McQuillan (1998) analyzed a more recent report from the same district and also concluded that children were not doing very well under the "immersion" plan. The district, for example, claimed that 81% of the immersion students could understand English in specially taught classes. McQuillan points out, however, that three-quarters of the children were already advanced enough in English to do a modified program before the new program began! In addition, only six of the 3,549 students were ready for regular classes after one year (the time limit imposed by Proposition 227), a dismal 1% reclassification rate, and, in agreement with my findings, only about half who began with no English were ready for "sheltered" classes after one year. Finally, once again, Orange Unified did not compare their students' progress in the new program to progress under older programs.

Westminster School District. The Westminster School District in California claimed that "after 18 months of instruction only in English . . . pupils have made better academic progress and learned more English than they did when taught in their native languages" (*Long Island Newsday*, November 28, 1997). But gains were modest (3 NCE points in one year), and no comparisons were ever made with previous programs. In fact, the Westminster district actually increased the amount of first language support provided to pupils, in the form of paraprofessionals (Krashen 1999).

TAFT SCHOOL. In another case, the comparison group was completely inappropriate. Children at the Taft School in Santa Ana, California, scored at the 48th percentile in English reading on the CTBS in Spring 1997, well above the district average of 22.5 and the highest in the district. Taft's principal credited the school's English immersion philosophy for some of this performance (*Education Week,* January 14, 1998). But Taft's students are clearly more advantaged than others in the Santa Ana district, as revealed by the following data:

	CTBS Reading, grade 5	% free/reduced lunch	LEP
District	22.5 (11.09)	80.1 (17.9)	77.8 (20.1)
Taft	48	43.8	36.2

Source: *Los Angeles Times,* August 28, 1997, A1, A16, A18.
Key: CTBS = Comprehensive Test of Basic Skills; LEP = limited English proficient.

Taft lies two standard deviations above the mean for free/reduced lunch as well as for percent of limited English-proficient students. The correlation between reading scores and SES status (as measured by % free/reduced lunch) was nearly perfect ($r = .926$) (Krashen 1999).

Taft's "success" most likely has nothing to do with the absence of bilingual education. In fact, some of it could be due to de facto bilingual education, the superior education in the primary language that more advantaged children tend to have.

DID LA STUDENTS "TAKE TO IMMERSION?" An article appearing in the *Los Angeles Times* on January 13, 1999, added to the confusion over immersion. The article itself was reasonably well balanced. Interviews were conducted in the Los Angeles Unified School District, and the *Times* reporter concluded that children were picking up "verbal English at a surprising rate" but also reported that there were concerns that children were falling behind in their studies. Many teachers were questioning "whether most of the youngsters have acquired the language skills necessary to comprehend math, reading, or history lessons in English." One teacher noted that children were picking up "social English," not academic English, that new concepts still had to be presented in the primary language, and that "we won't have as many readers in our class as we did last year" (under bilingual education). Other teachers said that they had to "water down" core subjects. This report was not a true evaluation. It was based on only thirteen interviews, and no test scores or any other kind of statistics were reported. Further, the *Times* reporter did not point out that children typically pick up conversational English with any kind of program, even with no special help: The challenge is to help them develop what Cummins (1989) calls "academic language," the language of school. Nevertheless, the headline of the article proclaimed: "L.A. Students Take to English Immersion," and the first paragraph stated that "teachers are delivering promised reports that their children are learning English more quickly than anticipated," overstatements that are inconsistent with the rest of the report and that encouraged the perception that Proposition 227 had been an unqualified success. Unfortunately, these are not isolated examples of sloppy reporting (see Krashen 1999 for more examples).

The Delaware–Massachusetts Analysis. Glenn (1998: 6) also presents an inappropriate comparison: "Massachusetts mandates bilingual education, for example, Delaware prohibits it, but Hispanic achievement is not notably higher in one state than in the other; indeed, the gap between Hispanic and non-Hispanic white scores on the National Assessment of Education Progress was substantially larger in Massachusetts than it was in Delaware."

There are a lot of problems with this comparison, as my colleagues and I have documented elsewhere (Krashen and Crawford 1999). First, it appears that the groups compared may be quite different: There are about 62,000 Hispanic students in Massachusetts and 43% are LEP (1996-1997 data), but there are about 4,000 in Delaware and only 30% are LEP. Clearly, Delaware has a lower percentage of LEP Hispanic students, which suggests that the groups differ in other important ways.

Second, we may actually be comparing bilingual education with bilingual education. Even though bilingual education is officially banned in Delaware, this ban is not enforced (see Crawford 1995: 42). Red Clay Consolidated District in Delaware does bilingual education, and 795 out of Delaware's 1,725 LEP children, and 762 of the 1,299 Hispanic LEP children, were enrolled in Red Clay in 1996-1997. There appears to be plenty of bilingual education in Delaware.

Third, we have no description at all of what kind of bilingual education was done in either state.

Finally, Hispanics in Massachusetts actually scored higher than Hispanics in Delaware on the NAEP reading exam, both in 1994 (194 to 190, a small difference, not "notable," as Glenn points out) and 1992 (a larger difference, 201 to 187). Glenn notes that the gap between Hispanics and non-Hispanic whites was larger in Massachusetts than in Delaware. This was true in 1994, but not in 1992. In 1992 the difference between non-Hispanic whites and Hispanics was larger in Delaware than in Massachusetts. Thus, even if we accepted the Massachusetts-Delaware comparison as a true experiment, which it is not, the data does not consistently support Glenn's assertions.

The 6% argument. Perhaps the most bizarre argument used by critics of bilingual education is the 6% (or 2%, depending on the state) argument. The California version was this: Bilingual education has failed because "each year only about 5% of school children (in California) classified as not proficient in English are found to have gained proficiency in English—the current system of language education has an annual failure rate of 95%" (*English for the Children* brochure).

The figure referred to is the percentage of limited-English proficient children who are reclassified as English proficient each year. (The precise percentage was 6.2% in 1996, up from 5.7% in 1995.) To be reclassified means to reach a high enough level of English literacy to be considered fully English proficient. Calling this a "failure rate" is inaccurate and misleading. As Jeff McQuillan has pointed out, using this definition, a four-year college would have a 75% failure rate, even if all students graduated in four years.

The 6% figure does not represent the success of bilingual education. The California figure was based on all limited English children in California, not just those in bilingual education. The real issue is whether children in full bilingual programs, about 30% of those classified as LEP, had a lower reclassification rate. This is, in other words, a study with no clear experimental group and no clear control group. It is counter to all scientific practice.

It also needs to be pointed out that reclassification is not easy to do: Some districts require that children place in the upper 2/3 of tests of English reading, which by definition 1/3 of the native speakers fail to accomplish. Many limited English proficient students are doing challenging academic study in English well before official reclassification.

Is bilingual education responsible for dropouts? The circumstantial argument is this: Hispanic students have a large dropout rate. Hispanic students are the biggest customer of bilingual education programs. Therefore bilingual education causes dropouts.

False. Only a small percentage of Hispanic students are enrolled in bilingual education: In California, for example, only 15% were in full bilingual programs. In addition, the only empirical study of the impact of bilingual education on dropouts, Curiel, Rosenthal, and Richek (1986), reported fewer dropouts among bilingual education students than among comparison students.

What accounts for dropout rates? Not surprisingly, lack of competence in English (McMillan, Kaufman, and Klein, 1997). But if bilingual education results in better English development, as claimed above, this finding is an argument for bilingual education.

A large number of studies confirm that other factors count, such as socioeconomic class, time spent in the United States, the presence of print, and family factors. Hispanic students are well behind majority children in these areas. What is especially interesting is that these background factors appear to be responsible for much if not all of the difference in dropout rates among different ethnic groups. In other words, when researchers control for these factors, there is little or no difference in dropout rates between Hispanics and other groups (Rumberger 1983, 1995; Fernandez, Paulsen, and Hiranko-Nakanishi 1989; Warren 1996; White and Kaufman 1997; Pirog and Magee 1997). Rumberger (1995: 605), for example, concluded that "Black, Hispanic, and Native American students have twice the odds of dropping out compared to White students . . . however, after controlling for the structural characteristics of family background—particularly, socioeconomic status—the predicted odds of dropping out are no different than those for White students." Rumberger (1983) confirms that Hispanic students often drop out because they have to go to work. When dropouts were asked why they dropped out, only 4% of the Hispanic students mentioned poor performance in school, compared to 8% of comparisons. But 38% of the Hispanic students mentioned economic factors, compared to 22% of the other students.

Bilingualism, bilingual education, and earnings. Lopez and Mora (1998) claim that Hispanics who participated in bilingual education programs earn significantly less in their late twenties than comparison subjects who did not participate in bilingual education. Jeffrey McQuillan and I have argued that this conclusion is not correct (Krashen and McQuillan 1998), based on the following observations of the Lopez and Mora study:

- Earnings differences between former ESL and bilingual students were small and not statistically significant.
- Comparison group subjects, those with no ESL and no bilingual education, probably included English-only native speakers of English: Subjects were allowed into the comparison group if they reported that a language other than English was spoken at home, even if they themselves didn't speak it or understand it.
- We have good reason to believe that subjects' self-reports were not accurate. The subjects were sophomores in high school when they were first interviewed, which was in 1980. Twenty-seven and a half percent claimed they had been in bilingual education, which would have occurred in the early 1970s. But there were few bilingual programs in those days. Jim Crawford has pointed out to me that only 6.5% of the schools in California, Arizona, Colorado, and Texas had bilingual education at that time, and the programs reached only 2.7% of the Mexican-American population.
- We have no information on how bilingual education was done at that time. It is not even clear whether "bilingual education" included ESL as a component.
- Lopez and Mora include third-generation enrollees in ESL and bilingual education. By then, language shift is nearly always complete.

Chiswick and Miller (1998) suggest that bilingualism itself leads to lower earnings. On the basis of an analysis of data from the 1990 census, based on males between the ages of twenty-five and sixty-four born in the United States, they claim:

1. Those who speak only English earned more in 1989 than those who reported that another language was spoken in their home, even when factors such as schooling, years in the labor market, amount worked, marital status, and urban or rural residence were controlled. Overall, English-onlys (those who only heard English at home) earned about 8% more.
2. Even those who grew up in homes with another language who reported that they spoke English "very well" earned less than English-onlys.

Chiswick and Miller (1998: 15) conclude that there is "no statistical support for the proposition that bilingualism, as measured in this study, enhances earning in the United States. It does provide support for the proposition that whatever detracts from full proficiency in English has an adverse effect on earnings." However:

- Those who really suffered were Native American, Hispanic, and "Mexican" men ("Mexican" was considered a separate category from "Hispanic"). Even those who reported they spoke English "very well" earned less than English-onlys, 16%, 9%, and 7%, respectively. Other groups had either a much smaller gap (3% for white non-Hispanics and none at all for men of African and Asian origin). Chiswick and Miller also found that Hispanics who speak English "very well" but who live in states with high concentrations of Spanish-speakers earned 11% less than English-onlys, but those in other states were only 4% lower. These results suggest that language may not have been the central issue in determining earnings, a possibility that Chiswick and Miller present.
- All other studies of heritage language show rather positive effects of bilingualism. Those who develop their heritage language, in addition to acquiring English, do slightly better in school and on the job market (research reviewed in Krashen 1998). The overwhelming majority of children of immigrants report higher competence in English than in the heritage language by the time they are in high school (Krashen 1996). Thus, most of those who speak another language at home probably do not develop it to high levels, for a variety of factors. Language shift is powerful. Most of Chiswick and Miller's subjects were, most likely, weak heritage language speakers. Their data is thus consistent with the hypothesis that high development of the heritage language is positive, and that weak development of the heritage language is a disadvantage.

Public opinion. Our discussion of theory helps us interpret some opinion polls on bilingual education. The polls clearly show that the public is not against bilingual education. Respondents last year in both Los Angeles and Texas agreed either that "students should be taught in their native language for a brief time—a year or two" (Texas poll by the *Dallas Morning News* = 38% agreement; *Los Angeles Times* poll = 39%), or that first language instruction "should last as long as teachers and parents think it is necessary" (Texas poll = 36% agreement; *Los Angeles Times* poll = 25% agreement). Thus, 74% of Texans surveyed supported some use of the first language in school and 64% of those surveyed in Los Angeles. Only a small percentage supported English only (Texas = 24%; Los Angeles = 32%) (details in Krashen 1999.)

A series of studies by Fay Shin also suggests that the public is not against bilingual education. Shin did not ask people if they supported bilingual education; instead, she targeted the underlying principles, asking whether people thought "developing literacy through the first language facilitates literacy development in English" and whether "learning subject matter through the first language helps make subject matter study in English more comprehensible." Results were encouraging; these principles apparently make good sense to a lot of people:

> Developing literacy through the first language facilitates literacy development in English.
> Percent agreement:
>> Hispanic parents = 53% (Shin and Gribbons 1996)
>> Korean parents = 88% (Shin and Kim 1998)
>> Hmong parents = 52% (Shin and Lee 1996)
>> Administrators = 74% (Shin, Anton, and Krashen 1999)
>> Teachers = 74% (Shin and Krashen 1996)

> Learning subject matter through the first language makes subject matter study in English more comprehensible.
> Percent agreement:
>> Hispanic parents = 34% (33% were "not sure") (Shin and Gribbons 1996)
>> Korean parents = 47% (Shin and Kim 1998)
>> Hmong parents = 60% (Shin and Lee 1996)
>> Administrators = 78% (Shin, Anton, and Krashen 1999)
>> Teachers = 70% (Shin and Krashen 1996)

It is important to note that Shin's subjects were not recent graduates of language education programs, nor were they bilingual teachers: Most were, in fact, "civilians." When polls seem to indicate that the public is against bilingual education, a closer look reveals that this is not so.

- In some cases, the public is simply expressing support for children learning English, a goal we all agree with. In fact, this explains much of the success of Proposition 227: Many people thought they were simply "voting for English" (Krashen 1999). When parents say they want children to learn English, this should not be interpreted as a rejection of bilingual education.
- When parents reject bilingual education explicitly, they reject versions of it that few bilingual education advocates would support, that is, versions in which all instruction is in the first language "until children are ready to learn English." As noted earlier, I think children are ready for English the first day of school (Krashen 1999).
- Some polls ask if parents are willing to delay subject matter for English, that is, take time for English study before children learn subject matter. This is an unreasonable question: In good bilingual education programs, children get both maximum subject matter instruction and make maximum progress in acquiring English at the same time. The former helps the latter, as explained earlier in this paper.

Some polls ask if parents are willing to delay English while the children are instructed in their native language. This is also an unreasonable question: In good bilingual programs, there is no delay of English.

Postscript: What happened in California? I suspect that many voters did not know what they were voting for when they supported Proposition 227. They thought that a "yes" vote was simply a vote for English. My evidence comes not only from the countless number of people I talked to, people who told me that they were voting for Prop. 227 because "I'm for English," but also from the *Los Angeles Times* poll of April 13, discussed in the text, which showed clear support for the use of the first language in school and little support for "English-only."

If voters had known what was really in Prop. 227, they would have voted differently. This was confirmed in our study. Jim Crawford noted that the following kind of question, closely following the description of Prop. 227 on the ballot, was typically asked of voters in polls: "There is an initiative on the June primary ballot that would require all public school instruction to be conducted in English and for students not fluent in English to be placed in a short-term English immersion program. If the June primary were being held today, would you vote for or against this measure?"

This kind of question can be easily interpreted as "Are you in favor of children getting intensive English instruction?" and did not reflect what was in

Proposition 227. A more accurate question, Crawford suggested, would be one like this: "There is an initiative on the June primary ballot that would severely restrict the use of the child's native language in school. This initiative would limit special help in English to one year (180 school days). After this time, limited English-proficient children would be expected to know enough English to do school work at the same level as native speakers of English their age. The initiative would dismantle many current programs that have been demonstrated to be successful in helping children acquire English and would hold teachers financially responsible if they violate this policy. If passed, schools would have sixty days to conform to the new policy. If the June primary were being held today, would you vote for or against this measure?"

Students in my language education class asked 251 voters either question 1 or question 2 and the data were analyzed by Haeyoung Kim. The difference between the responses to the two questions was huge (and statistically significant): While 57% supported the original version, only 15% supported the modified version, a result that confirmed our suspicions that few people knew what was in Prop. 227, and if they had known, most would have not supported it.

N = 251	for	don't know	against
Original question	74 (57%)	17 (13%)	39 (30%)
Modified question	18 (15%)	17 (14%)	86 (71%)

chi square = 51.51, df = 2, p < .001

Unfortunately, despite numerous attempts, we were unable to get crucial information about Prop. 227 to many voters.

REFERENCES

Appel, Rene. 1984. *Immigrant children learning Dutch.* Dordrecht, Netherlands: Foris.
Burnham Massey, L., and M. Pina. 1990. Effects of bilingual instruction on English academic achievement of LEP students. *Reading Improvement* 27: 129–32.
Chiswick, Barry. 1991. Speaking, reading, and earnings among low-skilled immigrants. *Journal of Labor Economics* 9: 149–170.
Chiswick, Barry, and Paul Miller. 1995. The endogeneity between language and earnings: International analyses. *Journal of Labor Economics* 13: 246–288.
Chiswick, Barry, and Paul Miller. 1998. The economic cost to native-born Americans of limited English language proficiency. Report prepared for the Center for Equal Opportunity, August.

Crawford, James. 1995. *Bilingual education: History, politics, theory and practice,* 3rd edition. Los Angeles: Bilingual Educational Services.

Cummins, Jim. 1989. *Empowering minority students.* Los Angeles: California Association for Bilingual Education.

Curiel, Herman, Walter Stenning, and Peggy Cooper-Stenning. 1980. Achieved reading level, self-esteem, and grades as related to length of exposure to bilingual education. *Hispanic Journal of Behavioral Sciences* 2(4): 389–400.

Curiel, Herman, James Rosenthal, and Herbert Richek. 1986. Impacts of bilingual education on secondary school grades, attendance, retentions, and drop-out. *Hispanic Journal of Behavioral Sciences* 8(4): 357–367.

Espenshade, Thomas, and Haishan Fu. 1997. An analysis of English-language proficiency among U.S. immigrants. *American Sociological Review* 62: 288–305.

Fernandez, Roberto, Ronnelle Paulsen, and Marsha Hiranko-Nakanishi. 1989. Dropping out among Hispanic youth. *Social Science Research* 18(2): 21–52.

Ferris, M. Roger, and Robert Politzer. 1981. Effects of early and delayed second language acquisition: English composition skills of Spanish-speaking junior high school students. *TESOL Quarterly* 15(3): 263–274.

Fitzpatrick, Finbarré. 1987. *The open door.* Philadelphia: Multilingual Matters.

Gardner, Sheena, Eleoussa Polyzoi, and Yvette Rampaul. 1996. Individual variables, literacy history, and ESL progress among Kurdish and Bosnian immigrants. *TESL Canada* 14: 1–20.

de la Garza, J., and M. Medina. 1985. Academic achievement as influenced by bilingual instruction for Spanish-dominant Mexican-American children. *Hispanic Journal of Behavioral Sciences* 7(3): 247–259.

Gersten, Russell. 1985. Structured immersion for language minority students: Results of a longitudinal evaluation. *Educational Evaluation and Policy Analysis* 7: 187–196.

Glenn, Charles. 1998. Rethinking bilingual education: Changes for Massachusetts. *READ Abstracts, Research and Policy Review,* August.

Gonzales, L. Antonio. 1989. Native language education: The key to English literacy skills. In D. Bixler-Marquez, J. Ornstein-Galacia, and G. Green (eds.), *Mexican-American Spanish in its societal and cultural contexts.* Rio Grande Series in Languages and Linguistics 3. Brownsville: University of Texas, Pan American. 209–224.

Goodman, Kenneth. 1982. *Language, literacy, and learning.* London: Routledge Kegan Paul.

Krashen, Stephen. 1991. Sheltered subject matter teaching. *Cross Currents* 18: 183–188.

Krashen, Stephen. 1996. *Under attack: The case against bilingual education.* Culver City, CA: Language Education Associates.

Krashen, Stephen. 1998. Heritage language development: Some practical arguments. In Stephen Krashen, Lucy Tse, and Jeff McQuillen (eds.), *Heritage Language Development.* Culver City, CA: Language Education Associates.

Krashen, Stephen. 1999. *Condemned without a Trial: Bogus arguments against bilingual education.* Portsmouth, NH: Heinemann.

Krashen, Stephen, and James Crawford. 1999. The research, the scientific method, and the Delaware–Massachusetts argument. *NABE News* 22(5): 14–15.

Krashen, Stephen, and Jeffrey McQuillan. 1998. Do graduates of bilingual programs really earn less? A response to Lopez and Mora. *NABE News* 22(3): 506.

Lopez, Mark, and Marie Mora. (1998). The labor market effects of bilingual education among Hispanic workers, *READ Perspectives* 5(2): 33–54.

McMillen, Marilyn, Phillip Kaufman, and Steve Klein. 1997. *Dropout rates in the United States: 1995.* NCES 97-473. Washington, DC: U.S. Department of Education.

McQuillan, J. 1998. Is 99% failure a "success"? Orange Unified's English immersion program. *Multilingual Educator* 21(7): 11.

Modiano, N. 1968. National or mother tongue language in beginning reading: A comparative study. *Research in the Teaching of English* 2: 32–43.

Moore, Fernie Baca, and Gerald Parr. 1978. Models of bilingual education: Comparisons of effectiveness. *The Elementary School Journal* 79(2): 93–97.

Mortensen, Eileen. 1984. Reading achievement of native Spanish-speaking elementary students in bilingual vs. monolingual programs. *Bilingual Review* 11(3): 31–36.

Pirog, Maureen, and Chris Magee. 1997. High school completion: The influence of schools, families, and adolescent parenting. *Social Science Quarterly* 78: 710–724.

Rumberger, Russell. 1983. Dropping out of high school: The influence of race, sex, and family background. *American Educational Research Journal* 20 (2): 199–220.

Rumberger, Russell. 1995. Dropping out of middle school: A multilevel analysis of students and schools. *American Educational Research Journal* 32 (3): 583–625.

Rossell, Christine. 1990. The effectiveness of educational alternatives for limited-English proficient children. In G. Imhoff (ed.), *Learning in two languages.* New Brunswick, NJ: Transaction. 71–121.

Rossell, Christine, and Keith Baker. 1996. The educational effectiveness of bilingual education. *Research in the Teaching of English* 30 (1): 7–74.

Shin, Fay, M. Anton, and Stephen Krashen. 1999. K-12 administrators' views on bilingual education. *NABE News* 22(8): 11–12, 29.

Shin, Fay, and Barry Gribbons. 1996. Hispanic parent perceptions and attitudes of bilingual education. *The Journal of Mexican American Educators*: 16–22.

Shin, Fay, and Simon Kim. 1998. Korean parent perceptions and attitudes of bilingual education. In R. Endo, C. Park, J. Tsuchida, and A. Abbayani (eds.), *Current issues in Asian and Pacific American education.* Covina, CA: Pacific Asian Press.

Shin, Fay, and Stephen Krashen. 1996. Teacher attitudes toward the principles of bilingual education and toward students' participation in bilingual programs: Same or different? *Bilingual Research Journal* 20: 45–53.

Shin, Fay, and Bo V. Lee. 1996. Hmong parents: What do they think about bilingual education? *Pacific Educational Research Journal* 8(1): 65–71.

Smith, Frank. 1994. *Understanding reading,* 5th edition. Hillsdale, NJ: Erlbaum.

Tse, Lucy. 1997. A bilingual helping hand. *Los Angeles Times* (December 17).

Verhoeven, L. 1991. Acquisition of biliteracy. *AILA Review* 8: 61–74.

Warren, John. 1996. Educational inequality among White and Mexican-origin adolescents in the American Southwest: 1990. *Sociology of Education* 69: 142–158.

White, Michael, and Gayle Kaufman. 1997. Language usage, social capital, and school completion among immigrants and native-born ethnic groups. *Social Science Quarterly* 78 (2): 385–398.

Educating English language learners in U.S. schools: Agenda for a new millennium

Rosalie Pedalino Porter
Institute for Research in English Acquisition and Development (READ)

Introduction. The special "bilingual" programs that are being provided in U.S. schools for immigrant, migrant, and refugee children remain far from meeting the equal education goal for these students and actually run counter to the original intent of the Bilingual Education Act, Title VII of the Elementary and Secondary Education Act of 1968. Radical changes in education policy and dramatic improvements in teaching strategies are urgently needed. I offer concrete suggestions for legislative changes at the state and federal level, and on necessary improvements in teaching strategies and curriculum. My recommendations are based on research conducted by colleagues during the past thirty years and on my experience of twenty-five years in the field as a classroom teacher, program administrator, and consultant to U.S. school districts.

Scope of the Problem. Passage of Proposition 227 by the voters of California in June 1998, the "English for the Children" initiative, has focused national attention on the plight of limited-English proficient (LEP) children who have been given years of native language instruction with the purpose of improving their learning of English and their mastery of academic content. The increasingly apparent problem is that the more special instruction in the primary language and the longer the delay in using English for classroom work, the less English language is learned, with no measurable gains in academic achievement in the school subjects reported for these students. It is not a lack of special help, but that the help is mostly of the wrong kind. Proposition 227 was ill-received by the education establishment and wrongly characterized as an anti-immigrant measure. Although I do not support every detail of the new law, I do believe a drastic action of this sort was the only remedy to remove the dead hand of bureaucratic mandates on California school districts, state edicts that rarely allowed deviation from the established native-language instruction model.

Close to four million children in mainland U.S. schools do not have a sufficient command of the English language to do ordinary classroom work in English. Since the late 1960s, this group of students has constituted the fastest growing part of our school population, due to the highest levels of legal immigration in U.S. history, a high rate of illegal entrants, and the admission of refugees fleeing war and persecution in their native lands (U.S. General Accounting Office 1994). In the letter and the spirit of federal and state laws, bilingual education is the special effort to remove the language barrier to an equal educational opportunity. Originally intended to help poor Mexican-American children learn English, the 1968 Bilingual Education Act's goal was "not to keep any specific language alive . . . but just to try to make those children fully literate in English," in the words of Senator Ralph Yarborough of Texas, author of the bill (1967).

Throughout the era of bilingual teaching efforts, two-thirds or more of the limited-English students have been children of Spanish-speaking families. In fact, it is fair to say that bilingual programs have been developed almost entirely for this language group, although legally, bilingual programs may be provided for the speakers of all 327 languages represented in the U.S. population (U.S. Department of Commerce 1990). Latino children are the most likely to be enrolled in native-language programs, and, therefore, are the greatest recipients of bilingual schooling. Unfortunately, Latino students have the highest school dropout rates in the country, with little or no signs of improvement. The final report of the Hispanic Dropout Project, published in February 1998, states that "[w]hile the dropout rate for other school-aged populations has declined, more or less steadily, over the last 25 years, the overall Hispanic dropout rate started higher and has remained between 30 and 35 percent during that same time period . . . 2.5 times the rate for blacks and 3.5 times the rate for White non-Hispanics" (U.S. Department of Education 1998: 5). It would not be accurate to say that bilingual education is the cause of the high dropout problem, but it may reasonably be said that since it does not appear to be improving the educational success of Latino students, it may be one of the contributing factors.

Theories of bilingual education. Ten years after the passage of the 1968 Bilingual Education Act, theorists developed the rationale for the U.S. policy on language minority education (Rossell 1998: 5). This rationale truly requires a willing suspension of disbelief, that is, we are asked to disregard most of what we have learned about language teaching and language acquisition. The main theories and hypotheses supporting bilingual instruction are the following:

1. A second language is not learned best in the early years of a child's schooling but will be acquired more effectively over a period of several years, after oral language development and literacy skills are first mastered in the child's primary language.
2. The time-on-task principle—more time spent studying a subject results in better learning of that subject—does not apply to the learning of English as a second language.

3. Five to seven years of participation in native language instruction (with gradual introduction of English) will result in the optimal achievement for language minority students: Better learning of English, the ability to do grade-level work in English, and higher levels of academic performance later on in high school.

4. Literacy skills must be developed in the primary language first, before attempting to teach reading and writing in the second language.

5. Extended native language instruction produces higher self-esteem and reduces stress of learning in a second language, which leads to better school performance and may also result in lowering dropout rates.

Not one of these theories/hypotheses has been definitively confirmed by objective, reliable research. Nor has any reliable evidence yet been published that shows native language instruction programs consistently producing better results in students' academic achievement and in second language proficiency (see appendix).

Although the theories described above gained currency over the past two decades, they are now increasingly coming under careful scrutiny. Some counterarguments follow:

1. While it is widely accepted among educators and linguists that older students and adults are capable of studying a new language intensively and efficiently, there is also general agreement that young children learn a new language easily and naturally when placed in a rich, second-language environment and are given maximum opportunities for natural interaction with native speakers, such as a school setting. Nothing in my twenty-five years in this field has yet convinced me that delaying the focus on second language in favor of primary language instruction for children starting school in the United States in the early grades is a wise policy. Most persuasive in this regard has been my involvement with public school programs from preschool classrooms through senior high schools.

2. That the time-on-task principle does not apply to second language learners is one of those ideas that is so contrary to good, common sense that it does not merit discussion. The obvious conclusion that limited-English students who are given more opportunities for interaction with native speakers and more direct instruction in the English language and more instruction in the school subjects in English are able to learn English more quickly and effectively and are able to do school work in English is borne out by at least these two studies: the El Paso Bilingual Immersion Project (1992) and the New York City Public Schools study published in 1994.

3. The five-to-seven-year hypothesis propounded mainly by Virginia Collier and Wayne Thomas has no basis in fact (Rossell 1998). Russell Gersten at the University of Oregon recently stated, emphatically, that "the cornerstone of most contemporary models of bilingual education is that content knowledge and skills learned in a student's primary language will transfer to English once the student has experienced between five and seven years of native language instruction. Yet absolutely no empirical research supports this proposition. Methodological problems so severe that the question cannot be adequately answered plague the research on the subject" (Gersten 1999: 43).

4. Literacy skills need not be developed first in the primary language, if one of the major goals of language minority schooling is the development of English language literacy for full inclusion in mainstream classrooms and for equal educational opportunity. The prestigious National Academy of Sciences report reviewing thirty years of bilingual education research (August and Hakuta 1997: 177) reveals the lack of empirical support for native language instruction in the early grades in this cautious statement: "We do not know whether there will be long-term advantages or disadvantages to initial literacy instruction in the primary language versus English, given a very high-quality program of known effectiveness in both cases." The authors also note that "it is clear that many children first learn to read in a second language without serious negative consequences. These include children who successfully go through early-immersion, two-way, and English as a second language (ESL) based programs in North America" (August and Hakuta 1997: 23).

5. The self-esteem level of students in native language instruction classrooms versus LEP students enrolled in English immersion programs is approximately the same, as reported in comparative studies in Dade County, Florida (Rothfarb, Ariza, and Urrutia 1987), Bethlehem, Pennsylvania (Simons-Turner, Connelly, Goldberg 1995), and El Paso, Texas (Gerston and Woodward 1992), to cite a few.

Effects of K-12 schooling on Hispanic adults. A new study of the labor market effects of bilingual education among Hispanic workers analyzes the earnings, ten years after high school, for adults principally enrolled in English-language programs compared with those who received native language instruction. Although the authors, Lopez and Mora (1998: 33) readily acknowledge the preliminary nature of this study, they do report that "utilizing data from *High School and Beyond,* we find that first generation and (to a lesser extent) second generation Hispanics who attended a bilingual education program appear to earn significantly less (30%) than otherwise similar English-immersed peers who received monolingual English instruction, *ceteris paribus."* Lopez and Mora also report that in regard to job sorting, adults who were in bilingual education programs are in less skilled jobs than English-language educated peers from the same background. Certainly much more research must be done on the economic and social effects of different school programs on LEP students later in life, assuming that reliable data become available.

Most Promising Educational Approaches. My professional experience in this field strongly suggests the following language teaching strategies and curricular designs hold the greatest promise for "leveling the playing field" for limited-English students:

1. Early immersion in a carefully structured, content-based English language program produces the best and quickest second language acquisition for school purposes. This is not a novel idea but an approach that has been widely known for years but not so widely applied because of the political and legal imposition of the native language teaching ideology. Now that thirty years of research has not confirmed the superiority of native language instruction programs, it is time to allow diversity of educational options.

2. Teaching all the language skills concurrently in the second language—listening comprehension, speaking, reading, and writing—from the first day of school will provide English language learners with the strongest base for literacy in the second language, for learning of school subjects taught in English, and for *thinking* in that language. The most promising curricular design would include these features: a literature-rich reading program, language lessons focused on school subjects, as much linkage as possible between lessons for limited-English students, and the grade-appropriate curriculum for each subject—an integration of linguistic and cognitive development in the mainstream setting rather than a separate, segregated education.

3. The highest level of interaction between limited-English students and their English-speaking peers—in both classroom and informal situations—provides essential opportunities for second language development and for practice with formal and informal speech patterns. The Transitional Bilingual Education model segregates by language and ethnicity for 50 to 80% of the school day for several years, unnecessarily delaying both second language learning opportunities and integration of diverse student groups.

More professional development for experienced teachers, administrators, and auxiliary staff, as well as better preparation of new teacher candidates, is necessary to make all school personnel knowledgeable about language minority children. Given the rapid increase in the enrollment of limited-English students in U.S. public schools in the past two decades, all school personnel need an understanding of the special needs of these students, of the different cultural backgrounds and how they affect children's school readiness and adaptation to American ways, of reasonable expectations for linguistic and cognitive progress according to each child's age, previous educational experience, family background. Too often well-meaning teachers set unrealistic standards for limited-English students, either impossibly high or ineffectually low, simply from a lack of accurate information.

To avoid misunderstandings, I will clarify my position on a few issues often raised by bilingual education advocates. Learning English is not the only priority for bilingual children. Of course, they must learn subject matter content as well. But, in my view, learning English early and well is the absolute prerequisite to academic achievement in that language and in the mainstream school, community, and larger social settings. Developing literacy in the primary language of the family is a desirable but secondary priority that should be offered as a voluntary activity where a speech community actively requests such a program.

It must also be acknowledged that no single school program, whether bilingual or ESL or two-way, is guaranteed to ensure student success for all children. A large percentage of the children who begin school without a sufficient knowledge of the common language—immigrant, refugee, or native-born nonspeakers of English—are children from families of poverty. Often their parents do not know English, do not have a high level of education, and are forced to move the family frequently to seek better living conditions (U.S. General Accounting Office 1994). All of these factors have an effect on a child's ability to achieve his or her highest potential in academic achievement, no matter what kind of special program is being provided. It is well to bear these facts in mind when determining which interventions will best serve the needs of children for self-realization, for upward mobility, and for eventual inclusion in a broad civic and social community.

Recommendations for changes at federal and state levels. Assuming there is general agreement that the improved schooling of limited-English students will result in higher academic achievement and lower dropout rates for Latino students, as well as greater numbers of formerly limited-English students going on to higher education and skilled jobs, I would suggest a number of changes at the federal and state levels that are most likely to effect these improvements.

Federal. On April 27, 1998, Secretary of Education Richard W. Riley announced a major shift in education policy for limited-English students. He recommended a goal of English language proficiency in three years for virtually all English language learners. He said at the time that "new immigrants have a passion to learn English, and they want the best for their children" (Riley 1998: 2).

Director of the Office of Bilingual Education and Minority Languages Affairs (OBEMLA) Delia Pompa stated at the opening session of GURT '99 that federal policy does not mandate native language instruction programs but supports flexibility in program choice at the local district level. I, personally, concur with both policy statements, but I have, for too long, seen a discord between policy and implementation.

If flexibility in program choice is indeed the policy of OBEMLA then it must be communicated to the Office of Civil Rights, whose compliance reviews have been inflexibly aimed at supporting bilingual education programs and pressuring districts to engage in more native language instruction than the district deems suitable for its students (Littlejohn 1998). This was not intended under the 1974 *Lau v. Nichols* decision of the U.S. Supreme Court (cited in Chavez 1991: 14–15). *Lau* made no requirement that language-minority children be taught in their native language, but instead mandated that they receive special help to remove the language barriers to an equal education. It appears that the Office of Civil Rights needs to be told to stop exceeding its legal responsibilities.

Another major area in federal policy that needs a drastic overhaul is OBEMLA itself. To implement Director Pompa's announced flexibility policy it is now time to remove the restrictions on funding at OBEMLA. Currently 75% of all grants are restricted to native language instruction programs and 25% are allocated to special English-language focus programs. And this is an improvement over the policy in effect up to 1988, where 96% of grants were given to native language teaching programs and only 4% to "alternative" programs, meaning English language focus.

There is no justification for the current funding policy to continue, since it is the Department of Education's funded research that has found no superiority for native language instruction programs (see appendix). I recommend that the major part of OBEMLA funds be awarded directly to states with limited-English students, in the form of block grants, to be disbursed on a per capita basis according to each district's enrollment numbers. That would be the equitable way of providing extra funding to school districts specifically to be used for these children, with state monitoring, and without dictating a pedagogical approach. Emergency Immigrant Education Act funds are administered in this fashion. Such a plan would eliminate OBEMLA's present grant procedure, which is cumbersome, time-consuming, and rewards only a few districts each year.

State. To bring this educational enterprise up to date with what we have learned since 1968, the most essential changes must occur at the state level. Legislation drafted in a dozen states, beginning with Massachusetts in 1971, either mandates bilingual education programs exclusively or coerces school districts to provide bilingual programs through funding regulations or strong-arm pressure by state education departments. Of the ten states enrolling three-fourths of the limited-English students in the country, four mandate bilingual education: Illinois, Massachusetts, New Jersey, and Texas. Three states—Michigan, New Mexico, and New York—do not have a mandate but only provide funding for bilingual programs. Arizona and Florida fund all programs for limited-English students. California, the state with 43% of all LEP students in the United States, currently has a legal mandate to teach these children in an English immersion program (Center for Equal Opportunity 1997).

The time has come to acknowledge the very limited success of the bilingual teaching experiment and for state initiatives to move forward seriously on two fronts: flexibility and accountability. State laws must remove the imposition of the bilingual model on all communities—the "one-size-fits-all" approach—and allow all districts with limited-English students the right to exercise local choice, giving the many skillful people teaching these children the freedom to use their best talents to make the necessary changes and improvements. States must provide extra resources to ensure support for professional development, curricular innovations, and extra learning opportunities after school and in summer, and leave the actual planning of program details to the districts. Coupled with local program choice is the obligation on schools to do careful, consistent monitoring and reporting on student achievement. It is a national disgrace that the evaluation of bilingual children has been so widely evaded over the years, even by Massachusetts, the state that started bilingual education (Massachusetts Bilingual Education Commission 1994), and California, the state with the largest concentration of limited-English students (Berman et al. 1992).

Conclusion. In an *Education Week* article dated April 29, 1998, Michael Kirst of Stanford University pinpointed the problem with bilingual education that must be overcome through rigorous accountability for student progress. He said, "From its inception . . . in the 1970s, bilingual education has been oriented toward inputs, process, and compliance. . . . The assumption was if you have this input, the outputs would take care of themselves. So . . . [we monitored] whether you mounted the program, and not its results" (quoted in Schnaiburg 1998: 16).

Fortunately for the future improvement of language minority education, the accountability movement is now beginning to include limited-English students. During the past five years, Texas has invested in developing statewide curricular frameworks and the Texas Assessment of Academic Skills (TAAS). In 1993, Massachusetts passed an Education Reform Act that has poured hundreds of millions of dollars of new money into state curriculum improvements and the testing of all fourth, eighth, and tenth graders through the Massachusetts Comprehensive Assessment System (MCAS). California developed a Standardized Testing and Reporting (STAR) program to measure academic progress of all students, in grades two through eleven every year, beginning in 1998. All of these well-funded, large-scale projects will gather useful data on student progress and, potentially, provide the impetus for curricular and pedagogical improvements.

The needs of language-minority students are serious and pressing, especially for Latino children who make up two-thirds of the limited-English students in our schools and for whom native language instruction is almost exclusively provided. In a recent *New York Times* feature (January 31, 1999), James Traub argues that Latino students spend far too much time in native language instruction, and that "bilingual education seems to be hurting Latino students the most—the one group it was initially designed to help" (33).

For earlier immigrant groups living in concentrated communities speaking Italian, Greek, or Yiddish, the transition from native language to English and from unskilled labor to professional careers was expected to take three generations. We cannot wait three generations today; we must do it in one. The schools must help students to master the English language, learn their school subjects, and become competent in the technology skills required even for entry-level jobs, at a minimum. Schools must also prepare the most motivated and hard working students for higher education and professions. The highest goal, in my view, is to give all children who start school as limited-English students the equal educational opportunities to become capable, successful citizens involved in the civic, cultural, and economic life of this most multi-ethnic, multilingual, and multicultural country. Anything less is not good enough. Finally, our efforts must be concentrated not on saving the bilingual education system—the status quo—but on giving our children the best educational opportunities.

References

August, Diane, and Kenji Hakuta, eds. 1997. *Improving schooling for language-minority children: A research agenda.* Washington, DC: National Academy Press.

Baker, and DeKanter. 1981. *Effectiveness of bilingual education: A review of the literature.* Technical Analysis Report Series, U.S. Department of Education. Washington, DC: Office of Planning and Budget.

Berman, P., J. Chambers, P. Gandara, B. McLaughlin, C. Minicucci, D. Nelson, L. Olsen, and T. Parrish. 1992. *Meeting the challenge of language diversity: An evaluation of programs for pupils with limited-English proficiency,* vol. 2, *Findings and conclusions.* Berkeley: BW Associates.

Board of Education of the City of New York. 1994. *Educational progress of students in bilingual and ESL programs: A longitudinal study, 1990–1994* (October). New York: Board of Education.

Center for Equal Opportunity. 1997. *Parents' guide to bilingual education/Guia para los padres sobre la educacion bilingue.* Washington, DC: Equal Opportunity Foundation.

Chavez, Linda. 1991. *Out of the barrio: Toward a new politics of Hispanic assimilation.* New York: Basic Books.

M. Danoff, G. Coles, D. McLaughlin, and D. Reynolds. 1978. *Evaluation of the impact of ESEA Title VII, Spanish/English bilingual education program: Overview of the study and findings.* Palo Alto, CA: American Institute for Research (AIR).

Gersten, Russell. 1999. The changing face of bilingual education. *Educational Leadership* (April): 41–45.

Gersten, Russell, and John Woodward. 1992. *Bilingual immersion: A longitudinal evaluation of the El Paso program.* Washington, DC: The READ Institute.

Littlejohn, Jim. 1998. *Federal control out of control: The Office for Civil Rights hidden policies on bilingual education.* CEO Policy Brief, Washington, DC: Equal Opportunity Foundation.

Lopez, Mark Hugo, and Marie T. Mora. 1998. The labor market effects of bilingual education among Hispanic workers. *READ Perspectives* V-2(Fall): 33–54.

Massachusetts Bilingual Education Commission. 1994. *Striving for success: The education of bilingual pupils.* Boston: Executive Office of Education.

Riley, Richard W. 1998. *Helping all children learn English.* Washington, DC: U.S. Department of Education, Office of Public Affairs. (April 29).

Rossell, Christine H. 1998. Mystery on the bilingual express: A critique of the Thomas and Collier study "School Effectivenss for Language Minority Students." *READ Perspectives* V-2(Fall): 5–26.

Rossell, Christine H., and Keith Baker. 1996. *Bilingual education in Massachusetts: The emperor has no clothes.* Boston: Pioneer Institute.

Rothfarb, Silvia, Maria Ariza, and Rafael Urrutia. 1987. *Evaluation of the bilingual curriculum project: Final report of a three-year study.* Miami: Dade County Public Schools.

Schnaiburg, Lynn. 1998. What price English? *Education Week* 1: 16.

Simons-Turner, Judith, Mark Connelly, and Ann Goldberg. 1995. The Bethlehem, PA, school district's English Acquisition Program: A blue-print for change. *READ Perspectives* 2(2): 53–121.

Traub, James. 1999. The bilingual barrier. *New York Times Magazine* (January 31): 32–35.

U.S. Department of Commerce, Bureau of the Census. 1990. Language spoken at home and ability to speak English for United States, Regions and States: 1990. Washington, DC: Population Division, Economic and Social Stratification Branch, 1990 Census Special Tabulation.

U.S. Department of Education. 1998. *Executive summary, No more excuses: The final report of the Hispanic dropout project.* Washington, DC: U.S. Department of Education (February).

U.S. General Accounting Office. 1994. *Limited-English proficiency: A growing and costly educational challenge facing many school districts.* Washington, DC: U.S. General Accounting Office (January).

Yarborough, Ralph. 1967. *Congressional Record,* 90th Congress, 1st Session. Washington, DC: U.S. Government Printing Office (December 1).

APPENDIX. A SUMMARY OF MAJOR BILINGUAL EDUCATION STUDIES

Prepared by Rosalie P. Porter, Ed.D., for New York University Law School Symposium February 28, 1997

1978—American Institute for Research report concludes that limited-English proficient (LEP) students in bilingual programs have less success in learning English than students receiving no special help at all; LEP students learn math equally well if they are taught in Spanish and English or only in English (Danoff et al. 1978).

1981—Baker and DeKanter report (U.S. Department of Education): The case for the effectiveness of Transitional Bilingual Education (TBE) is so weak that exclusive reliance on this instructional method is clearly not justified (Baker and DeKanter 1981).

1988—Dade County, Florida, 3-Year Curriculum Content Project: Limited-English students learned as much subject matter if they were taught in English or if they were taught in Spanish—no advantage for native language instruction (Rothfarb, Ariza, and Urrutia 1987).

1992—El Paso Bilingual Immersion Project: LEP children in English immersion classes consistently out-performed children in TBE classes in learning English and in learning school subjects over the ten-year study (Gersten and Woodward 1992).

1992—California State Study: Results based on twenty years of bilingual education reveal generally a poor quality of bilingual programs, no evidence that native language instruction is beneficial, lack of accountability, lack of data collection regarding academic progress of LEP students, and keeping LEP students in bilingual programs for too many years (Berman et al. 1992).

1994—Massachusetts State Study: Results based on twenty-three years of bilingual education show lack of accountability, no evidence that TBE programs produce good or poor results, no data evaluating performance of limited-English students compared with other groups of students (Massachusetts Bilingual Education Commission 1994).

1994—New York City Study: LEP students in English as a Second Language classes exited their special program faster and did better in mainstream classrooms than students taught in their native language in TBE classes (Board of Education of the City of New York 1994).

1996—Rossell and Baker analysis of research: "After reviewing the results of these studies [n = 72], we find no consistent research support for transitional bilingual education as a superior instructional practice for improving the English language achievement of LEP children" (Rossell and Baker 1996: 49).

1997—National Research Council conclusion on examining twenty-nine years of research: "We do not know whether there will be long-term advantages or disadvantages to initial literacy instruction in the primary language versus English" (August and Hakuta 1997).

The Official English movement and bilingual education reform

Eric J. Stone
U.S. ENGLISH Foundation

Introduction. Unfortunately, despite the fact that the federal government has been funding bilingual education programs for thirty years, the question of whether that is the best way to educate children with limited English is still unanswered. Regardless of what the long-term studies eventually show about bilingual education, there are steps that can be taken now to correct some of the more obvious flaws in the current system. Reforms are also necessary at the state, school district, school, and classroom levels, but federal policy must be changed to remove some of the barriers to reform at the state and local level. "Bilingual education" carries a lot of political baggage, both for and against. Unfortunately, that makes it hard to focus on the real issue—preparing children of limited English proficiency to lead successful lives by unblocking the door to opportunity.

Types of programs. The debate over bilingual education can be confusing because "bilingual education" means different things to different people. To some it means programs that use the student's native language to teach other subjects. To others it means any program designed to educate Limited English Proficiency (LEP) students.

Supporters of native language based programs take advantage of this confusion. They equate opposition to bilingual education with opposition to any help for LEP students. Federal law does not make things any clearer—funding for any type of program to assist LEP students comes under the Bilingual Education Act.

Let me make it absolutely clear: U.S. ENGLISH supports funding to help students become proficient in English. Our opposition to failed bilingual education programs does not mean we advocate placing LEP students in regular classrooms with no help to learn English. We believe a combination of structured English immersion for children with little knowledge of English and ESL classes for those with a greater knowledge provides the most effective and efficient way to use limited educational resources to help LEP students obtain equal educational opportunity.

Demographic characteristics of limited-English students. Nationally, among the LEP school population, the two largest groups are Asian and the Hispanic students. Great diversity exists among the populations of both groups. Within the Asian group, about 20% are Filipino, 17% are of Chinese origin, and 13% are from Southeast Asia. Students with Korean, Pacific Islander, and Japanese backgrounds form other large subgroups. About 75% of the Asian students live in families that consider themselves bilingual and rate themselves as having a low proficiency in their native language. A high socioeconomic status correlates positively with high English proficiency (SIAC 1993–1994: tables 6 and 7).

Within the Hispanic student population diversity also exists. Students of Mexican background, about two thirds of the Hispanic population, make up the largest subgroup. Puerto Rican students account for 11% of the Hispanic population, and Cuban students form 4% of this group. The remaining 23% are from "other" nationalities.

Supporters of bilingual education often claim that the majority of LEP students do not receive any help. This is simply untrue. There were 2,980,463 students in the public schools identified as LEP by local school districts in school year 1993–1994. Of these LEP students, 2,274,021 (82.4%) were in special programs designed to meet their needs. The remaining 486,801 LEP students were in no specially designed program of instruction (SIAC 1993–1994: tables 6 and 7).

The diversity of languages can lead to problems designing a program to meet the needs of all LEP students. Students from a language group with large numbers may receive more help than students who speak a language that is less common in the school district. While federal law, including the equal protection clause of the Fourteenth Amendment, requires that all students of limited English proficiency be given an equal educational opportunity, bilingual education advocates focus mainly on those whose language groups are of sufficient size that transitional or maintenance bilingual education is feasible.

Misplaced priorities. Imagine a five-year-old boy who speaks only his native language. On his first day of school, he is placed in a classroom where the teacher and the other students speak a completely different language, one that he has never even heard before. There is no special program to help him learn the language. The boy's father asks the school to transfer him out of the class into one more suited to his needs, one where he can actually understand what is going on in the classroom. The school refuses. Bilingual education's defenders would probably say that this story is a perfect example of why we need bilingual education. They would be wrong, because it is actually about a bilingual program run amok. In this case, five-year-old Travell Louie is an English-speaking African American who was placed in a Cantonese-speaking kindergarten class in Oakland, California. His father is now suing the school district, trying to get his son moved into a regular English classroom (Schorr 1998).

Bilingual education programs rely on the still unproven theory that a child must spend years becoming literate in his native language before he or she can properly learn a second language. Under their own theory, bilingual educators should not have placed an English-speaking child in a Cantonese-speaking class. But they did, and they then refused his father's request to move him into an English classroom.

Why didn't the school transfer Travell out of the Cantonese class once they realized he had been put there by mistake? Because it wasn't a mistake! It was intentional. School officials admit that they sometimes put English-speaking students like Travell into bilingual classes that have extra spaces in order to round out the class size.

What motivates the bilingual education bureaucrats to make such a decision? Under normal circumstances, educators would be looking for ways to reduce the size of classes, rather than pulling in extra students to fill them up. Why would the school want to increase the size of its bilingual classes? Perhaps the perverse incentives found in current federal bilingual education policy are part of the explanation. Because extra funds are available for bilingual education, schools have an incentive to place (and keep) students in bilingual classes. While our goal should be to make sure every child of limited English proficiency learns English quickly and well, schools are not rewarded for doing so. Instead, they are rewarded for being inefficient at teaching English—the longer a student is not proficient in English, the longer the school can receive extra funding.

Is there a federal role? In the 105th Congress, one of the proposed bills (H.R. 3720) dealing with bilingual education simply repealed the Bilingual Education Act and stopped all federal funding for programs to assist LEP students. Proponents of that bill argued that education is something that should be handled on a local level, and that the federal government did not have a role. While education is generally considered a local issue, there are reasons why it is particularly appropriate for the federal government to appropriate funds to assist LEP students. LEP students are not distributed evenly among the school districts of the nation. Instead, they are concentrated in areas with a high proportion of immigrants. Immigration policy is made at the national level, not the state or local level. However, the effects of national immigration policy are felt disproportionately by certain states, and even more disproportionately by certain localities. Schools in high immigration areas are required by federal law to help LEP students achieve proficiency in English. If the federal government does not assist the local schools, such a requirement would amount to an unfunded mandate.

What reforms are needed? In June 1998, California voters overwhelmingly passed Proposition 227, which drastically altered the state's methods of teaching LEP students. Under the "English for the Children" initiative, all LEP students are placed in structured English immersion programs. (There is a waiver process to allow students to be placed into native language-based programs.) This drastic reform came about because for several years the state legislature refused to pass bilingual education reform legislation. Because there is no federal initiative process, the voters cannot pass a federal version of Proposition 227. However, such drastic reform is unnecessary. There are three simple reforms at the federal level that would dramatically improve the situation:

Increase local control. The federal government currently earmarks at least 75% of its bilingual education funding for programs that spend most of the time teaching children in their native language. Federal funding should continue, but the federal government should allow the local school jurisdiction to choose the education program they find most effective.

Make schools accountable. Require schools to track and report on the progress of students in each type of program for LEP students. Funding should be withdrawn from programs that are not succeeding at rapidly teaching English and given to programs that are.

Give parents a choice. Require educators to get consent from parents of LEP children before placing them in bilingual education programs. Parents must also have the right to withdraw their children from such programs.

In addition to these three major reforms, there are minor reforms that, although not essential, would be helpful. For instance, renaming the Bilingual Education Act to something like the English Learners Act or the English Proficiency Act would help clear up some of the confusion over the term "bilingual education," as well as giving a clear signal that the major goal of the act is to help students achieve English fluency. For similar reasons, the Office of Bilingual Education and Minority Language Affairs (OBEMLA) should be renamed.

Increasing local control. Under the current Bilingual Education Act, federal funding for programs to assist LEP students is currently distributed on an application grant model. This means that grants are made directly from the federal government to local education agencies. In order to receive a grant, local education agencies must submit an application detailing the planned educational program. The Secretary of Education then decides whether or not to approve the grant. The application grant model does not guarantee that any particular state will receive funding proportional to the number of LEP students it must serve.

The funding preference for native language based programs affects the approval of grants. Section 3282(b)(3) of the Bilingual Education Act provides that of the money available for grants, "the Secretary may reserve not to exceed 25 percent for special alternative instructional programs." This leaves 75% or more of the funding to native language based programs. If too many local educational agencies request grants for English based programs (which fall under the term "special alternative instructional programs"), the secretary has no discretion to exceed the 25% limit. On the other hand, if grant applications for native language based programs exceed the 75% threshold, the secretary does have discretion to award funds that could have gone to English-based programs and use them for native language-based programs.

Such a bias in the funding arrangement discourages school districts from offering alternatives to native language based programs. If a school wishes to apply for a federal grant to assist in the teaching of their LEP students, it is more likely that they will receive funding if their program is native language based.

Removing program type restrictions. The most fundamental change to the current law would be to remove the funding restriction on alternatives to native language-based programs. The record of research compiled over the past thirty years does not support a preference for native language-based programs. Removing the restriction would encourage schools to try different approaches that might be better suited to the needs of their students.

Coupled with some form of reporting and accountability, a removal of the funding preference would bring a measure of competition to the education of LEP students. Programs that work would receive more funding, and programs that were failing would be forced to change.

Although there are some who advocate a ban on federal funding for native language-based programs (or, less drastically, a reversal of the current situation by giving funding preference to English based programs) such a dramatic change is probably not politically feasible in the face of opposition from the educational establishment. More importantly, although research does support the idea that English-based programs produce better results, it has not been proven conclusively (Rossell 1990). The best solution is to allow all types of programs to compete for funding. Eventually, schools will gravitate toward whichever program best fits their needs.

Block grants to states. In order to fairly distribute the funding to assist LEP students, funds should be allocated to each state on the basis of the number of LEP students in the state. Block grants have been used successfully with other federal funding problems to ensure an equitable distribution of funding and allow states to experiment with different implementation strategies. In order to ease transition from the current funding mechanism to block grants, local educational agencies that are currently receiving funding under approved grants should continue to receive funds until the grant term ends. (Current law allows grants up to three years in length.) By switching from the current application grant to a block grant program, states would gain more control over their educational programs for LEP students. The federal government's role would shift to oversight and accountability.

Accountability. The accountability provisions in current federal law are very weak. Strengthening accountability would help ensure that students are actually getting the help they need. Rather than continuing to pour money into failing programs, successful programs can be given the money to expand their services.

Current law includes a requirement that applications for grants include specific educational goals and a proposed method of measuring achievement of the goals. However, the Bilingual Education Act does not require that such information be reported when reapplying for a grant—or at any other time. Programs that are failing to meet their own educational goals are not under any federal statutory obligation to report that fact to anybody.

Furthermore, there are no real guidelines as to what those educational goals are to be or how they must be measured. Achieving competence in English does not even have to be one of the listed goals, and thus measuring a student's progress in learning English would not even be necessary. So a grant could be renewed for a program that was meeting the goals listed in the application, even if children were completely failing to achieve competence in English.

Tracking and reporting progress. In order to have a useful system of accountability that allows comparison between different program types, the specific goals to be achieved by programs for LEP students and the method of measuring achievement must be defined at the federal or state level. Different programs must be required to track the same data, and that data should be reported at regular intervals to the state educational agency overseeing the grants.

All programs for LEP students have as their nominal goal the achievement of academic competence in English so that students are capable of taking mainstream classes in English. (Although dual language immersion classes may have the added goal of producing competence in a second language, it must be acknowledged that if the program fails to produce competence in English, the program has failed in its most important goal.) Therefore, any system of accountability should require programs to track the progress of individual students in gaining competence in English.

Periodically, parents should be given reports that show how their children are progressing toward competence in English. Parents should also be given information comparing the progress of students in the same program as their children with the overall progress of students in alternative programs.

Time limits. How long does it take a child to learn sufficient English to be able to transition to mainstream classes? Many supporters of native language-based instruction argue against setting any sort of time limit on the basis that the important thing is *whether* a child learns English, not *how fast*. Although it is true that the most important thing is whether a child learns English, how fast the child learns English is also very important: Given that funding for programs to help LEP students is not unlimited, a program that can transition a student to mainstream classes within three years can serve approximately twice as many students for the same funding as a program that takes six years to transition students. A program that takes only two years can serve three times as many students. Since there is a shortage of teachers with the proper training to teach LEP students, the more rapidly LEP students transition into mainstream classes, the more students can be taught per trained teacher. The variety of classes, particularly college preparatory classes, is wider for students in mainstream classes. The sooner a student can attend mainstream classes, the sooner he or she can take advantage of those resources. Advocates of native language based education may argue that more funding can solve all the above problems. The simple fact is, if the goal of English competence can be achieved quickly rather than slowly, it can result in substantial financial savings.

In discussing time limits on federal funding, opponents of the limits raise the specter of children being forced into mainstream classes while still lacking the English proficiency they need to succeed. This is a red herring. Even though many studies show that this might actually be preferable to leaving the students in transitional bilingual education, schools are still required by federal law to provide special help to LEP students even when there is no federal funding.

Without some form of time limit, schools have no incentive to transition students into mainstream classes, as this would reduce the federal funding they could receive. With time limits on federal funding, schools have an incentive to help students achieve English competence within the time limit so they are not forced to continue special help for the student without federal funding.

Current limits. The current Bilingual Education Act sets a three-year goal and a five-year limit on how long an LEP student can remain in a federally funded program (except for dual language immersion programs, on which there is no limit.) If a comprehensive evaluation of a student indicates that after three years of the program he or she is still not ready for mainstream classes, the student can remain for a fourth year, and after a further evaluation with the same result, a fifth year. After that time, the student cannot remain in a program funded under the Bilingual Education Act.

While a violation of that time limit would theoretically be grounds for the Secretary of Education to deny an application for grant renewal, the time limit is easily ignored, because there is no mandatory reporting mechanism by which the secretary could determine that students were not being transitioned within that time limit.

What should the limit be? Current law sets a limit of five years. California's Proposition 227 set a one-year time limit. Some researchers say transition can take ten years. A model transitional bilingual education is supposed to complete the transition in three years. With all these numbers, what is a reasonable time frame in which to expect schools to transition their students into mainstream classes?

During the debate over Proposition 227 in California, the Clinton administration declared its opposition to the one-year time limit, suggesting that three years was a reasonable time limit. In theory, a properly implemented transitional bilingual education program should be able to succeed within three years, so the three-year limitation makes sense—a program taking longer than that is not working properly and should not be subsidized to continue its failure. In order to ensure that programs are on track to help their students achieve competency in English within three years, students should be evaluated each year to determine their progress, rather than waiting until the end of the third year.

Withdrawal of funding. True accountability requires some consequence for failure to meet requirements. Lacking such consequences, grant recipients are unlikely to fulfill requirements that they find burdensome or contrary to their preferred method of operation. The leverage that the federal government can exert to ensure that the law's requirements are met comes from the power of the purse. Funding must be withdrawn from grant recipients that are willfully or consistently in violation of the requirements outlined in the law.

With a block grant, states must agree to monitor the compliance of their local educational agencies that receive grants. States must withdraw funding from programs that fail to meet the standards set in the law and reallocate those funds to programs that are in compliance. By the same token, the federal government would monitor compliance at the state level and withdraw funds from states that were not fulfilling their responsibilities.

Parental Choice. Federal law currently provides that parents must be informed that their child is going to be enrolled in a bilingual education class and that they have the option of declining enrollment for their child. Although this is intended to allow parents to make an informed choice about their child's education, in practice it does not. Even if the school does inform the parents (and there is plenty of anecdotal evidence about parents who have not been informed), the information is generally presented in such a way as to influence the parents in favor of allowing their child to be enrolled in a native language-based program.

Opponents of bilingual education reform often claim that since parents already have a choice under the current law, no reform is needed. This glosses over a highly significant nuance of the current law: Although parents have the right to choose to decline their child's enrollment in a bilingual program, *there is no right to withdraw the child from the program.*

True parental-choice legislation must allow parents to withdraw their children from bilingual education classes if they believe their children would be better served by an alternative program. Combined with reporting requirements that allow parents to see what types of programs are successful, parental choice will allow children to move from failing programs to successful programs.

Conclusion. Most people agree that students of limited English proficiency should receive help in learning English. With the current Bilingual Education Act up for reauthorization, now is the perfect time to improve it to help ensure that every student learns English, so he or she can take advantage of the wonderful opportunities this nation has to offer.

Advocates of bilingual education blocked reform in the 105th Congress because they are single-mindedly committed to one form of education. People who are truly committed to the goal of helping LEP students to become fully proficient in English should care less about the instructional method and more about whether a program of any type is succeeding.

The federal government has a legitimate role in achieving that goal. Since the number of limited English proficiency students is directly related to our national immigration policies, it is only fair that the federal government help states and localities to deal with the impact of those policies. While the current law regarding the teaching of English to students with limited English proficiency has led to poor results, Congress cannot merely wash its hands of the subject and turn the issue back to the states. Instead, Congress has the responsibility to reform federal law to create a sensible policy that will help immigrant students to learn English.

Reasonable reform measures will not prescribe the methods to be used to help students to learn English—but it will require tracking how students are doing and shifting funds from programs that are not working to programs that are. This will give schools an incentive to make sure that their programs actually are helping students achieve competence in English.

Parental choice reform would allow parents to remove their children from programs upon request. This important item introduces an element of market competition to programs teaching English to LEP students. With the accountability and reporting requirements of this bill, parents will be able to see how well different programs perform in teaching English and will be able to move their children from programs that fail to programs that succeed. Ultimately, that is what reform of the bilingual education system is about—unblocking the door to opportunity so our nation's children can succeed.

REFERENCES

Rossell, Christine H. 1990. The effectiveness of educational alternatives for limited English proficient children in the Berkeley Unified School District. In Gary Imhoff (ed.), *Learning in two languages: From conflict to consensus in the reorganization of schools.* New Brunswick, NJ: Transaction Books.
Schorr, Jonathan. 1998. School district in race lawsuit: Anti-bilingual group takes on Oakland. *Oakland Tribune* (April 29).
SIAC. 1993–1994. *Summary of Bilingual Education State Educational Agency Program Survey of States' Limited English Proficient Persons and Available Educational Services 1993–1994.* Report to fulfill contract to the U.S. Department of Education Office of Bilingual Education and Minority Language Affairs. Special Issues Analysis Center.

Literacy development in high school English language learners

Anna Uhl Chamot
The George Washington University

High school English language learning (ELL) students with little schooling in their native countries face severe obstacles to school achievement in the United States. The most critical of these obstacles is limited literacy in both their native language and English. In contrast, students who arrive well-prepared academically and highly literate in a language other than English possess conceptual knowledge and skills such as reading and writing that can be transferred from their native language. Adolescent students lacking an appropriate educational background must develop literacy as quickly as possible so that they can use reading and writing as learning tools to acquire the concepts and skills they have missed by not having had access to formal schooling in their native countries (Chamot 1998). Information about effective instructional practices for developing literacy with high school English language learners is lacking, yet a significant number of non-English-speaking students with limited or no native language literacy are currently enrolled in secondary schools (Chamot, Keatley, and Schiavone 1997). These students come from countries that include, but are not limited to, Spanish-speaking areas and some parts of Africa. The reasons for students' lack of prior schooling are in most cases due to war, civil unrest, cultural customs, or a combination of these factors.

The most effective and efficient approach to developing literacy in English for secondary students lacking native language reading and writing skills is an unresolved question. Much more is known about young children's second language literacy development. While research points to the desirability of developing literacy first in young children's native language so that they can transfer reading and writing skills to English (August 1998; Collier 1992; 1995; Crawford 1997; Krashen 1993; Ramírez 1992; Thomas and Collier 1999), little is known about the most effective instructional approach for adolescent students. Logic indicates that older English language learners, like their younger counterparts, would find it much easier to learn to read and write first in the language they can already speak, and that skills developed in the first language could be transferred to literacy acquisition in the second language. However, there has not yet been any research to confirm this hypothesis. It could be that secondary school English language learners' developmental and cognitive maturity facilitates literacy acquisition directly in English. Adolescent attitudes and motivation are also developmentally different from those of young children. Since teenagers are attempting to establish both independence and a sense of their own individuality, they might be less likely to accept what they may perceive as a slower path to English literacy by developing initial literacy in their native language.

This paper reports on an ongoing study that is examining the effects of language-of-literacy instruction on the development of English literacy in low-literacy Spanish-speaking adolescent students.[1] The results of this study will have applications to all populations of older students with limited native language literacy.

Background and Research Questions. High levels of literacy are essential for meeting the nation's needs for productive citizens and workers in the new century, yet many immigrant youth are unable to complete high school because they lack the academic language and literacy skills needed for successful school achievement. Of these, the largest group comes from Spanish-speaking countries, comprising about 75% of limited English proficient students in the United States (U.S. Department of Education 1992). School-aged students with Spanish language backgrounds comprise about 12% of all students in U.S. schools (NCES 1995). The school dropout rate for students who did not speak English well was over 35% for Spanish-speaking students aged sixteen through twenty-four in 1991 (NCES 1993). For students who did not speak English at all, the dropout rate in 1992 was over 83% (NCES 1994). Only one in ten recent immigrant youth were enrolled in college in 1989, and of these, Spanish speakers were half as likely to enroll in college as other immigrants (NCES 1994).

Since published information about numbers of low-literacy immigrant students enrolled in secondary schools was not available, a telephone survey was conducted of the twenty-nine school districts in the United States with the largest numbers of English language learners (Chamot, Keatley, and Schiavone 1997). Each school district was asked the number of secondary school students enrolled in ESL and/or bilingual education programs. Then, the school district was asked what percentage of this number had been identified as having limited literacy in their native language. The responses were tallied, with the result that just over 10%, or 17,579 students out of a total of 172,128 secondary school ESL students, were identified as low literacy. This survey and the other statistics cited paint a bleak picture of the current prospects for Spanish-language background students to complete high school and continue into college. The picture is equally bleak for low-literacy students with other language backgrounds.

Educators acknowledge the need for identifying effective instructional practices for low-literacy adolescent English language learning (ELL) students. The research of Cummins (1981, 1984, 1993, 1996) and Collier (1992, 1995) has documented the length of time needed for ELL students to reach grade-level norms in school achievement. The average number of years ranges from four to seven for students with schooling in their native language, to up to ten years for students without native language schooling. Since older students do not have an extended time period to develop academic English skills, it is important to find ways to accelerate their literacy development and, through literacy, their access to the academic curriculum.

One instructional approach is to develop literacy first in the students' native language so that they can transfer reading and writing skills to English. Extensive research supports the transfer of literacy from a first language (L1) to a second language (L2), and it may be that explicit instruction in learning strategies for reading and writing can increase students' ability to transfer comprehension and composition skills from L1 to L2.

Literacy and transfer of skills from L1 to L2 have been studied thoroughly with elementary school students. The most extensive study of K–6 students to date found that students provided with extensive native language instruction would eventually reach higher levels of achievement than students who are exited quickly into all-English instruction, and that the native language instruction did not hinder the acquisition of English literacy (Ramirez 1992). However, the gains favoring a bilingual approach only appear over the long term, as in the first few years of English acquisition, students receiving all-English instruction appear to be making faster progress (Collier 1992; Thomas and Collier 1999).

We do not know if the research findings at the elementary school level will hold equally true for secondary school students. In addition to the factors mentioned above involving differences in level of cognitive development and possible motivation issues for older students, there are practical concerns as well. Most school districts do not have the resources or licensed teachers needed to provide native language instruction at the high-school level in subjects such as mathematics, science, and social studies. Therefore, at this secondary level, it would be an easier task to provide native language support rather than a complete bilingual curriculum. This support could consist of intensive literacy development in students' native language coupled with explicit instruction on ways to transfer skills to English. On the other hand, given the short number of years that secondary students are in school before they can legally drop out, it may be more beneficial to provide them with intensive instruction in literacy exclusively in English in the hope that initial faster progress (if this holds true as for elementary students) will foster feelings of success that will motivate students to stay in school. These as yet unanswered questions are being investigated by Project Accelerated Literacy (PAL).[2]

In addition to the need for identifying the most effective instructional approach for low-literacy adolescent ELL students in general, effective instruction for ESL students with special needs also has to be considered (Brice and Roseberry-McKibbin 1999). Identifying special needs of native language low-literacy and non-English speaking students is especially challenging, as it is difficult to separate difficulties due to limited literacy and those caused by other factors. Culturally and linguistically diverse students continue to be both over- and under-represented in special education classes (Baca and de Valenzuela 1998). This is of concern, because students receiving inappropriate placement are more likely than others to fail.

Low-literacy ESL students may be over-identified for special education through the use of literacy skills as the main criteria for assessing cognitive development. Similarly, under-identification of ELL students who really need special education services is equally serious. Educators have been known to misinterpret the work of Cummins (1981, 1984, 1996) and Collier (1987, 1989), citing their research as a reason for not referring ELL students to special education assessment under the mistaken idea that ELL students may somehow outgrow a real disability as they develop academic proficiency in English. For such ELL students, early intervention is needed and special education services would be beneficial.

These special education issues are an important component of Project Accelerated Literacy (PAL)[3] in its investigation of the impact of all-English literacy instruction (referred to as the monolingual condition) compared to English literacy instruction with native language support (referred to as the bilingual condition). No comprehensive research studies on the acquisition of English literacy have previously been conducted with adolescents with low literacy in their native language. The PAL study is documenting how Spanish-speaking adolescents with low or no literacy in their native language acquire literacy in English in each of the two conditions and the relationship of each condition to referrals for special education. The research questions for the PAL study are as follows:

1. Do low-literacy, adolescent, limited-English-proficient, Spanish-speaking students make greater gains in English literacy in one school year in a bilingual condition (instructional support in Spanish) or in a monolingual condition (instruction in English alone)?
2. Are there differences in self-efficacy between bilingual and monolingual groups?
3. Is instruction in each language perceived as effective by (a) teachers and (b) students?
4. After one year of instruction, are there differences between students in the monolingual and bilingual instruction conditions in the development of cognitive abilities/skills associated with the development of literacy, such as phonemic awareness, speed of semantic processing, complexity of elaboration while reading, and use of learning strategies?
5. In examining the relationship between the two instructional conditions (bilingual and monolingual) and students with special needs,

a. What is the rate of referral of students for special education assessment in the monolingual and the native language support classes?
b. How confident are teachers in each approach in identifying students with special needs?
c. Do participating teachers refer students they suspect have special education needs for special education assessment during the year of instruction? Why or why not?
d. Are participating teachers receiving support from special education services (such as special education, speech and language, occupational therapy, physical therapy, or counseling)?
e. Do students' levels of phonemic awareness in Spanish have a relationship to teachers' perceptions of special education needs?

Research Design Overview.[4] The PAL study is primarily a pretest–post-test design with two experimental conditions. The independent variable is language(s) of literacy instruction, which has two levels: English monolingual instruction and English instruction with native language support. The impact of language of instruction on the dependent variables will be measured separately for each variable. The dependent variables are: (a) level of skill in reading and writing in English (RQ #1), (b) feelings of self-efficacy related to literacy in English (RQ #3), and (c) proportion of students referred for special education (RQ #5).

The study is being conducted over a three-year period (1997–2000). In the first year, participating teachers completed two graduate level courses at the George Washington University (GWU) as preparation for implementing the literacy curricula in the second year. This same process is being repeated in the second year with a new cohort of teachers, who will then implement the curricula in the third year. During the implementation years, teachers enroll in a six-credit-hour graduate practicum course at GWU in which their classes are observed and they meet for a biweekly seminar. The two cohorts of students (years 2 and 3) will be combined for data analysis purposes to increase the size of study participants. This is necessary because of the high rate of attrition of low-literacy high school ELL students.

Context and Participants. The PAL study is being conducted in a linguistically and ethnically diverse setting. Participants include high school ESL teachers and their beginning-level students with low native language literacy.

Context. Three school districts in the Washington, D.C., metropolitan area, representing both urban and suburban settings, are participating in the study. The school districts have been receiving large numbers of immigrant students for a number of years and are therefore experienced in meeting the needs of ELL students. Across the three school districts, approximately 130 different languages are represented in the ELL population. Of these, the predominant (about 75%) language background is Spanish. In recent years, each school district has become aware of the needs of older immigrant students with limited prior education and have established "literacy" or "special needs" classes where numbers of students are sufficient to support a separate class. These classes are likely to be composed of predominantly Spanish-speaking students, though they may also include speakers of languages such as Somali or Amharic. Within each class, students are at different literacy levels in their native languages, though all are beginners in acquiring English proficiency. Students in literacy classes may arrive or leave at any time during the school year, and the number of students in a class at any given time may range from four to fifteen. These factors, among others, make both teaching and research extraordinarily challenging.

Teacher Participants. Teachers in the PAL study are certified in teaching English as a second language (TESL) in their respective school districts and have been recommended for project participation by their school district and/or by GWU faculty. Teachers in the native language support condition are fully bilingual in Spanish and English. All PAL teachers are completing twelve graduate credit hours during their participation in PAL. This course work is designed to acquaint teachers with issues and approaches in literacy instruction for adolescent ELL students, to reach consensus on instructional approaches, and to develop monolingual and bilingual literacy curricula. Fourteen teachers are participating in the study over the two years of implementation of instruction.

Student Participants. Students in the PAL study are native-Spanish speakers, aged fourteen to twenty, and enrolled in public high schools in participating school districts in the Washington, D.C., area. All student participants have been identified by their school districts as low literacy, meaning that they have experienced significant gaps in their prior education, making enrollment in the regular beginning ESL class impossible. Native countries represented by participating students are El Salvador, Bolivia, Nicaragua, Honduras, Guatemala, Mexico, and the Dominican Republic. Parental permission was obtained for all study participants younger than eighteen, and informed consent to participate in the study was given by students eighteen and older.

Twenty-nine students participated in the first year's cohort, and forty-five were in the second year's cohort. The attrition rate was about 25 percent and was due to factors such as returning to the native country, moving to a different location, or dropping out of school.

Instruments. Measurement instruments are standardized measures, instruments developed by adapting instruments used in previous studies, and instruments developed for this study. They include:

1. *The Woodcock Language Proficiency Battery—Revised: Spanish and English Forms;*
2. *The Language Assessment Scales—Reading and Writing, Spanish and English;*
3. a researcher-constructed reading test in English with oral recall and comprehension questions in Spanish;
4. a think-aloud protocol conducted in Spanish to reveal learning strategies used when reading in English;
5. a test of phonemic awareness in English and Spanish that includes segmenting, blending, and deleting initial phonemes and rimes in single syllable words;
6. an oral questionnaire-interview (administered in Spanish) designed to elicit personal history and background information;
7. the Pintrich Motivation Strategies Questionnaire (MSQ), translated and adapted;
8. a protocol for interviews with teachers to assess their perceptions of the effectiveness of instruction in the language conditions in which they have participated;
9. a protocol for interviews with teachers to assess their perceptions of the special education needs of the students in their classes; and
10. a questionnaire/interview (bilingual) to assess students' perceptions of the effectiveness of instruction in literacy in the particular language condition in which they participate.

Procedures. The components of the PAL study include development and implementation of a monolingual and a bilingual curriculum; professional development of teachers; pre- and post-testing of students' literacy skills to assess the impact of each curriculum; and an investigation of how each curriculum affects special education students.

Professional Development of Teachers and Instructional Model. In order to maintain as much consistency as possible in instruction across classrooms, a common curriculum is being implemented. This curriculum has two versions: One provides instruction exclusively in English (the monolingual curriculum), and the other provides the same curriculum with native-language support (the bilingual curriculum). It was considered important to involve teachers in the curriculum development process for two major reasons. First, the expertise of ESL teachers experienced in working with literacy students provided invaluable practical insights for meeting student needs. Second, we believed that teachers would be more likely to implement a curriculum that they had had a hand in developing. The curriculum development process took place during the first two graduate-level courses ("Foundations of Reading Development" and

"Diagnostic Teaching of Reading in the Secondary School") completed by participating teachers.

During the first course, it became apparent that teachers from participating school districts had differing philosophical and methodological views. Some of the teachers were strong proponents of a whole-language approach to literacy development; others argued in favor of a phonics-based approach. This issue was resolved through discussion and study of relevant research, and a decision was reached to develop a balanced reading approach that would include reading authentic texts and practicing word attack skills in context. In addition, vocabulary development and explicit instruction in learning strategies for reading and writing are provided in each lesson.

The instructional model underlying the curriculum is based on a cognitive approach in which learners are viewed as active and strategic processors of information and skills. The balanced reading approach acknowledges that different individuals have unique needs and learn in different ways and at different rates. A rich variety of learning experiences is an essential component of learner-centered literacy development. The Cognitive Academic Language Learning Approach (CALLA) is used as the instructional model for developing and implementing the PAL curriculum. This model integrates appropriate content topics, development of academic language, and instruction in learning strategies (Chamot 1996; Chamot and O'Malley 1994; Chamot et al. 1999). CALLA lesson organization is in five recursive phases. In the first, *preparation,* the focus is on identifying and building students' prior knowledge of the lesson's content. In the second phase, *presentation,* teachers use a variety of techniques to make new information and skills accessible and comprehensible to students, such as demonstrations, modeling, and visual support. This is followed by or integrated with the third phase, *practice,* in which students use the new information and skills (including learning strategies) in various activities. The fourth phase of the CALLA instructional design sequence is *evaluation,* in which students assess their own level of understanding and proficiency with the content and skills they have been practicing. Finally, in the fifth phase, *expansion,* students engage in activities that apply what they have learned to their own lives, including other classes at school, families and community, and their cultural and linguistic background. Because these five phases are recursive, lesson planning is flexible and can be adjusted to focus on specific lesson objectives. The CALLA model has proven to be an effective organizational tool for developing the PAL literacy curriculum.

Teachers decided on the scope and sequence of content topics, which include typical beginning ESL topics (e.g., school, weather, seasons, clothing, daily activities, family, home) and some content-based topics (e.g., health, community, the senses and observation in science, geography). Teachers worked in cross-school district groups to develop thematic units for each topic. These units went through an extensive revision process as teachers and researchers worked together to create a balanced literacy curriculum for an entire school year. The first cohort of teachers developed thematic units for approximately three quarters of the school year, and the second cohort developed units for the last quarter. Table 1 describes the types of activities included in each thematic unit.

In addition to planning the lessons for each unit, teachers and researchers also conducted a comprehensive search for appropriate instructional materials. Most important was the selection of reading materials for both class reading and classroom libraries for independent reading. The final selection included trade books in both English and Spanish and school-district developed storybooks in English and in English and Spanish. Genres included in the books selected are realistic fiction, folktales and legends, informational texts, and children's literature appropriate for older learners. Students read these materials in class and engage in a number of reading activities, such as making story maps, identifying

Table 1. PAL curriculum scope and sequence

Lessons address objectives in the following categories:

Content	school, feelings, weather, foods, geography, science
Patterns	*be,* pronouns, plurals, *a/an,* contractions, questions, negations
Word Attack	names and sounds of letters, word families, syllabification, blending sounds, silent *"e"*
Writing	writing letters of the alphabet, handwriting, punctuation, spelling, clear expression, journals, personal experiences, stories, poems
Reading Comprehension	understanding factual information, identifying elements of a story, finding main idea, identifying fiction and non-fiction, reading for pleasure
Vocabulary	receptive vocabulary development, meaning and spelling of core vocabulary in each content area
Learning strategies	decoding, identifying patterns, using imagery, cooperating with peers, using cognates, predicting, making inferences, planning, revising

main ideas, retelling, and writing personal reactions. In addition, the classroom libraries are used for regular periods of sustained silent reading (SSR).

Materials used for teaching vocabulary, word attack skills, language patterns, learning strategies, and writing have been developed by the teachers and researchers. Table 2 illustrates the time allotments in each daily ninety-minute period in the bilingual and monolingual classrooms.

In the bilingual condition, the portion of the lesson in Spanish is designed to teach concepts and skills needed for the English part of the lesson. In addition, during the Spanish part of the lesson, students have opportunities to enjoy literature from their own cultural background, to learn about different genres and basic

Table 2. Monolingual and bilingual lesson time allocations

1. Each of four weekly ninety-minute lessons is organized as follows

English Monolingual		**Spanish Support (Bilingual)**	
Warm-up	5 minutes	Spanish Patterns: Word Attack	15 minutes
Content/Patterns	30 minutes	Spanish Reading and Writing	15 minutes
Word Attack	15 minutes	English Warm-up	5 minutes
Additional Practice Activities	20 minutes	English Content and Patterns	30 minutes
Reading and Writing	20 minutes	English Word Attack	10 minutes
		English Reading and Writing	15 minutes

2. On the fifth day of each week, the 90-minute lesson is structured by the teacher and includes activities such as:
Writing Projects
Sustained Silent Reading
Review Activities
Assessment Activities

literary analysis, and to compose their own stories and poems. Learning strategies for reading and writing are taught in the Spanish portion of the lesson and reintroduced during the English part for additional practice and to encourage transfer. Grammatical contrasts and similarities between the two languages are also addressed during the Spanish portion of the lesson. After about thirty minutes of instruction in Spanish, the bilingual teacher switches to English and teaches the same activities as in the monolingual English classes, though somewhat less time is allocated to some activities (see table 2).

In the monolingual English condition, slightly more time is allocated to word attack (five minutes) and reading in English (five minutes) than in the bilingual condition. In addition, up to twenty minutes of additional practice activities are available in the English condition. The extra thirty minutes devoted to these types of activities in the English monolingual condition provide for additional explanation, modeling, demonstration, and practice that are necessary when native-language support is not provided.

Both the monolingual and the bilingual curricula were implemented by participating teachers. Classroom observations by researchers were conducted on a regular basis, and teachers met with researchers in a biweekly seminar. This seminar served as a vehicle for identifying any difficulties encountered with the curriculum, sharing of information about student progress, and suggesting ideas to be incorporated in future weeks of the curriculum. An issue that concerned both teachers and researchers was the need for each teacher to teach the curriculum as written, rather than to make spur-of-the-moment individual adaptations. In order to make valid comparisons across classrooms, it was felt necessary to keep the instruction as parallel as possible, so teachers were asked to follow the curriculum lesson plans exactly as they and the researchers had developed them. In order to provide teachers with some flexibility and opportunities for creativity and "teachable moments," lessons were planned for only four days in each week. Teachers used the fifth day in any way they liked—for review, sustained silent reading, writing projects, catching up, or additional practice activities. In addition, any requests by teachers for modifications, substitutions, or additions were incorporated into future lessons. We told teachers, "Please don't change this week's lessons. But tell us the changes you think are necessary, and we will incorporate them into next week's lessons."

Data Collection. The impact of language-of-instruction on reading and writing in English will be measured by (1) the *Woodcock Language Proficiency Battery—Revised, English and Spanish Forms,* (2) the *Language Assessment Scales (Reading and Writing), English and Spanish,* (3) an experimenter-constructed test on reading in English that measures recall and comprehension (literal, inferential, and critical) (post-test), (4) a think-aloud interview with students (in Spanish as they read in English) that is designed to reveal their learning strategies (post-test),

(5) a test of phonemic awareness in Spanish and English that includes ability to segment, blend, and delete onsets and rimes in single syllable words, and (6) writing samples in English and Spanish.

Feelings of self-efficacy are measured using (1) a translated, modified version of the Pintrich Motivation and Strategies Questionnaire (MSQ) and (2) specific direct questions about feelings of self-efficacy, motivation to study English, and students' perceptions of their parents' or guardians' attitudes about the importance of studying English, accompanied by Lickert-like scales.

Background information was collected at the beginning and end of each year on each student through individual interviews. These include information such as country of origin, age, educational history, interests, hobbies, work, family, family literacy, friends, feelings about moving to the United States, feelings about school in the United States, attitudes towards native language support in their ESL class, perception of parents' attitudes toward native language support, and plans for the future. Students are also asked about what other classes they take, whether any assistance is provided to help them understand the content of these classes, and how much they believe they have learned in these classes. This extensive structured interview is providing qualitative information to supplement the quantitative data collected through standardized measures.

Additional quantifiable qualitative information was collected at the end of each school year through student and teacher evaluations of the language-of-instruction condition in which they participated. This information was collected through structured individual interviews with all participating students and teachers.

A sample of students from the first cohort (1998–1999) was studied during the next school year (1999–2000) to determine the effects over time of the literacy instruction provided with and without native language support. These follow-up students were interviewed using some of the same instruments as those for the 1998–1999 cohort.

Structured interviews were conducted with all participating teachers to record their perceptions of the effectiveness of the language-of-instruction conditions. Teacher evaluations of effectiveness will be compared across language-of-instruction conditions (RQ #3a). A questionnaire or interview was completed by participating students to record their perceptions of the effectiveness of the language-of-instruction condition in which they participated. The student responses to the questionnaire also will be compared across language-of-instruction conditions (RQ #3b).

The impact of language-of-instruction on referrals to special education will be evaluated through (1) the proportion of students in the study actually referred by teachers in the study for special education evaluation, (2) the proportion of students in the study who were suspected by participating teachers of perhaps having special education needs (whether they were referred or not), (3) the proportion of students in the study who were referred to special education and received evaluations as needing special education services. Case studies of students suspected of needing special education services will be conducted using the data collected on reading, writing, and phonemic awareness in English and Spanish.

The proportion of students referred either during or directly after one year of instruction will be calculated and compared across the two language-of-instruction conditions (RQ #5).

Summary of Procedures. Research questions 1 and 5 (the effects of language-of-literacy instruction on literacy attainment in English and on the proportion of students referred to special education), constitute the basis of the research. Research questions 2 (self-efficacy) and 4 (development of cognitive skills related to literacy) focus on testing possible explanations for differences in student performance or referral rates in the two language-of-instruction conditions. An examination of the development of these factors may reveal why one language condition may be more effective than another in teaching English literacy to ELL students. Research question 3 (teacher and student perceptions) is included as a check on the more formal assessment measures and as a source of qualitative information about literacy education in the two language-of-instruction conditions.

Pretest data for the first cohort of students were collected in September 1998, and post-test data for this group were collected in May 1999. The process was repeated in the 1999–2000 school year, and data from the two cohorts were collapsed and are being analyzed.

Significance of the PAL Study. This study will provide important information about instruction for low native-language literacy, beginning-level ESL students. The study is wide-ranging in the types of measures used to assess student learning and motivation, yet it is focused on only one difference in the literacy curriculum implemented: the presence or absence of native language support. The study is controlling variability of instruction across classrooms by using a set of detailed lesson plans that are followed by participating teachers. We do not expect the results of this study to be simple. Rather, a complex interaction between literacy development and instructional approach will likely be evident. A better understanding of the relationship between language of instruction and special needs students will be another outcome of this study. The findings of the PAL study will provide the groundwork for future research with low native language literacy secondary school populations. This study will also have implications for the professional development of ESL and bilingual secondary teachers and for curriculum development at this level.

REFERENCES

August, Diane. 1998. Attributes of effective schools and classrooms for English language learners. In María del Rosario Basterra (ed.), *Excellence and equity for language minority students: Critical issues and promising practices.* Chevy Chase, MD: Mid-Atlantic Equity Consortium. 27–42.

Baca, Leonard, and J. S. de Valenzuela. 1998. Development of the bilingual special education interface. In Leonard M. Baca and Hermes T. Cervantes (eds.), *The bilingual special education interface,* 3rd edition. Upper Saddle River, NJ: Prentice Hall. 98–118.

Brice, Alejandro, and Celeste Roseberry-McKibbin. 1999. Turning frustration into success for English language learners. *Educational Leadership* 56(7): 53–55.

Chamot, Anna Uhl. 1998. Effective instruction for high school English language learners. In Russell M. Gersten and Robert T. Jiménez (eds.), *Promoting learning for culturally and linguistically diverse students: Classroom applications from contemporary research.* Belmont, CA: Wadsworth. 187–209.

Chamot, Anna Uhl. 1996. The Cognitive Academic Language Learning Approach (CALLA):Theoretical framework and instructional applications. In James E. Alatis (ed.), *Georgetown University Round Table on Languages and Linguistics 1996.* Washington, DC: Georgetown University Press. 108–115.

Chamot, Anna Uhl, Catharine Keatley, and Janet Page Schiavone. 1997. Literacy development in adolescent English language learners. Proposal submitted to Field-Initiated Studies Educational Research Grant Program, National Institute on the Education of At-Risk Students, U.S. Department of Education Office of Educational Research and Improvement, Washington, DC.

Chamot, Anna Uhl, and J. Michael O'Malley. 1994. *The CALLA handbook: Implementing the cognitive academic language learning approach.* White Plains, NY: Addison Wesley Longman.

Chamot, Anna Uhl, Sarah Barnhardt, Pamela Beard El-Dinary, and Jill Robbins. 1999. *The learning strategies handbook.* White Plains, NY: Addison Wesley Longman.

Collier, Virginia P. 1987. Age and rate of acquisition of second language for academic purposes. *TESOL Quarterly* 21:617–641.

Collier, Virginia P. 1989. How long? A synthesis of research on academic achievement in a second language. *TESOL Quarterly* 23:509–531.

Collier, Virginia P. 1992. A synthesis of studies examining long-term language minority student data on academic achievement. *Bilingual Research Journal* 16 (1-2):187–212.

Collier, Virginia P. 1995. Acquiring a second language for school. *Directions in language and education* 1:4. Washington, DC: National Clearinghouse for Bilingual Education.

Crawford, James. 1997. *Best evidence: Research foundations of the Bilingual Education Act.* NCBE Report. Washington, DC: National Clearinghouse for Bilingual Education,

Cummins, Jim. 1981. Age on arrival and immigrant second language learning in Canada: A reassessment. *Applied Linguistics* 2:132–149.

Cummins, Jim. 1984. *Bilingualism and special education: Issues in assessment and pedagogy.* Clevedon, England: Multilingual Matters.

Cummins, Jim. 1993. Bilingualism and second language learning. *Annual Review of Applied Linguistics* 13:51–70.

Cummins, Jim. 1996. *Negotiating identities: Education for empowerment in a diverse society.* Ontario: California Association for Bilingual Education.

Krashen, Stephen. 1993. *The power of reading.* Englewood, CO: Libraries Unlimited.

National Center for Educational Statistics (NCES). 1993. *Digest of education statistics.* Washington, DC: U.S. Department of Education.

National Center for Educational Statistics (NCES). 1994. *The condition of education: 1994.* Washington, DC: U.S. Department of Education.

National Center for Educational Statistics (NCES). 1995. *The educational progress of Hispanic students*. Washington, DC: U.S. Department of Education.

Ramírez, J. David. 1992. Executive summary. *Bilingual Research Journal* 16: 1–62.

Thomas, Wayne P., and Virginia P. Collier. 1999. Accelerated schooling for English language learners. *Educational Leadership* 56(7): 46–49.

U.S. Department of Education. 1992. *The condition of bilingual education in the nation*. Washington, D.C.: U.S. Department of Education.

NOTES

1. This study was funded by the Office of Educational Research and Improvement, U.S. Department of Education, under Grant # R306F970037. The content of this document does not necessarily reflect the views of the Department of Education or of any other agency of the U.S. government.
2. The research team at the George Washington University that participated in this study includes Anna Uhl Chamot, principal investigator; Amy Mazur, co-principal investigator; Catharine W. Keatley, senior researcher; Kristina Anstrom, project director; and research associates and assistants Mary Adonis, Teresa Jardines, Ximena Márquez, and Jennifer Simons. I would like to express my appreciation to these colleagues and also to the fourteen teachers who worked on the project.
3. The special education component of the PAL study was directed by Amy Mazur.
4. Catharine W. Keatley had primary responsibility for the research design of the PAL study.

Language in Israel: Policy, practice, and ideology

Bernard Spolsky
Bar-Ilan University

Introduction. A century after the beginning of a process of revitalization and revernacularization of Hebrew, we can attempt to trace the nature of policy and ideology and their effects on language practice in Israel. Supported by a strong ideology, Hebrew was established as the main language of the Jewish community in Palestine. As the principal language of the new state of Israel, Hebrew became dominant among the indigenous Arabic of the minority and the forty or so Jewish and coterritorial languages brought in by the huge numbers of immigrants. In its beginning, it overcame challenges of two world languages (German and French), but more recently is uneasily beginning to share major functions with English. At the same time, recently resistance efforts from Russian (with 800,000 recent immigrants) and Amharic, as well as the nominally official Arabic, are bolstering a growing ideological acceptance of multilingualism. Looking at this single but complex case within this model suggests ways of analyzing other problems of language in our time.

Distinguishing language practice, policy, and ideology. It is a great honor and pleasure to be able to participate again in a Georgetown Round Table, and an even greater privilege to share in the fiftieth anniversary of this major institution. I still remember warmly my first Round Table, just over thirty years ago (Spolsky 1968), when I had my first opportunity to address the distinguished audience gathered for this key event and to hear the exciting presentations and discussions that took place (Alatis 1968). It is a mark of the gap between the state of knowledge in our field and the state of practice in our society in matters affecting language education that many of the papers I heard then could well be repeated today, their messages about bilingualism and non-standard varieties and language education still ignored by much of the public. But rather than attempting to trace this issue through the recent tangled history of the bilingual education enterprise in the United States, I will talk today about the development of language policy over the past century in Palestine and Israel, with the goal of presenting a model of analysis that might be useful in other cases.

Let me start with a definition of the terms in my title. Under the term "languages" I include identifiable dialects and varieties. The very names of these varieties are controversial and ambiguous—many of the nearly extinct Jewish languages brought from the Diaspora now seem to have as many names as they have speakers. And a name like "Hebrew" or "Arabic" covers a wide range of varieties—historical, functional, social—that cries out for finer definition. By Israel, I refer to the current state, its borders awaiting definition, and to the historically preceding British Mandate and Ottoman region of Palestine.

It is also beneficial, I believe, to differentiate the terms "language practice," "language ideology," and "language policy." Language practice I define as the ethnography of communication, following Hymes (1974), or, to phrase it differently, the agreed linguistic repertoire of a defined speech community. Language ideology is a term I borrow from Silverstein (1979) through Dorian (1998) to mean the beliefs of members of a speech community about what their language practice should be, and language policy I define narrowly as any effort by someone who has or claims authority to modify the language practice or language ideology of other people. From this point of view, it is important to notice that linguistic hegemonies, such as the English hegemony studied by Phillipson (1992), fit under my definition of language practice or ideology. Planned linguistic imperialism and formally developed status or corpus or acquisition or diffusion activities (Cooper 1989), as so well described for French in Ager (1999), are what constitute language policy.

Essentially, then, I want to track the changes in language practice and ideology in one small but complex country over the past century or so and ask to what extent any changes can be accounted for by explicit policies or to what extent they were the results of demographic and political and economic and social changes.

The languages involved—a century ago and today. One oversimplified way to look at the topic might be to depict the language practice a hundred years ago and compare it to the present situation (Spolsky and Cooper 1991). In describing the language situation in late Ottoman Palestine, one would start with the Arabic spoken by the majority population, broken up into local dialects clustering into three broad groups, Bedouin, village, and urban. In Jerusalem, a city that already had a majority Jewish population, the indigenous Sephardi Jews also spoke Arabic alongside their intracommunity Ladino, and the rapidly swelling Ashkenazi population was starting to learn Arabic for intercommunity purposes (Kosover 1966) while maintaining Yiddish and a number of East European coterritorial vernaculars within their remarkably splintered community. The official language of government was Turkish, but knowledge of it tended to be limited to clerks and soldiers. Literacy in Classical Arabic was not widespread. A number of European languages had their special niches—English and German in the Protestant Mission, Russian as language of pilgrims, French as an elite language of high culture. In addition, French diffusion policies had instituted the language in schools in new Jewish agricultural settlements, where it was just starting to be replaced by Hebrew. Similar policies were inaugurating German in modern schools in Jewish towns. A hundred years ago, the ideologically supported movement for the revitalization and revernacularization of Hebrew was just getting under way in the new Jewish agricultural settlements, with support from afar by a few ideologues like Eliezer Ben Yehuda in Jerusalem (Fellman 1973).

A century later, the linguistic landscape is quite different (Ben-Rafael 1994; Spolsky and Shohamy 1999). Arabic continues—entrenched—as the main language (spoken and written) of Palestinians in the West Bank and Gaza (the region gradually coming under the control of the Palestinian Authority). For the Israeli Palestinian Arabic speakers who live within the green line, it is the language of home, education (as far as the end of high school), and community, but the Arabic spoken by Israeli Arabs is markedly influenced by Hebrew, a language in which most of them are bilingual and which is the language of higher education and work for many (Amara 1999). For Israel as a whole, Hebrew has become the dominant and dominating language for almost all private and public activities—the language of home, radio and television, government, education (up to the highest level), business, the army, and the health services. Only in marginalized niches (among some Hassidic sects, in Arab villages, among recent immigrants, foreign workers, and tourists, and in the two Circassian villages) does one find speech communities that function virtually without Hebrew. All but the most recent immigrant languages (those brought from the former Soviet Union and Ethiopia) now tend to be restricted to older speakers and to use in the home or ethnic enclaves. Given the large number of recent immigrants, there are still strong clusters of Russian and Amharic speakers, but there are clear indications that members of the younger generation are already moving to Hebrew. German in public use is minimal; French holds on, thanks mainly to the major metropolitan diffusion efforts as a peripheral cultural and school language, but even the schools founded by the Alliance Israélite Universelle give it second place to English. As in so much of the world, English has moved to the status of the major second language, to be used for education and culture and commerce and wider communication, and perceived as a necessary skill once Hebrew has been mastered.

How much was this complete change in a hundred years the result of direct language policy and how much was it the working of a myriad of factors concerned with the far-reaching demographic and social and political changes that have taken place over the past century?

The revitalization of Hebrew. The most obvious phenomenon that deserves careful study is the revitalization (Spolsky 1991, 1996a) and revernacularization (Fishman 1991) of Hebrew and the development of its current hegemony. Many scholars are tempted to treat this as the successful culmination of a long established policy. When one looks closer, however, one finds nothing to compare with say the millennium of French language policy activities documented in Ager (1996, 1999). True, a century or so ago Hebrew was selected as the symbolic national language (Mandel 1993) of a territorial nationalist movement (Zionism) at the same time that Yiddish was being selected as the symbolic national language of a competing largely nonterritorial nationalist movement (Fishman 1982, 1991). This ideological choice, although never proclaimed at a founding congress (Glinert 1993), led to a number of critical local policy decisions. One was the decision in a number of Jewish agricultural settlements in Ottoman Palestine at the end of the nineteenth century to replace French and Yiddish with Hebrew as language of instruction in the elementary school grades. A decade later, a second was the decision of one section of the labor movement in Palestine to use Hebrew rather than Yiddish for its publications. At the same time, the founding members of the new collective settlements were deciding to make Hebrew the language for all public use in the settlement, including the collective and public children's house. Shortly after, when the first new city of Tel Aviv was founded, its charter proclaimed that the city was to be hygienic and Hebrew-speaking (Harshav 1993). Individual schools, including high schools, founded by the originally German-diffusionist *Hilfsverein der Deutschen Juden* also switched in these early years of the century to Hebrew as language of instruction (Wahl 1996).

Under Ottoman rule, there was no central government interest in establishing language policy, but rather a tolerance of plurilingualism echoing the *millet* system (Karpat 1982), so that the small and growing secular Jewish community was left alone gradually to introduce Hebrew use into its institutions. The strength of the new ideology was asserted in the so-called language war of 1913, when a committee of the *Hilfsverein* planning a tertiary technical institute that would teach scientific subjects in German (using Hebrew for Jewish and general topics) was persuaded to change its mind. It was during the first World War that some very successful language policy activity took place, when the British were persuaded to ban German in the Palestine that they had conquered (Cohen 1918) and to set Hebrew as one of the three official languages, after English and Arabic, for the new mandate granted by the League of Nations after the war.

In practice, once the British Mandate over Palestine was in place, the government left the Jewish community of Palestine to conduct its own education. Its schools and educational institutions were free to institute local policies of Hebrew language use. Between 1923 and 1936, there was quite strong activity within the Jewish Yishuv to encourage the use of Hebrew. The active campaign for the diffusion of the language remained a central feature of Zionist and Israeli ideology. A youth legion formed in 1923 for the Protection of the Language continued its activities until 1936. During this critical period, strong campaigns were conducted against the two principal enemies, as Ussishkin identified them in this important speech at the 1923 third national conference of the legion, English, and Yiddish. He attacked those who used English in order to assert their elite status and closeness to the British rulers. His bitterest complaints, however, were against Yiddish, and one of the major accomplishments of the legion was to block the establishment of a chair of Yiddish at the Hebrew University.

By 1948, then, the Hebrew monolingual ideology was so firm that 80% of the Jewish population of Palestine claimed to know Hebrew, and over half claimed to use it as their only language (Bachi 1956). The change from plurilingualism to ideological monolingualism had taken about fifty years.

With the establishment of the state of Israel, Hebrew gained a solid official status and full institutional backing, but it was quickly confronted by the challenge of dealing with a massive influx of non-Hebrew-speaking immigrants. The only formal change in policy of the new state was to drop English from the list of official languages set by the mandatory government, leaving Hebrew and Arabic. By 1953, the percentage of adult speakers of Hebrew had dropped to 53%. Major campaigns for teaching Hebrew to new immigrants stressed the centrality of the language to Israeli identity, although in fact the main educational programs were those in the schools. The adult education *ulplan* program for professionals begun in 1949 reached only about 10% of the adult immigrants during the first stage of absorption. Gradually, the new immigrants and their children came to accept the status of Hebrew, and by 1972, the proportion who said it was their principal language was back to 77% (Bachi 1974).

During the periods of mass immigration, the major drive for adults to learn Hebrew revolved around the pragmatic requirement to enter the workforce. The power of the pervading ideology supported local decisions to insist on Hebrew and to discourage public use of immigrant languages. There was relatively little resistance to this pressure. While the immigrant settlement patterns allowed for home and neighborhood language maintenance, contact with school and government developed strong pressure for acquisition of Hebrew. Ben-Rafael (1994) has documented the speed of loss of immigrant languages, showing how large numbers of North African Jewish immigrants gave up rapidly not just their Jewish varieties of Arabic but also the French they had more recently acquired. Apart from maintenance by old people (and some longer continuation in homes where there were still monolingual grandparents), most immigrant groups rapidly moved through bilingualism to largely Hebrew monolingualism. There were exceptions—the immigrants from Germany in the 1930s who were deeply committed to their adopted language and culture held on longer than most; and the ultra-orthodox enclaves, particularly Hassidim of the southern sects like Vishnitz, Belz, and Satmar, continued to use Yiddish and worked to restore it in the policies of their separatist school system when their children, too, became Hebrew speakers (Heilman 1992; Isaacs 1998, 1999).

Essentially, then, the Hebrew ideology was strong enough without the formal attempts at policy enforcement that had been prevalent in the 1920s and 1930s.

Newspapers were permitted in all the immigrant languages, and radio news was regularly broadcast in many of them. There were individual and local cases of pro-Hebrew policy, such as the reduction in the time allocated to Yiddish decried by Fishman and Fishman (1974), the insistence that dissertations at the Hebrew University be written only in Hebrew, and the failures to encourage maintenance of the immigrant languages. But no efforts were made to ban the use of other languages in communities felt to be marginal, such as the ultra-orthodox Jews or the Arabs.

The case of Arabic shows much of the ambivalence. In 1948, the newly independent state of Israel took over the old British regulations that had set English, Arabic, and Hebrew as official languages for Mandatory Palestine but, as mentioned, dropped English from the list. In spite of this, official language use has maintained a de facto role for English, after Hebrew but before Arabic (Fishman, Cooper, and Conrad 1977). If government documents and public signs and notices are bilingual, they tend to be more often in Hebrew and English than in Hebrew and Arabic. But in spite of this, it is important to reiterate that Israel is one of the few non-Muslim countries where the Arabic language is officially recognized. There is an Arabic-language government radio station and the government television station broadcasts in Arabic three and a half hours a day. Arabic has remained the language of instruction in Arab and Druze schools, and it is taught in Jewish schools. In January 1948, four months before Israel was established, a recommendation brought to a meeting of the Education Committee proposed that the language of instruction should be Arabic for all Arab primary schools. These schools could choose to teach either Hebrew or English as a second language. Other formulas were proposed. The final decision reached at a meeting on May 12, 1948, two days before independence was proclaimed, laid down the principle that both minorities (Arab in the proposed Jewish state and Jewish in the anticipated Arab state) should have the right to elementary and secondary education in their own language and in accordance with their own traditional culture. As it happened, there was no Jewish minority left in the sections of Palestine over which Jordan and Egypt came to rule for the next twenty years, but this multilingual language policy was the one that was implemented for the Arabic-speaking minorities who remained in the new State of Israel. At the same time, because there was no provision for tertiary education in Arabic, it became essential for any Arab wanting higher education or employment outside the community to acquire Hebrew.

Changes in the last twenty-five years. It was in the 1970s, after the Six-Day War, that evidence started to accumulate of the weakening of the Zionist ideology that had built the community during the Mandate and that had helped integrate the mass immigrations of the first twenty years of statehood. From a linguistic point of view, the clearest sign of this has been the growing status and role of English.

Fishman, Cooper, and Conrad (1977) trace the early stages and Spolsky (1996b) describes and analyzes more recent developments. Part of this was the same kind of development as Fishman, Cooper, and Conrad (1977) and Fishman, Rubal-Lopez, and Conrad (1996) examined in other countries, the highly complex outcome of economics and globalization and the association of English with both. All of these have their effect in Israel, where the very success of Hebrew—a language restricted essentially to use within the country—naturally encouraged the need for an international language. In addition, the fact that the most active Jewish community outside Israel is English-speaking and the immigration of a significant number of English-speaking Jews strengthened the demand for English and the possibility of using it.

Even without the extra effects of more recent developments, the weakening of the Zionist ideology and the growing strength of English would no doubt have helped the growth of a new pluralism that has included some nominal recognition of multilingualism, as witness the newly founded and funded National Authorities for Yiddish and for Ladino. The beginning of the peace process played a major role too, providing encouragement for the teaching of Arabic in Jewish schools on the basis of its relevance in a peaceful Middle East. On top of this, the massive immigration of 75,000 Jews from Ethiopia and 800,000 from the former Soviet Union introduced major changes, not just in demography but also in linguistic ideology. The Ethiopian immigrants come from a quite different social and economic milieu, slowing down their integration. There are so many Russian speakers, and they are so convinced (like the German Jews before them) of the value of their culture and adopted language, that it is possible to argue for the beginnings of a major breach in the hegemony of Hebrew.

The new policy on language education (Ministry of Education, Culture, and Sport 1995, 1996) does in fact accept multilingualism as a desirable goal. Although asserting the primacy of Hebrew, it gives full formal recognition to the values of Arabic and of immigrant and community and heritage languages, and the importance of international languages to build national capacity. Hebrew is the language of instruction in the Jewish sector and Arabic the language of instruction in the Arab sector (about 20% of the schools). Hebrew is to be taught as a second language in the Arab schools, and four years of Arabic are now mandatory in Jewish schools. Of the international languages, English is recognized as first, but French also has a special place as a permissible substitute for English or Arabic or as a second foreign language. The policy encourages teaching new immigrants in their mother tongue and proposes the development of schools that concentrate on languages.

In practice, the picture is not as rosy as the policy suggests (Shohamy and Spolsky 1999; Spolsky and Shohamy 1998). The teaching of Arabic in Jewish schools is considered weak and unsatisfactory, and only half of the schools offer the minimum program—barely 2,000 pupils continue studying it to the end of high school. Few if any schools offer programs in languages other than Hebrew, Arabic, English, and French. Most Russian is restricted to upper levels (for immigrant pupils who have just arrived) or to afternoon schools conducted by parents. Little if any funding has been provided to implement the new policy.

Nonetheless, the policy itself is further evidence of the growing respect for linguistic diversity and of the weakening of the ideologically backed Hebrew-only approach. Previously, such freedom of language choice was limited to minority groups (Arabs, Druze, Beduin, and Circassians) or to marginal ultra-orthodox Hassidim (who continued to choose Yiddish). Now, there is encouragement of the teaching of Yiddish and Ladino in state schools, boosted by the recent establishment by law of a National Authority for Yiddish and a National Authority for Ladino. New textbooks and curricula have just been published for Russian and Amharic. Curricula have been published for some half a dozen of the other languages chosen by tiny groups of students.

Some principles for language policy. Looking at the complexity of linguistic situations in the world today, one can readily understand the need regularly perceived for formal policy making. While there is reason to suspect that the effective power of the nation-state is diminishing, eroded by regional groupings like the European Union, or nibbled at by growing globalization, there continue to be regular attempts to enforce or resist nationalistically inspired efforts at monolingual hegemony.

While there are many reasons for individuals, groups, and governments to choose a specific language policy, attempting by it to modify the language ideology or practice of a specific community, I suggest that any reasonable policy needs to be based on two distinct and competing principles. The first of these is uncontroversial. It is to arrive at the most efficient method of communication. It underlies programs to encourage all citizens of a state to develop mastery of the most common language and to gain the individual plurilingual competence that will assure them of access to needed information and jobs. In Israel, this provides support for the major efforts to teach Hebrew. It underlies also the encouragement or teaching of Arabic, English, French, Russian, and many other languages that can contribute to individual or national language capacity, a term we take from Brecht and Walton (2000). This principle is essentially pragmatic and instrumental. It can be met in part by provision of linguistic services; for instance, Israeli banks made sure they had signs and forms in Russian and interpreters able to deal with the 800,000 recent immigrants.

The second principle, associated as it is with the powerful symbolic function of languages as repository and token of group or ethnic or religious or national identity, is of necessity more controversial, and the cause of the conflicts regularly associated with language policy. There are essentially two contradictory expressions of this principle. One common, but I believe ultimately flawed, approach is what I will label the principle of "my language first" or of national (group) pride. In Israel, the strength with which this ideology was espoused by the early pioneers and the builders of the state made possible the unique revitalization and revernacularization of a language. Maintained unthinkingly after the goal of revival of Hebrew had been met, however, it led not just to the loss of many Jewish languages rich in tradition and culture, but also led to the serious weakening of national language capacity.

A better formulation of this second principle is starting to emerge, which I will characterize simply as respect for linguistic diversity or "my language alongside yours." While recognizing the central place in Israeli society of Hebrew, both as the most practical lingua franca and as the symbolic embodiment of national identity, it would find ways to show respect or even offer support for the many other languages of the population. Clearly, the details of this action would depend on the nature of the other languages, the number of speakers, and the practical possibility of making provision for them. But starting from this point of view, rather than from an uncompromising effort to assert the superiority of a single language, offers a better chance at a fair and effective language policy. This, we firmly hope, is what is emerging in Israel and in many other parts of the world.

REFERENCES

Ager, Dennis. 1996. *Language policy in Britain and France: The processes of policy.* Open Linguistics Series, Robin F. Fawcett (ed.). London: Cassell.
Ager, Dennis. 1999. *Identity, insecurity and image: France and language.* Clevedon, England; Philadelphia: Multilingual Matters.
Alatis, James E. (ed). 1968. *Report of the Twentieth Annual Georgetown Round Table Meeting of Languages and Linguistics.* Washington DC: Georgetown University Press.
Amara, Muhammad Hasan. 1999. *Politics and sociolinguistic reflexes: Palestinian border villages.* Amsterdam: John Benjamins.
Bachi, Roberto. 1956. A statistical analysis of the revival of Hebrew in Israel. *Scripta Hierosolymitana* 3: 179–247.
Bachi, Roberto. 1974. *The population of Israel.* Jerusalem: Institute of Contemporary Jewry, Hebrew University and Demographic Center, Prime Minister's Office, Israel.
Ben-Rafael, Eliezer. 1994. *Language, identity and social division: The case of Israel.* Oxford Studies in Language Contact, Peter Mülhäusler and Suzanne Romaine (eds.). Oxford: Clarendon Press.
Brecht, Richard D., and A. Ronald Walton. 2000. System III: The future of language learning in the United States. In Richard D. Lambert and Elana Shohamy (eds.), *Language policy and pedagogy: Essays in honor of A. Ronald Walton.* Amsterdam: John Benjamins. 111–128.
Cohen, Israel. 1918. *The German attack on the Hebrew schools in Palestine.* London: Jewish Chronicle and Jewish World.
Cooper, Robert L. 1989. *Language policy and social change.* Cambridge: Cambridge University Press.
Dorian, Nancy. 1998. Western language ideologies and small-language prospects. In Lenore A. Grenoble and Lindsay J. Whaley (eds.), *Endangered languages: Current issues and future prospects.* Cambridge: Cambridge University Press. 3–21.

Fellman, Jack. 1973. *The revival of a classical tongue: Eliezer ben Yehuda and the modern Hebrew language.* The Hague: Mouton.

Fishman, Joshua A. 1982. The role of the Tshernovits conference in the rise of Hebrew. In Robert L. Cooper (ed.), *Language Spread.* Bloomington: Indiana University Press. 291–320.

Fishman, Joshua A. 1991. *Reversing language shift: Theoretical and empirical foundations of assistance to threatened languages.* Clevedon, England: Multilingual Matters.

Fishman, Joshua A., Robert L. Cooper, and A.W. Conrad. 1977. *The spread of English: the sociology of English as an additional language.* Rowley, MA: Newbury House.

Fishman, Joshua A., and David E. Fishman. 1974. Yiddish in Israel: a case-study of efforts to revise a monocentric language policy. *International Journal of the Sociology of Language* 1: 126–146.

Fishman, Joshua A., Alma Rubal-Lopez, and Andrew W. Conrad (eds.). 1996. *Post-Imperial English.* Berlin: Mouton de Gruyter.

Glinert, Lewis. 1993. The first congress for Hebrew, or when is a congress not a congress? In Joshua A. Fishman (ed.), *The earliest stage of language planning: The "First Congress" phenomenon.* Berlin: Mouton de Gruyter. 85–115.

Harshav, Benjamin. 1993. *Language in time of revolution.* Berkeley: University of California Press.

Heilman, Samuel. 1992. *Defenders of the faith: inside ultra-orthodox Jewry.* New York: Schocken Books.

Hymes, Dell. 1974. *Foundations in sociolinguistics: an ethnographic approach.* Philadelphia: University of Pennsylvania Press.

Isaacs, Miriam. 1998. Yiddish in the orthodox communities of Jerusalem. In Dov-Ber Kerler (ed.), *Politics of Yiddish: Studies in Language, Literature and Society.* Walnut Creek, CA: Altamira Press. 85–96.

Isaacs, Miriam. 1999. Contentious partners: Yiddish and Hebrew in Haredi Israel. *International Journal of the Sociology of Language* 137.

Karpat, Kemal H. 1982. Millets and nationality: the roots of the incongruity of nation and state in the post-Ottoman era. In Benjamin Braude and Bernard Lewis (ed.), *Christians and Jews in the Ottoman Empire: the functioning of a plural society.* New York: Holmes and Meier.

Kosover, Mordecai. 1966. *Arabic elements in Palestinian Yiddish: The old Ashkenazic Jewish community in Palestine its history and its language.* Jerusalem: Rubin Mass.

Mandel, George. 1993. Why did Ben-Yehuda suggest the revival of spoken Hebrew? In Lewis Glinert (ed.), *Hebrew in Ashkenaz.* New York: Oxford University Press. 193–207.

Ministry of Education, Culture, and Sport. 1995. *Policy for language education in Israel (in Hebrew).* Jerusalem: Office of the Director General.

Ministry of Education, Culture, and Sport. 1996. *Policy for language education in Israel (in Hebrew).* Jerusalem: Office of the Director-General.

Phillipson, Robert. 1992. *Linguistic imperialism.* Oxford: Oxford University Press.

Shohamy, Elana, and Bernard Spolsky. 1999. An emerging language policy for Israel: from monolingualism to multilingualism. *Plurilingua* 21: 169–184.

Silverstein, Michael. 1979. Language structure and linguistic ideology. In Paul R. Clyne (ed.), *The elements: A parasession on linguistic units and levels.* Chicago: Chicago Linguistic Society. 193–247.

Spolsky, Bernard. 1968. Linguistics and language pedagogy— applications or implications? In James E. Alatis (ed.), *Twentieth Annual Round Table on Languages and Linguistics.* Washington, DC: Georgetown University Press. 143–155.

Spolsky, Bernard. 1991. Hebrew language revitalization within a general theory of second language learning. In Robert L. Cooper and Bernard Spolsky (eds.), *The influence of language on culture and thought: Essays in honor of Joshua A. Fishman's sixty-fifth birthday.* Berlin: Mouton de Gruyter. 137–155.

Spolsky, Bernard. 1996a. Conditions for language revitalization: a comparison of the cases of Hebrew and Maori. In Sue Wright (ed.), *Language and the state: Revitalization and revival in Israel and Eire.* Clevedon, England: Multilingual Matters. 5–50.

Spolsky, Bernard. 1996b. English in Israel after Independence. In Joshua A. Fishman, Alma Rubal-Lopez, and Andrew W. Conrad (eds.), *Post-Imperial English.* Berlin: Mouton.

Spolsky, Bernard, and Robert L. Cooper. 1991. *The languages of Jerusalem.* Oxford: Clarendon Press.

Spolsky, Bernard, and Elana Shohamy. 1998. Language policy in Israel. *New Language Planning Newsletter* 12(4): 1–4.

Spolsky, Bernard, and Elana Shohamy. 1999. *The languages of Israel: Policy, ideology and practice.* Clevedon: Multilingual Matters.

Wahl, Renee. 1996. *German language policy in 19th century Palestine.* M.A. thesis, English, Bar-Ilan University, Ramat-Gan.

Language and policy issues in the education of immigrant students

Donna Christian
Center for Applied Linguistics

Introduction. The impact of immigration on U.S. institutions and society has been widely noted and commented upon. The foreign-born constitute the fastest-growing segment of the population, reaching 25.8 million in 1997, just under 10% of the population, and the highest proportion since World War II (U.S. Bureau of the Census 1998). Even more striking than numbers, however, is the make-up of recent waves of immigration. Since the passage of the Immigration Act of 1965, which eliminated national origin quotas, Asia and Latin America have replaced Europe as the main sources of newcomers to the United States. The largest groups come from Mexico (over one-fourth of the foreign-born population), China, Cuba, India, and Vietnam. New immigrants to the United States come with diverse languages, cultures, and experiences.

These trends are by no means unique to the United States. International migration patterns show that while some countries, such as the United States, Canada, and Australia, have relatively larger proportions of immigrant populations, many other countries also have sizable numbers of immigrants. In fact, "migration is now global and no longer unidirectional. Today, few countries are not affected by either immigration or emigration" (Edmonston and Passel 1994: 23). This worldwide movement of populations across national borders is predicted to continue and will be the norm of the future. Projections for the United States tell us that immigration will remain an important influence on the composition of our society and will be the primary vehicle for population growth in the future, barring dramatic events in the world or changes in U.S. policy that alter the current course (Edmonston and Passel 1994).

In an increasing number of schools across the United States, the foreign-born also constitute a fast increasing segment of the student population. Recent studies indicate, however, that few schools are adequately and appropriately serving these linguistic and cultural minorities. In this paper, I discuss language, education, and policy issues concerning immigrant students and the opportunities (and challenges) presented to us by their presence in our schools. We need to develop strategies to achieve a "win-win" result for our society and for the school-aged immigrants who join us.

Can we move toward an orientation where we seek to build on the language and other skills that immigrants bring? It seems obvious to me that it is in everyone's best interest to help immigrant students prepare for success and productivity by giving them (and all students) an education that is responsive to their needs. It also seems like common sense that we would be better off if we could maintain and develop the language skills and other strengths that these students bring to school with them. To succeed, they must add English to their repertoire (a matter of wide agreement), but can we conserve and build on the languages they know when they enter our schools at the same time (as both their individual and our societal assets)? Our current language and education policies treat languages other than English as problems. Can we reorient these policies to see languages as resources?

In exploring these possibilities, I describe an initiative that the Center for Applied Linguistics has participated in since 1993, the Program in Immigrant Education. In addition to our findings about promising approaches for adolescent English language learners, these efforts are leading us to see that many of the reforms that make schools responsive to immigrants and diverse student populations in general are making schools better for all students, native-born and immigrant, linguistic minority and linguistic majority alike.

Immigrant students in secondary schools. While immigration has affected all aspects of American life, the changing demography of the United States is very keenly felt in education. In 1997, 2.3 million children between the ages of five and eighteen were identified as foreign-born by the U.S. Bureau of the Census (1998). By 2010, following current trends, 22% of the school-aged population (9 million in number) will be first- or second-generation immigrant children (Fix and Passel 1994). With over 90% of recent immigrants coming from non-English-speaking countries, schools are increasingly receiving students who do not speak English at home and who have little or no proficiency in English.

There is accumulating evidence that most school systems have not been able to give immigrant students access to experiences and learning that facilitate their success (considering dropout rates and other educational statistics that are frequently cited). Serving immigrant English language learners at the secondary school level is especially challenging. Faltis (1999: 1) notes that "bilingual and English as a second language (ESL) education at the secondary level is one of the most unexamined and overlooked areas of education in the United States." August and Hakuta (1997) in a review of research on educating language minority students also identified middle and high schools, along with programs for newcomers, as needing attention.

In order to provide schooling that is responsive to adolescent immigrant students, many language, academic, and social factors must be taken into account. U.S.-born secondary students entered school at age five or six and, if they remained in school, followed a relatively predictable sequence of coursework. As a result, educators can assume certain background experience and knowledge, and educational policies (such as graduation requirements) are developed for that context. But such assumptions cannot be made about immigrant students, who arrive with widely varying experiences and skills that may not directly translate into readiness for U.S. schools. They arrive at all ages. They may have had high-quality education, possibly even better than that available in the United States, or no previous educational experience at all. Differentiated responses are called for when the population includes both a fifteen-year-old who arrived at age thirteen with a strong academic background and a fifteen-year-old newcomer who had only two years of prior schooling (Lucas 1997).

Immigrant students of secondary school age, whatever their background, face serious challenges in acquiring English and succeeding in school (Peyton and Christian 1997). The skills they bring with them are not typically highly valued, especially their language. If they are newcomers, they have less time than students who entered the United States during or before elementary school to learn academic English and to master the academic content required to graduate from high school. They are confronted by tests that require English skills they do not have. They must study subjects such as biology, history, economics, and geometry that require high levels of English academic language, using texts and other materials that require a high level of English reading ability. Most secondary schools do not offer native language support for these academic subjects, nor is instruction often provided that accommodates their level of English-language proficiency. The students may also find it difficult to be accepted in well-established groups of English-speaking students (including those who share their country of origin but have been in this country longer). Finally, preparing for life after high school brings additional concerns. If college is in their plans, they must try to succeed in classes that are required for college acceptance and sort out other requirements such as admissions tests and the application process. In the few short years available to them in secondary school, immigrant students are faced with learning (and quickly using) a new language for academic purposes, adjusting to a new life, and making more progress each year than their fellow native-born students in order to meet the expectations of schools.

Secondary schools have, unfortunately, not kept up with the needs of their changing population. These schools are typically characterized by:

- Programs that fail to give immigrant students access to academic concepts and skills. Students need to learn academic content while they are learning English, but typically they are not offered a full educational program. A study in California, for example, found that only six of twenty-seven secondary schools examined provided full coverage of content classes through the native language or through sheltered instruction, to make the content comprehensible for English language learners (Minicucci and Olsen 1992).

- Few program or curricular alternatives for students with limited prior schooling and low literacy skills. Because of war, poverty, or a variety of other reasons, many immigrant students lack basic skills, though they have had rich life experiences on which they can build formal school knowledge and around which they can shape a successful life in the United States. Development of literacy is a key, and responsive programs are needed to prepare students for opportunities beyond high school in the relatively short time available (Mace-Matluck et al. 1998).

- A school structure that does not ensure smooth transitions from program to program, school to school, or school to college or work. Lucas, Henze, Donato (1990) found that high schools that were successful in working with Latino students provided assistance with such transitions—academic support programs to help students move from bilingual and ESL classes to mainstream classes; guidance counselors to offer assistance in exploring post-secondary opportunities, and so on.

- Teachers and administrators who are not prepared to meet immigrant student needs. All educators who work with English language learners need to know about second language development, cross-cultural issues, and methods to teach both language and academic content. The National Center for Education Statistics (1997) reports, however, that only 30% of teachers in the United States who instruct English language learners have received any preparation in these areas, and only 2.5% have a degree in ESL or bilingual education.

- A lack of appropriate assessment policies and procedures. Assessments in English cannot accurately measure the knowledge or skills of English language learners. Temporary exemptions from testing can have negative consequences (such as preventing students from qualifying for advanced placement courses or certain categories of diplomas). Much attention is focused on assessment issues, but unfortunately few strategies have been implemented with positive results.

Lucas (1997: 1–2) helps us understand these issues better through a glimpse at the life of Eduardo:

> He arrived in the United States from Colombia when he was 13, the oldest of three children. His family moved to a poor neighborhood in a poor city in the Northeast. He and his brother and sister went to urban schools that were overcrowded, understaffed, and without human or financial resources to educate the largely poor, immigrant student body. Both of his parents

worked long hours, and as soon as the children were old enough, they helped. . . . The school system did not help Eddie and his siblings develop their native Spanish abilities, nor did it adequately develop Eddie's English writing abilities or give him access to technological skills. While Eddie liked the idea of a career in computers, he had never actually used one, because the school had only a few and his family had none. . . . Eduardo finished high school . . . having completed all his credits with a C-minus average. But to his . . . surprise, he did not actually receive his diploma, because he had not passed the writing portion of the state's high school competency exam.

This is just part of Eduardo's profile, but it illustrates the realities that we need to keep in mind.

The Program in Immigrant Education. The Program in Immigrant Education was developed to create ways to respond to the situation described above. With funding from the Andrew W. Mellon Foundation, a collaborative network of local demonstration projects worked to improve the education of immigrant students at their sites by:

1. improving English language and literacy development,
2. improving mastery of academic content and skills, and
3. improving access to postsecondary opportunities (including preparation for higher education and the workforce).

These were no small goals, of course; the intent was to look comprehensively at schools, policies, and practices, and to design reforms that would lead to success in school and afterward for immigrant students of secondary school age. It was clear from the diversity of situations and students involved that there would be no one single response.

Local demonstration projects were directed by Jodi Crandall from the University of Maryland, Baltimore County; Laurie Olsen from California Tomorrow; and David Ramirez from California State University, Long Beach, who worked with Joy Peyton and others at the Center for Applied Linguistics. The local projects worked with schools in Maryland, northern California, and southern California, in a range of demographic contexts (for example, in one urban district, two-thirds of the students came from Spanish- or Khmer-speaking backgrounds; in another, only about 20% of the students came from homes where English was not the primary language, but they represented over 100 different languages). In each case, school and district educators (teachers, aides, and administrators) formed teams as a central mechanism for reform (called task forces, working groups, or action teams) (these are described in Adger and Peyton 1999). With the support and encouragement of the outside facilitators, these teams examined their own schools and students, studied relevant research, and identified priority areas for action. Based on emerging findings, we can point to some strategies that show promise of positive effects. These and other approaches are described in Adger and Peyton (1999) and Crandall et al. (in press).

Accessible Content Courses. As mentioned previously, it is critical for immigrant students to have access to content that they can understand in courses that advance them toward graduation while they are developing their English language skills. They cannot wait until they learn academic English to study academic content. One option is to increase the availability of subject area courses in the students' primary languages. This option is particularly helpful for recently arrived students with low levels of English proficiency, and it also facilitates the ongoing development and conservation of the students' native languages (Brecht and Ingold 1998).

However, for many reasons having to do with resources and other factors, it is not often possible to offer full curricula in languages other than English in our high schools. One viable alternative is to provide content classes in English that are specially designed for students who are learning English as an additional language. In project schools, new core content courses were developed that were offered by teachers trained in "sheltering" instruction—courses in biology, chemistry, history, and other subject areas that provided credit toward graduation and, in the best cases, formed part of an articulated sequence that allowed students to move through school to graduation. There is a growing literature on effective strategies for sheltered instruction (Echevarria, Vogt, and Short 2000). Some of the strategies incorporated in project schools included defining both language and content objectives, eliciting student prior knowledge to build on, scaffolding instruction with frequent checks for understanding, incorporating multiple forms of interaction and hands-on experiences, and assessing learning effectively.

In one district in the program, sheltered courses were developed to help students learn material covered by state-level tests required for graduation (among others). At one high school there, ESL students who took the sheltered courses (government and math) passed the state tests at higher rates than the overall pass rate for their school. In another school, new sections of sheltered science and math courses increased access to these subjects for English language learners. (For example, the percentage of tenth-grade ESL students enrolled in science classes rose from 34% to 82% over the three years of the project.) Sheltered courses provide access in at least two ways. First, when these courses exist, students have the opportunity to take subjects that might otherwise not be open to them. Second, by modifying instruction appropriately, the courses give students better access to the content itself.

Instructional practices for equity and active participation. All teachers need to develop strategies for working with students at different English proficiency levels. Making classroom routines predictable can allow students to concentrate on the content presented in their second language, rather than struggling to figure out what they are supposed to do. Increasing wait time is another strategy that helps students participate, especially those at early stages of language learning. Giving students five to seven seconds to respond (a big increase for many teachers, particularly at the secondary level) often leads to a wider variety of students participating and longer responses. Such practices are essential to sheltered content instruction, but they can be incorporated by all teachers to improve instruction for English language learners at different proficiency levels.

Programs for students with limited prior schooling. Many immigrant students are placed in secondary schools in the United States because of their age, even though they have had little formal schooling and have low literacy and numeracy skills. They cannot participate successfully in age-appropriate grade-level instruction. Refugees who have experienced traumatic events in war or oppression, for example, may have had little chance for schooling before their arrival. Specially designed programs can address their linguistic and social needs and provide academic training to help them succeed.

These programs offer basic skills instruction in a manner that is suitable for adolescent learners. Literacy development is critical, ideally in the native language with a subsequent transfer to English. This allows students to use the cognitive and language resources they already have as a foundation on which to build new skills. Flexibility in time and extending the amount of time of instruction is also important for these students. More opportunities to engage in academic learning, through after-school, weekend, and summer programs are very valuable but often difficult because the students must work or care for other family members.

In one project school, students with limited prior schooling now have access to a sequence of courses focused on literacy that they may follow in addition to their English language classes (Crandall and Greenblatt 1998). Depending on existing skills, students may take the entire sequence or enter where appropriate. The first level is for non-literate students with little formal education; the second builds on the skills of English language learners with low literacy. The third offering provides specially designed instruction for students who already have native language literacy skills or who have taken one of the earlier courses. Project staff report that an advantage of focused literacy classes is that students may progress more rapidly to more challenging English language classes. In the past, they were held to beginning ESL because of their lack of literacy skills. These literacy courses have also assisted the students in passing the state-required functional reading course, which has the added benefit of encouraging them to remain in school.

Restructuring use of time. Many project schools found that the typical comprehensive secondary school schedule does not provide optimum learning experiences for immigrant English language learners. Several sites made structural changes in the school day, providing longer blocks of time for class sessions. In one school, three class periods per day of one hour and thirty-eight minutes replaced the traditional day of six periods of fifty-four minutes each. Most teachers and students found the change to be beneficial. Teachers saw fewer students per day for longer periods of time and thus could develop closer relations and better knowledge of their strengths and needs. Students could focus on fewer subjects at one time, which gave them the chance to pursue understanding in depth.

Block scheduling does not, of course, change the need to use time in school effectively. There were some noticeable improvements once the schedule was restructured in the school just mentioned, however. In the first year after restructuring, there were improvements in discipline, grades, and credit accrual (the average number of on-campus suspensions went from 165 per day to 15, for example) (Olsen et al. 1999). Looking at options like block scheduling, as well as other ways of structuring time to fit the needs of immigrant students, can provide a key ingredient to creating optimum learning environments.

Attention to post–high school opportunities. Immigrant students and their families often lack information that is taken for granted by those who have grown up in the U.S. school system. Even those who are academically successful may not be aware that college is an option for them, or that steps need to be taken to meet certain requirements in order to be eligible (course selection, admissions tests, and so on). They may not know how to manage the application process or seek financial aid. Changing federal and state policies concerning immigration status and higher education may complicate the picture. Similar information needs arise in career planning.

Project schools found that specific and consistent attention to opportunities beyond high school could make a profound difference in the futures of immigrant students. At one school, task force members developed international councils that began as an after-school club with activities focused on college and career planning for international (immigrant) students. Later, the activities were recognized as important enough to be incorporated into the regular school day. Participation in the councils had profound effects: One year, all twenty-seven seniors who participated applied to and were accepted at universities, many with scholarships. The following year, twenty-nine out of thirty achieved the same result. (In prior years, few English-language learners had applied or even considered college as an option.) Supporting activities increased the impact of these efforts, including the creation of courses to help students prepare for critical tests such as the Test of English as a Foreign Language (TOEFL) and the SAT. Later, an elective course on preparing for college was instituted as well. Access to information and supportive guidance can open up paths beyond high school that immigrant students would otherwise never know about.

One school's experience. To give a snapshot of the impact of these reforms on immigrant students, consider this description from a California high school.

> Regular teacher collaboration time allowed ESL, bilingual, and sheltered teachers across academic departments to meet monthly to discuss LEP student issues during the "On-Site meetings." The combination of school reform and the project's focus on LEP students led to providing extended time to learn by encouraging LEP students (and all students) to take a fourth block class and to double up on English until students catch up to their grade level in a sheltered or mainstream class. More time to learn resulted in gaining more credits earned for graduation, higher grades, more access to science and math, and the ability of more LEP students to complete a full college prep English sequence in high school (Olsen et al. 1999: 267).

Policy Contexts. The experiences of the projects underscored the impact of policies on our ability to provide strong educational opportunities for immigrant students. The California projects were greatly affected by state-level propositions that were proposed and passed during the implementation of their activities (Proposition 187, which sought to restrict publicly funded services for undocumented immigrants, and Proposition 227, which aimed to end the use of bilingual education for English language learners). While these were particularly dramatic and disruptive, policies at federal, state, and local levels have directly and indirectly affected the opportunities of all immigrant students to succeed and of schools to help them. A few examples will serve to illustrate.

After Californians passed Proposition 187 (even though it was prevented from implementation by ongoing court cases), one project school experienced a 50% drop in the rate of families reporting use of a language other than English at home in the home language survey. The local staff did not believe that the community had changed in any way comparable to the survey results. This survey, a local policy used to assist the placement of students into appropriate programs, was considered dangerous in a climate perceived as anti-immigrant. Families were unwilling to have their children identified as immigrants because of a non-English home language, even if that meant that they did not receive the language services they needed. Thus the local policy, which sought to assist immigrant students, was compromised by the climate created by a state-level policy.

In another example, some school-to-work programs in project schools ran into a compatibility problem with a broader-based policy, in this case at the federal level.

One way to expand post-secondary opportunities for immigrant students is to build career preparation opportunities into the school curriculum through vocational and school-to-work programs. These educational programs with work components are very valuable in providing experience in the workforce. Two issues arise, however, related to the documentation status of immigrant students (a factor that cannot be considered in providing educational services, according to the *Plyler v. Doe* Supreme Court decision). First, some federally funded programs are by law specifically limited to U.S. citizens and other legal residents (such as the Joint Training Partnership Act; JTPA). Undocumented immigrants are ineligible, but schools cannot discriminate. Second, under a variety of school-to-work programs, employers offer compensation to students who work while they study. However, the Immigration Reform and Control Act requires that employers check to ensure that noncitizens have legal work papers. Schools cannot ask, but employers must. This interface of federal policies and school programs presents a dilemma for schools seeking to help students prepare for the workforce, and it became a troublesome roadblock for some career preparation initiatives in the project schools.

At a more general level, the broad range of language and education policies enacted at federal, state, and local levels create the context within which secondary immigrant students, especially those who are not yet fluent in English, are served by schools (Christian 1999). Laws, regulations, and budget allocations influence the use and learning of English and other languages, as well as the educational options that can be offered to the diverse groups of students in our schools. Policies of all kinds need to be taken into account, from the federal Elementary and Secondary Education Act, to state student assessment policies, to local district policies on providing transportation for students, to an individual school's rules about scheduling classes.

Whatever the level, though, when it comes to language issues, the prevailing orientation is to see "language as problem." For secondary immigrant students and their fellow non-native speakers of English, the orientation is toward eliminating limited English proficiency as a barrier to opportunity. The goal is to "fix" the problem and then these students can join the others in the so-called "mainstream." Maintenance and further development of the language skills they bring with them are not supported (and, depending on the local climate, may be actively discouraged). Language is not viewed as a potential societal resource, with planning and policy-making undertaken to maximize the benefit of that resource. Many speak of the practical limits to our ability to foster growth in so many students and so many languages. However, we have seen in some of our schools that a "language as resource" orientation can make a big difference; where all language skills are valued, their persistence can be celebrated, not lamented.

Conclusion. Diversity in our schools is clearly not a passing phenomenon. The situation for secondary immigrant students perhaps crystallizes for us the critical factors of time, language, and disposition that must figure into reforms that will offer the best opportunities for learning and success for all students.

While we respond to the challenges of diversity, however, we should not lose sight of the promise. In particular, the language skills possessed by immigrants from non-English backgrounds (especially those who are in later stages of language development) constitute a valuable resource for our society that should not be squandered (Campbell and Lindholm 1990). While we bemoan the sad state of competence in languages other than English in the United States, we fail to provide opportunities for speakers of other languages to conserve and develop their language skills as they add English. Instead, we treat their native languages as problems to be overcome, rather than as resources to be further developed. A new orientation in policy and practice could have profound effects. We see some hope in the growing popularity of two-way immersion programs (Christian et al. 1996), where students from two language backgrounds learn together in classrooms and a goal is bilingualism for all students.

The Program in Immigrant Education has demonstrated that comprehensive reforms can be developed and implemented that make secondary schools more responsive to the needs of immigrant students, giving them access to experiences, language skills, and subject area knowledge that will help them succeed in school and beyond. This paper offers only a glimpse of what has been learned through the program. More of the details (and first-hand accounts) can be found in the publications listed in the references and at the web site of the Center for Applied Linguistics (www.cal.org).

REFERENCES

Adger, Carolyn Temple, and Joy Kreeft Peyton. 1999. Enhancing the education of immigrant students in secondary school: Structural challenges and directions. In Christian J. Faltis and Paula Wolfe (eds.), *So much to say: Adolescents, bilingualism, and ESL in the secondary school.* New York: Teachers College Press. 205–224.

August, Diane, and Kenji Hakuta. 1997. *Improving schooling for language minority children.* Washington, DC: National Academy Press.

Brecht, Richard D., and Catherine W. Ingold. 1998. Tapping a national resource: Heritage languages in the United States. *ERIC Digest.* Washington, DC: ERIC Clearinghouse on Languages and Linguistics/Center for Applied Linguistics.

Campbell, Russell, and Kathryn Lindholm. 1990. Conservation of language resources. In William Van Patten and J. F. Lee (eds.), *Second language acquisition—foreign language learning.* Clevedon, England: Multilingual Matters. 226–239.

Christian, Donna. 1999. Looking at federal education legislation from a language policy/planning perspective. In Thom Huebner and Katheryn A. Davis (eds.), *Sociopolitical perspectives on language policy and planning in the USA.* Amsterdam: John Benjamins.

Christian, Donna, Chris Montone, Kathryn Lindholm, and Isolda Carranza. 1996. *Profiles in two-way immersion education.* McHenry, IL: Delta Systems/Center for Applied Linguistics.

Crandall, JoAnn, and Les Greenblatt. 1998. Teaching beyond the middle: Meeting the needs of under-schooled and high-achieving immigrant students. In Maria del Rosario Basterra (ed.), *Excellence and equity for language minority students.* Chevy Chase, MD: The Mid-Atlantic Equity Consortium. 43–60.

Crandall, JoAnn, Ann Jaramillo, Laurie Olsen, and Joy Kreeft Peyton. In press. Diverse Teaching Strategies for Diverse Learners: Immigrant Children. In Helene Hodges (ed.), *Educating everybody's children,* vol. 2. Alexandria, VA: Association for Supervision and Curriculum Development.

Echevarria, Jana, M. Vogt, and Deborah Short. 2000. *Making content comprehensible for English language learners: The SIOP model.* Boston: Allyn & Bacon.

Edmonston, Barry, and Jeffrey S. Passel (eds.). 1994. *Immigration and ethnicity: The integration of America's newest arrivals.* Washington, DC: The Urban Institute Press.

Faltis, Christian J. 1999. Creating a new history. In Christian J. Faltis and Paula M. Wolfe (eds.), *So much to say: Adolescents, bilingualism, and ESL in the secondary school.* New York: Teachers College Press.

Fix, Michael, and Jeffrey S. Passel. 1994. *Immigration and immigrants: Setting the record straight.* Washington, DC: The Urban Institute.

Lucas, Tamara. 1997. *Into, through, and beyond secondary school: Critical transitions for immigrant youths.* McHenry, IL: Delta Systems/Center for Applied Linguistics.

Lucas, Tamara, Rosemary Henze, and Ruben Donato. 1990. Promoting the success of Latino language-minority students: An exploratory study of six high schools. *Harvard Educational Review* 60: 315–340.

Mace-Matluck, Betty J., Rosalind Alexander-Kasparik, and Robin M. Queen. 1998. *Through the golden door: Educational approaches for immigrant adolescents with limited schooling.* McHenry, IL: Delta Systems/Center for Applied Linguistics.

Minicucci, Catherine, and Laurie Olsen. 1992. *Programs for secondary limited English proficient students: A California study.* Washington, DC: National Clearinghouse for Bilingual Education.

National Center for Education Statistics. 1997. *A profile of policies and practices for limited English proficient students.* Washington, DC: U.S. Government Printing Office.

Olsen, Laurie, Ann Jaramillo, Zaida McCall-Perez, and Judy White. 1999. *Igniting change for immigrant students: Portraits of three high schools.* Oakland: California Tomorrow.

Peyton, Joy Kreeft, and Donna Christian. 1997. Introduction to the series. In Tamara Lucas, *Into, through, and beyond secondary school: Critical transitions for immigrant youths.* McHenry, IL: Delta Systems/Center for Applied Linguistics.

U.S. Bureau of the Census. 1998. *The foreign-born population: 1997.* [Online: available at http://www.census.gov/population/socdemo/foreign/97 (April 9).]

The pragmatic implications of "boilerplate" in news coverage of California ballot initiative controversies

Colleen Cotter
Georgetown University

Introduction. A good news story is more than just scandal, victory, upset, or a tale of woe or triumph. A good news story is also marked by how artfully it is compiled. In fact, well-formed news discourse—the kind found in stories that would be considered well-reported and well-written by news practitioners themselves—is structured by a fairly strict set of rules that govern how information is selected and presented. Three interrelated discourse requirements are especially relevant in the case of controversial long-running news stories, such as those I consider here, because they can unwittingly work against the clarity that journalists are striving for. The injunctions of newswriting—(1) to simplify, (2) to maintain an authorial distance or neutrality, and (3) to summarize previously reported details of a story when reporting it afresh—are all made manifest in "boilerplate." Boilerplate is recurring material that is inserted into stories extending longer than a single day to remind readers of prior context.

Boilerplate summarizes, simplifies, and is presented as non-evaluatively as possible according to reporter codes of balance. Because of its very ordinariness and relative unimportance in relation to the "main point," or the most recent or newest dimension of a story (the lead), boilerplate is easy to overlook. Nonetheless, as an identifiable component of news discourse, it follows certain constraints on content and placement within the text. Its discourse purpose, while backgrounded to other goals, is orientational, orienting the public to the status of a story to date. My point is to show how the "shorthand" language and text design that result from the pragmatic requirements of news discourse may end up shaping public debate and even actions on important issues. The pragmatic implications of discourse rules become especially significant when the underlying propositions of the language of a news story become linked to more divisive issues within the culture in which the discourse is situated.

To illustrate the features and implications of boilerplate and other types of background or explanatory material, I will use examples from a corpus of stories that dealt with a major hot-button issue in California in 1994—Proposition 187, a ballot measure that, as it has been described, "banned state benefits and public education for illegal immigrants," and whose implications are in the news to this very day. I will also make reference to another ballot measure passed two years later in 1996, which banned preferences in hiring and other situations based on race and gender. This measure, Proposition 209, known variously and somewhat problematically as the anti-affirmative action or anti-quotas measure, or California Civil Rights Initiative, is often linked with Prop. 187 in terms of its social impacts and underlying racist presuppositions. This ideological link was forged in the in-between, non-election year, 1995.[1]

All of the articles in the corpus appeared in the three major California papers, the *Los Angeles Times,* the *San Francisco Chronicle,* and the *Sacramento Bee,* from June through November of 1994 and 1996, with selective sampling in 1995, and were collected using the Lexis-Nexis database. More than 2,000 articles are in the corpus, from which examples have been selected primarily to illustrate fundamental issues concerning boilerplate.

I begin with a discussion of the requirements for well-formed news discourse that motivate the use of boilerplate and help to construct its genre conventions. Then I outline and illustrate the defining characteristics of boilerplate in terms of content and structure. Finally, I consider the implications of boilerplate as a textual device that reports and thus represents the world to its readers. This work is intended to underscore the value of looking at media discourse as a multifunctional, interactionally grounded system (Cotter, Unpublished), and to show how one textual component is revealing of the complex relationship of journalists, their texts, and their audiences and the emergence of public understanding of social and political issues.

Requirements of news discourse. Reporters, who comprise their own discourse community and thus share norms of interaction across the profession, are grounded in the principles of reporting and editing, or the selection and presentation of information about the world, in ways that nonjournalists are not (Cotter 1999). They learn, internalize, reproduce, and reinforce "ways of speaking" that are indigenous to the journalism profession. In terms of worldview, a reporter in Florida would likely have more in common with a colleague in Alaska than he or she would with someone behind them in line in the grocery store in Tampa or Anchorage. Indeed, there is a mismatch between how the public perceives what journalists do and how journalists view their craft. This mismatch has been substantiated empirically by an ambitious "credibility" research project initiated by the American Society of Newspaper Editors (see ASNE 1999 and Woo 1999).

Academic researchers traditionally have focused on examining the media from the public or end-user perspective. It is important to expand our knowledge of how the media works by taking an ethnographic approach, as I do here, to better understand what communicative behaviors constitute membership in the professional community and to consider how journalistic practice intentionally or not relates to the public. Explicitly or implicitly, a well-socialized journalist knows the requirements behind producing a good news story. These requirements vary according to story genre; for example, there is more latitude in a feature story and even more in a column, and the least flexibility in a news story, a correlation that intensifies according to the extent of controversy. On the textual level, then, the rules that involve simplification, neutrality, and provision of sufficient explanatory information—operating factors behind the production of all stories—also lead to the production of boilerplate.

Simplification. The injunction to simplify derives from the general rule of brevity. Daily, a reporter is charged with grasping the significant particulars about a complex situation, synthesizing those particulars, and writing accessibly about them—with a minimum number of words, often in a minimum amount of time, and for readers with a minimum amount of time and attention. For example, the descriptions of Propositions 187 and 209 in all three of the newspapers in the study amounted to a couple of short paragraphs at most, as subsequent examples will show, whereas the language of the propositions themselves were much lengthier and reproduced in entirety, as a public document, in the paper usually once or twice during the election season.

Distance. Another interactional and thus discursive goal is to maintain an authoritative distance between reporter and story. Through discursive means a reporter should convey a sense of distance—of relation and ideology—between him- or herself and the material being reported. I call this the Principle of Neutral Authority, because the reporter adhering to the profession's ethical code will attempt to be neutral or balanced—to speak from a more distanced institutional or professional position rather than a personal one. This effort simultaneously supports the authority of the report as a compiled, vetted, multisourced, and neutralized text and suppresses the potential perspective of the reporter as an individual self.

Various textual strategies allow manifestation of this principle, which tie into linguistic assessments of evidentiality, or the distribution of responsibility for knowledge or the claims of an utterance (a relation that invites discussion beyond what I provide here). The principle in particular governs lexical choices and influences the use of quoted material. Value-laden words relating to the ballot initiatives are supposed to be eliminated or marked. For example, before propositions are assigned numbers, like 187 or 209, they are given identificatory names by their authors—typically, names that frame the initiative so as to appeal to particular voters. By using quotation marks and phrases like "so-called" and "dubbed" when referring to these names, the reporter marks that portion of the utterance, distancing the journalist from the partisan conceptual context with which the meaning of the word or phrase is associated, as in the following examples:

(1a) *8/4/95 Chronicle*: The ideological divide was most evident on the issue of illegal immigration, the subject of November's Proposition 187, the *"Save Our State"* initiative.

(1b) *8/12/94 Bee*: Venegas said he opposes Proposition 187, the *so-called* "Save our State" measure set for the November ballot that seeks to deny public education and social and health services—except for emergency medical care—to undocumented immigrants.

(1c) *8/15/94 LAT*: In addition, the council will consider endorsing Proposition 187 on the November ballot. The controversial initiative, *dubbed* Save Our State, would bar illegal immigrants from receiving public schooling, non-emergency health care and social services.

The examples in (1) illustrate the use of particularly identifiable and obvious distancing devices. The quotative nature of these devices, like quotes themselves, represents the material as coming from the source, and not the reporter.

Background. Another discourse requirement is to provide necessary background. In the case of long-running stories that appear before the public frequently, or in stories that have been out of the public eye for a long while, this background material—sometimes referred to as boilerplate by the general public as well as journalists—is used as an efficient way of getting readers up-to-date. Boilerplate, defined by its unreflective, unoriginal replications, works in conjunction with the fact that reporters are to assume that each day's readers are unfamiliar with the previous material, and yet they must also simultaneously background the previous information *and* highlight the new information.

As a story progresses over time, relatively little attention is given to boilerplate by reporters or editors if it is factually accurate. Boilerplate allows different reporters to cover a story at different points because it is assumed to be a comprehensive, neutralized summary of the main issues of the story to date—it is assumed to be given or rhemic information—and is repetitively inserted into stories. Boilerplate is one textual aid that allows reporters to focus on breaking news or to develop a new angle without having to do all the reporting work from scratch.

The placement of boilerplate, in modifying clauses on first-mention and in paragraphs at or near the end of a story (where, if necessary, they could be cut), demonstrates its secondary importance to the main angle of the story and allows an easy apprehension of the story's given-new hierarchical relation, as example (2) shows.

(2) *8/14/94 LAT*: Supporters and opponents of the Nov. 8 ballot measure—*which would deny schooling, non-emergency health care and other public benefits to illegal immigrants*—have spent the summer gearing up countywide campaigns aimed at winning over voters.

The underlined material is the background material, set apart from the main framing of the story not only by the clausal structure of the sentence, but also by punctuational means, through use of the dashes.

The discourse rules noted here work together in the construction of boilerplate, which represents an extreme distillation of the simplicity rule as it eases the textual workload and reader comprehension: active goals of the newswriting enterprise. Its characteristic generic, non-evaluative, and non-attributed format, as well as its subsidiary and thus expendable relation to the *current* installment of the story (its rhemic nature means it becomes optional in relation to more salient issues, such as newness) follows the Principle of Neutral Authority. Additionally, the summary structure of boilerplate as a piece or pieces of text repeated almost verbatim from story to story allows unmarked repetition over time, also easing the work of comprehension. But what boilerplate allows a reporter to achieve in relation to the larger requirements for the story (primarily those relating to newness) and for reader comprehension may have other consequences, which invite examination, particularly when the story is controversial.

Features of boilerplate. Reporters are taught explicitly about presenting background and context within a story, and, indeed, students in beginning newswriting classes often have difficulty interpreting what counts as contextual and necessary and what is expendable, as some sorts of background material often are. Unsurprisingly, this difficulty occurs even when novices are provided textbook definitions that describe background in part as "material placed in the story that explains the event, traces its development and adds facts that sources have not provided" (Mencher 1996: 252). This writing facility problem suggests that to be viewed as communicatively competent (and employable), a reporter must consciously learn the full range of conventionalized aspects of newswriting. Sacrificing chronology of events to the highlighting of the most newsworthy aspect of a story is a primary rhetorical characteristic of news genres, one that a reporter must learn how to do successfully, and one that also serves as a constraint on background or boilerplate material.

Boilerplate, because of its often "canned" nature, can be viewed as a particular, more conventionalized form of background. Mencher's definition refers to the explanatory, additive, and chronological nature of background—necessary to the extent that its addition makes news-of-the-moment intelligible. To call something "boilerplate" suggests additional features: it is repetitious, unattributed, identificatory, descriptive, often expendable, and summarizes what have been interpreted as key "complicating actions" of a story (to refer to and to situate news discourse in Labov's [1972] narrative framework).

The following paragraph from the April 27, 1999, *San Francisco Chronicle* will stand as a reference example (3a) of boilerplate from which I will make other comparisons:

> (3a) Proposition 187 bars illegal immigrants from receiving social services and government-paid nonemergency health care. Federal law already forbids them getting those benefits.
>
> The measure also bars illegal immigrants from public schools, even though the U.S. Supreme Court has ruled that unconstitutional.

Example (3a) bears structural and informational resemblance to examples (1b), (1c), and (2), illustrating one feature of boilerplate: it is *repetitious*. Almost every example in the pre- and post-election corpus, as well as randomly selected 1999 stories, contain mention of the following informational components down to the very words chosen:

- illegal (or undocumented) immigrants
- deny (or bar, ban, restrict)
- health, schooling, social services (or public benefits)

The examples also show how the boilerplate summary is repetitious: from story to story, both across newspapers and within newspapers, and across time. Additionally, this information is *not attributed* to a source, another characterizing feature. Attribution is a primary discourse requirement of a news story, except in cases of common knowledge, and boilerplate is thus viewed by the reporter—and viewable by the reader—as received information. Further, these examples show the *identificatory* positioning of boilerplate. Boilerplate identifies or describes what has occurred, avoiding interpreting or explaining, which allows brevity and repetition. Because it refers to the most observable, concrete aspects of a story, it is more *descriptive* than evaluative. It *summarizes* the story's key events (as in disaster, accident, or crime coverage) or the main necessary propositional information to date (as in coverage of government or legal news). Example (3a), from 1999, contains information similar to examples (1b), (1c), and (2), from 1994. But after the measure passed in 1994, and challenges were subsequently filed in court, the measure's legal relationships were highlighted in news stories, and thus the 1999 example (3a) contains relevant additional phrases as listed in (3b), which themselves are unattributed, identificatory, descriptive, and summarizing:

(3b) Federal law already forbids them getting those benefits. . . . even though the U.S. Supreme Court has ruled that unconstitutional.

The physical-conceptual placement of boilerplate within the structure of a news story also positions it as background and allows for its potential *expendability*. It is material that can easily be cut to fit the fluctuating exigencies of the "news hole," the space allotted for that day's stories. Most boilerplate is placed near the bottom of the story[2] where it can be cut (or ignored) if necessary without sacrificing the completeness of the story. For instance, example (3a) represents paragraphs 14 and 15 in a 17-paragraph story. (Final paragraphs 16 and 17 contain additional background material, dating from after the election in which Proposition 187 passed; extra material is usually presented in continuing stories if there is sufficient space.)

I have also considered the nature of the summarizing material appearing on first reference, which could be termed "first-reference boilerplate," as in examples (4a) and (4b), which are separated by nearly five years:

(4a) *8/13/94 Chronicle*: San Francisco's Social Services Commission voted unanimously Thursday to support a resolution by Supervisors Susan Leal and Tom Hsieh that would oppose Proposition 187, *which would deny public benefits to illegal immigrants.*

(4b) *4/27/99 Chronicle*: While the whisperers and fingerpointers worked the Capitol corridors and phone lines, the federal appeals court accepted Davis' request for the mediator, a low-key method of handling the court challenge to the 1994 measure, *which banned state benefits and public education for illegal immigrants.*

When repetitious, unattributed, identifying material appears on first reference in the story itself, it is often in a modifying clause at the end of a paragraph, as in (4a) and (4b). Modifying clauses are easy to cut, often gaining the copy editor (who will generally do the cutting) an extra line. But given its informational value in first-reference position, this would be the last resort and only if the copy editor assumed a general knowledge within the readership. Interestingly, only stories in the corpus that appeared *after* the elections and passage of the propositions regularly eliminated first-reference boilerplate, suggesting that journalists were assuming a fair degree of shared knowledge on the part of readers (and pointing up the journalists' own mutable view of carefulness, affected when something is officially or ritually disputed or under contention, as all electoral contests are).

There is even a hierarchical relationship within boilerplate itself, which relates to expendability. The information in (3b), by its very location in the text—at the end of a paragraph, in a modifying clause at the end of a paragraph—is positioned as possibly expendable and thus subsidiary to the primary summary (see [3a]), which has been integral to the Proposition 187 story from its beginnings. This relationship is made clearer in example (5), which more extensively shows the text from which examples (3a) and (3b) are extracted. Example (5) also illustrates the extent to which boilerplate is restricted as to *placement,* and points to the distinctions between boilerplate and background elements secondary to the story. Note that the underlined material in the example marks the primary summary of the issue, which predates the election, and the italicized material marks the additional facts of the issue, which occurred after the election. The most recent development in the story—the reason for publication—is marked by boldface type in the lead or first paragraph.

(5) *4/17/99 Chronicle*

HEADLINE:

Point Driven Home In *Prop. 187* Feud

Davis, Bustamante at odds over how to handle appeal of case

PARAGRAPH (#)

(1) SACRAMENTO—A **feud** sparked by differences over *Proposition 187* between Governor Gray Davis and Lieutenant Governor Cruz

—> *lead, new* Bustamante took a **new turn yesterday over parking.**

(2—5) [. . .]

(6) While the whisperers and fingerpointers worked the Capitol corridors and phone lines, the federal appeals court accepted Davis' request for the mediator, a low-key method of handling the court challenge to the *1994 measure, which banned state benefits and public education for illegal immigrants.*

(7) *Nearly all of Proposition 187, passed by 59 percent of voters, has been blocked by U.S. District Court Judge Mariana Pfaelzer in Los Angeles.*

(8–13) [...]

(14) *Proposition 187 bars illegal immigrants from receiv-*
ing social services and government-paid nonemer-
gency health care. Federal law already forbids them
getting those benefits.

(15) *The measure also bars illegal immigrants from public*
schools, even though the U.S. Supreme Court has
ruled that unconstitutional.

(16) *Pfaelzer blocked the ban from taking effect, saying*
that regulating immigration is solely the job of the fed-
eral government.

(17) *Davis said mediation would allow the state and*
the measure's opponents a chance to negotiate a
settlement.

The first five paragraphs of the story develop the lead, or new aspect of the ongoing story. Paragraph 6 is interesting as it relates the immediate situation of the parking feud ("While the whisperers and fingerpointers worked the Capitol corridors") to the current status of the proposition (it is in mediation) and reminds readers what the proposition (passed in 1994, five years earlier) was designed to do. It is in a pre-emptive position: the reader must not be left too long to wonder about the relation of Prop. 187 to the immediate story. Nonetheless, the clause in the last sentence of paragraph 6 highlights the given or rhemic nature of the information, implying a status as background shared by the majority. As first-reference boilerplate, the clause contains identificatory elements that have gone along with the story since its inception ("ban," "benefits," "illegal immigrants"), mentioned in the examples in (1). Paragraph 7 builds on the background function of the text and the preceding paragraph, summarizing the court challenge, the most salient dimension of the story since the election.

Paragraph 7's position in relation to the identificatory material reaffirms the temporal order of the story, which serves reader comprehension and narrative coherence, and, by its second-order placement, also marks the identificatory facet of the proposition in Paragraph 6 as essential and possibly immutable. This pattern is repeated in the concluding paragraphs (paragraphs 8 through 13 develop the feud story line) and follows the general order of the "inverted pyramid," the basic structure of news texts in which information is placed in diminishing order of importance or salience, the least important in last place. The story could easily be cut after paragraph 13 and still be well-formed; indeed, it could be cut after paragraphs 6 or 7 and still count as a fully fledged news story. Of course, what is cut out—either on the page at any optional moment or in the formulation of boilerplate as a standardized summary—influences what information the public has access to.

Implications of boilerplate. Boilerplate has implications for public understanding as it both responds to and frames the nature of a news story and its social entailments. Beyond its role in information structure affecting the reader and the public record, boilerplate also has a bearing on the reporter's own position in relation to the information being reported. It supports the ideology or professional stance of "being a reporter," because it marks a form of neutrality and distance. It is contingent—on the story process, its placement, and expendability—creating various editing options depending on what else needs to be addressed that day. It is only a partially representative summary that is never overtly evaluative. Nonetheless, boilerplate as read or interpreted by both reporter and reader serves to background what can be viewed as a more covert evaluative dimension that may be embedded within the text and within the production of news.

Given and new status. Boilerplate's reflection of the general rules of well-formed news discourse as well as its unique characteristic features jointly support the backgrounding of what is presented. This backgrounding essentially renders uncontested (or incontestable) the information it sets apart, making the issue of given information key when one considers how the structure of texts and the meaning of their constituent parts have an impact on public understanding.

Boilerplate is essentially information about some facet of the story that predates the new angle being freshly reported; it is given or rhemic information that is assumed to be generally known but cannot be left out because it explicitly gives background or a history of the issue to date. As the given information that accompanies stories that are long-running, boilerplate is a standard textual element because reporters are always to assume a new and uninformed audience at the same time they must background the previously presented material and foreground the new information. Not knowing what prior discourse the audience has had access to, the reporter has boilerplate as a tool to serve a multifunctional discourse purpose. Its features (repetition, nonattribution, identification, structural placement) lead to an interpretation of genericness that allows a reader to either skim or ignore the information as given at the same time it can be read for its informational value by a first-time or forgetful reader. Either way, the framing of the issue, as we have seen in the example case of Prop. 187 in two different years, becomes part of the public record. If a story is an ongoing one, as most stories that have an impact on the sociopolitical sphere are, the preliminary depiction of the issue gets replicated and repeated through boilerplate.

The neutral authority model. Reporters spend a fair amount of professional and thus discursive energy distancing themselves from the claims, propositions, narratives, and beliefs they are reporting on. Concurrently, an utterance has more credibility when it is directly or indirectly viewed as coming from a source other than the reporter, hence the tremendous emphasis placed on attribution of information. The reporter thus positions himself or herself as a neutral authority, using professional identity and the resources of the text to do so. As mentioned earlier, the principle of neutral authority would account for words such as "so-called" or "dubbed," as in "Prop. 187, dubbed the Save Our State initiative." These quotative textual markers isolate the phrase that follows as not of the journalist's creation— "Save Our State" and its accompanying "SOS" acronym are value judgments. These textual devices (including scare-quotes) allow the perpetuation of a neutral authority and distance the reporter from the evaluative stance of the source.

Of course, despite the professional-ideological constraints governing personal affiliations to the matters being reported, the boundary between social self and professional self is semi-permeable, as are the issues of authorship in the discursive process of reporting the news in which one story is the outcome of many contributing participants. Boilerplate, despite the features that lead to a generic or neutral reading, nonetheless owes its origin to the primary framing of an issue. In the case of a ballot measure, the authors of a ballot proposition provide a baseline definition of an issue, creating and setting the terms for debate against this baseline. Given the source of what ends up as boilerplate, the use of "neutral" or unattributed information can better be seen as representing the journalist's *intention* to hold to a neutral authority model rather than instantiating a neutral authority alone.

Contingencies in the story process. The majority of news stories are keyed to cycles—seasonal, economic, legislative, historical, meteorological, and so on— and their coverage becomes routinized (Cotter, to appear). There are markers (constructed by either the journalist's world or the larger social world) in the process of reporting over time that influence how a story is reported. (Thanksgiving travel stories, which involve large numbers of Americans and play simultaneously to reader interest and journalistic news values of importance and effect, are a case in point.) In the case of a ballot initiative, election day becomes a defining event in the story process.

Boilerplate is contingent on the story process as it unfolds over time and changes to meet changing informational needs. There were substantive changes in the presentation of boilerplate after the elections, when modifying clauses after first mention—as in examples (1a) through (1c)—fall off and acronyms such as CCRI (the California Civil Rights Initiative) or SOS (Save Our State) to refer to propositions 209 and 187 all but disappear. One could hypothesize that after the proposition becomes ratified by voters, its presence becomes unmarked and viewable as shared knowledge; or that editors and reporters are less careful. More care is generally taken with stories before an election—by reporters *and* editors—because of the potential loss of credibility and a status as neutral authority, which newspapers (and individual reporters) want to maintain.

Boilerplate usage changes not only in response to actual events, but also in connection with developing social attitudes. In fact, the meaning of Prop. 187 and its implications changed over time from a legislative proposition with specific consequences for a specific group of people to a symbolic marker that invoked a larger and more abstract set of social meanings. The related stories that ran in 1995, the year after the proposition's passage, began to cite Prop. 187 in passing as tangential to the main point of whatever the current story was—as a way to illustrate what was viewed as a general decline in tolerance, particularly toward immigrants and minority communities generally. In this way, Prop. 187, which was viewed by detractors as punitive and racist, became linked to the next election cycle's Prop. 209, itself viewed by detractors as racist and exclusionary. The boilerplate remained the same, but the contingencies of its use changed. Boilerplate can thus be viewed as a highly contingent and situated discourse element on a number of levels.

Partial representation. Related to its contingent status, boilerplate is only a partial representation of the fuller meaning of what it is characterizing. Although it does not carry an overt evaluative stance, it offers a position by its presence. I have already noted that boilerplate in Prop. 187 coverage functions to identify the proposition by articulating what it will do (limit benefits for a particular segment of the population). This information is drawn from the actual language of the ballot initiative, which itself does not include the social agenda or rationale of its authors. The implications of Prop. 187 are not included within the boundaries of boilerplate because implications are evaluative and therefore not compatible with "neutral," unattributed information.

There are a number of features of Prop. 187 that seldom appear in the majority of the hundreds of summaries (i.e., background and boilerplate) presented in the three California papers. These include the following:

- that it is a measure to get federal attention with the hopes of changing national immigration policy,
- that federal laws would supersede the state initiative (this fact comes out in boilerplate well after the election, as example (5) shows,
- who the detractors and supporters of the measure are,
- the fiscal impacts,
- the partial unanimity across the opposing camps that the issue of illegal immigration needs to be addressed,
- the most dire implications raised by either side (at their worst: zero-sum diminution of life-as-we-know-it vs. diseased, uneducated, underserved underclass), and

- its relation to other events and anti-immigrant attitudes from California's recent past, such as Japanese-American internment during World War II.

These details, which are less identification and more socially complex, are often relegated to invisibility because they are not currently "new," and because they cannot easily be summarized without all the apparatus of proper reporting (e.g., balance, attribution, fairness to all positions, fresh quotes), they go unrepeated. Example (6) from the *Los Angeles Times* shows the points that are seldom raised or represented in boilerplate about Prop. 187 (issues under debate, jobs and the border, and the viewpoints of authorities outside of the political sphere):

> (6) *8/10/94 LAT*: But even as polls show the measure gathering widespread support among voters, its very *premise*—that public services and schools draw illegal immigrants—remains a matter of fierce *debate*. The initiative doesn't directly address *jobs*, widely considered by *scholars and other authorities* to be the principal lure for immigrants. Nor does Proposition 187 do anything about the porous U.S.–Mexico *border*.

One could also look at the presence of boilerplate in relation to a host of intertwined agendas, themselves inherently partial. Proponents and detractors have their own complicated political agendas, which become the content of what is reported, while journalists themselves, under the mantle of neutral authority, have a stated position of balance that is intended to supersede personal political agendas. But the issue of balance itself is a negotiated and conventionalized notion, entailing a certain *kind* of balance: getting an equal number of (two) sides; quoting the originator of a claim, which is preferable to a third-party spokesperson quote; verifying and testing claims against the other side; giving the person singled out a chance to respond, to voice another view.

From this perspective, journalistic partiality is rarely overt and instead becomes reflective of a mainstream orientation to a topic and of professional practice. But as the requirements of discourse stand, the neutrality or balance rules sometimes work against balance when the issue is complicated and the meanings are negotiable or contested. This is where journalists can pause: Not only are assumptions embedded within boilerplate, but more importantly, the summary of story is only partial. It is good to keep this in mind: the elements of a "complete," well-formed news story represent an interpretation of what is considered important—on the journalistic level as well as on the level of shared, public knowledge.

Discourse-level evaluation. Although every effort may be made to eliminate value judgments on the levels of semantics and journalistic practice, there are discourse-level issues that can be seen as privileging an evaluative stance because they inherently contextualize information and how it may be interpreted. Quotes and repetition are two components of narrative structure that orient an audience to the material being presented. I have already mentioned the relation between the repetition of boilerplate and given vs. new information. From the journalistic perspective, repetition might be better viewed not so much a reinforcement of the propositions, but as a way of marking elements of the story so that a reader has what he or she needs to process the news of the moment—the emphasis being on what is new and not on what is comprehensive.

The use of quotes by reporters serves not only to disavow responsibility for an utterance but to sometimes also point to a frame of reference or perspective that cannot be expressed personally or within the parameters of the reporter's textual participation (otherwise the "intrusion" or violation of expected norms will be noted by editors and disallowed before it reaches print). In the Prop. 187 coverage, restricted material such as the rare overtly racist or "politically incorrect" comment by sources was carried within quotations, as in examples (7a) and (7b).

> (7a) *8/10/94 LAT:* "Illegal *aliens* are killing us in California," said Ronald Prince, a Tustin accountant who heads the Proposition 187 campaign. "Those who support illegal immigration are, in effect, *anti-American.*"

> (7b) *8/13/94 LAT: "Thanks for sticking up for white people!"* says a call-in listener from Del Mar Vista to Buck's radio show, pleased with the host's support of Proposition 187, which would take away most public benefits to illegal immigrants. [Note: the caller is being ironic.]

Even so, reporters may be so grounded within the professional ethic in which quotes are predominantly viewed and used as distancing devices that they do not also see another perspective: that reporters are co-responsible—along with the speaker being quoted—for the content they produce, including their choice of what they include within quoted material (cf. Tannen 1990). But the responsibility does not only reside with the reporter and newsmaker. If the quote is an implicit way reporters can present information about the participants in a story without violating the discourse-level norms governing news writing or the reporter's own perceived role in the discourse, the reader is also implicated. The reader becomes part of the inferential process, distributing responsibility for the construction of meaning beyond the newsroom and into the living room (or coffee shop or commuter train).

Failing to directly point out a potentially discriminatory reading in a source's comment or quote would not be viewed as unbalanced or irresponsible to most journalists, but an exercise of First Amendment rights by all involved, provided that the competing perspective is also offered. But it may also be viewed as reprehensible by others, including a significant portion of the public for whom the balancing routines and evidentiality processes of journalism practice are not made explicit.

Conclusion. The discourse requirement to provide accessible synopses and background information in news stories leads to textual elements like "boilerplate" and other shorthand devices of reference. General journalistic writing rules—simplification of complex issues or events, authorial distance and the value of neutrality or balance, and the recurrence of sufficient given information to render all new versions of a story intelligible by the majority of intended readers—guide the production of boilerplate, which has intrinsic characteristics. It is repetitious, unattributed, identifies and describes, summarizes, and is potentially expendable as text.

Nonetheless, there are implications for the transmission of meaning that are inherent in even the most innocuous or expendable forms of text. For example, Santa Ana (1999) argues that the issues of immigration were formulated rhetorically by journalists to ultimately minimize humanitarian responses in discussions of Prop. 187, whether it was consciously intended or not. These meanings, which likely extended beyond journalists' intentions, were also potently mediating with social values held by the larger public collective (the proposition, after all, was voted in). Nonetheless, they are potentially replicated in each iteration of the story because background material—which carries the story's history over time—is seldom challenged on behalf of its content. Boilerplate, for its part, contributes just as significantly to the orientation of the public debate as does the lead and other textual components of a story.

Because boilerplate assists in responding to and framing the nature of public discourse, it is worth noticing by journalists, linguists, and the public. Like all linguistic and discursive elements situated contextually, it plays a multilevel role in shaping social action. Considered generic and uncontested information, boilerplate is also a textual device that allows the reporter to distance authorially from the material and helps establish the professional persona of a neutral authority. As a summarizing mechanism, it only partially represents what it is characterizing, a feature that may have greater significance when the issue is complicated, socially contested, and relates to issues of authority, power, and responsibility in society.

On their own, mainstream journalists generally resist changing or tinkering with the rules that they perceive as supporting free speech. But perhaps linguists can argue the point for them, by pointing out the rituals and routines of news production and texts, exploring the connection of text-level behaviors to social meaning, and thereby bringing the discussion to another footing—one that could offer alternative readings and meanings in the presentation of contested issues to the public.

REFERENCES

American Society of Newspaper Editors (ASNE). 1999. *Examining our credibility: Perspectives of the public and the press.* Reston, VA.: ASNE.
Cotter, Colleen. 1999. Language and the news media: Five facts about the Fourth Estate. In Rebecca S. Wheeler (ed.), *The workings of language: From prescriptions to perspectives.* Westport, CN: Praeger.
Cotter, Colleen. Unpublished. *News values, news practice: Shaping the language of the news.*
Labov, William. 1972. *Language in the inner city.* Philadelphia: University of Pennsylvania Press.
Mencher, Melvin. 1996. *News reporting and writing.* New York: McGraw-Hill.
Santa Ana, Otto. 1999. Like an animal I was treated: Anti-immigrant metaphor in U.S. public discourse. *Discourse and Society* 10(2): 191–224.
Tannen, Deborah. 1990. *Talking voices: Repetition, dialogue, and imagery in conversational discourse.* Studies in Interactional Sociolinguistics 6. Cambridge: Cambridge University Press.
Woo, William. 1999. Credibility is built by a *paper,* not just a newsroom. *The American Editor* (May–June): 7–8, 26.

NOTES

1. Stories in the 1995 corpus illustrate this link, although I will not discuss it here. Additionally, I use Prop. 209 only as a point of comparison at this stage, although it is worth examining in the context of the subject of boilerplate and its ramifications.
2. News practitioners' use of the metaphorical term "bottom," rather than "end," suggests a physical, spatial orientation to the story rather than a more *literarily* narrative one—another difference between the perceptions of practitioners and nonjournalistic writers. With a different metaphorical frame in operation, the entailments for the text and how to shape it would also vary.

Involuntary language loss among immigrants: Asian-American linguistic autobiographies

Leanne Hinton
University of California at Berkeley

Despite the fact that some 97% of the American population knows English "very well" or "well," according to the 1990 census, there is a constant fear expressed by various public figures that the English language is somehow endangered in the United States, and the only way for English to maintain its status is for other languages to disappear. Despite decades of research findings to the contrary, a large portion of the American public, the educational system, and the government believe that bilingualism is both bad for children and unpatriotic, and that the only way to be a true American is to leave behind any other language and allegiance that might be in your background.

As we will see in this paper, children also buy into this belief system—both long-term Americans and immigrant children. Yet at the same time, there is a strong feeling among immigrant families that it is important to maintain ties with the old country and to maintain the heritage language. Among the children of immigrant parents, this conflict between assimilation and heritage maintenance is played out in various ways at different stages of life. I look at the ages between birth and college—only the beginning of life, but the most important time in terms of language development. This paper is based on a set of about 250 "linguistic autobiographies" of Asian-American college students, done over the last several years in a class at the University of California at Berkeley. Quotes from the autobiographies themselves make up the heart of this paper. In this self-reporting mode, we see the human, rather than the political, side of language shift.[1]

It is usually the goal of the parents for their children to be bilingual: to learn English fluently but not forget their heritage language. To the parents' disappointment (and ultimately to the regret of the child, as we shall see) this goal is only rarely fully achieved. We will see that it is commonplace that fluency in the first language declines as English improves, so that by the end of the high school years, the child is a semi-speaker of his heritage language at best. I will examine the pattern of language shift that takes place in the young first- or second-generation student, and why this shift takes place. I look at the kinds of efforts made by families to keep the heritage language strong, and why they are usually

doomed to failure. I also examine those relatively rare people who have succeeded in becoming bilingual, and what happened to make it work for them. Finally, I discuss policy implications.

Parental goals. Immigrant parents have relatives, friends, a lifetime of associations and customs in their home country, and perhaps generations of family
history there. They may even intend to return someday. Often, the families see
their arrival in the United States not as an abandonment of their old country but
rather as a process of making a bridge between the two countries. The language of
their country may be the language the family has spoken since time immemorial.
Typically, the parents want their children to adapt to the United States, but at the
same time retain the knowledge and values of the old country as well.

> Our family was the first one [among our kin] to leave the main-
> land of South Korea. The day we left for United States, every-
> body was pretty emotional at the airport, but I remember one
> single thing my aunt shouted down the airport corridor (in Ko-
> rean), "Don't forget Korean!" (K-9)

Learning English. The most frequent experience of the students has been
that they knew little or no English when they started school in the United States.

> At the age of ten, my family on my mother's side immigrated to
> America and this is when I learned my second language. Going
> to school made me feel deaf, mute, and blind. I could under-
> stand nothing that was going on around me. (C-6)

> Although I did know some useful phrases, such as, "Could
> you prease point to the bathroom?" and "Sorry, I don't speake
> any Engrish," besides those handy phrases, I survived the first
> few months by utilizing the art of hand gestures and various
> body language. (K-9)

> I was not able to communicate well at first. Smiling was the
> best language for me to show other Americans. Whenever I didn't
> understand, I smiled. I felt stupid, but I didn't look bad. (K-18)

> I came to the United States when I was just ready to begin
> preschool and the only language I spoke was Hindi. My first ex-
> posure to American-English was with another young Indian girl.
> She spoke only in English and I only in Hindi, but amazingly
> enough the language barrier was unable to prevent us from some-

how communicating and playing games. However, when I went home, I remember feeling bad for the girl because I thought she had a language deficiency and could not speak. I thought Hindi was the universal medium of communication and the concept of speaking a different language was unfathomable. (I-5)

Language shock. The students entering school without knowing English often undergo shock and depression.

I started as an eighth grader in a junior high school and soon my burning desire and hope of a brilliant novel life [in America] began to fade away. I faced an unexpected obstacle of miscommunication between my fellow students and teachers. Back in Korea, I and my friends thought that after living in the U.S. for only [a few] months, you would be perfectly fluent in English. . . . But soon I found out that several years of studying English is needed to speak it fluently. Unprepared to meet the dilemma, I was quite depressed and in a condition of despair for the beginning year. . . . I used to be very active and popular in my school in Korea and here I was nothing. (K-6).

I got my very first impression of the American culture and language at third grade. I went to an elementary school where there were virtually no Asians and predominately whites. At first, I was excited to see kids with blond hair and pale colored skin like those people in the movies. However, my excitement didn't last long as I began to realize that there was no way I could communicate with them because I spoke no English at all. I began to dread going to school the few months in America. I was so miserable because all the kids looked at me as if I was a monkey in the zoo. I didn't have any friends at all because nobody spoke Chinese. How I longed to go back to Taiwan and to see familiar faces and to hear my native language being spoken. I never expected so much difficulties in assimilating into a brand new culture with a brand new language. (C-64)

ESL. Virtually no one who wrote these autobiographies had ever been in a bilingual education program, showing that despite all the controversy about bilingual education, true bilingual education programs are a rare breed, at least for Asian Americans. For some children, however, ESL (English as a Second Language) classes were available in school.

> Thirteen years ago, my family and I escaped from communist Vietnam and arrived at Michigan, USA. At that moment, we found ourselves lost in a new environment where no one spoke Chinese, the only language that we knew. It was a tremendously hard task to communicate with anyone. Fortunately, our church sponsor felt it necessary for my sister, brother, and I to be enrolled in school to learn English, the impossible foreign language then. The administrators gave me a program, English As A Second Language, to aid me in learning English. I was gradually acquainted with this peculiar language, and within one year, my attendance at school allowed me to communicate in English a little. (C-8)

The general impression one gets from the autobiographies is that there is a hodge-podge of approaches to teaching English. Many schools are inadequately prepared for the students who needed to learn English, and some bizarre solutions were offered at times:

> When I started kindergarten, I did not know how to speak the English language. I didn't even know my own name in English. (Pretty sad, huh?) . . . The only [classes] offered to non-English speakers were ESL for Spanish speakers and Sign Language for the deaf. Since I couldn't be put in the ESL classes, I was taught sign language. That was the only way I knew how to communicate with all the white people who talked so differently than myself. Gradually I began to learn English from my classmates. (K-39)

Television. There are several other sources from which children learn English as well. Chief among these are television and friends. On television:

> Until the age of abut four, I spoke entirely in Korean with my parents. Shortly thereafter, I rapidly began to learn English. Television shows, like *Sesame Street* and *Mister Roger's Neighborhood* greatly contributed to my learning process. The English sounds that had once been so foreign before soon became my own. (K-16)

> For a couple of months [as a newcomer to the U.S. who spoke no English] I continued my cartoon ritual. Cartoons served as my foothold into English, and I understood more and more as the weeks passed. For a brief, interesting while my vo-

cabulary consisted of words and phrases like "x-ray vision," "transformation," and "radio controlled drones." American television helped me learn English, but more importantly it eased the shock of transition as I struggled to bring American culture into harmony with my Chinese identity. (C-15)

In our household we use Mandarin mainly, but we watch Taiwanese-speaking or English-speaking programs as well. Ninety-five percent of the programs are with Chinese subtitles, and I personally think that's a great way to learn a language. We use the subtitle machine which is for deaf people to know what's going on on the television, to improve our English listening ability when we just arrive this country, and this helps us understanding videos and shows much better. (C-65)

Friends. Friends may play the biggest role of all in helping children learn English.

One day I found my first true friend in the states. His name was Jason and he was Hispanic. He liked me for who I was, not where I came from. He was not only my best friend but also my teacher. He always invited me to his house and taught me English. I guess if it wasn't for him, I would have really had a hard time adapting to the new language. (K-2)

When I was in junior high in the United States [having arrived at age 14], I hardly had any Korean friends. I had a couple of American friends who I played with all the time. One of them was a deaf person. I learned some of the basic words in sign language, but most of the time I wrote him notes to communicate. Not having Korean friends helped me a lot to learn English fast. I was out of ESL by the end of 8th grade. (K-19)

The students often consciously cultivated friends who did not speak their language, in order to learn English better.

I avoided speaking Korean as much as I could. I started hanging out with people to whom I could speak English. (K-31)

There were a few Koreans who hanged around together and spoke Korean only. I thought I couldn't be able to speak English quickly if I started to hang around with those Koreans.

> So I played with English-speaking friends—mainly Chinese
> and Americans. (K-21).

In the zeal of the incoming children to learn English, sometimes mistakes
were made:

> I can still recall that during the first few weeks in my new
> school, I befriended a group of Vietnamese kids. Because I did
> not understand what they were saying, and that they looked
> Asian, I mistakenly assumed that they were ABCs (American-
> Born-Chinese) who couldn't speak any Chinese. So, in my ig-
> norance, I started to learn from them what I thought was
> English. (I did wonder why the "English" I was picking up
> from them sounded different from the one I was simultaneously
> learning in the classroom.) Not until later on in the semester,
> when I met a fellow Taiwanese immigrant, did he point out to
> me that my group of friends were speaking Vietnamese instead
> of English! (C-43)

Family involvement in the child's learning of English. The family helps the
children fight their battle toward English fluency. Siblings play an especially
important role in English acquisition: younger siblings always learn English at
an earlier age than older siblings, because the older siblings teach the younger
ones.

> I have two older sisters who started school before me, and my
> oldest sister still has memories of first starting school and not
> knowing the language. By the time I started school, it is possi-
> ble that I had already learned to speak English from my sisters
> who had learned it at school, because I can't particularly re-
> member being teased for not speaking English when I started
> preschool. . . . Therefore, I am certain that I picked up English
> before I started formal schooling thanks to the precedent of my
> two older sisters. (K-26)

Since (as will be shown below) the use of the heritage language at home is an
important factor in children retaining that language, parents have a conflict in
whether to use English at home or not. Even if they have not made a conscious
decision to use the heritage language at home for language maintenance purposes, they have other reasons not to use English. They may not know English
themselves or may speak with a heavy accent and grammatical errors that they
fear would be picked up by their children. Or, they may not know English well

enough to allow the intimate level of communication families enjoy. But while some families opt against the use of English at home, others play a big role in their children's English education—and of course all families support their children in whatever way they can toward the goal of English fluency.

> [D]uring my early years in L.A., my parents encouraged the use of English at home, both to help me, and to help themselves. Actually, my father didn't need much assistance—he was an English major in college, who actually considered teaching it in Korea. He was, and still is, a nearly perfect bilingual. My mother, on the other hand, was a completely different story. Being an extremely intelligent and proud woman, she didn't like the idea of her being "ignorant" in English. Thus, she watched cartoons and PBS shows like *Sesame Street* and *The Electric Company* with me. We were essentially learning English together.
>
> By the second grade, my English skills were proficient enough to enable me to skip the third grade. My parents had a lot to do with it. Even my mother's faculty in English had grown by leaps and bounds. She served at my elementary school as a teacher's aide, for my class in fact. So, she and I would go to school together and spend the whole day in each other's company. Our entire family was slowly, but surely, becoming a bilingual team. (K-23, arr. age 6)

First-language attrition. While some students, especially those that came as teenagers, still struggle to perfect their English even at college, most of their worst difficulties with the language are behind them, and they certainly know English well enough to have been admitted to a top American university. The majority of the students are dominant in English at this point in their lives but find that their heritage language has suffered. These heart-felt reminiscences are in keeping with findings at the other end of childhood by Wong Fillmore (1991), who looks at the stage when language attrition begins. This phenomenon of first-language attrition is discussed in almost everyone's writing about their personal language history. Here are a few statements about language loss selected out of dozens.

> My family immigrated to the United States on a summer's night of 1980 in search of the American dream. I remember that night clearly because as I stepped foot on to "American soil," I clung to my mother's arms and cried. Years later, my mother told me I

wept, "Let's go home, let's go home." That was fourteen years ago; home is now Torrance, California, Korea is now a place I vaguely remember and the Korean language is slowly slipping away from my tongue, day by day. (K-13, arrived age 6)

By the end of my first year in the U.S., I spoke English semi-fluently. And by the second year, I was totally "anglicized," with no joy from my parents because at the same time, my Korean speaking and writing ability was slowly deteriorating. (K-10, arrived age 8 or 9)

I can still vaguely remember possessing a stunning comprehension of Mandarin before I started school, but now, it has mostly left me. Often, since I have such perfect examples of pronunciation and grammar before me, I can mentally play a wonderful copy of what I want to say; when it comes out of my mouth, though, I can hear a semi-terrible American accent distorting my words. Sometimes I put words in the wrong order, which gives my messages a much different meaning than what I originally intended. (C-12)

I noticed that I began to think more and more in English. Now, the only thing that is still Chinese in my mind is the multiplication table. I wish I had kept up with my reading skills in Chinese. It felt as though my Chinese heritage was fading away with my Chinese literacy. (C-19)

Before I learned English, I felt comfortable, secure, and confident speaking Mandarin because Mandarin was my only communication language. As I learned English, I spoke Mandarin grammatically incorrect and pronounced each word with a foreign accent. (C-28)

It was also during this crucial period of my life that I had gradually lost contact with my Chinese culture. Unlike Taiwan, the American public schools didn't teach the Chinese language, history, art, or culture. But rather, more emphasis were placed on European History instead. Eventually I also abandoned many forms of Chinese entertainment such as music, cartoons, or movies in my personal life. Since my family had no other relatives living in the US with us, I felt it unnecessary to keep my native tongue of Taiwanese. Due to these factors, my writing and reading skills diminished dramatically in just three brief years. (C-5)

Just recently I realized how much Cantonese I have forgotten. Last week, I went over to my relatives' house to celebrate Chinese New Year in San Jose. I have not seen them for about five years now. When I was there, I could not communicate with them very well because they speak Cantonese and a little English. Even when I was able to figure out what they were saying to me, I could not answer them back in Cantonese because I did not know how. Instead, I replied in English hoping they would figure out what I was saying. At times, my younger cousins serve as translator for me since they were able to remember more Cantonese than I. (C-70)

My fluency in Gujrati has diminished tremendously since the age of five. At home, both my sisters and I speak in English with our parents. I am unable to read or write Gujrati, and can only speak a few words, phrases, and sentences. (I-1)

The feeling of knowing what to say in one language, but not in the language being spoken, still remains. Now, the situation is often reversed. My proficiency with Hindi today is comparable to my ability in English when I was in second grade. While I can understand almost all levels of spoken Hindi, when I converse with my grandmother, who can only understand Hindi, I often find myself groping for the right words and incorrectly conjugating Hindi verbs; I listen enviously to recordings of myself speaking fluent Hindi as a four year old child. Unfortunately, now that I am older, it is much harder to regain the familiarity with speaking Hindi I once took for granted. (I-4)

Despite my parents' constant efforts in preserving the use of Tagalog in our household, my older brother, my younger sister, and I still cannot communicate to our parents in "their" language. However, we can clearly understand every word that is communicated to us in Tagalog. I have discovered that the same holds true for many of my fellow Filipino-American friends. Some of them do not even understand a single word spoken to them in Tagalog. I have also observed that together we have one major thing in common; we are all second generation Filipino-Americans. (P-4)

Passive knowledge. One typical outcome is that children get to the point where they can understand the home language in a basic way but cannot speak as well as they understand.

The languages that I heard spoken in my household as a child were English, Telegu, and Hindi. The only language I can speak fluently is English. I understand Telegu completely, but I do not speak it. If I tried with effort I could probably be able to speak it. Hindi is not spoken as frequently as Telegu or English in my household, so I only understand a few words of it. I use English every day. It is the only language that I can use to communicate without having to think about what I am saying. (I-9)

[M]y parents and I ventured for a better life in the United States when I was two years old. During the formative years between five and twelve, I was primarily exposed to English due to my enrollment in school. While English was being imprinted onto my psyche, my parents fluently spoke Tagalog at home. Due to my home life, I strangely was able to understand almost everything my parents spoke in Tagalog but could not speak nor write it. This situation has boggled my mind for years. I have always wondered how I can be exposed to the sound of Tagalog words for so long and not be able to speak a word of it. To this day I still cannot speak nor write in my native language. (P-3)

Mixing languages. Another typical outcome is that the children speak a mixed language. Mixed Korean and English is often called "Konglish" or "Korenglish," as one student prefers to call it—spin-offs on the first word in this genre, "Spanglish." Chinese-English mixing is sometimes called "Chinglish," and so on.

I spoke only English in school and progressively spoke less and less Chinese at home. I actually started my own language, "Chinglish," which is a mix of Chinese and English. I only spoke this way to my parents and my brother who always laughed whenever I spoke it. My Chinglish started off innocently enough, but more and more English got thrown into my conversations. The reason for this is that I forgot how to say certain words in Chinese and didn't want to bother giving it much thought. (C-23)

It wasn't long until, I interchanged words in Cantonese for words in English. It was my mother who always called it "half broken English" and "half broken Chinese." According to her, I was changing into a "white ghost," a literal transaction of the word, Caucasian. (C-24)

Although I have been speaking Cantonese all through my life, sometimes I find that I can no longer converse at total ease with others without mixing my speech with one or two English words. When talking to my Cantonese Speaking friends here in the States, we usually use "Chinglish." Sometimes it is easier to express something in English while at other times we just cannot express some feelings in any language but Cantonese. (C-40)

USE OF MIXED LANGUAGE AS MAIN LANGUAGE OF HOME.
Sometimes, this mixed language actually becomes the main language used at home.

[M]y family and I still speak more English than Hindi at home. We have even developed a sort of "Hinglish," which often consists of a mixture of the two languages. "Mom, is *khana* (food) ready yet?" (I-3)

My father is the only one in the family who speaks Chiou-Chou without switching to other languages, but lack of communication with him has put me out of practice. It is an unspoken rule in our family that out of respect, all of us switch to Chiou-Chou when addressing our father; otherwise, our conversation with each other is a mixture of English, Vietnamese, Chiou-Chou, and occasionally some Mandarin and Cantonese. (C-69)

Sadly, I use my Chinese rather sparingly these days. Even with my parents I speak English. Interestingly enough, they use just as much English as Chinese when talking to me (I like to call the mixture "Chinglish.") I think this is an effort (either conscious or unconscious) on their part to reduce the generation gap that has widened because of the cultural gap resulting from having grown up in different countries. (C-33)

INVOLUNTARY CODE-MIXING. The literature on code-mixing often fails to distinguish between the stylistic switching done by balanced bilinguals and the involuntary mixing done by people who command one language better than the other. The majority of students in this corpus are only semi-speakers of their heritage language and report language mixing as the best they can do with their language. This "involuntary code-switching" is often used with their Asian-language dominant parents.

When I communicated with my siblings, I usually used mixture of Korean and English referred to [by] many Korean Americans as "Konglish." I basically felt insecure with both languages that I wasn't fluent with either Korean or English. (K-11)

Although I speak English fluently, I speak to my parents only in Korean. Well, actually, I speak a sort of mixed language that, apparently, was developed from Korean speakers like me who do not speak Korean so well. Many people refer to it as Konglish (Korean-English). Konglish is when people say some words in Korean and some words in English all in one sentence. Speaking Konglish is quite fun but I know it grieves my poor old father when I pervert his native language when I speak. Konglish is spoken by many people especially among the Koreans of Los Angeles (I am from Los Angeles). (K-25)

My native language became harder and harder to speak and understand. It was often too difficult for me to communicate with my parents purely in Korean, so a new mixed language, Konglish, began to be used around the house. "Um-ma (mom), when's juh-nuk (dinner)?" "Um-ma, I'm going to haac-gyo (school) now!" Without a second thought, my sisters and I were speaking by interconnecting words from two varying languages, and my parents were starting to actually understand us!! (K-28)

[W]ithout me even noticing, I was starting to forget Korean. By the time I was in sixth grade, I was speaking in Konglish, which is a mixture of Korean and English combined in speaking. Thus, when I got home from school, I would tell my mom, *"Um-ma,* I'm home, but *na ching-gu-naa* house *gal-gu-ya,"* or translated "Mom, I'm home, but I'm going to my friend's house." However, Konglish was not a convenience, but a necessity. My parents and grandparents did not speak English too well, but they did know enough of the basic English vocabulary to roughly communicate with other Americans. At the same time, I was fluent in English, but I had lost fluency in the Korean language. Thus, in order to communicate with my parents and grandparents, I spoke in Korean but substituted very few words, but as the years went by, more and more words were substituted. (K-36)

The degree to which I am proficient in English is quite high but my command of Tagalog is if anything but flawless. I can understand a majority of the vocabulary but putting together phrases and sentences is something I find difficult. The only time I am required to use my knowledge of Tagalog is when I speak with my "Tagalog only" fluent great-grandmother. My communication with her is a comedy in itself since I mix together Tagalog, English, and my own ad-libbed version of sign language. (P-6)

Illiteracy. Even when children can speak their heritage language, they are usually unable to read and write in their language unless they came over at a late age.

The problem I face now is that I have difficulty with the Korean language. My reading skills are equivalent to a first grader in Korea, and my writing skills are even worse. In order of what I can do best to what I am worst at would be that my understanding is the best, followed by speaking, then reading, and finally writing. (K-26)

Even though I can speak one Chinese dialect and understand a little of another, I never learned to read or write the Chinese language. (C-3)

The languages that I speak are Hindhi and Punjabi at home I speak Punjabi much more fluently and better than Hindhi. Regretfully I cannot write in either language. (I-2)

Although I am fluent when it comes to speaking Vietnamese, I never had the chance to master its written language. (V-4)

Problems created by first language attrition. Heritage language attrition creates many problems for the child, who finds him- or herself personally frustrated, unable to communicate effectively with relatives, alienated from peers in the old country, and humiliated in front of visitors to the home.

Unfortunately, at this point in my life, my lack of versatility in Mandarin is probably one of my greatest regrets. For one thing, while I can communicate with grandparents and relatives, it's not unlike stuttering every few words trying to get a few simple ideas across. In addition, hot having the language at my disposal limits my options for the future, although I plan to take some classes and try to use Mandarin with friends. One of the most significant aspects of my lack of fluency in the language is the fact that China is one of the major players in world politics today, and I have less potential at this point to effect the outcome of the nation. In the end, I realize that I missed a golden opportunity in not learning the language well. (C-36)

There were three staff writers (at a Korean-American newspaper) who knew as much Korean as Dan Quayle knew Tagalog. Needless to say, they were constantly insulted and ostracized by the other workers. These writers themselves felt a strong sense of shame in their inability to speak their native language. No matter how well they wrote in English, they told me, they would never be accepted as an "American," because on the outside they were obviously "Korean." They told me that they would do anything to be able to go back and study Korean when they were younger. (K-23)

I know that I have been extremely fortunate to have been able to learn English so easily, but I have paid a dear price in exchange. I began my English education with the basics, starting in first grade. As a result, I had to end my Chinese education at that time. I have forsaken my own language in order to become "American." I no longer read or write Chinese. I am ashamed and feel as if I am a statistic adding a burden and lowering the status quo of the Asian community as an illiterate of the Chinese language. (C-7)

Logically, one would assume I had been chastised and ridiculed for my ignorance while I visited Sri Lanka. This then led to humiliation which progressed to such remorse that bodily deformation became a fair price for the instant knowledge of Singhalese. However, I encountered only kindness and respect from the people. In addition, knowledge of the language is not vital for survival in Sri Lanka since so many of the natives are bilingual. So why such anguish? One of the saddest feelings I have experienced in my eighteen years is to feel a tourist in my own country, Sri Lanka. Already a "Westerner," language was perhaps the only real and significant bond I could share with the people there. Unlike some others, religion and physical similarity did not create enough of a bond for me. I found it profoundly sad to witness such a breathless beauty and experience such rich culture, yet realize I had no rightful claim to it. (I-7)

I regret, however, that I was not able to learn any of my native Filipino languages fluently. I believe that I am missing out on an important part of my own cultural identity by not being able to speak Tagalog or Bicol. (P-1)

If there is one regret in my life thus far it would be my inability to speak the language of my parents, grandparents, and ethnicity for that matter, Tagalog. (P-6)

"I believe in immersing the Indians in our civilization and, when we get them under, holding them there until they are thoroughly soaked" [quote of a previous BIA commissioner; Crawford 1992: 44]. The problem was that many students drowned in the process. I, too, have been drowned in the process of Americanization and Anglicization. But, unlike the Native Americans, I was not dragged into the water by the throat and submerged. I made the choice myself to plunge into the pool. It was my decision to commit this suicide-of-sorts. (P-8)

POOR COMMUNICATION BETWEEN GENERATIONS. One of the worst problems that comes about with first language attrition is its impact on communication in the family.

Trying to speak proper Korean to adults when one can barely speak the language can be extremely embarrassing. My family is very involved in a Korean church, and many times the reverend, elders, and deacons come to visit. When I find myself stuck at home on these unfortunate nights when guests are over, I have to introduce myself and speak to them in Korean. The trouble really begins when they talk to me and ask me questions—I'm usually stuck there in a most awkward position, trying to understand what they are saying, and trying to answer back in the most polite way possible. What usually comes out of my mouth is a mixture of English and informal Korean, which causes all the adults to laugh at me. (K-15)

There are a lot of things that my parents say in Haka that I do not understand, and my parents, despite having immigrated to the United States some twenty-five years ago, are not fluent in English. My father understands a little more English than my mother, so sometimes when my mother and I don't understand what the other is trying to say, we have my father translate for us. (2nd-generation student autobiography [C-3])

To this day, I cannot speak the Chinese language fluently. A guilty conscience has ruled over me ever since I lost part of my culture. Every time I visit my Chinese-speaking grandparents, I have a greater desire to regain my ability to speak Chinese fluently because I barely understand a word they say. There has been a tremendous communication gap between my grandparents and I for most of my life. When I communicate with my Chinese-speaking father who understands very little English, my mother often plays the role of the translator. My communication with my father is a combination of Chinese and English words due to my ignorance of my native language.

To regain this vital part of my lost culture is very important to me. I would like to break the communication barrier and gain more access to my grandparent's lives and experiences. . . . Becoming familiar with the Chinese language would also help my relationship with my father. (2nd-generation student [C-4])

My parents often emphasized to me the social and economical advantages of knowing dual languages, but I seldom paid little attention to their advice. Little did I realize this, until I saw the ineffectiveness and the lack of coherency in my speech. I was no longer able to even communicate to my parents basic, everyday Cantonese. The only way they could understand me was for them to decipher my English using what little English they knew. (C-24)

This has been the base of a minor communication problem in our family. For although I can have an intricate and serious discussion with my parents, my sister is limited to casual conversations with my parents, who, even though they can speak English, can never have the same fluency and grasp on the language as my sister due to the fact that they came here at an age when learning a new tongue was difficult. And my sister's lack of proficiency in Chinese hinders her from expressing herself fully in front of my parents. I feel that this language barrier has been the basis of many unnecessary misunderstandings. (C-43)

Even with the Chinese that I can speak, I am limited to the normal yet shallow "everyday" conversations I have with my parents and do not have enough of a vocabulary to have meaningful talks with them. Such was the case just the other night when they asked me what my major at Berkeley was but I did not know the words or phrase for "Biology," much less, "Molecular and Cellular Biology." The best I could manage was "Science" in Chinese and explained the rest in English; I could not communicate to them why I selected this major, what I was going to do with it, and so forth—we ended this discussion by changing the subject. (C-76)

INTERGENERATIONAL CONFLICT. For many students, parental insistence on retaining the language and values of the old country has become a very sore point in the household, and has become the source of real intergenerational conflict.

> Between my parents and my siblings and myself, there has been constant tension—a pressure that is always existent, though perhaps not visible or audible—for my younger sister, younger brother, and me to use Korean among ourselves and with our parents at least when we're in the house. Yet, we neglect it and use the more comfortable English . . . until we hear another lecture. (K-29)

> The cultural values of both ethnic groups are at opposite extremes. What I acquire at school and what I am taught at home are completely contradictory. My teachers at school discourage me to speak Korean because they feel that it might have a negative effect on my ability to become a well-spoken intellectual. In contrast, my parents stress that I should not conform to the American ways. If I follow the American way of life, they feel that I might drift away from my actual roots and lose my Korean cultural values. They constantly emphasize that I should retain my Korean linguistic skills. Furthermore, my parents constantly reiterate that their sole reason for coming to the States was to provide me with an opportunity for a better education. Because I am being taught by the American educational system, I am destined to learn the American ways which my parents resent so much. As a Korean student attending an American school, I should be left alone to make my own choices. (K-38)

CRITICISMS FROM RELATIVES AND ACQUAINTANCES. Young people who have lost their first language are also subject to the embarrassment of criticism from other people from their home country.

> I cannot begin to count how many times people have ridiculed my language and my ethnicity by making fun of how spoken Chinese sounds and by mimicking a "Chinese accent" when speaking English. On the other hand I have also experienced linguistic prejudice from Chinese people because I am of Chinese descent but

do not speak the language very well and must resort to English when talking to these people. (2nd-generation student [C-3])

To [people of my parents' generation] my command of the Korean language showed whether or not I was a true Korean or just a yellow-skinned boy without a cultural identity or pride. And did I resent that attitude. Whenever relatives would visit I'd always get the same show; first the initial looks of surprise, second the question (Don't you know how to speak Korean?), and finally reprimands of shame and pity from anyone and everyone, even my younger, Korean-speaking cousins. The thing that bothered me the most was that I felt I could do so little about my problem. (K-32)

"Your Chinese is *awful!*" An elder cousin whom I had not seen for eight years directed this comment to me several summers ago while we both were in my parents' presence. I was filled with indignation as I thought to myself where this jerk got off at telling me about my Chinese deficiencies and how eight years was too short of a time to see this creep again. Of course, this cousin wrote and spoke Cantonese, the dialect of Chinese my family spoke fluently. "Can't you learn more?" he added. After that one, I thought that I had discovered the so-called Missing Link of the evolutionary process between ape and man. I glanced over to where my parents were sitting only to see them nod in agreement. They not only thought he was right, they knew he was right; but for that matter, so did I. Moreover, these were the same comments my parents themselves made to me ever since my family moved from Hong Kong to San Francisco in 1978. My cousin's comments served a reminder to me from that day of a language's potential to be a barrier or a bridge. (C-76)

I have even encountered prejudice from Filipinos because of my linguistic background. Sometimes, even my peers' parents and other elders look down on me for not speaking in a native tongue. (P-1)

People in the home country also feel strongly that people who come to America should not forget their heritage.

When I went to Korea during my summers, I felt proud that I could speak well and easily. In Korea the society used to look up to those who lived in America and could speak English, however, at present they are disappointed by the many youths who have become "Americanized," and have forgotten their heritage. (K-35)

Factors relating to first language retention and attrition. What happened that created this language shift, against the will of the family and, often, to the ultimate regret of the child? In this section, I discuss the factors that might tip the balance one way or another in attrition or retention of the heritage language.

The language of the home. There is a direct connection between fluency in a language and the degree to which that language is used. In the effort to help their children assimilate to the new country and learn English, the parents have a dilemma: To what extent should they speak English with their children? Should they speed their children's English education by speaking it with them, or would that hurt their children's chances of retaining the heritage language? This is a painful choice, for it is clear that children who don't know English suffer emotionally and educationally, at least for the first year or so; and often schools strongly encourage parents to use English at home. Yet while parents who decide to use English at home find that their children learn English faster, the student autobiographies show very clearly that at the same time, knowledge of the heritage language never develops or else deteriorates rapidly once the English-at-home policy is introduced.

> My parents took the liberty to teach me English as I grew up, as opposed to Korean like most of my cousins. At the age of five, only after my ear and mind completely operated in English did they then decide that it might be time to mix it up. They tried speaking to me in English in public while speaking to me in Korean at home. Soon they realized, though, that I would never truly be bilingual. (K-32)
>
> I have asked my parents many times why they did not teach me to speak Marathi fluently, and this is what they always tell me. While growing up, my parents wanted my sister and I to be able to speak English like all of the other children. They had heard stories about Indian parents only speaking the Indian language at home, and their children not learning proper, conversational English. My parents did not want this to happen to us, so they limited how much they spoke Marathi around us. I would say this has worked to my advantage and to my disadvantage. All throughout my past education, I have felt that I can speak

English just as well as all of my classmates. Not once have I felt that I lacked any English-speaking abilities. The drawback though is that I do not know Marathi fluently. I can understand most of what is spoken in Marathi, but I can probably only speak as well as a first or second grader. I am basically illiterate also, and cannot read or write the language. (I-11)

Those children who retained fluency or near-fluency in their native tongue come from homes where the heritage language was spoken by matter of policy. These quotes are all from children born here who became bilingual.

My parents taught me Cantonese first, and English was something I learned later on in school. My parents constantly insisted that I learn Chinese until I was in second grade, because they felt that they might want to return to Hong Kong after my father got his Ph.D. from UCLA. They even went to great lengths to teach me the language. My parents acted as part-time teachers, having ordered a set of language books from China. They taught me enough to allow me to survive if I had to return to schools in Hong Kong. These lessons not only taught me the language, but also taught me a lot about the history and culture of China. From these books I learned more about Chinese values as well. (C-45)

Chinese was still the dominant language in our household; English was a forbidden taboo. My parents had wanted to ensure the fact that I would never forget my language and culture. (C-66)

As a preschooler, I was not familiar with any English at all. My parents had chosen to teach me Hindi first, because they knew I would inevitably learn fluent English in school. Being born and reared in the United States, I value what my parents did for me, because it has enabled me to stay fluent in Hindi, the only language I spoke for the first three years of my life. (I-3)

My parents have always felt that its harder to learn Punjabi because in our everyday lives in the United States we are not as exposed to it, except in the home. If they could succeed in teaching us Punjabi at home, we would easily pick up English at school. This was absolutely true. I began school knowing hardly any English and I picked it up quickly. I soon became completely fluent in both Punjabi and English and speak both without an accent. (I-8)

> I learned English in nursery school and from listening to my older siblings practice their English at the dinner table. On the other hand, I learned Vietnamese through my parents. I was forbidden to speak to them in anything other than Vietnamese. This was because my parents were afraid that I would grow up to forget my roots. All in all, I consider myself to be equally fluent when it comes to both languages. (V-4)

INSUFFICIENCY OF PARENTS AS SOLE SOURCE OF HERITAGE LANGUAGE. The parents' decision to use the heritage language at home is a necessary condition for raising a bilingual child, but it is not sufficient. Many of the families of the students who wrote these autobiographies in fact did choose to use the heritage language at home, and yet still found that their children were losing fluency. With siblings starting to talk to each other and even answer their parents in English, the home language begins to slip away.

> My first memory is of learning the correct way of pronounce "Kung Hee Fat Choy," the Cantonese way of saying "Happy New Year," with the intent to charm the socks off the listener and cause him to give me a packet of lucky money. My mother tells me I was a paragon of a baby, usually silent, but when I spoke, I spoke in Chinese. I got along will with all the relatives who visited from Hong Kong (or at least the ones I wanted to get along with by enchanting them with my baby-talk).

> This delightful time when I was the perfect Chinese daughter did not last long. Spending time with my older siblings and hearing them speak in English, I soon began to lose my first language. I, in turn, helped speed the deterioration of Chinese in my baby sister. My older siblings first learned English when they started formal education. In contrast, by the time I entered kindergarten, I had no trouble making friends by using this new second language. I also began using the derogatory term "F.O.B" (fresh off the boat) to describe peers who spoke only their native Oriental tongue because they had not been in Hawaii long enough to know better. (C-11)

> After graduating from elementary school, I made a lot of new friends. All the friends that I made were English speaking people, so for about six years my main language was English. Only time I spoke Korean was at home because my parents

> didn't speak any English. . . . I imagined myself always retain-
> ing the Korean language, but to my surprise I almost forgot
> 50% of the language. (K-2, arrived age 11)

ONE PARENT, ONE LANGUAGE. A fairly common approach for families trying to raise bilingual children is the "one parent, one language" approach. It is a good compromise for families who want their children to be bilingual but at the same time want to keep them from suffering by arriving at school not knowing English. Dopke (1992) (whose study took place in Australia) reports that the one-parent, one-language approach worked in some families but not in others. She points out that those families whose children did succeed in maintaining fluent bilingualism throughout the period of the study differed from the others in two key ways. First, the parents were consistent about the approach and most importantly did not let the children respond to them in the inappropriate language. If the child responded to the heritage-language-speaking parent in English, the parent might just say "What?" until the child repeated the message in the heritage language. Second, the successfully bilingual child had other people to talk to in the heritage language besides the parents. Other relatives, or neighbors, or social or religious groups that use the heritage language provide necessary language support that provides both further exposure and motivation to the child. Several students in my classes reported the "one parent, one language" policy in their homes.

> Gujrati was the first language I learned, and spoke fluently until
> the age of five. At home, my mother would speak to me in Gu-
> jrati, and my father would speak to me in English. . . . Thus,
> when I attended preschool at the age of three, I didn't have a
> problem learning English. Before I entered kindergarten, I was
> completely fluent in both Gujrati and English. (I-1)

Of course, this approach can be found anywhere in the world where two languages are important. One trilingual student recalls her parents employing this method when she was a child in Taiwan:

> As a child, I spoke Mandarin and Taiwanese at home. Some-
> times it was very confusing to know two names for every item
> so in an attempt to diminish the confusion in my young mind,
> my father only spoke in Mandarin while my mother spoke Tai-
> wanese. (C-57)

Language rejection. A factor that may be even more important in language attrition than any of the above is language rejection by the children themselves. The children are subjected to tough assimilative pressures at school, mainly from their classmates. They are made to feel "different" and "not normal," and their language or their accent is ridiculed. The children begin to develop a strong sense of shame about their language and their heritage culture and accordingly make every attempt to suppress it.

> It was the Korean language, and "Korean-ness' in general, as the ugly monster that kept me from being "normal," isolated me from my peers, and ate away every opportunity to "belong" with people my age. . . . I learned to hate hanging out with my family because they reminded me that I wasn't "American." I had learned to hate being a "foreigner" and I saw no reason to speak Korean except to keep my parents content enough to leave me relatively alone. (K-27)

PEER GROUP PRESSURE TOWARD LANGUAGE REJECTION. The most important factor causing language rejection among children is peer pressure. Children can be heartless teases, and most immigrant children have tales of the cruelty that was aimed at them for being "different." Just a small sample:

> It was two heartless comments, from a group of small boys in my "white" neighborhood for me to want to deny my language let alone my culture, as well. How was I to react to a racist comment of "Ching chong chooey go back home to where you belong. You can't even speak English right." Sixteen small words which possessed so much strength and contained so much power caused a small, naive child to want to lose her heritage—to lose what made her. (C-2)

> I didn't use Korean whenever possible, as I tried to become as Americanized as I could, as well as avoid the cruel comments kids could inflict on Asian languages. (K-1)

> [T]he Caucasians would try to mock us with the incomprehensible jumble of sounds, trying to mimic our language. (K-3)

> One thing I remember experiencing was that I was always picked on because I couldn't speak English well, but then, I used to let my fists do all the talking. Many of my childhood acts of violence were results of linguistic harassment's or misunderstandings. (K-9)

> "Gook."

> "Chink."

"Flat-nosed Oriental."

"How do you blind-fold a Chinese person?" "You use dental floss."

"Ha, ha, ha . . ."

(Back in the 1980s, *every* Asian was believed to be Chinese.)

Taunting and ridiculing, the harsh voices of my worst memories belonged to small elementary children who found diversity just as unfavorable as I did. . . . My sisters and I spent two years attending [school name] that was mainly dominated by Anglo-American students. Our ears burned daily from their words of malicious content, but somehow, this stirred up our motivation to grasp the English language even faster. (K-28)

My painful road to achieving fluency in English took a few years, during which I sometimes felt alienated from the society around me. I discovered the disrespect, that antipathy, and the hatred that could be directed on a non-English speaking and non-white immigrant. It was then, after countless mockeries from American kids in school and other uncomforting episodes that I became convinced that America, despite the Statue of Liberty, the Constitution's proclamation for equality of all men, and its advertising as a melting pot and a land of freedom and opportunity, was a racist and xenophobic nation. (C-43)

TEACHING RESPECT FOR CULTURAL DIVERSITY IN THE SCHOOL. On a more hopeful note, there are a few Asian-American students who went to schools that were able to instill respect for cultural diversity among their students; these students remember positive experiences instead of peer discrimination and ostracism.

At Independence High School, cultural diversity was cherished. Every year a multi-cultural assembly and a food fair is held to celebrate and to promote the diverse cultures at Independence as well as to teach students to respect and appreciate cultures different from their own. With respect to the history of race and language in the United States, I was very fortunate in that I did not encounter any discriminations. Prior to the 1980s immigrants and "racially inferior" people were discriminated and denied of opportunities enjoyed by others. All the credits can be attributed to earlier African Americans, Hispanics, and other ethnic groups who had fought a long struggle to win equal rights for everyone. (V-8)

MAINTAINING PRIDE IN HERITAGE. Some children managed, through the help of their parents and grandparents, to maintain pride in their heritage despite the teasing and rejection of their peers.

> When I was younger I felt embarrassed to speak my native languages in the fear of being mocked or ridiculed. It was bad enough that I was an immigrant but speaking such a hideous languages was incomprehensible and rude to other "American" children. However, I learned to deal with all the mocking because my parents taught me to be proud because I was a unique person in knowing such beautiful languages. I could speak three languages at the age of six while my friends only knew one. I felt gifted and soon was no longer was being ridiculed but envied. (I-2)

> My parents had just moved the family from Taiwan to America. Even though the Mandarin Chinese I had grown up speaking seemed useless now, I felt no remorse because I couldn't speak English. I knew I was part of the rich, beautiful, and complex Chinese culture, a culture that has taken thousands of years to develop. And my grandparents had told me many times that I belonged to a proud family. (C-15)

THE DRIVE TO ASSIMILATE. But for most, attempts to "fit in" are as paramount in immigrant children's minds as they are with any other child. Thus the drive toward complete assimilation is overwhelming, and rejection of the heritage language is associated with that drive.

> In the effort to assimilate into American society, especially in a place such as Lincoln where cultural diversity was extremely small, however, I found myself trying to shed my linguistic background in order to overcome alienation and teasing. Although I do not specifically recall isolated incidents, I am confident that my parents pushed me to excel in English in order that I would not encounter the difficulties they did due to their limited competence in English. (C-44)

> To get rid of my accent and speak perfect Californian-surfer-English is my proudest accomplishment in life, since it demonstrated not only my hard work, but also my acceptance by my peers. (C-61)

I spent the next few years trying desperately to linguistically assimilate into my new society. I did not want to sound like an immigrant in public and tried my hardest to sound "American." I did not realize my clear neglect to maintain my native tongue. During that time, I did not mind because I knew I was not going back to the Philippines anytime soon and I wanted to quickly integrate myself to my new country and learning how to speak the language without an obvious accent was a preliminary step. I believe that the wish to "speak" like the majority is a common desire for most foreign country immigrants coming into the United States. Proficiency in English is somehow connected to upward social mobility and a higher class status. It is the goal to have a "better life" than the lives they had in the country they fled from that drives immigrants to learn English. This is when newcomers, especially the younger people, begin to forget their native language. This pattern certainly happened to me and will continue to repeat itself in the years to come. (P-2)

I can see how my eagerness to Americanize and my quick pace to Anglicize (which began from my younger days in the Philippines) killed the Filipino in me. (P-8)

FEELINGS OF SHAME. Being an immigrant, looking different, and speaking English with an accent are all sources of shame to children. They become deeply ashamed of their heritage language and cannot bear to speak it in public with their families. At the same time, they are ashamed in front of their relatives and relatives' friends because they do not know their heritage language and culture. They blame themselves for all these problems.

I wish I can tell you that I'm a fifth generation Chinese American. I wish I can say that my ancestors have been here just as long as your ancestors have, and therefore I am as much an "American" as you are. I wish my Asian Cultures teachers would stop assuming that I am a living Asian History textbook because I'm Chinese. I wish my fellow classmates would quit picking on me because I'm different from them. I wish I can somehow reassure myself that it isn't my fault that I am ignorant of my own culture. But I can't. There is certainly no reason that I can't recall a single event in the Chinese history. There is absolutely no excuse for me to speak Chinese with a horrible accent since I've only lived in the States for a decade. (C-5)

SHAME ABOUT PARENTS. The awareness of being "different" has a profound effect on the immigrant child's feelings about his or her heritage. They also become very self conscious of their parents' lack of fluency in English (if such is the case).

> The fact that my parents do struggle with English has been at times difficult for me to grow up with. Many times I have even been ashamed of them. . . . This is an illustration of the effects of immigrating to a different country, and some of the social "problems" that have to be dealt with. (K-26)

> When I entered [name] Junior High School, my attitude toward the Chinese language changed dramatically, partially because I was no longer protected by the innocence of childhood and partially because [name] was located in a less racially diverse neighborhood. When some of my classmates began to ridicule and throw racist remarks at Chinese people, I began to distance myself away from Chinese culture. I felt ashamed when my parents spoke to me in Cantonese at a supermarket. I got into heated arguments about why only English should be spoken at home. My dad was fluent in English but my mom had this heavy accent and I began to question my mom on why she would not learn English as well as my dad did, even though I knew perfectly well—she did not go to school here like my dad did. I continuously tried to fit in, even if it meant abandoning culture and identity. I was probably most hostile to my background during those years in junior high. (C-45)

> Not only was I obviously different in my physical appearance, but I had to deal with a separate culture as well. And my linguistic background was one of the only things I could suppress, by speaking only in English. I used to get so embarrassed whenever anyone asked me what language I spoke, or for that matter, even brought up anything Indian. I mean *really* embarrassed. My face would get very hot. I learned to change the subject faster than anyone else I knew. (And I have to say that that has been a very useful skill!) (I-12)

> I believed in the superiority of American English. Indeed, I even went further as to believe in the superiority of the white man. It is no wonder that I am more fluent in English than I am in my native language, Tagalog. (P-11)

LANGUAGE SHYNESS. In a kind of "reverse shame," language rejection may also occur or be intensified as a result of discouragement over one's lack of knowledge of the heritage language; non-fluent children try not to speak the language at all for fear of being criticized or laughed at by those who speak it better. This is called "language shyness" by Krashen (1998).

> [M]y American accent has in a way, made me less willing to speak my native language. One of the bad experiences ¡hat I have encountered was when my family and I went over to Hong Kong and Macao to visit relatives. Naturally, I had to speak Chinese throughout the entire visit. My aunts and uncles soon found me to be a great form of entertainment because my Chinese sounded so funny to them. To them I was their niece, the "toa-gee," which simply means that I was born in America or they would get really creative and call me an "A-B-C" which is an acronym for "American-Born-Chinese." I was really offended by their constant harassing, but I soon got over it when I realized my Chinese sounded to them much their English sounded to me—bad. (C-23)

> I am even afraid of re-learning Filipino. (I tried last year here at Berkeley.) I wish that I could at least answer my mother in Filipino. I try, but what results is an English-Filipino mix that makes me feel like a fool. (P-8)

FEELINGS OF USELESSNESS OF FIRST-LANGUAGE MAINTENANCE. For a smaller number of students, language rejection is less emotional and more pragmatic. Students who have lived in the United States most or all of their lives often simply see no use in using their heritage language.

> In terms of my values, I think that perhaps I have lost zeal for Korean because I don't see so much a practical use for it as I do for English. I no longer see speaking Korean as a "part" of my identity, although my parents would probably be crushed to hear such a thing. (K-29)

> I am more fluent in English than in Taiwanese. My other dialect, Mandarin, is almost nonexistent. A part of me wants to keep my language alive, but a big part of me wonders if it really matters. I am sure I'll be living in American for the rest of my life. I guess I just don't really care. (C-22)

Efforts at language maintenance. When parents see their children losing their heritage language, they often make strong efforts to remedy the situation.

> Though I came to America when I was little over a year old, I am fully fluent in my mother-tongue (Bengali). Ever since a young age my father has stressed the importance in retaining my culture and rich heritage. To this end, he has spent much time and effort educating me on aspects of my culture which I cannot learn in school. (I-10)

The two most common means of trying to stem the loss of the language is through increased insistence on language use at home, and sending the kids to language school. But in general, these remedies are "too little, too late."

Increased insistence on language use at home. The autobiographies describe parents as punishing, lecturing, cajoling, or doing whatever they can to get their child to speak the heritage language at home.

> This trend [of becoming a balanced bilingual] took a turn for the worse when my knowledge and fluency in English started to usurp that of Korean. My Korean friends had long ago abandoned the Korean language for English. Thus, my parents no longer had assurance that I would maintain respect for my mother tongue. They drastically reversed their stance on language in 1987, when I was in the seventh grade. I was prohibited from using English at home. If I asked my parents for anything in English, my request would fall on deaf ears. I had to ask for water in Korean, otherwise I would die of thirst. The emphasis had shifted from learning English to salvaging what little I remembered of Korean. From the local Korean bookstores in the neighborhood, my parents bought me tons of Korean magazines, noels, and comic books. Every day after school, my mother and I would sit and read Korean stories together. Whatever words I didn't understand, she would make me look up in the English-Korean dictionary. And late at night, the three of us watched the Korean station on television. They made me view everything from sit coms to cooking shows, hoping I would learn the language through hearing it spoken. The language war was on. My parents' ultimatum was, quite simply, "English at school, Korean at home." (K-23)

Language schools. A great many immigrant children are sent by their parents to a language school—"Chinese school," "Korean school," and so on. These schools teach literacy and oral skills in the heritage language as well as values and culture. Children go to these schools after regular school or else on Saturdays.

> As a child, I was taught both English and Mandarin. I went to a Chinese school in the San Fernando Valley every Saturday with many other children, teenagers, and adults who were there to learn Mandarin or Cantonese. I attended this form of schooling for many years, but because of the little time we spent each week actually learning the language, most of us never fully got a grasp of the technical skills. (C-38)

A small minority of children have positive memories of their language school experiences:

> Although I lived a typical American kid life, my parents began to feel that my first language, Chinese, would be lost since my daily interactions evolved around English. In order to preserve my Chinese culture, my parents enrolled me in a Chinese school in L.A. Chinatown. At the age of eight, I began attending Chinese school every weekend. There I learned two dialects of Chinese, Cantonese and Mandarin. Although I was very young at the time, I found myself very interested in learning my ancestral language and culture. So for eight years, I continuously went to school seven days a week, learning both languages. After graduating from Chinese school at the junior high level, I was able to read and write in Chinese fluently. (C-55)

> [M]y Korean began to deteriorate, and almost died had it not been for my parents who sent me to Korean school for a couple of months. Even though I attended only a short while, those couple of months are greatly responsible for my ability to speak and to some degree read and write Korean today. (K-1)

Most of the students were sent against their will; but many are glad in retrospect that their parents insisted that they go:

> [My parents] sent me to a Korean language school when I was seven years old; in the beginning, I remember dreading the thought of going to school on Saturdays for two hours, being completely at the mercy of a strict teacher who punished his

pupils for getting an answer wrong with a sharp hit on the wrist. Although I only ended up attending the school for three months, I owe my ability to read and write in Korean to the twelve, two-hour sessions I attended with that time as well as to my parents' insistence that I attend Korean language school.

But most students found these Saturday schools or after-school programs boring or useless, and whether they stuck with the school or not, felt they did not learn a great deal.

> Against my appeal, my mother coerced me to go to Korean school at my church. Every Sunday I practiced my alphabets with children three or four years my younger. Back then, I didn't realize the great importance of keeping the Korean language in me, all I knew was the frustration of having to learn a language I felt was insignificant in my life and the awkwardness of being stuck with younger kids. I quit after two years, an action I now regret. (K-13)

> At the ages of ten and eight, my older siblings were placed into Chinese school, which met for two hours every day after school. Even now, they talk about the sheer boredom and strictness they were forced to endure in mixed tones of amusement and dread. (C-11)

> My parents made me go to Chinese school but I didn't learn much. Every week for about five years I went. Once a week doesn't help but to learn a few phrases. Chinese school was a waste of time. I probably won't send my children to Chinese school. I didn't get much out of it, and I feel that they won't either. (C-22)

> It wasn't that we were discarding our heritage, but rather we were unhappy for being forced to attend Chinese school on Saturday mornings, instead of being allowed to watch the Saturday morning cartoons, or of being able to go out to play. This mental block caused me to forget much of the Chinese which I had learned as a child, and ever since then it has been difficult for me to return to the level of Chinese I was at before, low as it may appear. (C-41)

> My life followed a pattern. English at school and with my friends; Chinese at home with my parents. I was by now

comfortable with both languages and no longer confusedly mixed the two in my sentences, as I had done in my earlier years. At about this time, when my parents saw the ease at which I had become accustomed to both languages, promptly enrolled me in Chinese school to learn how to write in Chinese so that I would be able to write to my relatives. I suppose my parents had only been doing what was right, but at the time, I had not been so sure. English had become my first language, pushing Chinese into second place. I had no desire nor saw any need to waste all my Saturdays at Chinese school. In other words, I was becoming "Americanized." After a school year of learning to write Chinese, I was blissfully rewarded with a summer break. But to my parents' shock and to my dismay, the results of the registration tests in September showed that I had to start all over again in Class 1. Apparently the summer break of writing absolutely no Chinese had its consequences. After three more years of Class 1, I was thankfully given a reprieve as my parents gave up on me. Besides, I had been at the beginning of my teenage years, and felt that there were more important things in life than learning something that I felt I would never use. (C-66)

Some refused to go altogether.

Throughout middle school and high school, my mom would always urge and sometimes even force me to attend Mandarin school or write Chinese characters at home. But I would never take her seriously and rebelled against the language. I would tell her Taiwanese was all I needed. During those years, I wanted to fit in American society and in my narrow point of view, learning Mandarin would only distance me from the rest of the crowd, I deeply regret my decision back then. (C-25)

Television again. Television, cited by so many as the great teacher of English, also sometimes helps in the maintenance or improvement of the home language:

Even though I had an effortless time understanding Mandarin, this did not mean that I was fluent and comfortable with it. The accents of people from Mainland China were quite different from those from Taiwan. People from Mainland China appeared to curl their tongue more, making the words that come out more incomprehensible. Television again came to the rescue. It was the medium that lead me to become more fluent and confident with Mandarin since most Chinese television shows on TV were spoken in Mandarin. (C-74)

Ethnic community. An important factor in language maintenance is having peers with whom one can speak the language. Earlier in this chapter, I quoted students who were glad to attend schools that had few other students of their ethnicity, because it allowed them to learn English more quickly. Yet we have also seen a darker side of that story, in the discrimination and shame suffered by the students in all-white schools. Another problem with living in white neighborhoods and attending white schools is that children begin to think that their heritage language has no use. This student is very glad he attended a high school with a large minority representation, where he was able to develop a sense of ethnic pride as well as tolerance for others:

> Looking back at my use of language historically, I am now careful to look at things differently. I will now even question things which I usually take for granted such as my choice of language. I have gradually changed my perspective. Fortunately, I went to a high school where the majority of the students were minorities. Many of the misconceptions I had about other minorities were shattered because I went to school with them every day. I ate lunch with them, played music with them, talked politics and debated over it with them. I think that it is only through living together can we truly understand each other. As a result, I began to lose the shame I had for speaking Tagalog. I spoke Tagalog with friends at school whenever I could and began speaking Tagalog to my parents instead of answering in English. Today, I love telling ghost stories in Tagalog with my cousins. (P-11)

In the same vein, students who grew up in an ethnic enclave with neighbors who spoke their language were much better able to retain their heritage language.

> Coming from an immigrant family, Cantonese was the first language I learned. My learning was greatly reinforced since I lived in San Francisco's Chinatown and attended a Bilingual day care center. (C-23)

Nevertheless, intensive early childhood learning of the language does not mean that the language will be retained without continued reinforcement throughout childhood. The student quoted above moved out of Chinatown later and her Cantonese began to go downhill.

Some students have had membership in churches or clubs whose membership is primarily ethnically defined. These organizations provide an important social motive for keeping the heritage language strong and also allow more exposure to and practice with the language.

> Even while living in the United States, my parents always encouraged my siblings and I to speak Korean in the home so that we wouldn't forget our native language. Thanks to my parents, I can proudly say that all three of us are fully bilingual. . . . There are many opportunities for me to practice Korean. I attend a Korean church, so I always speak in Korean to the older members of the church and also to the very young members when I teach Sunday School. I also taught at a Korean language school for a while, and through this, I not only had the chance to test and improve my own knowledge of Korean, but also to teach it to the younger kids who were just learning. (K-4, arrived age 7)

Lacking school support of bilingual development, the retention of the heritage language is up to the family, and as we have seen, success is rare. All in all, it appears that heritage language retention is successful only if there are multiple situations where the language is being used, which not only allows for sufficient input for continued language development but also helps the child realize the usefulness of the language and keeps his or her motivation high.

Visits to the homeland. There is certainly nothing better for family retention of the heritage language than being able to make return trips to the homeland. For most immigrants, this is probably impossible, either due to economic considerations or in other cases political problems in the homeland. However, some families are wealthy enough to make occasional or even regular visits to the old country a reality. Those families able to retain these close ties are those where bilingualism is most likely to thrive.

> Learning English was tough; however, because the environment assists me in learning English, I began to catch up quickly. After moving to the United States, I still go back to Taiwan about once a year. Through these experiences, I retain my ability to speak Mandarin and the little bits of "Ka-Cha-Hwa" and Taiwanese. After years of study, I became more fluent in English. Now I have become bilingual. This fact changes

my perspective on languages. Now I can communicate with two groups of people of totally different language and culture. The newly acquired ability made me think that Mandarin should not be my only language [besides English]. I should learn as many languages as possible. (C-32)

After years of living in the United States where the heritage languages are not valued, we have seen that Asian-American children tend to reject their language. Sometimes a visit to the homeland is a wakeup call that gives them a new motivation to learn.

Of the many activities and events I have taken part in to retain my "Indianness," it is one in particular which stays most on my mind: a journey through parts of India. (I-10)

In 1988, we visited Korea . . . to view the Olympic Games. . . . My three months in Korea were really bizarre. To survive, I had to speak Korean. Actually, my knowledge of Korean has always been sufficient enough to keep me alive. I didn't have a difficult time of communicating with people; I just had a tough time adjusting to the harsh reality that I had to use it ALL THE TIME. But I can't tell you how much my Korean improved under such demanding conditions. My anglicized accent disappeared, my vocabulary increased tremendously, and my writing skills were honed and sharpened. (K-23)

I always felt different from everyone else. It wasn't until two years ago, when I returned to Taiwan that I came to learn about my heritage and come to appreciate it. It was then that I came to realize that I wasn't simply Chinese or American. I was Chinese-American and that mix was in its own right, an advantage. (C-56)

Many students report their deep chagrin upon returning to the old country only to find that they can no longer communicate in their heritage language.

After my trip to Taiwan this past winter break, I discovered that my Taiwanese was no longer what it used to be. My Mandarin was a complete joke. It is not hard to imagine what a difficult time I had communicating, even with my own family and relatives. I broke a sweat after each conversation and dreaded being asked questions by family friends, who assumed I was fluent in Taiwanese and Mandarin. I can't count how many times I felt

> embarrassed because I couldn't complete a sentence and had to
> resort to English to bail me out. I was truly a foreigner among
> my own people. I decided that I needed to learn Mandarin,
> since it is the dialect taught everywhere. I want and need to re-
> discover my roots, and the basis for doing that would be to
> learn the necessary language, plain and simple. (C-25)

While for most students, a trip to the homeland resulted in greater motivation to
maintain their heritage language, it also made some of the same students realize
how much they loved the English language:

> [After visiting other Korean-American friends in Korea] long
> after we went our separate ways, I was reminded of my love for
> English. I began to yearn for MTV, "Saturday Night Live," and
> "Monday Night Football." I had had enough of Korean melo-
> dramas, documentaries, and movies. By the end of August, I
> was dying to read American novels. . . . It got so bad that I
> wanted to return to my junior high school in a suburb of L.A.
> known as the San Fernando Valley (the birthplace of "valley
> girl talk")! (K-23)

And for a few, the trip was more like the closing of a door on their homeland,
making the student realize that s/he didn't belong there anymore.

> [student first mentions Korean customs that he found he dis-
> liked]. . . . Finally, I was incapable of communicating with the
> teenagers in Korea. The slangs and jargons that were used by
> everyone sounded very strange to me. Although I spoke Korean
> quite well, there were several times when I couldn't understand
> what my friends were saying. From these experiences, I real-
> ized that I can no longer find any means of fully relating to the
> customs of my own people because I have already been greatly
> affected by the American way of life. (K-38)

The university. These students, all at the University of California at the time
they wrote their autobiographies, found when they came here a richly diverse student body, with a strong impetus toward learning about their heritage. Campus
clubs and nearby church groups allow the students to form bonds with people of a
similar background. A large number of the students have found groups of friends
of similar ethnic identity and language background, which awakened a new desire
to improve their skills in the heritage language. Also, for the first time, most of
them were at a school where their languages were taught, so it was their first op-

portunity (other than the dreaded language schools mentioned above) to take classes in their language. Here are a few out of scores of comments by students newly-awakened to the pleasures of their heritage:

> Although my parents saw their goal accomplished when my brother, then I, entered U.C. Berkeley, and though I made my goal of becoming fluent in English, the cost for all of us has been emotionally painful. One of my great goals in college is to get close to my family and show them my support by getting in touch with my native culture and becoming as learned as possible in the Korean language. (K-28)

> Not until I came to college was I able to speak Korean fluently. I was very glad of what the new college environment brought me, my old language. . . . Now after attending college for two years I am becoming very fluent in Korean, as fluent as English. Most of the time I can talk in Korean or in English but I still search for words to speak in Korean. The new experience of coming to a new country and learning a new language will always stay with me, but the one thing that will keep me intact is the times I almost forgot my first language. (K-2)

> After beginning my studies at Cal, a richly diverse campus and community, I began to realize that my "lost" Chinese would have been very handy to me. I joined a Chinese club, to regain what I "lost" and to retain what I still had left in me, which was not very much. . . . The majority of the students in the club spoke Cantonese and thus led me to feel very handicapped since I could not hold a very long conversation without having to revert to English. This was the point at which I told myself that I would try to learn Chinese again. Now if an opportunity is given to me, I will try to utilize what I can of my native language, but obviously, regardless of how "Americanized" or "Chinglish" I sound, I am aware of the necessity to maintain and practice one's own culture. . . . I think I found my motivation here at [the university]. (C-1)

> I come from a linguistically diverse family, I wish I had been able to learn more from them, but now I constantly hear the nagging voice screaming—It's too late! Now with the pressures of school, I really don't have time. I've tried to enroll in classes here at Cal, but I've been on the waiting list for the fourth semester now and still I have been unable to get in. (C-7)

Recently, I have become interested in Vietnamese again. I am interested in learning to read and write in Vietnamese; next year, I am considering to take a Vietnamese class at Berkeley. Thanks to my godbrother, I have gotten the confidence to practice my Vietnamese and renew my primary language. (C-73)

I'd like to take a Hindi-Urdu class at Berkeley next year, to enable me to understand the language in greater depth. Learning the alphabet and scripture will open up more doors in comprehending the language. (I-3)

Nevertheless, it was only until college that I started to actively seek my true culture; valuing Tagalog came hand in hand. Before this time, I did not know any better; and although I knew I would never let go of my Pilipino heritage, it was not until college that I could tell anyone why.

This change of attitude that takes place at college, and the subsequent drive to take courses in one's heritage language is not unique to the University of California. Universities around the nation cannot help but be aware that a large proportion of students taking courses in Asian languages and some of the Middle Eastern languages, and also a large proportion of students taking Spanish, are students who have had some exposure to the language at home. Some come to class fluent but illiterate; some come with knowledge of only some phrases and idioms, but with excellent pronunciation, comprehension, and mimicking abilities. Language teachers agonize over how to balance the needs of the heritage language students and the true beginners in the same classroom. Heritage language students cannot begin in an advanced class despite their background, because their grammar and literacy skills are usually too low, and yet they are miles ahead of the beginners. The larger departments have begun to have special sections for "heritage language" students. In the Spanish department at Berkeley, for example, there is one track for beginners with no home background, another for "Spanglish" speakers, who speak Spanish but cannot avoid dropping English words in, and another for fluent home speakers (who still need a great deal of education in grammar, reading and writing). Similarly, there are special classes for Chinese, Japanese, Vietnamese, Korean, and Tagalog heritage speakers, who now form the majority of students taking those languages.

Benefits of bilingualism. We have seen that some first- and second-generation young people feel that retaining their first language has no practical value. On the other hand, those students who are fluent in their heritage language have found that their bilingualism is a great benefit to them. There is a feedback relationship between being bilingual and finding bilingualism useful; each begets more of the other. Here is a sample of the dozens of statements about the benefits of bilingualism.

> I feel that my linguistic background is something to be proud of and that there are many advantages of being bilingual. Being bilingual allows me to be able to communicate with people of two different countries, to experience and understand the cultures of two lands, and as an added bonus, if I ever get tired of speaking in one language, I have the option of switching to the other one! In addition, I can enjoy Korean TV programs and Korean music a well as American TV programs and music, I have the opportunity to read old Korean folk tales in the original language, and I've been useful as an interpreter when needed, because of my ability to speak two languages. (K-4)

> The usefulness of languages are infinite, but the most useful form of it to me has been either to help others or myself. One of the more grateful memories that I have to my ability to speak Korean was during a summer in Seoul. My friends and I needed to take a taxi. Well it is known to happen that if a taxi driver suspects that he is driving a group of non-native students, he will drive and extra long route to get where one needs to go. Luckily, my accent was decent enough to get us to our destination in reasonable time. A more satisfying use for languages has been at the times when I can help people with translations at stores, or other places. It is this which has motivated me to volunteer to help translations for immigrants and tutor English to Korean students as well. (K-35)

> Many times, I do play the role of translator and go between for my family. For example, even though my father can read and understand simple letters, when he receives documents or little more complex letters in the mail, I attempt to translated it for him. . . . Bilingualism also helped me in other ways. Since I live in an area that is heavily populated with Koreans back at Home, my proficiency in Korean becomes significantly useful. Last summer, I worked in a Korean American community center. The agency deals with many Koreans as well as other ethnic groups. Whenever I received a phone call from someone, either Korean or non-Korean, who was in need of assistance, I used my language skills to communicate with that person so that I can help in any way possible. (K-11)

Learning Korean can be very beneficial. Speaking two languages is definitely better than speaking one. Also, I have a certain interest in International Business, particularly concerning U.S. and Korean affairs. (K-15)

After the recent L.A. riots, many people were devastated, specifically Korean-American store owners. Many were hopeless and confused as they faced their burnt establishments and the endless insurance reports. Confronted with this unexpected dilemma, hundreds of non-English speaking Koreans sought help from bilingual interpreters. Last year, I had an opportunity to put my bilingual tongue to constructive use. Even with my Konglish, I was able to aid many people in those desperate times. With such great diversity in the U.S. today, multilingualism, with English as one of the languages, is a useful tool in communication. (K-28)

I strongly feel that the more languages you know, the more advantageous it is. For me, I am planning to establish businesses in Burma and Japan. Hopefully, my knowledge of their languages would help me in the future. I think that when we learn a country's language, we also get to understand its culture better, thus, broadening our minds. As a result, we would become more able to communicate and associate with different kinds of people and form many different kinds of friends. Since I feel that the knowledge of a language is so valuable, I will definitely encourage my children to learn as many as possible. (C-54)

In my situation, my ability to speak Cantonese fluently has enabled me to have a very close relationship with my family and all my relatives. (C-55)

Through all nineteen years of my life I never thought that learning Chiou Chou was for acceptance in my family. It was not until I wrote this essay that the thought struck me. From the use of Chiou Chou, the relationship between my family and I has been very close. We usually joke around, tell stories, or where our experiences at dinner time. My acceptance into my family proved to be very rewarding. Because America is a land of prejudices and not everyone is willing to lend a helping hand, one must stick together with one's family to help each other out. For me, I like to learn new languages to be accepted by other groups, but I would never alienate myself from my family. Because learning Chiou Chou has brought my family and I so close together, learning any new language to be accepted by any group can never break us apart. (C-71)

Love of the heritage language. At this point in their lives, most first and second generation students who have come to the university, whether they are bilingual or whether they are limited in their first language, and whether or not they underwent language rejection at one time, now have a sense of love for their heritage language.

As for English, I do speak the language but I don't think I'll ever talk it. English is the language that flows from the mind to the tongue and then to the pages of books. It is like a box of Plato blocks which allows you to make anything. But a Plato house cannot shelter human lives and a Plato robot cannot feel! I only talk Vietnamese. I talk it with all my senses. Vietnamese does not stop on my tongue, but it flows with the warm, soothing lotus tea down my throat like a river, giving life to the landscape in her path. It rises to my mind along with the vivid images of my grandmother's house and of my grandmother. It enters my ears in the poetry of *The Tale of Kieu,* singing in the voice of my Northern Vietnamese grandmother. It appears before my eyes in the faces of my aunt and cousins as they smile with such palpable joy. And it saturates my every nerves with healing warmth like effect of a piece of sugared ginger in a cold night. And that is how I only talk Vietnamese. (V-1)

Searching for identity. Asian-American students undergo an intense and poignant effort to reconcile the conflicting forces in their lives and find a comfortable sense of identity. Some Asian Americans who have spent their lives becoming as "Americanized" as possible still feel that racial attitudes in the United States keep them from assimilating completely.

I am Korean-American. Not American or even American-Korean, but simply Korean-American. I have black hair, brown eyes, and a yellowish complexion. No matter what I did to my outside appearance, my inherent outer characteristics did not allow me to be purely American like Caucasians. I tried to hide some of the differences in my appearance and culture and tried to be American-Korean, but as I got older, I realized I could not ignore my heritage.(K-36)

I realize that the color of my skin already paves a road of not being accepted one hundred percent in the American society. In general, monolingual Americans look at me and already presume that I am illiterate in English. Suddenly, they raise their voice when speaking, slow down the speed and enunciate every syllable. I feel like saying, "I'm Korean, not hard of hearing!" Then, when people realize I speak fluently, they would stop screaming but start talking in simple English as though my comprehension level is that of a second grader. Sometimes these little things would insult me but generally, I am amused. This is also the reason why no matter how much "American" I become, I am still Korean because my skin can't . . . more importantly, won't hide what I am. (K-13)

An important question popped in my mind, "Do I want to live the rest of my live feeling unattached from my first spoken language? to the culture that passed down in my family for generations? Do I actually belong in any culture?" True, I guess to the last question, I feel that I do belong to a culture, one that consists of individuals who feel most identified with America. Yet do Anglo-Americans accept this fact? Many may not because although we all share the same culture, we look drastically different in appearance. I might consider myself an American, but will they? This is not a sign of insecurity, but instead a reality faced by an Asian-American in a white, male-dominated society. (C-35)

My English speech background has definitely made me more comfortable in society. I feel it protects me, in some ways, from those who don't look upon the Chinese in a favorable light. Verbal abuse or remarks are still expressed every now and then, and it almost takes me by surprise. It's sad to realize that there are still many people who choose to be racist in society. It simply shows that society is still trapped by racism and its progress is not as developed as some may think. (C-38)

The college years are often a time when students begin to look at their heritage identity positively and make efforts to reclaim it.

About my senior year in high school, l began to realize what a shame it was that I did not know my own native language well enough to even communicate easily with my parents and grandparents. When I thought about it more, I realized I did not even know my own culture that well either. I had totally neglected my own heritage. Thus, I am now in the process of learning my own language and culture again. However, this does not mean I will forsake all the things I am now; I am only seeking a modification. I count my American culture important too. (K-36)

In my junior year, I began to realize the importance of my culture. Being Korean is part of my identity. I saw the folly of anglicizing my name and at that point I made a mental note to change my name back to [Korean name] in college. Now, thinking of my parents who had immigrated to find a better life in America, I find my parents' decision to cross over to be tragic. By coming here, they had risked the losing of my own cultural identity and theirs as well. Looking ahead into my own future as a near adult, I determinedly know that no matter how long I stay in America, I will always be a Korean. Nevertheless I feel a need to return to Korea. I know that I can study hard and soon become equally fluent in both languages, and by then, I will return and live in Korea. (K-3)

One of my innermost desires is to learn how to speak the language of my heritage. There are several reasons for my passionate desire to learn Tagalog. For one thing, I feel like a complete stranger in my own house; I would like to communicate with my parents without speaking English. Secondly, I would like to be able to communicate with my relatives in "their" language whenever a visit to the Philippines is possible. Thirdly, I would like to be proficient in two languages rather than one. Last but certainly not least, I would like to preserve the language that has been a part of my cultural heritage for years. (P-4)

Some strongly embrace their American identity but argue that knowing other languages is not "un-American" and are very happy to be bilingual, or sad if they aren't.

I don't have the blond hair nor the white skin; I had lived three fifths of my life in Korea, not in the U.S.A.; and also, I definitely speak better Korean than English. All of these segregate me from being a white American. However, who are the true Americans? Isn't the U.S.A. a country for everyone? I truly believe that being a white American is not the only reason that makes a person a true American. It's the willingness. If a person

> is willing to be an American, obeys all the laws, and takes the responsibilities as an American, he/she should be called as a true American. Speaking another language other than English is the matter beyond Americanism and I think it is a very good advantage for the persons. (K-21)

While the examples show that students struggling with English care more about improving their English skills and less about their skills in the heritage language, many of those who have lost or never attained fluency in their heritage language feel ashamed and incomplete. Those who are satisfied with their language skills in both languages tend to have a more positive self-image.

> Being bilingual in Korean and English has truly made me feel fortunate for several very important reasons. Not only do I not have to worry about serious language barriers between my parents and I, but I do not feel a sense of shame or even a void in my life because I am somewhat fluent in my native language. (K-22)

First and second generation Asian-American students at the university are struggling to define their identity. The internal conflicts that some of them are still waging is clearly present in their writings.

> So growing up as a Korean-American has had its disadvantages, but it also has advantages, that I can now speak two languages proficiently. I don't wish to abandon my culture and heritage, and neither do I want to be a separatist. My great struggle will be to find the balance between these two conflicting halves of my self. (K-26)

> I find it alarming that with this loss of language, I might also be losing a part of my cultural identity. I don't feel like I'm truly Chinese and I don't feel like I'm completely American either. (C-75)

> When I go back to India for visits people tell my parents that I am "Americanized" but they appreciate that I am still fluent in my native Indian language. For my generation, the bridging between our old culture and the American culture is difficult and sometimes we feel like we are a part of neither. This feeling of being an alien raises the question "Who am I?" and the need to seek and identify becomes apparent. The Hindi language helps reaffirm my identity in that group and it is yet

another means of expressing my East Indian culture, whose preservation is essential to me. (I-5)

For some, the rejection of heritage language and culture still stands, and they see themselves not as Asian-Americans, but simply as Americans.

My father once told me that America is now his country and that his allegiance belongs to America, yet the only thing that gives him his identity and affiliation to being Korean is his language. I do not know the land where I was born, and, personally, I do not care to. I was raised here in America and my allegiance belongs to America. . . .

I write, speak, converse, and dream in nothing but English and I know no other way of doing these things. (K-25)

Many see themselves as having a dual identity, and seek to find the balance between them.

In truth, I consider myself "Korean-American." It's true I was born in Korea and I'm not a U.S. citizen yet but I've spent most of my life here. I probably won't be able to "survive" back in Korea anymore. I'm a Korean with American values, lifestyle, and mind. To me, being a Korean-American means to nurture Korean traditions and customs but also to assimilate into the American culture as much as possible. (K-10)

The loss of one's cultural language symbolized the loss of one's cultural identity. Many Asian Americans pride themselves for successfully turning their kids into "complete" Americans who speak English in flawless American accent. In my perspective, this actually is something that they should be ashamed of. Without doubt, fitting oneself into the mainstream is important; yet retaining one's cultural language is not at all trivial. To me, I will try my best to excel both in English and my mother tongue, Cantonese. (C-26)

I feel very lucky and enriched to have parents who believed in teaching their children how to speak their native languages. Many of my Chinese-American friends cannot speak their native language. I am proud to be Chinese (Taiwanese) and am very thankful that I do speak my native languages fluently. I feel that knowing my native languages has helped me as a person and has reaffirmed my ties of being Chinese. Language plays an important role in a person's history, background, culture, and ethnicity. It enables the person to understand themselves or other people better. Learning a language at a young age takes the work out of this otherwise tedious task. I was fortunate enough to grow up in household full of people with versatile tongues. I am proud to be Taiwanese, Chinese, and as an American citizen, I am also proud to be American. (C-30)

I do regard multilingualism, or at least bilingualism, as an important part of anyone's lives. I am an American, but we all have our heritage to maintain. Each one of us is filled with a mixture of various cultures and ethnicities; this is what makes America so unique. If we all blend as one, there is nothing to separate our individual lives. There must be something which sets us apart from everyone else, something which allows us to stand out, and this is our ethnicity. We are all Americans, but to me, being an American means that we are all individuals from numerous ethnic backgrounds which have come together to live in peace and harmony. (C-41)

Learning the universal language and a native language ensures that no one person will grow up ignorant of their cultural identity. In America, knowledge of English is necessary to succeed, but each individual should not be forced to abandon his/her cultural roots. The United States, though standing for equality and democracy, has often been blinded by prejudices and racism into believing that linguistic minorities should abandon their heritage and become "Americanized" in order to prove their loyalty or else be excluded from society. But America should not become a "melting pot" where each person loses his/her identity while conforming to the majority. Rather America should become a "salad bowl" where cultural differences are appreciated and not oppressed by mixing cultures in which each retains a unique flavor and creates an enriched society. (C-64)

I have experienced prejudices because of speaking the Indian language in the public. When my family and I go to a public place and speak languages other than English we are given glares and rude stares. Majority of the American society feel it is rude of us not to speak English when we are out of our homes and associating with "Americans." They feel uncomfortable because they think we are talking about them. They have often said that this is America and not India and that we should only speak English. I feel that is not what America is. It is a land of freedom and everyone has the right to free speech as long it does not hurt other people. We came to this wonderful country precisely for those rights. It is not fair tell Americans to speak *only* the language of a country that they are visiting or living in. If we are not hurting anyone than we have the right to speak any language that we please. That is America. (I-2)

Thoughts for future generations. Although there was a great deal of variation in heritage language fluency among the students and many different views about identity, almost everyone agreed that they wanted their children to know the heritage language if at all possible.

> I hope that when I have children of my own, they would appreciate the Chinese language as much as I do. Although they will be much more Americanized, I wish that beside English, they would also learn the Chinese language, without one more dominant over the other. I fear that if they only know English, they would lose a part of their culture identity. And not only that, there will be a tremendous communication gap between them and my parents. And at that time, I would have to play the role of a translator between my kids and my parents. That will be horrible! (C-13)

> I'm scared to lose a part of who I am. But more importantly, I realize that I have the awesome responsibility of one day passing on a precious language, that really is more than just a language, to my own children. (C-25)

> I was determined to teach my kids only English so that they would not have to go through this bilingual experience. But in hindsight, I think this experience was more positive than negative. I am lucky to be able to speak both Cantonese and English fluently. (C-45)

> Now I am having second thoughts about teaching my kids only English, because Cantonese for me was a source of identity. Bilingualism to me means dual identity. If I do not teach my kids culture a great part of which is language, then I will be breaking this vital link that has held generations of my family together. (C-45)

I want to teach my children Cantonese because I want them to preserve some of our ancestral culture. In essence, I want my children to know and understand who they are. I do not ever want them to lose their Chinese identity even if they become completely Americanized. (C-70)

Conclusions. The changes in language attitudes that these students report are in keeping with Tse (1998), who discusses three stages of ethnic identity formation: (1) unawareness, (2) ethnic ambivalence or evasion, (3) ethnic emergence, and (4) ethnic identity incorporation. Most of the people writing these autobiographies are in stage 3 or 4, but the language journey for these college students is far from complete. Most will probably continue to go through different periods of life when their heritage language is more important to them and others when their heritage language is less important. Some will go on to careers where their contacts with the homeland are enhanced or where their heritage language plays a role, others will not. Some will marry people of the same language background, others will not. While almost all the students write that they hope to help their own children grow up bilingual, we know from past experience that second-generation and third-generation Americans are increasingly likely to know very little or nothing of their heritage language, and so the intergenerational struggle so clear in these autobiographies is likely to be repeated between these students and their children, or else the families will "surrender" to English.

Policy implications. The response of some to the points I have made here will be that it is a good thing that language shift is occurring so rapidly, and that the United States should be comforted by this fact. It is good for our country that immigrants are abandoning their languages, they will say. And after all, these are successful students, now in the university—so if they rejected their language, it seems like it must have done them good. But we need to look at the human cost of what is happening. As this paper has shown, the first language loss that so many students have experienced has been accompanied by a loss of family intimacy and communication, a sense of bitterness toward a system and people that the students have come to see as racist, and a sense of personal inadequacy. The bitterness in the student autobiographies is clear. These students have learned English, but they have grown up with a sense that no matter what they do, they are not being accepted as Americans. They have grown up with a strong feeling that this is a racist country that does not want to make room for them. Is this sense of bitterness and alienation good for our country?

There is no doubt that the school experience in the United States is the most important factor in the pressure on children to abandon their heritage language. We have seen in this paper that peer group teasing and ostracism is the pressure of which the immigrant youths are most aware. But implicit policies of the schools back up this pressure in many ways, not the least of which is the fact that school teachers and officials turn a blind eye to students' racist slurs (Benjamin 1997). In Benjamin's study of Spanish at an elementary school in New Mexico, she writes "The older siblings [of the students in the study] recounted the terrible experiences they had had in middle and high school. For those who were unwilling or unable to shift to English or conform to a more assimilated identity, the consequences were frequently rejection, suspension and even expulsion." Thus, although there is no necessary direct relationship between first language abandonment and success in education, the peer-group ostracism suffered by minority students works against success in the education system by students with a strong sense of ethnic identity—the very students who would be most likely to retain their heritage language. The one student who came from a school that celebrated multiculturalism could serve as a model for how our schools might begin to combat the intolerance that creates this bitterness.

Immigrant families are offering the United States a great resource of bilingual offspring, which the United States is rejecting, not only through the schools, but also through political intolerance within the government (witness the congressional efforts to make English the official language and the present legislative attacks against bilingual education and other bilingual services). And yet, bilingual citizens are increasingly needed as we become more involved with other nations diplomatically and economically. It would appear to be in the interest of the United States to foster and encourage bilingualism, through such programs as strong maintenance-oriented bilingual education programs (a hopeless thought, in the wake of California's Unz Initiative). Nor should America fear the development of the dual identity that many of these students are attempting to work out. The desire to be an American is not diminished by the desire to maintain a sense of identity with one's ethnic heritage. To end with a final quote from one of the student autobiographies:

> The lesson that I have learned is the value of language. It identifies the character and heritage of an entire group of people, and serves to bind them together. It is a precious gift that withers away if it is not used. It is often said that a mind is a terrible thing to waste. The same can be said about a language. (C-9)

REFERENCES

Benjamin, Rebecca. 1997. Si hablas espanol eres mojado: Spanish as an identity marker in the lives of Mexicano children. *Journal of Social Justice* 24(2): 26–44.

Crawford, James. 1992. *Language Loyalties: a source book on the official English controversy.* Chicago: University of Chicago Press.

Dopke, Susanne. 1992. *One parent, one language: an interactional approach.* J. Benjamin's.
Krashen, Stephen D. 1998. Language shyness and heritage language development. In Stephen D. Krashen, Lucy Tse, and Jeff McQuillan (eds.), *Heritage language development.* Culver City, CA: Language Education Associates. 41–49.
Tse, Lucy. 1998. Ethnic identity formation and its implications for heritage language development. In Stephen D. Krashen, Lucy Tse, and Jeff McQuillan (eds.), *Heritage language development.* Culver City, CA: Language Education Associates. 15–30.
Wong Fillmore, L. 1991. When learning a second language means losing the first. *Early Childhood Research Quarterly* 6: 323–346.

NOTE

1. Numbers following each quote reference the particular autobiography. "C-6" stands for Chinese autobiography #6, etc. K= Korea, I= India, P = Philippines, V = Vietnam.

Ebonics and standard English in the classroom: Some issues

Salikoko S. Mufwene
University of Chicago

Introduction. The Oakland Unified School District Board's resolution about using Ebonics in the classroom in order to help its speakers develop more proficiency in standard English and perform better academically brought to the surface a number of questions and issues on this vernacular. Among these was the question of whether Ebonics is an American English dialect or a separate language altogether. Reactions to the resolutions included myths about its development. I focus on two of them in this essay.

First, some of those claiming that African-American English (AAE) is a separate language have argued that it is a Niger-Congo language mistakenly identified as English (e.g., Smith 1998). Therefore standard English should be taught to its speakers using second-language teaching techniques, more or less in the same way that English is taught to speakers of Niger-Congo languages in Africa, for instance.

The second myth has to do less with use of any special techniques for teaching standard English to AAE-speakers than with negative opinions about African Americans. This myth considers African Americans to be less skilled at acquiring the English language in North America, unlike members of other ethnic groups. Putatively, White Americans have inherited English intact from England and have restructured it little, if at all, whereas African Americans have misshaped it, perhaps beyond recognition, and only their laziness or mental inferiority must be blamed for the problems experienced by their school children.

It is not clear whether these unfounded myths are clearly different from each other, except regarding the ethnic affiliations of their authors and their attitudes to using federal or state funds to help the relevant school children. The Ebonics qua Niger-Congo language position has been advocated especially by some African Americans since Williams (1975), whose definition, discussed below, has provided good justification for requesting allocation of funds from Limited English Proficiency (LEP) programs to teaching standard English to AAE-speakers (Baugh 1998). Since LEP programs were designed for speakers of languages other than English, they argue that AAE can also be treated as a separate language, and techniques for teaching standard English to its speakers must be at least similar to those used for teaching it to children of immigrants from non-Anglophone countries.

The misshaped English position is an older and more popular myth, held mostly by the average nonlinguist White American and some successful African Americans who have an opinion on the subject matter. Those who subscribe to it assume that the average White American speaks standard English and this is little restructured, if at all, from English as brought over from England in the seventeenth century. Accordingly, all it should take African-American school children to speak standard English is being more dedicated to schoolwork and working harder at the task at hand to succeed like everybody else.

I take issue with both positions, arguing that all American English varieties are contact-based, restructured varieties. Everything we have learned, and will learn, about the development of AAE makes us more aware of questions we should be addressing about the development of White American English varieties (Mufwene 1996a, 1999a). The Niger-Congo identification of AAE is quite a romantic idea that is undermined, on the one hand, by communicative difficulties between Anglophone Africans and basilectal AAE-speakers, and, on the other, by the often observed structural similarities between AAE and White Southern English (Mufwene, in press a). I also argue that the debate on Ebonics in the classroom has been unduly ethnicized. It should have been no more than a question on whether or not nonstandard English vernaculars can, or should, be used in the classroom. Aside from further stigmatizing AAE-speakers, the debate as conducted to date has also been at the expense of underprivileged White children whose condition in the classroom has probably not been better off than that of African-American school children.

What we should remember about the development of American English varieties. The tradition of singling out AAE as the only restructured variety of English in North America is bizarre, because there is no White American English variety that matches a British English variety of today or of the past few centuries (Mufwene 1996a). As far as contemporary varieties are concerned, part of the explanation for this diversification lies in the fact that British English itself has changed since the seventeenth century. The population movements that brought European populations over to the New World started in Europe. Migrations of British indentured servants to North America were typically extensions of labor migrations in the British Isles, by which English, Irish, and Scottish populations moved around in search of jobs and often wound up unemployed in port cities such as London, Bristol, and Liverpool, and then decided in desperation to try a chance in the New World (Bailyn 1986; Fischer 1989).

In England, these population movements also entailed dialect contacts, and the latter led to the restructuring of British English into its present dialects. In the case of the United States, the population movements led to new contacts among English dialects (Algeo 1991) and with other languages, European and non-European. Although English prevailed over the other European languages, such as French, German, and Dutch, its victory was a pyrrhic one. It prevailed in a restructured form. The socioeconomic history of North America suggests that even if British English dialects had not changed over the past four centuries, American varieties of English would still not be identical with them. Indirect evidence for this conclusion comes from new Englishes in places such as Australia, New Zealand, and the Falkland Islands (Trudgill 1986). Although they developed from later, eighteenth- and nineteenth-century varieties of British English, novel contacts of (subsets of) these dialects have produced varieties different from both American and British Englishes.

The situation of AAE is a compounded one, with the still unanswered question of what role African languages played in the selection of its features, even if the features themselves did not necessarily originate in the African languages (Mufwene 1999b). AAE has remained very close structurally to White English varieties that developed on the tobacco and cotton plantations of the southern states, as well as on the rice fields of coastal South Carolina and Georgia. Gullah must have diverged earlier from other American varieties, because segregation was instituted early in coastal South Carolina, in 1720, when the colony was proclaimed a crown colony. The reasons for segregation were that the Blacks made up the majority of people in the region, and, as a result, Whites thought there were constant threats of uprising against slave-owner oppression (Wood 1974). Nonetheless, Gullah remains close to plantation White speech, despite the kinds of differences observed by Rickford (1985).

African-American vernacular English (AAVE) seems to have diverged rather late from White Southern English, to which it has remained very close. The divergence, attributed mostly to White varieties undergoing changes in which African Americans have not participated, is the consequence of the institutionalization of segregated life styles since 1877, at the end of Reconstruction and after the passage of Jim Crow laws (Schneider 1995; Bailey 1997). The fact that AAVE shares several of its features with White American varieties (e.g., Appalachian English) suggests that its peculiarities were selected from English—undoubtedly under partial corroborative influence of some African languages (Mufwene 1999b)—by the principle of convergence qua congruence (Thomason and Kaufman 1988; Mufwene 1996b).[1]

There is thus no reason to assume that the AAE—both Gullah and AAVE—developed by any structural processes peculiar to it, although it has selected a set of structural features that only overlaps with sets selected by other dialects. This observation applies to any English dialect, because none is identical with another. Despite the following definition of Ebonics proposed by Williams (1975) and adopted by Smitherman (1997) and Smith (1998), it remains that AAE-speakers sound more like speakers of other American English varieties than like those of Caribbean or African English varieties:

> Ebonics may be defined as "the linguistic and paralinguistic
> features which on a concentric continuum represents the com-
> municative competence of the West African, Caribbean, and the
> United States slave descendants of African origin. It includes
> the various idioms, patois, argots, ideolects [sic], and social di-
> alects of black people" especially those who have been forced
> to adapt to colonial circumstances (Williams 1975: vi). *Ebonics*
> derives its form from ebony (black) and phonics (sound, the
> study of sound) and refers to the study of the language of black
> people in all its cultural uniqueness. (Williams 1975: vi)

Structural linguistic facts, especially those features that AAE shares with
other American nonstandard vernaculars (e.g., Poplack 1999; Bailey and Thomas
1998), suggest that AAE is a regular American linguistic phenomenon, and it
need not be disfranchised because of the race of its speakers (Mufwene 1997). A
pilot survey I conducted recently (Mufwene, in press b) shows that, overall, its
speakers think they speak English and not some form of a separate African (-
American) language.

AAE in the classroom. The typical solution proposed to date to improve the
proficiency of many African-American school children in standard English has
been conceived on second-language teaching techniques. To be sure, there is a
sense in which standard English, an elusive target that I will not attempt to define
here, is a second-language variety to most English speakers. One of the reasons is
that it is primarily written with structures more consistent with writing as a
medium of expression, whereas other English varieties are primarily oral, with
structures more consistent with orality. For instance, the latter have fewer complex sentential structures and certainly fewer instances of complex subordination.
Wh-relative clauses and Pied-Piping are more typical of written texts than of spoken discourse. As a matter of fact, *wh*-relatives in spoken discourse are a byprod-
uct of literacy. They are rather uncommon in nonstandard vernaculars, except for
where and *what* in a sentence such as *everything **what** Mary said.* However, some
vernaculars are structurally closer to the standard than some others are, and
speakers of such varieties have fewer problems developing proficiency in standard English. One may also argue that one of the reasons some native speakers
fail to acquire perfect command of standard English is their inability to perceive
differences between some structures of their vernaculars and those of standard
English. For instance, to the extent that *ain't* is accepted as an emphatic negator,
one may miss the fact that standard English does not allow saying *I ain't seen Tom*
instead of *I haven't seen Tom.* Likewise, because *done* meaning 'finish' is
homonymous with *done* as past participle of the verb *do,* its use as a marker of
PERFECT in nonstandard vernacular English, as in *I done told you,* may easily be

transferred incorrectly into standard English discourse. Underdifferentiation and overgeneralization are phenomena common in second-language usage.

Similarities between learning a second language and developing proficiency in a second dialect end, perhaps, with the above observations. A native speaker still feels that he or she is learning to read and write, and even compose more structured discourse, within the same language. In the process of learning standard English, he or she brings into the classroom assumptions and expectations that are not the same as those of non-native speakers of the same language, such as being able to understand what is said in standard English and paraphrasing it in their own vernaculars. Such an expectation is to some extent validated by the exposure that a hearing child has typically had to oral media before going to school. The child has developed some passive competence in the media variety and an awareness of structural features that distinguish that variety from his or her own vernacular. Unfortunately, because of the passive nature of this competence in the media dialect, the child may not realize that he or she keeps slipping back to patterns of his or her own vernacular while intending to speak or write standard English, especially when differences between the two varieties are subtle and the relevant nonstandard features are strongly stigmatized. The question here is: how should teachers handle such situations? Should they treat speakers of nonstandard vernaculars in the same ways as they do speakers of languages other than English? Are the psychological dispositions so similar in both cases?

The literature reports all sorts of humiliating experiences in which the child's vernacular has constantly been put down, his or her sense of identity and self-esteem shattered, and motivation for performing well in the classroom eroded (Delpit 1998). Based on Smitherman (1998), Judge Charles Joiner was right in treating the problem in the Ann Arbor Black English Trial more as a problem of attitude toward the vernacular of African-American school children than as a problem of another language or of significantly different structures. The position regarding structures is indeed what is supported by McWhorter (1997: 9–10) when he observes:

> It is a fact that Black English is not different enough from standard English to pose any significant obstacle to speaking, reading, or writing it. Black English is simply a dialect of English, just as standard English is. . . .
>
> It is mutually intelligible with standard English both on the page and spoken and its speakers do not occupy a separate nation. . . .
>
> We also must not make the mistake of equating Black English with mere "street slang." Black English speakers indeed often use a colorful slang . . . just as standard English speakers

> use slang. . . . African-Americans are often aware of the simi-
> larity between black speech and that of poor Southern whites,
> such speech is essentially as different from standard English as
> Black English is.

The way to interpret McWhorter's position constructively is that AAE is not alone in being different from standard English and that the differences between AAE and American standard English are not necessarily greater than between the latter and other American nonstandard English vernaculars. The position implies correctly that techniques for teaching standard English to African-American school children need not be different from those used for teaching it to other American school children who speak English natively, though they should be adapted to subcultural differences. This position does not of course entail that school systems should continue business as usual. It simply suggests that AAE need not be treated as an exceptional or uniquely deviant case in the classroom.

In a way McWhorter's position invites us to situate elsewhere than in structural differences the problem with the failure of school systems to make many African-American school children proficient in standard English. The kinds of attitudinal problems discussed, especially by Delpit (1998), deserve more attention. She points out that solutions proposed to date to address underproficiency in standard English have typically eroded the positive disposition of African-American school children in one way or another. The very fact of singling out their vernacular as the only or most deviant one from standard English is a problem in itself, because we know that every vernacular deviates from standard English in one way or another. It boils down to a problem of tolerance of linguistic variation, reflecting negative attitudes of some members of the American society to speakers of some specific varieties (Lippi-Green 1997). It is indeed a problem when the child is led to wonder why some ethnic ways of speaking are accepted but not his or hers. Adopting special solutions that privilege other ethnic and cultural backgrounds over those of African-American kids is a serious psychological problem that can kill the student's motivation for learning.

Solutions that insist on treating AAE as a separate language of the Black Diaspora have derived support from cultural differences that distinguish the average African-American population from the majority White American population (e.g., Smith 1998: 55). They have, however, ignored differences within the White American population, for instance, the fact that Appalachian and rural White Southern school children apparently face problems similar to those of African-American children, unless their teachers are from their own backgrounds and use educational materials that pay attention to these particular backgrounds. Overemphasis on structural differences between White and African-American ways of speaking, sometimes suggesting that most Whites speak standard English, gives the historically incorrect impression that unlike other Americans,

African Americans have failed in the acquisition of English as brought from England. It contributes unwittingly to the myth that African Americans are lazy or mentally inferior and had to develop their vernaculars through extraordinary processes. Despite their authors' good intentions, this approach disfranchises and stigmatizes African-American school children as much as those alternatives that are racially motivated and assign them to special remedial programs on the simple basis of dialectal differences.

Delpit (1998: 19) is correct in observing that constant negative comments about their vernaculars and constant zealous corrections of the ways they read or speak make African-American school children "increasingly aware of the school's negative attitude toward their community." This treatment of African-American children makes them resentful of being put down and unmotivated for learning. Indeed, as Delpit also observes, there are alternative, less humiliating, and more constructive ways of teaching standard English to AAE-speakers, as there are for speakers of other vernaculars. For instance, she suggests role playing, which should teach the kids "that there are many ways of saying the same thing, and that certain contexts suggest particular kinds of linguistic performances" (Delpit 1998: 19). Excessive corrections intended to discourage school children from speaking their vernaculars altogether often ignore the fact that the same children are subject to contrary peer pressures in their own backgrounds, such as stigmatization for "talking proper" or like a White person.

As a matter of fact, AAE has persisted, despite being stigmatized, because it has also functioned as a marker of ethnic identity in a society where integration has been more de jure than de facto. When an African-American child is put down at school, when he or she realizes that the chances for success in the socioeconomic system look grim despite promises associated with standard English proficiency, and when there is no rational motivation for losing one's ethnic identity, then the child may lose interest in learning. The goal of the school system in teaching standard English should not be to replace the child's native vernacular but instead—as in second-language teaching—to help him or her acquire command of an additional variety of English, in order to function adequately in settings where the vernacular is not accepted. In this respect, the typical approach to the problem of many African-American school children with standard English has failed and one can only empathize with the Oakland Unified School District Board's decision to seek alternative solutions. The board just did not have to claim that AAE is a separate language.

Conclusions. AAE is definitely not the only nonstandard vernacular spoken in the United States of America. Its excessive stigmatization and the related commitment on the part of some to eradicate it may have to do with negative attitudes inherited from the American colonial past, the period since which African Americans have often been thought of as less intelligent. The very fact that vernaculars of the White middle class have typically been identified by fiat as standard reflects the prejudice that everyone should adapt to White middle-class norms.

It is true that socioeconomic stratification has imposed a system in which command of either standard or White middle-class English has become a requirement for success in the professional world. However, developing proficiency in these norms need not be at the cost of abandoning one's vernacular for all communicative functions. Vernaculars have their own social identity functions; and many speakers are not ready, and certainly not eager, to renounce that social-indexical role of their vernacular. As observed by Delpit (1998), they see in the humiliations of excessive corrections and in the very style of the corrections themselves aggression against their own ethnic and cultural identities. Children's negative reactions to inadequate approaches to the standard English proficiency problem foster lack of enthusiasm, which in turn produces poor performance not only in standard English but also in the classroom in general, especially when they become self-conscious linguistically.

It remains imperative that school systems teach standard English more successfully to AAE-speakers. What I hope to have shown in this paper is that this effort should be consistent with the development of diverse nonstandard English vernaculars in North America since the colonial period and with the fact that AAE is only one among many nonstandard vernaculars. Perhaps excessive concern with AAE is in itself a negative factor that has ethnicized the more general question of how to teach standard English efficiently to speakers of nonstandard vernaculars in general without bruising their speakers' self esteem and eroding their enthusiasm and interest in being educated.

REFERENCES

Algeo, John. 1991. Language. In Eric Foner and John A. Garraty (eds.), *The Reader's companion to American history*. Boston: Houghton Mifflin. 637–640.

Bailey, Guy. 1997. When did southern American English begin? In Edgar Schneider (ed.), *Englishes around the world*, vol. 1, *General studies, British Isles, North America: Studies in honor of Manfred Görlach*. Amsterdam: John Benjamins. 255–275.

Bailey, Guy, and Erik Thomas. 1998. Some aspects of African-American vernacular phonology. In Salikoko S. Mufwene, John R. Rickford, Guy Bailey, and John Baugh (eds.), *African-American English: Structure, history, and use*. London: Routledge. 85–109.

Bailyn, Bernard. 1986. *The peopling of British North America: An introduction*. New York: Random House.

Baugh, John. 1998. Linguistics, education, and the law: Educational reform for African-American language minority students. In Salikoko S. Mufwene, John R. Rickford, Guy Bailey, and John Baugh (eds.), *African-American English: Structure, history, and use*. London: Routledge. 282–301.

Delpit, Lisa. 1998. Ebonics and culturally responsive instruction. In Theresa Perry and Lisa Delpit (eds.), *The real Ebonics debate: Power, language, and the education of African-American children*. Boston: Beacon Press. 17–26.

Fischer, David Hackett. 1989. *Albion's seed: Four British folkways in America.* New York: Oxford University Press.

Lippi-Green, Rosina. 1997. *English with an accent: Language, ideology, and discrimination in the United States.* London: Routledge.

McWhorter, John H. 1997. Wasting energy on illusion. *The Black Scholar* 27(1): 9–14.

Mufwene, Salikoko S. 1996a. The development of American Englishes: Some questions from a creole genesis perspective. In Edgar W. Schneider, *Varieties of English around the world: Focus on the USA.* Amsterdam: John Benjamins. 231–263.

Mufwene, Salikoko S. 1996b. The founder principle in creole genesis. *Diachronica* 13: 83–134.

Mufwene, Salikoko S. 1997. The legitimate and illegitimate offspring of English. In Larry E. Smith and Michael L. Forman (eds.), *World Englishes 2000.* Honolulu: University of Hawai'i and the East-West Center. 182–203.

Mufwene, Salikoko S. 1999a. North American varieties of English as by-products of population contacts. In Rebecca Wheeler (ed.), *Living English.* Westport, CT: Greenwood. 15–37.

Mufwene, Salikoko S. 1999b. Some sociohistorical inferences about the development of African-American English. In Shana Poplack (ed.), *The English history of African-American English.* Oxford: Blackwell.

Mufwene, Salikoko S. in press a. English in the Black Diaspora: Development and identity. In Braj Kachru (ed.), *Language in diaspora: Creativity and identity.* Urbana: University of Illinois Press.

Mufwene, Salikoko S. in press b. What is African-American English? In Sonja Lanehart (ed.), *Sociocultural and historical contexts of African-American Vernacular English.* Amsterdam: John Benjamins.

Poplack, Shana (ed.). 1999. *The English history of African-American English.* Oxford: Blackwell.

Rickford, John R. 1985. Ethnicity as a sociolinguistic boundary. *American Speech* 60: 90–125.

Schneider, Edgar W. 1995. Verbal -*s* inflection in 'early' American Black English. In Jacek Fisiak (ed.), *Linguistic change under contact conditions.* Berlin: Mouton de Gruyter. 315–326.

Smith, Ernie. 1998. What is Black English? What is Ebonics? In Theresa Perry and Lisa Delpit (eds.), *The real Ebonics debate: Power, language, and the education of African-American children.* Boston: Beacon Press. 49–58.

Smitherman, Geneva. 1997. Black language and the education of Black children: One mo once. *The Black Scholar* 27(1): 29–35.

Smitherman, Geneva. 1998. Black English/Ebonics: What it be like? In Theresa Perry and Lisa Delpit (eds.), *The real Ebonics debate: Power, language, and the education of African-American children.* Boston: Beacon Press. 29–47.

Thomason, Sarah G., and Terrence Kaufman. 1988. *Language contact, creolization, and genetic linguistics.* Berkeley: University of California Press.

Trudgill, Pater. 1986. *Dialects in contact.* Oxford: Blackwell.

Williams, Robert L. 1975. *Ebonics: The true language of Black folks.* St. Louis, Missouri: Robert L. Williams and Associates.

Wood, Peter H. 1974. *The black majority: Negroes in colonial South Carolina from 1670 through the Stono rebellion.* New York: Alfred Knopf.

NOTE

1. My current research shows that the term "convergence" is not terminologically adequate.

Ebonic need not be English

Ralph W. Fasold
Georgetown University

I believe it is a legitimate question to ask how I, an old white man with no claim whatsoever to being a part of the African-American community, can try to talk authoritatively about the language of African Americans and to make a recommendation about the status it might have within its own community. It is certainly not because there is any sense in which I consider myself entitled to have a part in the community. Rather, I see my role as a linguist as analogous to that of a BMW automobile technician. As a linguist, I believe I have insights into the technical inner workings of the language I will call Ebonic. Like the auto technician, I might know more about the inner workings of the device than most of its owners do. But like the technician, I will never know what it is like to own and use it. I confess I am envious of the users of Ebonic, like the technician might be, and for the same reasons. Having looked under the hood, as it were, I know the power and precision the device is capable of. But since I am not one of its owners, I have no practice, skill, or experience in driving it. I will return to the technical specifications of Ebonic later, explaining my admiration for it.

The label "Ebonic." Ebonic has been known by a number of names over the years, from the antiquated and ultimately insulting "Negro Nonstandard English" of the 1960s to "Black English" and "Black English Vernacular" to "African-American Vernacular English" (currently favored by most linguists who do research on the language) to the "Ebonics" of the famous controversy of late 1996 and early 1997. Since I am going to take the position that this language is not, or at least need not be, English, it will not be appropriate for me to use "African-American Vernacular English," which presupposes that it *is* English. The term "Ebonics" was not coined by a linguist, but by a psychologist in the 1970s, who combined "ebony" and "phonics," supposing that the result meant "black sounds." But "phonics" does not mean "sounds"—it is the name of a technique for teaching reading. Besides, a language is far more than just its sounds. Nevertheless, the coinage is actually very close to a natural way of naming languages. There are languages that end in "-ic," like Arabic or Amharic, as well as language family names of that form, like Slavic or Germanic. Without referring to "phonics" or the like, the coinage "Ebonic" would be a clear way to specify "black language." Besides, the use of "Ebonics" during the debate was ambiguous. It was used to refer both to a language and an educational method that utilized the language. In my usage, I will reserve "Ebonics" for the educational program and apply the term "Ebonic" to the language.[1]

The concept "a language." Linguists generally agree that status as a language or dialect is largely political. In January 1997, for example, the Linguistic Society of America (LSA) passed a resolution on Ebonic that included the following paragraph:

> The distinction between "languages" and "dialects" is usually made more on social and political grounds than on purely linguistic ones. For example, different varieties of Chinese are popularly regarded as "dialects," though their speakers cannot understand each other, but speakers of Swedish and Norwegian, which are regarded as separate "languages," generally understand each other. What is important from a linguistic and educational point of view is not whether AAVE [African American Vernacular English] is called a "language" or a "dialect" but rather that its systematicity be recognized.

Other linguists have taken a rather stronger viewpoint, however. Noam Chomsky (1982:14) made this remark about his view of the concept "language" as opposed to "grammar": "Language, whatever it may be, is a notion more abstract than grammar, more remote from actual mechanisms, consequently raising new problems which may or may not be worth trying to solve (personally, I am skeptical)."

In an editorial in the linguistics journal *Natural Language and Linguistic Theory,* Geoffrey Nunberg (1995) emphasized the role of national identities—other social identities—in determining what is or is not a "language": "Whatever people may suppose, that is, there are languages because there are nations, and not the other way around. So there are no linguistic conflicts that weren't first national (or ethnic, or religious) conflicts."

Reviewing a book on language in Africa, William Samarin (1996) made the same point even more starkly. Speaking of a hypothetical study of sub-Saharan Africa as it was before colonialism, he wrote:

> The map of Africa we would start with would be white, or gray, or black—whatever best iconized a "clean slate." A continent without languages. Yes, a continent without "languages." Of course, Africans used language in a linguistic sense to communicate with each other, and we have learned

that these are beautifully complex and awesomely elegant means of verbal expression, not the primitive jabberings that they were first taken to be. But they were not "languages" in the socio-cultural sense. There is little in our knowledge of Africa to suggest ethnolinguistic self-consciousness. Thus we can say that before literacy there were no "languages."[2]

Both Nunberg and Samarin realize that what it takes to make a language is not a set of structural linguistic properties or lack of intelligibility with related linguistic systems, but, at least in part, the conviction that the linguistic system is a symbol of nationalist or ethnic identity. Given this sociocultural property, a language is distinct from all others, no matter how mutually intelligible. Without it, you do not have a language, even if there is no other linguistic variety on the face of the earth that is at all similar.

In fact, there are cases around the world of both kinds—cases in which mutually unintelligible varieties belong to the same language and others where mutually intelligible varieties are separate languages. The LSA resolution cited previously mentioned one of each kind of case. The dialects of Chinese are very much distinct from one another. It is agony for a student from Guangzhou, for example, to study at Bejing University, because his Cantonese dialect will be of almost no help in understanding the Mandarin he encounters in the classroom. Yet, the two remain dialects and not distinct languages. Linguistics professors sometimes say that the Chinese dialects really are languages because they differ from each other as much as the Romance languages do. But that is just one perspective. I sometimes fantasize that somewhere in China a linguistics professor is telling her students, "Europeans think that the Romance languages of southern and western Europe are separate languages. But they are really just dialects because they differ from each other no more than the Chinese dialects do."

Arabic is a similar case. Although Classical Arabic is the same throughout the Arab world, it serves limited functions and has very few fluent speakers. The various modern varieties of Arabic are quite distinct from one Arab nation to another—so much so as to impede mutual intelligibility. I am told that a student in the United States from Morocco will find it easier to converse with a fellow student from Jordan in English than in Arabic, because their mutual Arabic varieties are too hard for them to understand. Nevertheless, there is a single language, Arabic, that unites all the Arab nations as one people.

There are any number of cases of mutually intelligible varieties that are separate languages. The LSA resolution mentioned Norwegian and Swedish, which have been estimated to be up to 80% mutually intelligible. But there are any number of other examples. During the half-century or so that Estonia was incorporated into the Soviet Union, Estonians were able to keep in touch with Western television news and other programming by watching Finnish television, which they could receive from Helsinki across the Baltic Sea. The fact that the television programs were in Finnish did not stop Estonian viewers from enjoying them, although there is no question that Finnish and Estonian are not the same language.

Hindi and Urdu are similar in this regard. At the level of everyday spoken usage, the two languages are mutually intelligible. I was told by an American that when she had just arrived in India from Pakistan, a baggage handler praised her ability to speak Hindi when she thought she was speaking Urdu. There can be no suggestion that Hindi and Urdu are the same language, because they identify different religious communities. Hindi and Urdu are in a way the mirror image of the case of the Chinese dialects. The Chinese dialects are all written in the same orthography so that written material is easily comprehensible across dialect boundaries. Hindi and Urdu are written with very different orthographies and neither can be read by speakers of the other language, unless, of course, they make the effort to learn the other script.

The constellation of Dutch, Flemish, and Afrikaans is yet another case. Each of these languages is easily understood by speakers of the others. On a trip to South Africa some years ago, I had occasion to take a tour in Johannesburg. A family of Dutch tourists were able to converse with the Afrikaans-speaking tour guide without a hitch. A Belgian colleague attending the same conference in Pretoria was interviewed on South African television, having only to adjust his native Flemish slightly to be heard as speaking perfect Afrikaans. For most Afrikaners, Afrikaans is certainly not either Dutch or Flemish, but a new language that grew from the South African soil. Nor are all Belgian Flemings inclined to accept Flemish as a dialect of Dutch.

Most of these examples suggest that linguistically similar varieties can be languages only if they are identified with different countries, like Swedish and Norwegian, Finnish and Estonian, or Dutch and Afrikaans. But the same situation can exist within the borders of the same country. The Nguni and Sotho language families of South Africa are an example. There are four Nguni languages— Xhosa, Zulu, Swati, and Ndebele—each of which is generally reported to be readily understood by speakers of the others. The same relationship exists among the three Sotho languages—Tswana, Pedi, and Southern Sotho. Nevertheless, in the 1940s and more recently in the late 1980s, proposals to unify the two groups into two standard languages met with massive resistance, partly because of a general popular belief that the seven languages to be placed in the two groups are each languages in their own right, with dialects of their own.

The circumstances in the case of Mayan languages of southern Mexico and Guatemala are similar. Despite mutual intelligibility and despite the fact that speakers of the different Mayan languages do not have their own countries, the linguistic systems are languages, not dialects, because they symbolize different ethnic identities for their speakers. There is another such case to which I would like to return after I address the case of Ebonic as a language more specifically, that of English and Scots—not Scottish Gaelic—in Scotland.

Ebonic and English compared. This being the case, there is no linguistic reason why Ebonic could not achieve status as a language distinct from English. Two major objections to this proposal would be (1) Ebonic is not a language or even a dialect, but English corrupted by bad grammar and excessive slang, and (2) Ebonic and English are far more similar to each other than any of the cases I have cited here. The first objection, that Ebonic is very bad English, is so obviously false to linguists who have studied it in detail as to be almost risible. Nevertheless, outside the realm of academic linguistics the idea that Ebonic is bad English is generally held to be uncontroversially true. Hence it is necessary for me to demonstrate the fact that the notion is untenable. The second objection, that Ebonic and English are too similar to be different languages, is overtly or tacitly considered valid even by linguists. So a demonstration that this is also not a cogent objection is also called for. It is clear on examination that Ebonic, far from being bad English, is actually superior to English in one of its subsystems, the verbal tense-aspect system. By superior, I mean that Ebonic provides its speakers with rich resources for making distinctions among kinds and times of actions and states that can be made in English only awkwardly via periphrasis. The Ebonic verb system has the same present and past tense, progressive and perfective forms that English does, although with certain differences in detail involving regularization of agreement, extension of contraction, and the function of the past perfect.[3] In addition to these forms, Ebonic has several aspect markers, of which three are the habitual, the remote past, and the resultant state.[4] The combinations of these forms gives Ebonic a powerful system for specifying verbal relationships.

Naturally, the Ebonic verbal aspects are less familiar to English speakers than the forms Ebonic shares with English. The habitual, remote past, and resultant state forms are exemplified here. The examples are taken from Green 1998.[5]

Habitual:

She be eatin.	'She is sometimes/usually/always eating.'
She dó be eatin.	'She ís sometimes/usually/always eating.'
She don't be eatin.	'She is not sometimes/usually/always eating.'

Remote past:

She bin eatin.	'She has been eating for a long time.'
She bin ate.	'She ate a long time ago.'
She ain't bin ate.	'She didn't eat a long time ago.

Resultant state:

She don ate.   'She has already eaten.'

She ain't don ate.   'She hasn't already eaten.'

These very forms are often used as illustrations that Ebonic is simply corrupt English. The habitual is invariably used ungrammatically in such illustrations, where it is taken as a "corruption" of "She is eating."[6] But of course the habitual progressive in Ebonic *contrasts* with the present progressive, which would be "She eatin" or, under emphasis, "She ís eatin." It also contrasts with the simple present. It would be perfectly reasonable, for example, for an Ebonic speaker to say: "She not writin right now but she be writin mostly every day and she write good."

This would mean that the person referred to as "she" is not in the process of writing at the moment, but that one would find her in the process of writing almost daily and she characteristically writes well. The habitual is very difficult to translate into English because it denotes habitual or intermittent actions distributed over time, but specifies nothing about frequency. As a result, Green gives English glosses that contain the three adverbs "sometimes, usually, always" as alternatives because any one of them would correspond only partially to the range of meaning of the habitual. Of course, if an Ebonic speaker wanted to specify frequency, he could also use a time adverb, saying "She usually be eatin," or the like.

Similarly, Green is forced to use an adverbial expression—"for a long time" or "a long time ago"—to render the Ebonic remote past construction. In most situations, this gives a reasonably accurate translation. But Ebonic speakers can use the remote past construction to *present* a predication as if it had occurred in the distant past in order to emphasize the fact that it is irrelevant to bring the matter up at the present moment. For example, one person, call her Carolyn, might tell someone else, call him James, that a mutual friend had just found a job. Perhaps a half-hour later, another friend named Wes might tell James the same news. It would be entirely appropriate for James to say "Wes, I bin heard that." This would be something of a put-down of Wes, meaning that James considers the news to be so old as to be no longer worthy of mention. If James were to say in English, "Wes, I heard that a long time ago" and Carol were to overhear, she could well say, "No you didn't, I just told you a half hour ago." Using the Ebonic remote past construction does not literally commit the speaker to the distant past and would not leave him susceptible to that kind of objection.[7]

The resultant state construction almost defies translation. The translation Green provides for "She don ate"—"She has already eaten"—makes it seem equivalent to the English present perfect. But Ebonic has the present perfect, and its use is quite similar to its use in English. One can perfectly well say "She have already ate" and the force would be clearly distinct from "She don ate" to any Ebonic speaker. The difference, though, is quite subtle. The resultant state aspect conveys a stronger sense of a thoroughly completed result than the present perfect does.

Under analysis, this very set of forms—so often seen in uninformed commentary on Ebonic as evidence of slovenly English—is revealed to fit into a most impressive system of precise time and aspect distinctions that functions much more efficiently in these respects than the English system does. Once this becomes clear, it is amazing to see Ebonic presented as inferior to English. Take, for example, the three-way distinction in Ebonic among the present, the present progressive and the habitual progressive, illustrated previously, which corresponds to a two-way distinction between the present and present progressive in English. One can only imagine what the result would be if Ebonic had a two-way distinction where English had a three-way difference. Racists would use that fact to support theories of the mental inferiority of Black people and White liberals would wring their hands over the impoverished verbal environments that cause Black children to lose a whole tense. As I have shown, however, the difference is actually in favor of Ebonic, but we still hear about slow linguistic development and impoverished verbal environments. It is this sort of state of affairs that has led M. K. Asante (1997) to say "I don't know of any other people in the world whose language is despised as much as this language."

Ebonic, then, is not a hopelessly snarled abuse of English, but an elegant linguistic system with a fascinating system of verbal distinctions. But we are left with the objection that this linguistic system, as elegant as it is, is just too close to English to be credible as a different language. I will address this objection below in a discussion of Scots and English.

Is Ebonic a language to its speakers? Neither the widespread but false assumption that Ebonic is corrupt English, nor the degree of relationship between English and Ebonic are sufficient to prevent Ebonic from being a language. There is, however, a crucial third factor that keeps Ebonic a dialect of English. That is the near-universal opinion, held not only by the English-speaking power-holders in the American social order, but also by most speakers of Ebonic, that Ebonic is certainly not a language, but a flawed dialect of English. Because status as a language is, as I have pointed out, not a matter of linguistic structure, but rather depends on whether or not a linguistic system is seen as a symbol of ethnic or nationalist identity, this fact is crucial. Ebonic is clearly not generally seen as a valid symbol of ethnic identity, and in consequence is not presently a language. During the Ebonics debate in the late 1990s, however, I encountered some evidence that this state of affairs need not be permanent. In February 1997, I joined Fay Vaughn-Cooke, then chair of the Department of Language and Communicative Arts at the University of the District of Columbia and now the dean of Graduate Studies at Florida A&M University, on a radio talk show broadcast by WUDC, then the radio station of the University of the District of Columbia. The topic was the "Ebonics" controversy. The host, who was a very talented and professional woman, was quite suspicious of the stance Vaughn-Cooke and I took on

Ebonic, which was congruent with the conclusions that every linguist who has studied the language system has reached. Much to the surprise of both of us, four of the seven callers from the predominantly African-American listening audience were very sympathetic to what Vaughn-Cooke and I had to say. The following exchanges are illustrative:

> Caller: Ms. _____, I think when you hear a replay of your comments concerning this discussion, I think you will surprise yourself. I think you are a very intelligent woman. But I think you, like Senator Specter, don't have a clue to the very simple statements that have been and are being made that Ebonics is not being touted as some second, third, tenth, twelfth language. It *is* a language. It *is* language. It is a starting point that teachers are encouraged to move from where the student is, to standard English. And I wish you would open your mind to that.

> Host: My mind is fully open to that, but the question is this. When you have children that are speaking a language that is not going to assist them in getting through this society successfully, and we know it as a corrupted form of standard English, do you elevate this particular language. I mean, you recognize it, it exists, people are speaking it. But it doesn't necessarily mean that you give it a formality. . . .

> Caller: I don't mean to offend you, or anything. I'm going to call you "sister" anyway. I want you to listen to what one of your callers said. You should take a tape of this program and listen to what you're saying. Because I can see you looking down your nose at this whole discussion about Ebonics. Because the first thing you said is you used adjectives like "ghetto" language and all that kind of stuff.

> Host: It *is* ghetto language!

> Caller: Well that's your attitude. OK?

> Host: It was in the ghetto I came from, that's the language we spoke.

> Caller: You're looking down your nose again, sister.

The points were not being made in proper academese, but it was clear to Vaughn-Cooke and me that these callers "got it"; they understood that it was not necessary to view Ebonic as deficient English, and that it could be used as a background for teaching standard English. In the 1960s and 1970s, these attitudes were virtually never heard from people who were not involved with the language and the education of Ebonic speakers. Now it appears that there are at least some "ordinary people" whose view of the relationship of Ebonic to standard English is quite close to the actual state of affairs. It is not inconceivable to me that in a generation or two Ebonic could be well on its way to becoming a language.

The case of Scots. A possible example of a speech system that is struggling toward language status is Scots, one of the three languages of Scotland. I am not speaking of Scottish Gaelic (another minority language spoken in Scotland), but the Germanic language, closely related to English, that was once the language of the court but has largely been displaced by English. At the present time, because of its relatedness to English, Scots is considered by many in Scotland to be a corrupted dialect of English, a similar attitude to the one directed toward Ebonic in the United States. The differences between Scots and English seem comparable to those between Ebonic and English, as the following example, from a website maintained by one Clive P. L. Young, illustrates:

> The wirdleet kivvers aboot 700 o the maist cowmon wirds in onie leid (A wisna luikin fur jist kenspeckle Scots wirds). The spellins come frae the School Scots Dictionary. A warnin thou, the file is muckle an maun tak a wee tae doonload.

> [The word list covers about 700 of the most common words in any language (I wasn't just looking for well-known Scots words). The spellings are from the School Scots Dictionary. A warning, though, the file is large and may take a while to download.]

To the naïve eye, the Scots version for the most part looks like English badly spelled and presumably badly pronounced. There are a few vocabulary differences, like "kenspeckle" and "muckle," but most of the excerpt contains words that are close cognates of English words. Historically, and in the view of present-day activists, however, Scots is not a degenerate form of English, but a language distinct from English. Merlin Press, a small publishing house that publishes instructional materials for teaching Scots, has posted the following questions and answers to its website:

> Q. In what form does Scots exist in the present day?

> A. It exists in a multiplicity of dialect forms but without a Standard Scots to correspond to Standard English. . . . There is noth-

ing linguistically wrong with the forms of Scots we have, but for political and social reasons our children have been discouraged from using them for nearly three hundred years, on the grounds that they are incorrect, inferior or corrupt forms of English.

Q. Isn't Scots just a form of slang?

A. Absolutely not. It has a history and a literature behind it and its forms have an etymology. Slang is universal and subject to fashion. Language is local and evolving. When teaching Scots, one of your first tasks will be to show children the difference between Scots and slang.

Q. What is the best way to teach Scots in the classroom?

A. The best way is to start with what you have . . . the children themselves hear Scots every day and many of them actually speak it without realising it. Start by recognising this and allowing its use in the classroom. . . .

Q. How can children be taught to write in Scots?

A. Start with how they speak, then try to write it down as it sounds, consulting a dictionary for help with spelling consistency. Get rid of apostrophes for "missed out" letters and try to capture the Scottish idiom, rather than stick in Scots words here and there on an ad hoc basis.

To those who followed the Ebonics debate, this discussion has an almost eerie familiarity. Scots has to be defended from charges that it is an incorrect form of English and that it is just a form of slang. Children grow up speaking Scots but are discouraged from using it. The suggestion in answer to the question "What is the best way to teach Scots in the classroom?" is almost identical to the proposal by the Oakland School Board that provoked the furor in late 1996 and early 1997, except that the Oakland Board proposed the use of Ebonic in the classroom as a bridge to English. Similarly, the suggestion on how to teach children to write in Scots is close to what many linguists have suggested as a way to teach Ebonic-speaking children how to write in English, by allowing initial writing skills to be developed in Ebonic and then gradually teaching children to replace the Ebonic forms with English ones. It is clear, of course, in the present political climate, that any suggestion that children be actively taught to develop skills in Ebonic would be met with enormously overwhelming resistance.

Another similarity is the ability and practice of Scots-English bilinguals to slide between Scots and English easily and fluently without being aware of it. Again from Clive Young's website:

> Scots and English form a linguistic continuum (i.e., they can be mixed easily). Speakers interchange Scots and English words freely, depending on the social circumstances. For example a simple sentence such as *I'm going home* could be rendered *A'm awa hame, A'm away hame, A'm gaun hame, I'm gaun hame, I'm goin hame, I'm going home* (and probably a few others!). This word-by-word 'switching' is so engrained that it is rarely noticed.

It is typical of Ebonic speakers to move between exploiting a wide range of the language's distinctive features to using fewer Ebonic and more English characteristics in a very similar manner. Just like Scots speakers, Ebonic speakers adjust their usage depending on social circumstances and do so without being aware of it.

We can see the case of Scots as an example of a linguistic variety widely viewed as a corrupted dialect of English being promoted by language activist groups toward language status. There are certain similarities, as we have seen, between the Scots linguistic situation and the one involving Ebonic. However, there are important advantages that Scots has that Ebonic lacks. Scots has a literary and national history and its own recognized grammar and dictionary. It is taught as a subject at several of Scotland's oldest universities and in some primary- and secondary-level schools. It is recognized by the European Bureau for Lesser Used Languages, a nongovernmental organization, as one of the five minority languages of the United Kingdom, along with Irish, Welsh, Scottish Gaelic, and Cornish. While not widely taught, it is not considered outrageous to teach Scots in schools and there are published materials for use in teaching it.

On the other hand, Ebonic has one great advantage over Scots. It appears that without successful efforts to maintain and revive it, Scots is in danger of dying out completely in a few generations. Ebonic—in spite of almost universal opinion against it, and in spite of the total lack of support in the educational system or by the government, in spite of being, in the opinion of M. K. Asante, despised more than any other language—is one of the most robustly maintained minority languages in existence. There is no hint that it is in any danger of dying out in the foreseeable future. Perhaps it is *because* of the opposition it faces that Ebonic is doing so well.

On the literary use of Ebonics. The activists promoting Scots are able to point to its literary past as a reason for preserving it. The Ebonic literary past is more limited, though it certainly exists. More to the point, Ebonic seems to have an encouraging present and future.

In *Imani All Mine,* a 1999 novel by Connie Porter, the protagonist narrates the entire novel in flawless Ebonic. Tasha, the main character, is a teen-aged single mother who lives in the inner city of Buffalo, New York, with her mother and baby girl, Imani. For example, in one scene, Tasha describes a teacher who makes the students speak "proper English":

> But Mr. Toliver take everything so serious. He be making us talk proper English in his class and keep on correcting us when we don't. We have to talk that way, he say, so we'll have a good future. Maybe he right. All I know is my head be hurting in his class when I concentrate on talking like that. It don't come natural to me, and it seem like I'm just putting on. Like I'm trying to be white. (p. 64–65)

There can be little doubt that Ebonic can be effective as a language of literature. For the moment, it appears that it works primarily as a language of first-person narration, but there is no linguistic reason why this has to be the only context for its use.

If Ebonic were a language. I have argued that Ebonic need not be English, but that there is every reason to suppose it is capable of being a language in its own right. Status as a language is not a linguistic matter, and the linguistic properties of Ebonic are comparable with those of other linguistic systems that are languages. Its most criticized features can be shown to be part of an intricate grammatical system that allows for precise distinctions to be made that are difficult to replicate in English. Although it is similar to English, it is not substantially more similar to English than other linguistic systems are to related languages, but are indisputably separate languages. The path by which Ebonic could become a language is perhaps being blazed by the case of Scots, another linguistic system taken as a corrupt dialect of English, but for which there is activist support in favor of recognition and maintenance. Ebonic is demonstrably capable of playing a role as a language of literature as the example by Connie Porter has shown. But are there any advantages to considering Ebonic a language separate from English, rather than as an orderly and systematic dialect of English?

My answer is that there are. The major advantage is that when one speaks of Ebonic as a language, rather than as a dialect, it reforms the discourse in a way that makes it easier to address the common misconceptions about Ebonic that have kept the debate at such a low level.

To begin with, when Ebonic is defended as a systematic and well-ordered dialect, it is inevitably contrasted with "standard" English. The idea of "standard English" is more complicated and controversial that it might first seem, and I cannot take up the issue here. But the term "standard" embodies an ambiguity which, to my knowledge, has never been addressed in discussions about standard and other dialects of languages. A "standard" comes in two flavors, MINIMUM STANDARDS and

ARBITRARY STANDARDS. Minimum standards are specifications that must be met or exceeded for acceptability. Safety standards for automobiles is one example. If an automobile does not have the right features and properties of structural integrity, it may fail the standards and the manufacturer may not be able to sell it. In short, minimum standards must be met in order for an item to be "good enough"; if minimum standards are not met, the item has failed and should not be put in use.

Arbitrary standards are entirely different. For example, the United States uses Fahrenheit degrees in measuring temperatures, including ambient air temperatures in weather reports. Most of the rest of the world uses an entirely different standard and measures temperatures in degrees Celsius. One could argue that Fahrenheit degrees are harder to use and interpret and are based on less sensible criteria than Celsius degrees are and that the Fahrenheit system is therefore inferior. However that may be, Fahrenheit degrees serve an important function. They serve as an agreed-upon arbitrary standard that everyone in the United States comes to understand and use. It is not so important that the best system of temperature measurement is used as it is that everyone agrees on the same—arbitrary—standard. To say that the air temperature is 30° may mean that a tee-shirt and shorts are called for, or it may mean we will need a winter coat. It is necessary for everyone to agree in advance which it is. That is the nature of an arbitrary standard.

When linguists use the term "standard language" they invariably and implicitly mean an *arbitrary* standard. Just as in the case of the measurement standard for temperature, there are advantages to have agreement on certain arbitrary standards for some language uses. In American English, there is a general tacit agreement on what these standards are. The standard language may not be the best possible constellation of linguistic features available; in fact, I have argued that in some ways standard English is demonstrably inferior to Ebonic. But just as there is general agreement in favor of the Fahrenheit standard, even if the Celsius standard is probably better, the arbitrary standards we have agreed on for American English are unlikely to be abandoned any time soon. It is general social acceptance that gives us a workable arbitrary standard, not the inherent superiority of the item it specifies.[8]

In general conversation about language standards, however, the assumption made by the vast majority of people, who have not studied the nature of language in depth, is that the term "standard English" refers to *minimum* standards. If there is any variation from what is understood to be the language standards, it is not seen as adherence to an alternative set of standards, but as a failure to achieve acceptable quality. Just like a house that fails to meet the building code standards, or an automobile that does not meet safety standards, nonstandard language is considered not fit to be used. The users of these dialects must, on this view, be brought up to the minimum standard, for their own good as well as for the good of the society in general. In such a context, it seems an oxymoron to speak of Ebonic or any variety other than standard English as "rule-governed." If a language fails to meet standards, it has *eo ipso* failed to be governed by the only rules that count. It is impossible to hold the minimum standards view of standard English and still believe that nonstandard varieties are rule-governed. A variety may either be rule-governed or it may be nonstandard. It cannot, for most people, be both. When linguists assert that nonstandard varieties are rule-governed, although nonstandard, the perceived contradiction prevents us from making sense, or from being taken seriously. For example, during the radio call-in show in which I participated in 1997, the host made it clear that she thought of language standards as minimum standards:

> Host: I think that if you have people who are supposedly the leadership in the community or the school system, they have to set a standard. *A standard that everyone rises up to.* Not we go the other way. [Emphasis added]

Another view of the same problem involves the term "dialect." For linguists, dialects are speech varieties that make up a language, somewhat the way the slices make up the pie. One of these "slices" often achieves the status as a standard. But for the linguist, this is an arbitrary standard. Given a different social history, one of the other dialects might have become the standard just as well.

For ordinary people, though, the term "dialect" and its relationship to the notion "language" is totally different. A "dialect" is either a speech system that is used by people who are considered primitive and that doesn't quite make it as a language (e.g., "the dialects of the indigenous people of the Amazon jungle"), or it is a perhaps quaint but surely faulty way of speaking a "language." In that sense, it is on a par with slips of the tongue, slang-laced conversation, excessive use of profanity, and other perceived abuses of language. Dennis Preston, a linguist who has spent years studying folk linguistics—the ideas about language that ordinary people have—compares the linguist's view of the relationship between language and dialect with the view of "real people" in figure 1. As Preston sees it, the folk model takes a language to be the real thing, the proper thing, the only really worthwhile thing. Then there are several ways of damaging the language, indicated in figure 1 by the broken lines. These include slips of the tongue, casual speech, drunken speech, and, of course, dialects.

The linguist's view is quite different. For us, there are several levels of analysis of a language, each just a different view of the same phenomenon. So the language is the largest level, but it doesn't have either more reality or value than the others. It can be viewed in greater detail as the dialects of which it is composed, and these, in turn, can be examined more closely as the various styles that exist in each dialect. Slips of the tongue, drunken speech, and the like are phenomena that take place when people are in the process of speaking one of the styles of one of

Figure 1. Folk (above) and linguistic (below) taxonomies of language. (From Dennis Preston, 1999, Linguists and real people in the educational process. Paper presented at the Linguistic Society of America Annual Meeting, Los Angeles, January 7.)

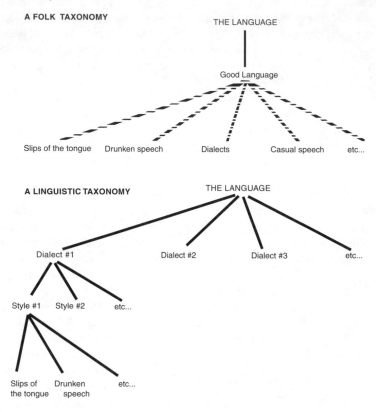

the dialects of the language. All of these levels are connected in Preston's diagram with solid lines, to show that all are a necessary part of the big picture.

If Preston is anywhere near right, imagine what happens when a linguist says that Ebonic is a dialect that is orderly, rule-governed, and worthy of respect. The term "dialect" fits into the folk taxonomy for the audience while the linguist is working with the linguistic taxonomy. The linguist thinks she has made a simple-to-understand statement that ought to be accepted on her authority as an expert on language. The statement is that the dialect Ebonic is one of a number of equally orderly dialects of English, including the standard one. It is not comparable to slurred speech or slips of the tongue, but should be viewed on a level of analysis two levels up from such phenomena. The "real person," though, hears the word "dialect" and interprets it in terms of his taxonomy. Since dialects are presupposed to be corruptions of language, the claim that Ebonic is orderly and rule-governed cannot make sense, unless it means that this particular way of corrupting the language has certain characteristics that can be described systematically. It may even be agreed that speakers of the dialect are worthy of respect. After all, you would not judge someone too harshly for the occasional slip of the tongue, so you shouldn't be too hard on someone who speaks a dialect once in a while. But the linguist's analysis will make no dent in the ordinary person's conviction that anyone who is able to speak only a dialect is in serious trouble. Such speakers have an immediate need to replace the dialect with the real language, perhaps being allowed to slip back into that particular kind of sloppiness in a few relaxed and casual settings, once the language is mastered. But the real person will never hear that the linguist is actually saying that the dialect Ebonic is on a par with the standardized dialect and, given different historical developments, might even have *been* the standard.

An exchange between me and the host of the radio talk show cited earlier shows that she implicitly held the folk taxonomy and that I became caught in the no man's land between the linguistic and folk taxonomic understandings of the term "dialect":

> Host: But in 1997 it just seems preposterous to present as a formal language to be taught in a school . . . broken English. Because that's what we're talking about.

> Fasold: No, it's not what we're talking about. If it were what we were talking about . . .

> Host: It's a DIAlect!

> Fasold: Uh, perhaps . . .

Given the yawning chasm between the linguistic and folk ideas "standard" and "dialect," for linguists to attempt to convey what we have learned about Ebonic while using terms like "standard English" and "African-American English dialect" starts us off immediately with a double handicap. Somehow, we have to dislodge the idea of minimum standard as applied to language and replace it with the alien concept arbitrary standard. At the same time, we have to redefine "dialect" from a kind of corruption of the real language to a notion of dialect as a legitimate component of language relevant at a particular level of analysis. This done, we have to persuade listeners that, by the way, Ebonic is one of these co-dialects of English that may deviate from the arbitrary standards imposed on

English while conforming to standards of its own. The likelihood of accomplishing all this, say, in an op-ed article or in a conversation with a reporter, is not significantly different from zero.

On the other hand, if Ebonic were a language and presented as such, much of the mismatch in presuppositions can be avoided. The Ebonic language would not be a dialect and would therefore not be assumed to be a corruption of anything, but something real in its own right. As a language, the question of its "rising up" to the standards of English would not even come up. A language has its own standards, and the standards, whether arbitrary or minimal, of some other language would be simply irrelevant. The way we discuss these matters would immediately change. Imagine the following hypothetical conversations:

"Real Person": Isn't Ebonic broken English?

Linguist: Of course it isn't broken English, it isn't English at all. It's another language, Ebonic.

"Real Person": Isn't Ebonic just bad English?

Linguist: Certainly Ebonic is bad English, in the same sense that good French is bad English. Good English is bad Ebonic, too.

"Real Person": Why don't these so-called Ebonic speakers inflect the verb *to be*. Why do they say "He be eating" when they mean "He is eating?"

Linguist: Unlike English, which has only one form *to be,* Ebonic has two words for *to be*. One of them is inflected and the other is not. The grammar of Ebonic makes a distinction not found in English, so that when we say "He be eating" in Ebonic, we mean something quite different from "He is eating." The difference is quite subtle and not easy for English speakers to master.

I have no illusions. Simply speaking of Ebonic as a language rather than a dialect will not immediately cause linguists' discoveries about Ebonic to become universally accepted. There will be massive resistance to the idea that Ebonic is a language, partly because people are so convinced that it is a despicable way to speak and because it is so largely interintelligible with English. Linguists would be accused of carrying political correctness to new and more ridiculous levels by presenting Ebonic as a distinct language. Even if by dint of charisma and eloquence linguists manage to convince some nonlinguists that Ebonic could be a language, the struggle would not be over. Now we would hear the arguments used to support suppressing immigrant languages. Arguments like: "We are all Americans here, and anyone who wants to share in the bounty ought to give up any other language, whether Spanish, Vietnamese, or Ebonic, and use only English. To do otherwise would fracture the country and turn the United States into Sri Lanka or Canada." All these difficulties would exist, but I must say I would find the new struggle easier to deal with.

Even by my own definition, Ebonic is not yet a language, because its speakers share with English speakers the folk view of English and its substandard dialects. But Ebonic is a *potential* language. There is nothing about it that can rule out its being a language. It may even become a language—on the criteria I propose—in several generations. I do know that I have been able to get across the linguistic perception of the nature of Ebonic much more efficiently by framing its relation to English as one of language-to-language. This newer discourse just seems to work better.

REFERENCES

Asante, M. K., quoted in Tamara Henry. 1997. Weighing in on the Ebonics debate. *USA Today* (January 13): 6D.

Blackshire-Belay, Carol Aisha. 1996. The location of Ebonics within the framework of the Africological paradigm. *Journal of Black Studies* 27: 1.5–23.

Chomsky Noam. 1982. *Some concepts and consequences of the theory of government and binding.* Cambridge, MA: MIT Press.

Fasold, Ralph W., and Yoshiko Nakano. 1996. Contraction and deletion in Vernacular Black English: Creole history and relation to Euro-American English. In Gregory R. Guy, John Baugh, and Deborah Schiffrin (eds.), *Towards a social science of language: Papers in honor of William Labov,* vol. 1, *Variation and Change in Language in Society.* Amsterdam: John Benjamins. 373–396.

Green, Lisa. 1998. Aspect and predicate phrases in African-American vernacular English. In Salikoko S. Mufwene, John R. Rickford, Guy Bailey, and John Baugh (eds.), *African-American English: Structure, history and use.* London: Routledge. 37–68.

Merlin Press. *Scots Language Materials.* http://www.sol.co.uk/m/merlinpress/.

Mufwene, Salikoko. 1992. Why grammars are not monolithic. In D. Brentari, G. Larson, and L. MacLeod (eds.), *The joy of language.* Amsterdam: John Benjamins. 225–250.

Nunberg, Geoffrey. 1995. Topic . . . Comment: Angels in America. *Natural Language and Linguistic Theory* 13 (2 May): 343–350.

Porter, Connie. 1999. *Imani all mine.* Boston: Houghton Mifflin.

Preston, Dennis R. 1999. Linguists and real people in the educational process. Paper presented at the Linguistic Society of America Annual Meeting, Los Angeles, January 7.

Romaine, Suzanne. 1982. *Sociohistorical linguistics.* Cambridge: Cambridge University Press.

Rickford, John R., and Christine Therberge Rafal. 1996. Preterite *had* + V-*ed* in the narratives of African American adolescents. *American Speech* 71: 227–254.

Rickford, John R., Arnetha Ball, Renee Blake, Raina Jackson, and Nomi Martin. 1991. Rappin' on the copula coffin: Theoretical and methodological issues in the analysis of copula variation in African-American English. *Language Variation and Change* 3: 103–132.

Samarin, William J. 1996. Review of Adegbija Efurosibina, Language Attitudes in Sub-Saharan Africa: A Sociolinguistic Overview. *Anthropological Linguistics* 38(2): 389–395.

Young, Clive P. L. *Scots on the Wab.* http://www.umist.ac.uk/UMIST_CAL/Scots/.

NOTES

1. My use of the term "Ebonic" does not refer to the same range of linguistic phenomena as does the term "Ebonics," as used by some writers. I use "Ebonic" to refer to what most linguists call "African American Vernacular English." "Ebonics" is sometimes taken to mean all the languages of people of African origin both in Africa and in the Diaspora. This would include non-English languages, on the one hand, and the American English used by middle- and upper-status African Americans in the United States and elsewhere, on the other (cf. Blackshire-Belay 1996: 20).

2. Samarin could have—and I believe would have—made exactly the same point if he had been speaking of Italy or Germany before nationalism arose in those countries. Africa is certainly not unique in this regard. I am not sure I agree with Samarin that literacy is a necessary condition for status as a language.

3. There is some controversy about whether or not the extension of contraction is the correct account of the absence of present-tense forms of *to be* in Ebonic. See Romaine 1982, Rickford et al. 1991, Mufwene 1992, and Fasold and Nakano 1996, for some discussion. For a discussion of the past perfect in Ebonic, see Rickford and Rafal 1996.

4. The terminology for these aspects varies somewhat in the linguistics literature. Here, I am following Green 1998.

5. I have modified Green's examples in certain noncritical ways.

6. I recently saw a sign in the window of a bar in Seattle that said "We be non-smoking." It was fairly clear that this was a blundering attempt to use Ebonic. If it meant what it means in Ebonic, it would mean that the bar doesn't allow smoking sometimes and at other times it does. If one wished to avoid being in a place that allows smoking, one would never know when it was safe to go to the bar.

7. As a graduate student some thirty years ago, I was once tutoring a young Ebonic-speaking boy in math. Full of youthful idealism, I began to teach him arithmetic by approaching addition as a set union operation, what was known at the time as "The New Math." The youngster was able to deflate me totally by saying, "Ralph, I bín knowin that." It was clear that his point was that I was certainly not teaching him anything new. In any case, he could not have learned about set union *too* far in the past—he was only ten years old!

8. Personally, I think the advantages claimed even for arbitrary language standards are exaggerated.

Whose "standard"? What the Ebonics debate tells us about language, power, and pedagogy

Denise E. Murray
Macquarie University

Although some linguists regard the concept of "language" as abstract, even epiphenomenal . . . and they can joke about language being a dialect with an army and navy, the truth remains that for most people the joke is far from frivolous. Regardless of what professional linguists say about the distinction between "language" and "dialect" to the general public the two words have different connotations.

Mchombo 1998

Introduction. As a result of the Oakland Unified School District Board of Education resolution on Ebonics in December 1996, a debate over Ebonics erupted in the U.S. media and was reported in many countries around the world.[1] This media-intense interest provided an opportunity for linguists and language educators to lead the public debate by their demonstrating an understanding of the "different connotations" held by the public and by demonstrating the sociopolitical bases behind assigning the labels language or dialect.[2] Furthermore, it was an opportunity to change the nature of the debate about the value of different languages and their varieties from an emotional, attitudinally based argument to one based on scientific data from sociolinguistic research. Linguists and language educators were interviewed, wrote op-ed pieces, and appeared on talk shows, a change from the usual media consultation of linguists about the correctness of split infinitives or the derivation of words. Professional associations (e.g., the American Association of Applied Linguistics, the Linguistic Society of America, Teachers of English to Speakers of Other Languages) passed resolutions, wrote articles in their own newsletters and journals, held conferences, and distributed press releases. Smitherman (1999) in her history of language rights policies of the Conference on College Composition and Communication (CCCC) claims that such activities of professional associations (and I would argue of professionals individually) are essential because policies of professional associations "provide the necessary intellectual basis and rhetorical framework for waging language debates and arguments. Further, since intellectuals provide the ideological rationale for public policy, it was and is important

for organizations like CCCC to go on record as supporting language rights."
(Smitherman 1999: 373).

Yet, neither our professional associations nor our individual efforts seem to
have changed the rhetoric of public debates or provided the ideological rationale
for public policy. Neither the name Ebonics nor the arguments associated with it
remain in public consciousness. Just over a year later, California businessman
Ron Unz proposed Proposition 227, the proposition to require structured English
immersion as the preferred instructional program for teaching students entering
California's schools with languages other than English. While the debate that surrounded this proposition did not involve differentiating (or not differentiating) between a language and a dialect, it did involve two issues in common with the
debate on Ebonics: the pedagogical soundness of the use of a child's home language as a basis for acquiring the language of the schools—standard English—
and the determination of who makes pedagogical decisions about the education of
language minority students.[3] This second public debate demonstrated again the
public's lack of understanding of the nature of language, language learning, or
sound pedagogical practices for language minority students.

Given the high profile of the Ebonics debate, the amount of air and print time
devoted to reasoned arguments supported by linguistics research, why did the
public still not "get it?" Why did we have to repeat the same arguments presented
during the 1974 *Lau v. Nichols* and the 1979 Ann Arbor decisions.[4] Despite the
scientific accuracy of our arguments, "'scientific' language, marshaled in the service of informing public policy, often reads and sounds irrelevant to policy and
administration; and administration language, marshaled in the service of making
things happen, often reads and sounds expedient" (LoBianco 1997). The critical
players in the education of language-minority children thus remain divided by
their own use of language, a division that can only be breached through frequent
interaction. Yet, policy makers, the public, and linguists rarely engage in dialogue, except when an immediate issue grabs media attention. This is especially
true because language education issues appear without direct input from linguists,
often as the creation of administrators trying to alleviate an immediate educational issue such as the poor performance of African-American students on standardized tests or the perceived low rate of acquisition of standard English by
speakers of other languages.

The lack of linguistic understanding starts with teacher-training programs,
which rarely include descriptive linguistics, let alone critical linguistics that discusses issues of power and ideology. For those of us involved in linguistics and
language education, this should be our first point of advocacy. We will have made
some progress toward improving the educational success of language minority
students if we can educate future teachers in an understanding of language and
power and in appropriate pedagogies for these students, so that teachers' praxis,
that is, their "informed, committed action" (Carr and Kemmis 1986: 190), sup-

ports learning for language minority students. There will still be public, political battles to be fought, but, as all educators know, what goes on behind closed classroom doors is mostly between teacher and student. Below I outline briefly such an agenda for what teachers need to know about language, power, and pedagogy.

Language. Probably the most difficult aspect of language for nonlinguists to accept is variability such as that displayed in text structure or in pronunciation, syntax, or vocabulary. This abhorrence for variability leads to a desire for standardization, resulting in folk notions that there are "correct" and "incorrect" forms, whether in spelling, syntax, pronunciation, or text structure. Of course, communities must have some agreed upon conventions, because I cannot choose my own meanings for words or my own rules of syntax. If I did, I could not communicate. But the desire for uniformity goes beyond agreement on conventions for mutual comprehensibility. The myth of a correct English holds that any deviation from this standard is impoverished and full of error. Historically, English language speakers were more tolerant of variability. In fact, after the Norman Conquest in twelfth- and thirteenth-century Britain, variability was across languages, with French used for literature, administration, and legislation; Latin for the church and scholarship; and English for more local and personal functions. In medieval England, variability in written texts was normal practice; spelling varied from text to text and within texts (often for aesthetic purposes to justify text). Over time, however, spelling and meaning became codified through dictionaries, creating a "standard" such that variations in spelling are less tolerated than variations in pronunciation. Grammar, punctuation, and other aspects of text structure also became prescribed in style manuals, so that adherence to these standards is highly valued.

Ebonics opponents refer to it as slang, broken English, or poor grammar and to its speakers as lazy or sloppy and so demand it not be used in schools (or even recognized as a legitimate communication system). At best, they say, it is nonstandard English. This variety of English, which has been assigned various names (Ebonics, Black English, Black Dialect, African-American Vernacular English [AAVE]), has been found by linguists who have studied it to be rule governed, with its own phonology, lexicon, and grammar (e.g., Labov 1972; Wolfram 1991). Calling it either a dialect or a language is a political question, not a linguistic one. That Standard American English (SAE) is the prestige variety is a result of nonlinguistic forces such as wealth and political power, not of inherent characteristics of SAE. So, the issue cannot be about being in favor of Ebonics or not. As Lisa Delpit so cogently argues, "I can be neither for Ebonics or against Ebonics any more than I can be for or against air. It exists. It is the language spoken by many of our African-American children. It is the language they heard as their mothers nursed them and changed their diapers and played peek-a-boo with them. It is the language through which they first encountered love, nurturance and joy" (Delpit 1997).

An additional dimension of language variation crucial for teachers to under-stand is the nature of genres, the culturally typical ways of engaging rhetorically with recurring situations. People learn new genres through social contexts. In dif-ferent communities, ways of representing and presenting knowledge vary. Differ-ent communities value different kinds of knowledge and display and package it in ways unfamiliar to those outside the community. One such example is narra-tive. Research on narratives in different cultural groups (e.g., Michaels 1981) shows us that not all culture's stories have a point; not all give a setting, present a problem, and then its resolution, the structure most common in middle-class America. In Western Australia, for example, Ian Malcolm (1994) has worked with aboriginal children, finding them silenced in the classroom setting but eloquent storytellers outside the classroom. They are silenced in the classroom because they are baffled by their teachers' expectations of them. Equally baffled are their teachers, who think these children have nothing to say. Malcolm recorded young aboriginal children in classrooms and as they told stories to each other in the dor-mitories of their residential schools. Some of the children he recorded are bilin-gual, others speak only Aboriginal English. In both cases, the aboriginal children tell stories structured very differently from those of their white classmates. The *story tells* consist of multiple narrations of going from one place to another and what happens when the participants arrive. The story tells are often accompanied by drawing in the sand using a stick or piece of wire. It is claimed that this story structure, with its two components of moving and stopping, reflects the tradi-tional aboriginal way of life—the nomadic life where moving and stopping are salient. Whatever its origin, the structure and values are different from those of the Western narrative, which helps explain the difficulties these children have at school.

Even as we talk about standard English, we have variability. Which standard? That of Britain, of the United States, of Australia, of Singapore? Kachru (1986) was the first to posit three concentric circles of English to categorize English users, based on their relationship with the language: the inner circle of countries where the majority of speakers use English as a first language (e.g., the United States and New Zealand); the outer circle of countries where English is one lan-guage among others in people's repertoires (e.g., India); and the expanding circle where English is learned as a foreign language (e.g., Japan). Graddol (1997) has estimated that there are around 750 million English speakers in the expanding cir-cle, and 375 million in each of the outer and inner circles.[5] Clearly, some English speakers consider only British and American as legitimate standards, with per-haps some tolerance for Australian or New Zealand standard usage. On a personal note, I was refused English teaching positions in Europe (including England) be-cause I spoke Australian. When I first arrived in the United States and was offered a position teaching adult ESL, for which I had extensive experience and training in Australia, Britain, and Thailand, I was informed during the interview that I would be hired because of my qualifications and experience, well above those required for the position, but that I would need to lose my accent. McArthur (1997) even posits an International Standard English (which, in retrospect, either I didn't speak or the interviewer didn't recognize) with five strands: international print standard; international media standard; international governmental, administrative, and legal standard; international commercial and technological standard; and international education standard.

Further, even within one national standard, language varies from situation to situation, depending on the speaker-hearer relationship, the topic, and the medium (written or oral). Many speakers competently code-switch orally between SAE and a nonstandard variety but have not developed competence in written SAE, which is not as variable as its oral counterpart, largely because of the codification and prescription of dictionaries and style manuals. Others may use a nonstandard variety in speech but be competent in SAE or the more international variety McArthur refers to.

Power. That one variety either is considered a language or a standard variety is a result of the history of the users of the language or standard variety. English has become a global language as a result of British colonial and industrial power, followed by U.S. economic power. The dominance of English continues even through the Internet, largely because computer technology and the Internet network originated with English speakers, and consequently,[6] the code used for protocols, called the American Standard Code for Information Interchange (ASCII), was developed for the English alphabet. To create even simple diacritic marks such as the accent on the name of my former university, San José State University, requires several keystrokes, and in transmission is often converted to *Jos?e*. To summarize, English is a global language today because of an accident of history. Similarly, for standard varieties the variety of the elite and powerful becomes the standard. In Australia, for example, Standard British English was long considered prestigious and used to identify speakers as the upper classes. To express solidarity with "real" Australians, a speaker would instead use "Broad Australian."

The choice and use of a language variety is never socioculturally or sociopolitically neutral, involving as it does the interaction between these two continua of power and solidarity (see, for example, Brown and Levinson 1987) as aspects of social identity. Languages and language varieties may "symbolize group identity and become emblems of that identity, especially when there is contact with other groups whose ways of being are different" (Heller 1982: 3). In describing English as a global language, Crystal (1997) identifies two different functions that bilingualism or bidialectalism can fulfill. One language or variety may provide the symbol of group identity of a community; the other may function to provide intelligibility across a wider range of communities. For speakers of nonprestigious language varieties or languages, there is the power of the in-group in using the variety, but there is equally the lack of power in situations where the prestigious variety is the only one acknowledged (e.g., schooling). Nelson-Barber (1982), for example, found that Pima Indian children's phonology most closely approximated the SAE of the teachers during grades one through three, but by grade four, even though they could use SAE competently, they chose instead to use the Pima English variety of their local environment. She hypothesized that by grade four students had decided to strongly identify with their own language variety group rather than with those in power, such as their teachers.

In all situations, but especially in education, we need to ask explicitly whose language or variety is accepted for what functions of communication and why. A number of scholars working in language education have begun addressing these questions of power in different aspects of language education: language planning (e.g., Tollefson 1991), language learning (e.g., Peirce 1995), ESL curricula (e.g., Auerbach and Burgess 1985), and the globalization of English (e.g., Phillipson and Skutnabb-Kangas 1996). Educators need to be ever mindful that our discursive practices perpetuate inequalities because they continually reproduce unequal power relations and social identities.

Sociolinguistic studies have identified attitudes toward speakers of different languages and varieties (e.g., Cazden 1988), attitudes that often shape opportunities for speakers of those languages and varieties. Other studies have examined not only the pronunciation, syntax, and vocabulary differences across varieties, but also the structure of texts both written and oral.

Although the study of language varieties has a long history, there is still much we do not know, especially about the use of dialect across different social settings and modes of communication. Although many educators (e.g., Delpit 1995) have advocated adding the standard to the repertoire students bring with them to the classroom in order to give them upward social mobility, we do not have research that shows the "costs and benefits associated with dialect choice" (Adger and Wolfram 2000: 393). We do not know whether a nonstandard variety is acceptable in certain settings, but we do know that the acquisition of a standard variety does not guarantee social mobility and success for language minorities. Further, we cannot assume that the language of the home is the child's language of affiliation, and it may not be the child's dominant language. Many adolescents, for example, claim a language affiliation other than their mother tongue and demonstrate expertise in yet another (Mobbs 1997). And, for second-language learners, the language of affiliation may be a nonstandard variety of English or of the mother tongue.

Pedagogy. A number of crucial pedagogical issues arise from the Ebonics debate: which variety is to be the explicit object of instruction; which variety should be used as a medium for instruction; which varieties are used for which functions; and which varieties should students have as part of their linguistic repertoire. These issues are important not only for the education of Ebonics speakers, but also for the education of any learner who does not use the prestige variety, such as:

- speakers of varieties of World Englishes,
- students coming to the United States and other English-dominant countries speaking an English-based creole,
- students speaking indigenous dialects (e.g., Aboriginal English),
- second-language learners who have acquired a nonstandard variety of English because of where they live or with whom they interact,
- students who may be able to code-switch between dialects in speech but who have not mastered SAE for writing, and
- students who speak a nonstandard variety of their mother tongue.

Language educators know that the most appropriate instruction builds on what the learner already knows, and so it is appropriate to begin with the language (or language variety) that students bring with them to the classroom. One of the misperceptions the public and media had of the Oakland School District approach to teaching Ebonics speakers was the belief that they intended to teach Ebonics to the children, just as Spanish, for example, is taught to Spanish-speaking children. Such teaching was not their intent. Rather their goal was to teach through the medium of Ebonics and use a curriculum that used the language already spoken by the students as a resource. Work on language awareness (e.g., Fairclough 1992) has shown that explicitly teaching learners to see differences between their language or variety and the standard, most powerful variety "gives students a knowledge base for developing a second language or dialect" (Adger 1997: 14). Wolfram, Schilling-Estes, and Hazen (1996) have shown that upper elementary and middle school students are fascinated by dialect awareness curricula and that they become aware that dialect prejudice is not justified by linguistic data. Through such study they also become aware of the rule-governed nature of their variety, of its viability, and of their own expertise as competent users of the variety. They come to realize that the standard is the standard for historical, political reasons, not because of any intrinsic attributes. They no longer feel a loss of self-esteem because others view their speech as slang or lazy.

But such contrastive study should not be confined to the curriculum for students who use a nonstandard variety; rather, contrastive language study should be part of the curriculum for all learners. Thus, speakers of prestige varieties come to realize the communicative effectiveness of all varieties, while speakers of languages other than English come to understand the variability of the English language they are learning. To provide the most appropriate instruction, educators need to understand the language and language varieties learners use in different situations, whether they be speakers of World Englishes, English-based Creoles, indigenous dialects of English, or their mother tongue.

It is precisely because of the role of a standard variety of English as a gate-keeper to better jobs and education in many societies that educators must take their responsibility seriously. In an ESL situation, it is essential for immigrants to learn the codes for success. The aboriginal story tell will not help those young aboriginal learners become successful in their academic subjects where a different genre is required. Similarly, an international student who uses extensive background information because in her culture it is related to politeness may not be successful in writing or conversation in U.S. mainstream culture. It is not that there is anything intrinsically better about the more direct, less background information genre privileged in U.S. education. However, the student who fails to use the appropriate genre will find her papers marked up in red pen and people not listening to her conversation, considering it to be rambling or not coming to the point. The very terms used to describe the writing of students who do not conform to the SAE written genre are value-laden. Educators have the responsibility not to withhold the knowledge of the genres and culture of power from students but to assist them in learning the languages and culture of power. At the same time, however, educators must help students to learn the arbitrariness of those standards and to understand the power relationships they represent and then let *them* choose.

On the one hand, we need to advocate respect for difference, difference in language, difference in varieties of English, differences in culture. On the other hand, we need to recognize that as we empower through teaching a standard, we also disempower. As Edge (1996: 16) says for teaching English to speakers of other languages, "Every time our students are successful in getting that TOEFL score that means that they can study at a U.S. college, we celebrate this step towards personal liberation. And, at exactly the same time, we have put another little brick in the wall that holds back all those other people who would have wanted to be a doctor, an architect . . . in their own country, but whose aspirations will be blighted because they failed to learn enough English".[7]

Conclusion. All language educators, whether we teach Ebonics speakers or not, need to understand these issues of language because they impact on our decisions about which variety or language should be taught explicitly, which should be the medium of instruction, what are the socioculturally appropriate situations for using one variety or language or another. These decisions are not unique to the United States or other English-dominant countries. They are relevant to all countries with multilingual and multidialectal populations.

What we need to focus on is intercultural communication, rather than multicultural education. The former involves communication across cultural boundaries; the latter is often "based on a prescriptive notion that multicultural education is a remedy for controlling students of color and other marginalized students in the classroom, [and] . . . instructional programs that view students as deficient and in need of compensatory models of instruction" (Grant 1999: 7). We need what

Zarate (quoted in Crozet and Liddicoat 1997: 3) calls "knowing how to relate to otherness." To achieve this, we need to make visible both the many varieties of otherness and of oneself. Such an approach removes what has been an exclusive focus on the model native speaker of standard English as the norm for education, including English language teaching and learning. Instead, we need to prepare learners to communicate outside their own linguistic and cultural boundaries, teaching how to make the home language and culture relate to the target language and culture so they are freed from a singular view of the world. So, the more appropriate norm is a bilingual-multilingual or bidialectal-multidialectal position, which we can think of as creating an intercultural space for the learner. But this needs to be taught *explicitly*. Education and even language learning does not *automatically* result in intercultural sensitivity and the breaking of stereotypes.

Meanwhile, we can, as Wong and Thomas (1993: 25) have observed about Malaysian English, "empower our students by building on these nativized items; in doing so, our students will be able to find their own personal and cultural voices, and at the same time will learn to transform their meaning into a language that is understandable to a larger audience. The classroom will therefore become an arena where, through an evolving dialogue with their inner selves, their peers and their teachers, learners will see themselves gradually becoming a part of a larger community whose strength lies not in its homogeneity but in its rich cultural diversity."

REFERENCES

Adger, Carolyn Temple. 1997. *Issues and implications of English dialects for teaching English as a second language.* Alexandria, VA: TESOL.

Adger, Carolyn Temple, and Walt Wolfram. 2000. Demythologizing the home–school language dichotomy: Sociolinguistic reality and instructional practice. In J. R. Peyton, F. Griffin, W. Wolfram, and R. Fasold (eds.), *Language in action: New studies of language in society.* Cresskill, NJ: Hamton Press. 391–407.

Auerbach, Else Roberts, and Denise Burgess. 1985. The hidden curriculum of survival ESL. *TESOL Quarterly* 19(3): 475–95.

Baugh, John. 1998. Linguistics, education, and the law: Educational reform for African-American language minority students. In Salikoko S. Mufwene, John R. Rickford, Guy Bailey, and John Baugh (eds.), *African-American English.* London: Routledge.

Brown, P., and S. Levinson. 1987. *Politeness: Some universals in language usage.* Cambridge: Cambridge University Press.

Carr, W., and S. Kemmis, 1986. *Becoming critical.* Lewes, England: Falmer Press.

Cazden, Courtney B. 1988. *Classroom discourse.* Portsmouth, NH: Heinemann.

Crozet, Chantal, and Anthony J. Liddicoat. 1997. Teaching culture as an integrated part of language teaching: An introduction. *ARAL* S(14): 1–22.

Crystal, David. 1997. *English as a global language.* Cambridge: Cambridge University Press.

Delpit, Lisa. 1995. *Other people's children: Cultural conflicts in the classroom.* New York: New Press.

Delpit, Lisa.1997. Ebonics and culturally responsive instruction. *Rethinking schools* 12(1). Available online: http://www.rethinkingschools.org/Archives/12_01/ebdelpit.htm.

Edge, Julian. 1996. Cross-cultural paradoxes in a profession of values. *TESOL Quarterly* 30(1): 9–27.

Fairclough, Norman (ed.). 1992. *Critical language awareness.* London: Longman.

Graddol, David. 1997. *The future of English?* London: British Council.

Grant, Carl A. 1999. The coming together of intellectual and physical space in the multicultural education movement: The importance of "A room of one's own." *Multicultural Perspectives* 1(1): 3–7.

Heller, M. 1982. *Language, ethnicity and politics in Quebec.* Ph.D. dissertation, University of California, Berkeley.

Kachru, Braj. 1986. *The alchemy of English: The spread, functions and models of non-native Englishes.* Oxford: Pergamon Press.

Labov, William. 1972. *Language in the inner city: Studies in the Black English vernacular.* Philadelphia: University of Pennsylvania Press.

LoBianco, Joseph. 1997. Ebonics, King's English and straight talking. *Australian Language Matters,* 5(1): 1–2.

Malcolm, Ian. 1994. Discourse and discourse strategies in Australian Aboriginal English. *World Englishes* 13(3): 289–306.

McArthur, Tom. 1997. The printed word in the English-speaking world. *English Today* 13(1): 10–16.

Mchombo, Sam A.1998. National identity, democracy, and the politics of language in Malawi and Tanzania. Paper presented at the Wars and Words: Political Change and Language Use in Africa Conference, Yale University, March 26.

Michaels, Sarah. 1981. Sharing time: Children's narrative styles and differential access to literacy. *Language in Society* 10: 423–442.

Mobbs, Michael C. 1997. Children's other languages: Expertise, affiliation and language use among second-generation British South Asian pupils. *NALDIC Occasional Paper* 9. Watford, UK: NALDIC.

Nelson-Barber, Sharon. 1982. Phonological variations of Pima English. In R. St. Clair and W. Leap (eds.), *Language renewal among Indian tribes: Issues, problems and prospects.* Rosslyn, VA: National Clearing House for Bilingual Education.

Peirce, Bonny Norton. 1995. Social identity, investment, and language learning. *TESOL Quarterly* 29(1): 9–31.

Phillipson, Robert, and Tove Skutnabb-Kangas. 1996. English only worldwide or language ecology? *TESOL Quarterly* 30(3): 429–52.

Tollefson, James W. 1991. *Planning language, planning inequality.* London: Longman.

Smitherman, Geneva. 1999. CCC's role in the struggle for language rights. *College Composition and Communication,* 50(3): 349–376.

Wolfram, Walt. 1991. *Dialects and American English.* Englewood Cliffs, NJ: Prentice Hall.

Wolfram, W., N. Schilling-Estes, and K. Hazen. 1996. *Dialects and the Ocracoke brogue. Eighth grade curriculum.* Raleigh: North Carolina Language and Life Project.

Wong, Lian-Aik, and Jacinta Thomas. 1993. Nativization and the making of meaning. In Mark N. Brock and Larry Walters (eds.), *Teaching composition around the Pacific Rim.* Philadelphia: Multilingual Matters. 15–27.

Notes

1. The term Ebonics was coined from Ebony and Phonics by Robert Williams in 1973.
2. I will use the term language as it is commonly accepted in linguistics, to describe languages that are termed such by their users. Except when contrasting language with dialect, I will use the

term variety for all language variation, including standard and nonstandard varieties. I will not capitalize standard except when referring to specific standard varieties by name.

3.   I use the term language minority throughout this article to refer to native speakers of nonstandard English and native speakers of languages other than English because both are not native speakers of national Standard American English. John Baugh (1998) makes a similar case. I acknowledge, however, the arbitrariness of the term native speaker.

4.   The former case supported the right of limited-English-proficient students to an equal educational opportunity and instructed educational agencies to overcome language barriers that might prevent that equal access. In the Ann Arbor case, Judge Joiner directed the Ann Arbor School District to use the home language of Black English-speaking children in teaching them to read Standard English.

5.   Such estimates vary depending on whether the definition of English includes pidgins and English-based Creoles and what measure of proficiency is used for non-native English speaker.

6.   The Analytical Engine originated with Charles Babbage and the Universal Machine with Alan Turing, both English. The Internet was an outgrowth of ARPANET, the network developed by the U.S. Department of Defense to connect it with research universities involved in defense research.

7.   TOEFL, the Test of English as a Foreign Language is the test used by most U.S. universities to determine (standard American) English proficiency for entrance.

From definition to policy: The ideological struggle of African-American English

Walt Wolfram
North Carolina State University

Introduction. A few years ago, I was conducting one of the many dialect workshops for practitioners that I have now done for over three decades. The reactions of the participants—ranging from curious bewilderment to hostile resistance—were little different from those I have routinely entertained from those introduced to sociolinguistic premises for the first time. Having encountered such responses on countless occasions, I fully expected these reactions. What I did not realize, however, was the fact that I had done a similar workshop at the same school a couple of decades earlier, and that, in fact, a few of the participants in attendance that day were present at the earlier workshop. I was concerned about my obvious lapse of memory, but I was much more disturbed by the fact that the reactions from the participants that day seemed no different from those of any other group confronting sociolinguistic premises for the first time.

Most sociolinguists who participated in the original deficit-difference debates of the 1960s or the subsequent periodic public controversies about dialect diversity had a strong sense of déjà vu when the so-called Oakland Ebonics controversy erupted in late 1996 and 1997. It seems surprising that so little has changed over several decades with respect to public opinions and attitudes about language differences. We are still arguing about issues that range from the definition of the variety, now named Ebonics or African-American Vernacular English (Mufwene forthcoming), to the significance of linguistic information about this variety for the socio-educational lives of its speakers (Rickford 1997; Wolfram, Adger, and Christian 1999). Furthermore, the institutional and individual effects of linguistic discrimination and subordination are still evident in virtually every social and educational arena. Lippi-Green (1997: 73) observes that discrimination based on accent remains "so commonly accepted, so widely perceived as appropriate, that it must be seen as the last back door to discrimination."

If nothing else, the controversy and media blitz surrounding the resolution of the Oakland Unified School Board on Ebonics has reinforced several important lessons about the status of dialect differences in American society. It exposed, once again, the intensity of people's beliefs and opinions about language and language diversity. In fact, a *Newsweek* article (Bridgeman 1998: 1) reported that an America Online poll about Ebonics drew more responses than the polls asking the public whether O. J. Simpson was guilty. Beliefs and attitudes about language derive from the same core of beliefs that govern religion, morality, and ethics, thus making them entrenched—and also largely unassailable. Furthermore, beliefs about the sovereignty of Standard English seem to be embedded in what Anderson (1991) labels a "sacred imagined community," where privileged access to truth and power are rooted in the Standard English script. In challenging the fundamental belief system about the way language is supposed to be, the Oakland Unified School District's resolution opened, or more accurately, reopened the intensive, heated discussion of language ideology and linguistic subordination.

The controversy further emphasized the persistent and widespread level of public misinformation about language variation in public life and in education. There is an entrenched mythology and "miseducation" about dialects that pervades the understanding of this topic, particularly with respect to the relationship between vernacular and standard varieties (Baugh 1988; Lippi-Green 1997; Wolfram and Schilling-Estes 1998; Wolfram, Adger, and Christian 1999). Furthermore, the factual misinformation is not all innocent folklore; it affects how we view people and how they view themselves on both a formal, institutional level and an informal, personal level. Operating on erroneous assumptions about language differences, it is easy for people to perpetuate unjustified stereotypes about language as it relates to class, ethnicity, and region—stereotypes as severe as any other racial and class stereotype.

The Ebonics controversy therefore underscored the need for a strong, proactive strategy to counter the deleterious institutional and personal effects that derive from the popular assumptions and factual misinformation that dominate the public understanding of sociolinguistic diversity. Language diversity is one of the most fundamental dimensions of human behavior still entrenched in such a pervasive mythology, yet there are few systematic and programmatic movements directed toward educating the American public about the "facts of dialect diversity."

Has such little progress really been made over the past several decades in the sociopolitical and socioeducational struggle against linguistic subordination and language-based discrimination? Can we realistically expect wide-scale change with respect to the consideration of dialect diversity in our social and educational institutions and in the treatment of those who speak vernacular varieties? What can we hope to accomplish and how must we go about it if we seek to effect change? In the following sections, I provide some perspective on the fundamental challenges for socioeducational and sociopolitical change and offer some proposals for change in policy and in practice.

The ideological context. To understand the full significance of the periodic controversies about dialect diversity that erupt in American society, we have to understand the fundamental ideology that frames such debates. By *language ide-ology* I mean an underlying, consensual, and unquestioned belief system about the way language is and is supposed to be (Woolard and Schieffelin 1994). In its most pervasive form, language ideology appears to make "common sense" so that no specialized knowledge or expertise is required to understand fundamental "facts" about language and its role in society. The primary socialization processes of an ideology (Eagleton 1991) naturalize and universalize beliefs so that they are self-evident. Furthermore, social reality is obscured in ways convenient to the be-lief system, so that alternative ways of thinking are excluded and denigrated. In Foucaultian terms (1972) "regimes of truth" legitimize a set of beliefs and prac-tices. In the case of language diversity, a set of perspectives and practices is es-tablished that is associated with asymmetric, heterogeneous groups. The beliefs about language need not be made explicit; in fact, as Fairclough (1989: 85) notes, language ideology is most effective when its workings are least visible. At the root of the struggle over the status of African-American Vernacular English (AAVE), then, is an entrenched ideology that recognizes the sovereignty of the standard variety and the linguistic subordination of vernaculars, particularly those associated with class and ethnic asymmetries.

From time to time, particular events in society may bring to the surface foun-dational beliefs about language, and language itself may become an object in an ideological struggle. In an important sense, the Oakland Unified School District's resolution (1996, 1997) was controversial because it challenged primitive beliefs about language and language diversity, offering an alternative, nonmainstream set of beliefs.

The questions and comments about Ebonics thus provided a forum for ex-posing alternative ways of viewing language and language diversity. The lan-guage of everyday conversations readily portrays the ideological struggle over language diversity and the status of AAVE.[1] For example, during the controversy I was routinely asked if I "believed in Ebonics," as if there were some article of religious belief attendant to the recognition of AAVE. In fact, one host on a radio talk show confronted my stance on the legitimacy of AAVE as a linguistic system with the comment, "You have to understand, professor, that I believe in a right and a wrong, a moral and an immoral, a correct and an incorrect, and Ebonics is simply incorrect English." Others have had similar experiences. After I gave one lecture on Ebonics at a university, the following day a person in the audience re-ported that she was greeted that morning by a colleague who observed, "I heard you went to the Ebonics lecture last night; so do you believe in Ebonics now?" Such a response to attendance at a lecture on Ebonics conjures up images of at-tendance at a religious revival meeting. But this semblance is not far-fetched. I have found that it is as difficult to dispute the linguistic validity of a vernacular variety such as AAVE as it is to dispute religion or politics. Everyone seems to have an opinion about dialect diversity, and these opinions are typically quite dogmatic. In fact, I found during the height of the Ebonics controversy that the question, "So what do you think of Ebonics?" functioned as an indirect speech act declaring that a person is about to offer you their opinion on this topic rather than a literal question. Furthermore, most people assume that any "reasonable person" would believe the same way as they do about language.[2] Such is the manifestation of language ideology—at its best or worst.

There is another characteristic of language ideology that may set language apart from some other domains of knowledge. Language is considered to be at once a collective and personal matter, a symbolic token of group identity as well as personal character. In its collective capacity, it is a shared, ordinary commodity, and no specialized knowledge or expertise is required for public commentary. This status means that authoritative critique on the topic is not limited to those with specialized expertise. In fact, the Ebonics controversy has taught us that social and political prominence is considered to be sufficient for the assumption of an authoritative stance on language. Fuel was added to the fire of the Oakland Ebonics controversy when prominent public figures ranging from the president of the United States to educators and leaders in the African-American community offered immediate and pronounced condemnation of the Oakland School Board for its resolution recognizing the linguistic integrity of Ebonics.

It is interesting to note that the Senate subcommittee hearings on Ebonics convened by Senator Arlen Specter included two well-versed, widely recognized sociolinguists, William Labov and Orlando Taylor, who argued in support of the Oakland resolution. Their position was, in turn, opposed by two antagonistic counter-testimonies offered by a columnist and a preacher, neither of whom had any formal training in linguistics or sociolinguistics. This scenario would be akin to two non-experts arguing with two well-credentialed research physicists about the ramifications of a particular law of physics in industrial manufacturing.

Without any safeguards that limit public discussion to those with specialized expertise in language structure, popular beliefs that include common myths about language can run rampant. And that is exactly what took place in the public furor over the Oakland resolution. In this instance, however, the issues involved broad-based societal beliefs about the nature of language and a specific set of misunderstandings about language diversity in Oakland. The controversy even unleashed a whole new public genre of linguistic racism, as documented in the Ronkin and Karn (1999) analysis of Internet parodies of Ebonics. Perhaps most revealing about such parodies was the liberty with which people distributed them on the Internet, apparently unaware of or insensitive to their linguistic racism. I personally was shocked to receive dozens of electronic mail messages containing forwarded linguistic parodies of Ebonics from colleagues and students who would not think of sending me a racist parody on another topic. As Ronkin and Karn (1999: 33, 34) note:

> Ebonics parody pages . . . distances producers and consumer
> from responsibility for language that would be highly offensive
> in other public venues . . . the Oakland resolution brought lan-
> guage ideology to the foreground in the entire United States in
> a dramatic way. The resolution, moreover, precipitated a na-
> tionwide discourse on language in which attitudes toward
> Ebonics served as a safe proxy for a discourse on the threats
> that racialized groups pose to dominant group power in the
> United States.

One of the ironies of the public commentary on Ebonics was the seemingly paradoxical alliances of public figures who commented on the topic. Public commentary brought together leaders from the African-American community known for their social activism and progressive sociopolitical perspectives and those known for their conservative, reactionary political stances. On what other topic have conservative icons such as the media commentator Rush Limbaugh and the social activist Jessie Jackson agreed upon in their public condemnation? Such alliances are, however, simply a testament to the depth of the entrenched language ideology.

In general, the American public has been socialized into the same language ideology, so that the principle of linguistic subordination cuts across the racial and class distinctions that seem to divide the population on most other issues. In fact, it is one of the few ideologies that seems to transcend race and class in American society. Americans of different classes and races therefore can stand united in totalitarian support of the sovereignty of Standard English—even as they may stridently disagree on other "moral" issues in our society, ranging from the guilt of O. J. Simpson to the sexual behavior of Bill Clinton. With such a consensual base, the small group of academic linguists and "radical" members of the Oakland School Board who seek to legitimize a vernacular dialect can safely be marginalized as a disenfranchised, out-of-touch groups who deserve no public voice in the language policy of the United States. In fact, one of the greatest challenges for linguists speaking out on Ebonics was their credibility as practically minded citizens who genuinely were interested in the academic success of AAVE-speaking students. As one reporter from *USA Today* put it, "People are simply going to say that this is the position of a bunch of radical, ivory-tower academics. What do you say to that?" As we shall see, the threat of marginalization is not an idle challenge, but an important consideration if we hope to translate our sociolinguistic axioms into public policy and practice.

The discussion of language ideology may seem to provide a rather imposing and pessimistic background for discussing change in the practice of linguistic subordination, but it is also the place where we must start. Such a perspective also may help us set realistic expectations in terms of a program of change. Major changes in belief systems regarding the "facts of life" take generations to be realized, and language ideology should not be expected to be different in this respect. It has taken generations for particular laws of nature to become publicly accepted doctrine; it is therefore not surprising to find that the fundamental premises of sociolinguistics have yet to be embraced by the general public. At this stage, perhaps we should be more concerned about the mobilization of effective strategies and policies for challenging the ideology of linguistic subordination than public opinion polls showing the acceptance of AAVE or other vernacular dialects. I therefore concentrate in the following sections on the examination of strategies and policies for bringing about change.

Language policy and language variation. Language policy typically includes a combination of official decisions and prevailing practices related to language use and education (McGroarty 1997; Cooper 1989). For various historical reasons, approaches to language policy in the United States are quite diffuse and "unofficial." McGroarty (1997: 68) offers two primary reasons for the diffuse approach: "First are the tensions inherent in the public ideologies related to language, which are strongly individualistic and pragmatic in character, though they include some provisions for protection of minority rights and implicit connections to the notion of pluralism. Second is the effect of the overlapping governance structures that affect all levels of education."

There is, of course, no official national language policy in the United States despite the well-publicized efforts of the English-only movement to add a constitutional amendment making English the official language of the United States. The Constitution currently has no reference to the language of government, and there is no national language academy to offer prescriptive proclamations about Standard English structures, as is found for European countries such as France and Spain. But the lack of an official policy seems to matter little in the instantiation of language practices. In fact, until recent media coverage and statewide votes regarding the English language amendment, most citizens were quite surprised to find out that English was *not* the official language of the United States, and that there were no authorities who mandated in an official capacity the forms of Standard English.

The relationship between the federal government and education, the primary venue for formal language service, is at once separate and intertwined at different levels of governance. Authority for formal, public education is granted to local school boards and educational agencies so that language-in-education policies in the United States are simply the sum of purely local decisions (McGroarty 1997: 68). This is quite unlike countries such as England, Australia, and New Zealand, which adopt national curricula in a top-down model of education.

At the same time, local school districts may be subjected to federal litigation related to language in the classroom under the authority of federal law. For example, the guarantee of equal protection under the Fourteenth Amendment (Section 1706, Title 20) states the following:

> No State shall deny equal educational opportunity to an indi-
> vidual on account of his or her race, color, sex or national ori-
> gin, by
>
> . . .
>
> (f) the failure by an educational agency to take appropriate ac-
> tion to overcome language barriers that impede equal participa-
> tion by its students in its instructional programs. 20 U.S.C.
> 1073f).

On the basis of this statute, a judgment granting language concessions for African-American students was made by the U.S. District Court judge in Ann Arbor, Michigan, in the so-called Ann Arbor Decision. In particular, Judge Joiner (Ann Arbor 1980: 11) ruled that the school board had to "take steps to help teachers to recognize the home language of the students and to use that knowledge in their attempt to teach reading skills in standard English." Such federal litigation is, however, relatively infrequent.

Although authority for formal education is quite localized in the United States, there is still a widespread, prevalent practice that excludes all varieties other than Standard English. The ideology of linguistic subordination discussed previously is so entrenched in American society that government officials, educators, and citizens see no need to state the obvious—that Standard English is the only acceptable language for handling the affairs of government and education on a national, state, or local level.

The actual practice, or "unofficial policy," with respect to Standard English is confirmed by the reaction to any institutional effort to recognize the legitimacy of varieties other than the reified standard. Such formal efforts are met with strong negative reaction and typically lead the way to misinterpretation, as exemplified in the reaction to the resolution of the Oakland Unified School Board. The actual wording of the board's position on Standard English and African-American language is this:

> BE IT FURTHER RESOLVED that the Superintendent in conjunction
> with her staff shall immediately devise and implement the best
> possible academic program for the combined purposes of facil-
> itating the acquisition of and mastery of English language
> skills, while respecting and embracing the legitimacy and rich-
> ness of the language patterns whether they are known as 'Ebon-
> ics,' 'African Language Systems,' 'Pan African Communication

Behaviors,' or other description (Resolution of the Board of Education, Oakland Unified School District 1997).

Although the resolution simply states that students' community dialects should be respected, affirmed, and used as a bridge to learn Standard English, it was consistently misinterpreted by the media and the public to mean that students and teachers were to use and teach the vernacular variety. Pedagogically, all this statement means is that educators should have specific knowledge about the community language patterns of their students in order to know where they are in the process of moving them towards standard English proficiency. As Orlando Taylor (1997: 2) put it in his testimony to the Senate subcommittee hearing, "taking students where they are to where they need to go is an educational principle that is as American as apple pie." But the ideology of linguistic subordination is so entrenched that such explicit acknowledgment is misinterpreted as a challenge to totalitarian sovereignty of the standard variety.[3]

My personal experience with proposals for implementing dialect awareness programs suggests that the popular interpretation of the Ebonics resolution with respect to teaching is not unusual. For almost a decade, I proposed to pilot an experimental dialect awareness program for primary and secondary students to school systems around the country. The goal of the program simply was to teach students to understand and appreciate the nature of language differences and the intricate and systematic patterning of all dialects and languages. No aspect of the programs ever endorsed teaching in a vernacular dialect or teaching students to use the vernacular in any productive way. Nonetheless, I was repeatedly denied permission to pilot these programs in the public schools—by principals, teachers, and parents who worried that the programs might teach students to speak "bad language." Once prevailing ideologies are challenged, the security of language quality control evaporates, thus opening the door for worst case scenarios with respect to the demise of Standard English.

Implementing language variation policy. Given the diffuse and unofficial approaches to language policy in the United States, it seems apparent that the implementation of policies with respect to language variation will follow a similar, varied course of action. What exactly can be done to implement practices and policies that ensure the equitable treatment of vernacular dialect speakers in society and in education? Even if it were possible by some national fiat to adopt a national policy on language and dialects, it would require extensive social and educational augmentation given the depth of the entrenched ideology of linguistic subordination in American society.[4] No single language policy can unilaterally overturn a pervasive, largely covert practice that derives from a foundational ideology of linguistic subordination. At the same time, there are some strategies that can be set in motion to counteract the current practices toward speakers of AAVE and other vernacular varieties of English. In the following sections, I discuss briefly some of the venues for adopted policies to counter current practices.

Litigation. The United States is a highly litigious society, which offers recourse for those who have been discriminated against through the legal system. Furthermore, there are protections against discrimination offered under the Civil Rights Act of 1964, which mentions explicitly the denial of equal opportunity "because of an individual's, or his or her ancestor's place of origin; or because an individual has the physical, cultural, or linguistic characteristics of a national origin group" (U.S. Equal Employment Opportunity Commission 1988: §1606.1).

Notwithstanding some notable exceptions, there are actually few cases involving dialect rights that end up in litigation.[5] In part, this is because language is often treated as a right derived from other demographic traits such as race, sex, or national origin, rather than language per se. However, as Matsuda (1991: 1391–1392) notes: "The way we talk, whether it is a life choice or immutable characteristic, is akin to other attributes of the self that the law protects. In privacy law, due process law, protection against cruel and unusual punishment, and freedom from inquisition, we say the state cannot intrude upon the core of you, cannot take away your sacred places of the self. A citizen's accent, I would argue, resides in one of those places."

Perhaps a more important explanation for the relative paucity of court cases related to dialect discrimination is found in the tacit accommodation of the linguistic subordination principle in the legal system. Lippi-Green observes (1997: 164) that the courts remain quite receptive to arguments that accents impede communication and therefore the ability to perform jobs, even though every case she examined in detail indicated no effort to make an objective assessment of the communication skills required for the job. This remains the case despite ample documentation of overt and covert discrimination based on language variation (Milroy and Milroy 1985; Lippi-Green 1997). As Milroy and Milroy (1985: 3) note, "[a]lthough public discrimination on the grounds of race, religion and social class is not now publicly acceptable, it appears that discrimination on linguistic grounds is publicly acceptable, even though linguistic differences may themselves be associated with ethnic, religious and class differences."

Dialect discrimination is ultimately a sociological rather than legal problem, but the United States has a long history of addressing such inequities through the court system, and it often serves as the incentive for implementing social policy. Exclusion on the basis of dialect has not really had its day in court. Or, as Lippi-Green (1997: 170) puts it, "linguistics and language-focused discrimination have yet to meet their Scopes Trial." It seems that we need to seize the opportunity to have a full hearing on issues of language variation so that legal precedents can be set to guide the society towards sociolinguistic justice. As with other areas of discrimination, such precedents cannot eliminate prejudice, but they can at least protect the legal rights of those affected by linguistically based discriminatory behavior.

Resolutions and position statements. In the wake of the Oakland United School Board Resolution on Ebonics, a number of major professional language organizations formulated supportive resolutions and position statements. For example, the Linguistic Society of America, the American Association of Applied Linguistics, and Teachers of English as a Second and Other Language were among the associations offering resolutions in support of the efforts of the Oakland Unified School Board to recognize the linguistic integrity of AAVE. As the event played out in the media, some of these resolutions became an essential part of the story. The resolutions, along with media interviews with linguists, were often used to present the other side of the public condemnation of the Oakland School Board's resolution. Linguists all over the United States were called upon to offer expert professional opinion on the controversy for local and national news stories, and the resolutions of these various professional organizations helped ground their expert opinion; they could point to the adoption of supportive resolutions by prestigious professional language organizations. Such resolutions also added professional credibility to the numerous web sites that were rapidly created in response to the controversy. Thus, the various resolutions and position statements by professional organizations certainly seemed to provide support for linguists throughout the country trying to take advantage of their fifteen minutes of media fame related to language variation.

The long-term effects derived from these resolutions and position statements are, of course, another matter. Position statements on language variation are hardly a new strategy for supporting changes in language policy and practice. For example, a subdivision of the nation's largest and most influential organization of English teachers, the National Council of Teachers of English (NCTE), adopted a strong position affirming students' dialect rights in 1974. The statement asserted that "teachers must have the experience and training that will enable them to respect diversity and uphold the right of students to their own language" (Committee on CCCC Language Statement 1974: 3). The American Speech-Language-Hearing Association (ASHA), the exclusive authoritative professional organization for speech and language pathology, also offered a strong position statement on social dialects, in which they insisted that dialects be considered differences rather than disorders. Thus, it was noted (ASHA 1983: 23) that "no dialectal variety of English is a disorder or pathological form of speech or language" and that "each social dialect is adequate as a functional and effective variety of English."

To what extent have such resolutions and position statements had any effect on the professional membership? Do they inspire change? Do they really make a difference in terms of language practice? Although it is difficult to answer these questions in a comprehensive way, it appears that such position statements are effective to the extent that they can be subjected to concrete appropriation. For example, the ASHA position statement on social dialects served as an important professional guideline for our implementation of an extensive training program for speech and language pathologists in the Baltimore City Public Schools (Wolfram, Adger, and Detwyler 1993: 1), as indicated in the following statement in the introduction of the handbook.

> The approach to language differences adopted by BCPS [i.e. Baltimore City Public Schools] is consonant with the position statement on social dialects formulated by ASHA.

> It is the position of the American Speech-Language-Hearing Association (ASHA) that no dialectal variety of English is a disorder or pathological form of speech or language. Each social dialect is adequate as a functional and effective variety of English. Each serves a communication function as well as a social solidarity function. It maintains the communication network and the social construct of the community of speakers who use it. Furthermore, each is a symbolic representation of the historical, social, and cultural background of the speakers. (ASHA 1983: 25(9), 22–23)

> The ASHA position on dialect differences adopted by BCPS has important implications for service delivery to a linguistically and culturally diverse student population. In particular, there are essential implications for the competencies of SLPs [i.e., speech and language pathologists] with respect to language differences. These are set forth by Cole (1983: 25) as follows:

> 1. knowledge of the particular dialect as a rule-governed linguistic system

> 2. knowledge of nondiscriminatory testing procedures

> 3. knowledge of the phonological and grammatical features of the dialect

> 4. knowledge of contrastive analysis procedures

> 5. knowledge of the effects of attitudes toward dialects

> 6. thorough understanding and appreciation for the community and culture of the nonstandard speaker.

The particular details of descriptive and applied sociolinguistic knowledge required to serve students equitably and effectively in BCPS cannot necessarily be assured on the basis of the SLP's previous academic training and background; hence it is usually necessary to augment their previous training with additional knowledge about linguistic-cultural differences. It is also necessary to adopt appropriate procedures for considering the dynamic nature of language variation in the Baltimore language community. In the following sections, we attempt to provide clinicians with relevant sociolinguistic descriptive information and procedural models for applying and integrating this information regarding linguistic-cultural differences into the service delivery model.

We appropriated the ASHA position statement primarily as a rationale for our training program. It provided a justification of the training for both the practicing speech and language pathologists who participated in the program and for the higher administrative offices within the BCPS system who might have questioned the training plan. We tried to ward off resistance by showing that our efforts were directed towards bringing local speech and language pathologists into compliance with the position statement adopted by the major professional organization responsible for certification and accreditation.

Another way in which the position statement on social dialects has been appropriated relates to the preparation of students. ASHA does not dictate specific, required courses for professional certification, but it does designate topical areas for coursework that now includes a core area related to language structure and language differences.

Perhaps an even more effective strategy for learning such information is the inclusion of examination questions about language differences on national certification exams. I admit, for example, that I have written questions in this area for the pool of questions to be selected for the certification exam and taught a section on social dialects as part of examination preparation courses. In American society, there is, unfortunately, no greater motivation for learning a topic than the threat of an examination. While I realize that there is an apparent inconsistency in my cooperation with the testing establishment while railing against the sociolinguistic biases of standardized testing (Wolfram 1976), I am willing to live with such personal paradoxes to promote change in the institutional treatment of vernacular dialect speakers.

In my opinion, ASHA's position statement on social dialects has made a difference in professional practice within the profession, though the change may not be as encompassing in terms of local practices as we would like to see. In fact, I personally think that ASHA as a professional organization has made more institutional progress over the last three decades with respect to their consideration of language differences than any other professional language service organization with which I am familiar.

In contrast, the NCTE statement on dialect rights has not had the same kind of professional and practical impact that the ASHA statement seems to have had. Surely, it has generated heated debate among some professionals, which in itself indicates some progress. But my personal experience working with language arts teachers in local school systems indicates that the policy has had little effect on how they conduct their business with respect to their students who speak vernacular dialects. There are probably a number of reasons for this, ranging from the loose relationship between local school systems and national professional organizations to the composition of the statement itself, but the bottom line seems to be the same. To my knowledge, the NCTE professional position statement has not been appropriated to a significant degree in the training of professionals nor in the local places of practice. It seems that position statements by professional agencies can have an effect in changing practice, but only to the extent that there is some institutional control exerted over appropriation—in the preparation of professionals and in the establishment and maintenance of professional standards of practice.

Establishing standards. One of the ways in which policy change is effected in American society is through the establishment of "standards" or objectives of behavior. These standards, which are often related to resolutions and position statements, may be applied to a wide range of behaviors in diverse settings, from broad-based socioeconomic standards for living (e.g., the establishment of a "poverty level") to objectives for specific competencies (e.g., literacy). Furthermore, the establishment of standards may involve varied levels of bureaucratic responsibility and authority, ranging from the highest levels of federal government to local education systems. The federal government may, for example, set a standard for raising the literacy level for the nation as a whole, whereas a local school board may establish a quite specific standard for reading competency for third graders. Given the system of governance within the United States, the federal government often has no say in state and local affairs, including education, but the allocation of money and other resources certainly affects state and local government systems. The federal government has little to say directly about state and local affairs related to language, but it certainly wields significant influence. For example, a Senate subcommittee hearing was held to consider the Oakland resolution, with possible implications for funding allocations. One of the primary reasons for the inquiry by the subcommittee of the Senate Committee on Appropriations: Subcommittee on Labor Health and Human Services of Education, in fact, was related to the issue of budgetary allocation, thus showing how the federal government may exert pressure over the educational practices of local school systems.

The establishment of standards for behavior on a national, state, or local level seems to be an effective venue for policy change, particularly with respect to language. National agencies, like the government and vested professional agencies, may provide overarching mandates for change, whereas state and local agencies possess the authority and responsibility to implement concrete change. Standard-setting may also be relegated to professional agencies responsible for language practice. For example, we saw in the previous section that ASHA, which holds exclusive authority for certifying speech and language pathologists and accrediting training institutions, holds the vested authority to ensure the local implementation of its social policy on dialects. Agencies that do not hold such regulatory power over training and practice naturally would have less authority in implementing change of various types.

In the best case scenario of a top-down model, a national agency adopts a set of standards with respect to language, a state, through its appropriate agencies, adopts a similar standard, and a local governing board follows this up by instantiating change on a local level. Adger (1999) exemplifies this hierarchy by documenting a national standard on language variation set forth by the National Council of Teachers of English and International Reading Association, a state-adopted standard related to language diversity for the state of Massachusetts, and a curriculum standard for fifth- through eighth-grade students adopted for a local school district, Lowell, within the state. This case even includes specific teaching examples that can be used to carry out the objective. Adger (1999) quotes the standards on these respective levels as follows:

National Council of Teachers of English and International Reading Association, Standards for the English Language Arts.

"Standard 9: Students develop an understanding of and respect for diversity in language use, patterns and dialects across cultures, ethnic groups, geographic regions, and social roles."

Massachusetts English/Language Arts Curriculum Framework.

"Students will demonstrate an understanding of how oral dialects differ from each other in English, how they differ from written standard English, and what role standard American English plays in informal and formal communication."

Lowell, MA, English/Language Arts Curriculum Framework, grades 5–8.

"Students will analyze how dialects associated with informal and formal speaking contexts are reflected in slang, jargon, and language styles of different groups and individuals."

Core knowledge/skills, grade 8.

"Students will carefully examine and explore the many ways in which variations and oral language impact on communication and determine the ways we understand the meanings derived from that communication."

Teaching Examples, grade 8.

"The teacher could ask students to choose a favorite sport or activity/hobby, generate a list of jargon specific to that field and share results with the class."

Adger's example underscores the significance of hierarchical support in setting and implementing a language policy. At the same time, she demonstrates that effective policy must be translated into concrete, localized practice. In effect, she demonstrates the adage of "thinking globally but acting locally" as popularized in other movements involving policy change.

Public Education. If nothing else, the Ebonics controversy has once again illustrated the dire need for general education about language issues. In other articles (Wolfram, Adger, and Christian 1999; Wolfram 1999a, 1999b), my colleagues and I have outlined the rationale for dialect awareness programs and provided numerous examples of curricular activities and products that might be used in implementing school-based and community-based dialect awareness programs. At the heart of public education should lie two concerns: truth and fairness. As noted earlier, there is an entrenched mythology and miseducation about dialects that distorts the understanding of this topic in American society, particularly with respect to the relationship between vernacular and standard varieties (McWorter 1998; Wolfram and Schilling-Estes 1998; Wolfram, Adger, and Christian 1999). Furthermore, the factual misinformation is not all innocent folklore; it affects how we view people and how they view themselves on both a formal, institutional level and an informal, personal level. As noted previously, it is easy for people to perpetuate unjustified stereotypes about language as it relates to class, ethnicity, and region. And this is where issues of fairness come to the fore.

I am constantly reminded that many people have never even considered alternative interpretations of vernacular dialects apart from the popular myth that speakers are simply too ignorant or lazy to speak better. As one host of a radio talk show commented surprisingly in our discussion of the nature of vernacular dialects, "So you mean to say that dialects have rules? I never knew that!" Certainly, it starts with the presentation of accurate information about the structural integrity of dialects, moving from there to a sense of fairness in terms of the speakers of such varieties. Many people, particularly children, have a strong sense of fairness in the treatment of others. One of the most common responses we get from elementary and middle school children in discussions of dialect attitudes is the observation that "it's not fair" to treat people badly because of their dialect. As one fifth-grade student in Baltimore wrote after viewing some vignettes illustrating dialect prejudice from the video *American Tongues*: "Today I learned that not all people speak the same. I like the way some people talk differently. I did not like the way some people teased others because of their language. I would like to see Dr. Wolfram improve the attitudes of the people in the video." In an evaluative summary of one of our dialect-awareness curricula, the learning experience most noted by the students concerned dialect prejudice and human relations related to dialect differences (Messner 1997).

As mentioned in the resolution passed by the American Association for Applied Linguistics (1997), "all students and teachers should learn scientifically-based information about linguistic diversity, . . . education should systematically incorporate information about language variation," and linguists and other language professionals "should seek ways and means to better communicate the theories and principles of the field to the general public on a continuing basis."

Implementing such programs is, of course, easier said than done; to my knowledge there presently are no large-scale dialect awareness programs in the United States. As we are discovering in our effort to implement such a program in the state of North Carolina, it takes great marketing skills, bureaucratic finesse, and a good sense of timing, to say nothing of sociolinguistic expertise and translation skills. First, we have to sell the notion that dialect awareness programs are essential and that they align with the extant educational objectives on a statewide and local level. We have, for example, aligned specific lessons and activities in our dialect awareness program with specific competencies in social studies and communication skills as set forth by the State Board of Education (Simmons et al. 1998). Some of the units meet the following competencies of North Carolina Standard Course of Study (NCSCS) Social Studies Goals:

- The learner will access the influence of geography on the economic, social, and political development of North Carolina.
- The learner will evaluate the effects of earlier contacts between various European nations and Native Americans.
- The learner will judge the continuing significance of social, economic, and political changes since 1945 and draw conclusions about their effect on contemporary life.

Some of the units that examine the history of dialects in North Carolina and the current changes taking place in post-insular dialect areas clearly fall within the goals for social studies. For example, geography is an important dimension of dialect diversity, and changing conditions within the state have clearly affected the dialect landscape of the state since 1945. At the same time, there are also a number of aspects of the curriculum that align with the NCSCS Communication Competencies Goals, including the following:

- The learner will use strategies and processes that enhance control of communication skills development.
- The learner will use language for the acquisition, interpretation, and application of information.
- The learner will use language for critical analysis and evaluation.
- The learner will use language for aesthetic and personal response.

It is not difficult to demonstrate how dialect awareness programs are consonant with the current state-mandated competency goals, such as critical analysis and use of language in responding to new information about language variation. This demonstration is a necessary step in the process of marketing the materials to teachers, curriculum designers, and state education administrators. Schools and teachers are highly aware of and responsible for attaining these mandated competencies, and this step cannot be ignored or bypassed.

It is also essential to package the text appropriately for students and teachers. At this point, cooperation with curriculum writers and publishers who might incorporate the materials into textbooks becomes critical for the implementation process. Over the past several years, I have maintained regular contact with the publishers of social studies texts for North Carolina in order to ensure that units on dialect diversity will, in fact, be incorporated into the next edition of a middle school text and/or the supplement to the current fourth- to sixth-grade text. I have also co-authored illustrative text with a curriculum writer.

The teachers must also be prepared for the challenge of teaching about language variation. I have attempted to orient teachers to the curriculum by presenting workshops on the dialect awareness materials at state and local conventions for teachers. We have even provided incentives, such as free maps of the dialect areas of North Carolina, for teachers to exhibit in their classrooms. The maps include sample text for the proposed curriculum for classroom teachers to become familiar with a sample of the content and presentation mode. And the staff of the North Carolina Language and Life Project have now taught a localized pilot curriculum on dialects in select classrooms in North Carolina for the past six years, including a week-long showcase unit in the Ocracoke School that I have personally taught every year since 1994. The preparatory stage requires marketing, networking, coordination, and perhaps most of all, patience. Such changes are not taken lightly, nor do they come quickly if they are to become a permanent part of public school education.

The implementation of dialect awareness programs in education cannot, however, take place exclusively through the education sector. As Kaplan (1997: xiii–xiv) notes, "language-in-education policy is subsidiary to national language policy, that national language policy is rooted in the highest levels of government, and that the education sector follows the lead of more powerful sectors." There is obviously a critical need to engage in broad-based informal education venues as well as school-based public education.

Our own efforts to promote dialect awareness in recent years have included community-based programs such as television and video documentaries (e.g., Alvarez and Kolker 1986; Blanton and Waters 1995), trade books on dialects for general audiences (Wolfram and Schilling-Estes 1998), museum exhibits (Gruendler et al. 1997), and presentations to a wide range of community organizations such as civic groups, churches, preservation societies, and other local institutions and agencies.

The Oakland controversy has clearly indicated the inherent interest and underlying concern that most people have about language issues as well as the need for public education on these issues. As the superintendent of the Oakland Schools, Carolyn Getridge (1997: 2) noted, this situation created "a teachable moment of national proportion"—an occasion to provide accurate information about dialect diversity to counter some of the misguided, popular interpretations. We now need to move beyond that moment to provide long-term, informal sociolinguistic education for the American public. There is simply no other insurance against the reincarnation of the kinds of controversies and misunderstandings that continue to arise. More importantly, there is probably no other road that will lead to an authentic understanding of the role of dialect diversity in American society. Such variation affects us all, regardless of the dialect involved. Dialect awareness programs should therefore be inclusive of the wide range of dialects that represent a full array of language diversity in American society, not just AAVE. In fact, our experience with programs in schools and in communities indicates that they are most effective and less threatening when they do not isolate a single language variety in the discussion of language variation. There are few "facts of life" more misrepresented in the public sector than those involving language variation; it seems only appropriate that a wide-scale, dedicated effort be made to counter this miseducation through using the full range of formal and informal public education venues.

Conclusion. Given the entrenched ideology that governs matters of language diversity, it is hardly surprising that the implementation of concrete, equitable sociopolitical and socioeducational language policies should take place so slowly. But we must keep things in perspective. Changes in primitive belief systems, such as those governing language, do not take place rapidly; major changes take generations to be effected, and even then there is continued, residual resistance. Thus, it has taken generations for the teaching of scientific theories of human development to be implemented in our schools, and there are still pockets of opposition. The fallout of the Scopes trial is still felt after well over a half century. We should not realistically expect a different timeline for the scientific understanding of sociolinguistic diversity to replace the entrenched mythology. Perhaps the most we can expect is incremental progress as more people gain an understanding and more institutions become cognizant of the orderly naturalness of language diversity independent of its association with particular regional, social, and ethnic groups.

It should also be clear from this discussion that change will not simply take place without intervention. There is a need for proactive involvement on many levels, ranging from broad-based government policy to individual practice. In this regard, Wren's (1997: 3) advice for the involvement of TESOL teachers in language policy seems to be quite generally applicable to those involved in issues pertaining to language variation:

- Convince them [i.e., practitioners] of the need to be interested in language policy issues.
- Make them feel they can make a difference in their own workplace.
- Develop their own skills in order to influence institutional colleagues.
- Provide them with knowledge, skills, and understandings to "act locally."

National language disputes such as the Oakland resolution, the English-only movement, and other national and local language controversies provide a measure of the current state of national language ideology, and a reminder of what still needs to be accomplished with respect to public knowledge, policy, and practice. While it might be easy to get discouraged about what has not yet changed with respect to the national consciousness about language variation, there are at least significant tasks for everyone to do in the effort to mold a more linguistically informed and equitable society with respect to language differences. I personally am thankful simply that I have had an opportunity to be present at the initial stages of a movement towards equitable sociolinguistic policies that might be realized sometime in the next millennium. The dawning of the new millennium at least gives a reasonable time frame for accomplishing the desired changes in policy and practice.

REFERENCES

Adger, Carolyn Temple. 1999. Race, ethnicity, and language in the school curriculum. Paper presented at American Association for Applied Linguistics, Stamford, CT, March 9.

Alvarez, Louis, and Andrew Kolker (producers). 1987. *American tongues.* New York: Center for New American Media.

American Association for Applied Linguistics. 1997. *Resolution on the application of dialect knowledge to education.* Annual Meeting of AAAL, Orlando.

American Speech-Language-Hearing Association (ASHA). 1983. Social dialects: A position paper. ASHA 25(9): 23–24.

Anderson, Benedict. 1991. *Imagined communities: Reflections on the origin and spread of nationalism.* London: Verso.

Ann Arbor Decision, Memorandum, Opinion, and Order and the Educational Plan. 1980. District Court, Ann Arbor, MI.

Baugh, John. 1988. Language and race: Some implications for linguistic science. In F. J. Newmeyer (ed.), *The Cambridge survey,* vol. 4, *Language: The socio-cultural context.* New York: Cambridge University Press. 64–74.

Blanton, Phyllis, and Karen Waters (producers). 1995. *The Ocracoke brogue.* Raleigh: North Carolina Language and Life Project.

Bourne, Jill. 1997. Language policy in the USA: National values, local loyalties. In William Eggington and Helen Wren (eds.), *Language policy: Dominant English, pluralist challenges.* 41–50.

Bridgeman, Cathy. 1998. Language, identity, and power: The Ebonics debate. Unpublished manuscript. Columbus: University of South Carolina.

Cole, Lorraine. 1983. Implications of the position on social dialects. ASHA 25(9): 25–27.

Committee on CCCC Language Statement. 1974. Students rights to their own language. *College Composition and Communication* 25 (separate issue, paginated separately). Champaign-Urbana: National Council of Teachers of English.

Cooper, Robert L. 1989. *Language planning and social change.* New York: Cambridge University Press.

Eagleton, Terry. 1991. *Ideology: An Introduction.* London: Verso.

Fairclough, Norman. 1989. *Language and power.* London: Longman.

Foucault, Michel. 1972. *The archeology of knowledge and the discourse on language.* New York: Pantheon Books.

Getridge, Carolyn M. 1997. *Statement of Carolyn M. Getridge.* U.S. Senate Committee on Appropriations: Subcommittee on Labor Health and Human Services of Education. Washington, DC: U.S. Senate.

Gruendler, Shelley, Charles Holden, Walt Wolfram, and Natalie Schilling-Estes. 1997. An exhibit on the Ocracoke Brogue. Ocracoke, NC: The Museum of the Ocracoke Preservation Society.

Kaplan, Robert B. 1997. Forward: Palmam qui meruit ferat. In William Egginton and Helen Wren (eds.), *Language policy: Dominant English, pluralistic challenges.* Philadelphia: John Benjamins. xi–xxiii.

Linguistic Society of America. 1997. *LSA resolution on the Oakland Ebonics issue.* Linguistic Society of America annual meeting, Chicago, January 4.

Lippi-Green, Rosina. 1997. *English with an accent: Language ideology and discrimination in the United States.* London: Routledge.

McGroarty, Mary. 1997. Language policy in the USA: National values, local loyalties, pragmatic pressures. In William Egginton and Helen Wren (eds.), *Language policy: Dominant English, pluralistic challenges.* Philadelphia: John Benjamins. 67–90.

McWorter, John. 1998. *The word on the street: Fact and fable about American English.* New York: Plenum.

Matsuda, M. J. 1991. Voice of America: Accent, antidiscrimination law, and a jurisprudence for the last reconstruction. *Yale Law Journal* 100: 1329–1407.

Messner, Kyle. 1997. Evaluative summary of Appalachian Dialect Awareness Program. Unpublished report. Boone, NC: Appalachian State University.

Milroy, James, and Leslie Milroy. 1985. *Authority in language: Investigating language prescription and standardization.* London: Routledge.

Mufwene, Salikoko S. forthcoming. What is African American English? In Sonja Lanehart (ed.), *Multidisciplinary perspectives on African American English.* Philadelphia: John Benjamins.

Oakland Unified School District. 1996, amended version, 1997. *Resolution on Ebonics.* Oakland, CA: Office of the Board of Education.

Rickford, John R. 1997. Unequal partnership: Sociolinguistics and the African-American speech community. *Language in Society* 26(2): 161–98.

Ronkin, Maggie, and Helen E. Karn. 1999. Mock ebonics: Linguistic racism in parodies of Ebonics on the Internet. *Journal of Sociolinguistics* 3: 360–380.

Simmons, Erin, Anita Ware, Alan Wark, and Pete Yount. 1998. Cohort 4 dialect project. Unpublished manuscript. Boone, NC: Appalachian State University.

Taylor, Orlando. L. 1997. *Testimony of Orlando Taylor on the subject of Ebonics.* U.S. Senate Committee on Appropriations: Subcommittee on Labor Health and Human Services of Education. Washington, DC: U.S. Senate.

U.S. Equal Employment Opportunity Commission. 1988. *Guidelines on Discrimination because of national origin.* Washington, DC: Government Printing Office.

Wolfram, Walt. 1976. Sociolinguistic levels of test bias. In Deborah Sear Harrison and Thomas Trabasso (eds.), *Seminars in Black English.* Hillsdale, NJ: Erlbaum. 265–287.

Wolfram, Walt. 1999a. Dialect awareness programs in the school and community. In Rebecca Wheeler (ed.), *Language alive in the classroom.* Greenwood Press. 47–66.

Wolfram, Walt. 1999b. Repercussions from the Oakland Ebonics controversy: The critical role of dialect awareness programs. In Carolyn Adger, Donna Christian, and Orlando L. Taylor (eds.), *Making the connection: Language and academic achievement in the education of African American students.* Washington, DC: Center for Applied Linguistics and Delta Systems.

Wolfram, Walt and Natalie Schilling-Estes. 1998. *American English: Dialects and variation.* Cambridge, MA: Basil Blackwell.

Wolfram, Walt, Carolyn T. Adger, and Jennifer Detwyler. 1993. Handbook on language differences and speech and language pathology: Baltimore City Public Schools. Washington, DC: Center for Applied Linguistics.

Wolfram, Walt, Carolyn T. Adger, and Donna Christian. 1999. *Dialects in schools and communities.* Mahweh, NJ: Erlbaum.

Woolard, Kathryn, and Bambi Schieffelin. 1994. Language ideology. *Annual Review of Anthropology* 23: 55–82.

Wren, Helen. 1997. Making a difference in language policy agendas. In William Egginton and Helen Wren (eds.), *Language policy: Dominant English, pluralistic challenges.* Philadelphia: John Benjamins. 3–28.

NOTES

1. Bridgeman (1998) notes that the prevalence of two metaphors dominated the media coverage used to describe Ebonics, namely fire and disease. These two share the entailment of "breaking out" and "spreading." As such, they pose a serious threat to others and need to be contained.

2. In the process of preparing this manuscript on a plane, I was asked by the person sitting next to me about my occupation. When I replied that I was a linguist, his first question was, "So did you have anything to do with that Ebonics stuff a couple of years ago?" When I replied that I did, his immediate response was, "What did you think? I thought it was stupid." Subsequent conversation indicated that the passenger was a fellow faculty member at North Carolina State University.

3. For all the rhetoric about the linguistic status of Ebonics, the underlying goal of the Oakland school actually was quite conservative, and even assimilationist with respect to its advocacy of proficiency in Standard English. The board never wavered in its goal of teaching proficiency in the dialect of mainstream, middle-class America. All it really proposed was recognition and respect for the intricate, systematic nature of AAVE, yet the resolution was popularly interpreted as advocating that students be taught in Ebonics and teachers be taught to use Ebonics in instruction.

4. In this respect, England seems to be a prime example of how quickly a government can retreat from an enlightened perspective on language awareness and language planning. In the mid-1980s, the National Education Curriculum adopted a strong set of language awareness materials only to retreat to a more traditional curriculum that now largely excludes explicit instruction in this area. As Bourne (1997: 41) puts it, "Language policy in education in English is now balanced on the knife edge between the most detailed and explicit language planning through legislation ever set in motion in the United Kingdom, and a return to a long tradition of inexplicit (some would say covert) control through funding mechanisms."

5. Although there are more cases regarding the rights of bilinguals that now end up in litigation, they still seem relatively infrequent for a society as obsessed with litigation as the United States is.

South Asian bilingualism: Hindi and Bhojpuri

Shaligram Shukla
Georgetown University

Throughout the history of South Asia, we find former common languages splitting up into many dialects, and then evolving into languages. For example, Sanskrit split up into many Prakrit dialects and languages, which then further split up into many modern languages of India, Nepal, Pakistan, and Sri Lanka. Furthermore, conquests, colonization, migration, and cast and class distinctions have brought languages into contact and have produced the condition for extensive bilingualism, which has led to inevitable sociopolitical and linguistic changes.

Mastering a single language in the fullest sense is difficult. Now imagine mastering two or three languages and then also having a receptive knowledge of a third or fourth language. But that is what many speakers in India, Nepal, Pakistan, and Sri Lanka had been doing for centuries. No wonder the life in South Asia begins with challenges. The speakers of these different dialects and languages accept a common socioeconomic condition around the common culture of market, town, or the capital city. They accept political subordination under a wider territorial administration, and social subordination under an upper class around a central elite. In the process they have no choice but to accept the common standard language of the market, town, city, or the elite. This languages could be Hindi, Urdu, Nepali, Bengali, or Sinhalese, above and along with their own language such as Bhojpuri, Gujarati, Punjabi, Newari, or Tamil or any one of the hundreds of South Asian languages. This association of two or more languages invariably creates varieties in the common standard language. Thus, under various bilingualisms, the common standard Hindi has split up into Panjabi-Hindi, Gujarati-Hindi, Bhojpuri-Hindi, Tamil-Hindi, Kannada-Hindi, and a few others. In the future, these hyphenated varieties of Hindi could eventually evolve into distinct cognate languages. Many of these new languages could be further replaced by one of the dominant varieties of Hindi, and thus the centuries-old cycle of split and dominance would continue. I believe that the Urdu language came into existence as a result of bilingualism when the Turkish- and Persian-speaking Muslims had no choice but to become bilingual and for their administrative language adopt the variety of Hindi spoken around Delhi. The influence of Turkish and Persian languages remains a defining feature of Urdu, just as the influence of Bhojpuri defines Bhojpuri-Hindi, the influence of Punjabi defines Punjabi-Hindi, and the influence of Tamil defines Tamil-Hindi. A similar case of bilingualism may have caused the split of Ancient Greek into many dialects. Thus, language split is caused not only by language change, but it is also caused by bilingualism, which modifies a language in different locations with new linguistic features. Hence, if Hindi and other South Asian languages ever split up into many dialects and languages, the South Asian bilingualism will have a positive hand in it.

If a bilingual can keep the languages apart, he or she would be two speakers in one person, but because of psychological and social factors many bilinguals do not succeed in keeping the languages apart and do not seem to care. When I hear a Bhojpuri, a Bengali, a Marathi, or a Tamil speaker speaking Hindi, I am in awe of their carefree attitude toward Hindi forms. They speak Hindi with freedom and ease and demonstrate that there is nothing sacred about the distinctive phonology and grammar of a language, and that variations are equally authoritative and expressive. Their speech underscores the fact that the fundamental grammar is universal and that variations are mere sociolinguistic conventions and conveniences subject to easy and harmless alternations and modifications. Thus, in this fashion in South Asia languages come in contact, ferment and flourish, and by filling many lexical gaps enrich each other. This kind of linguistic behavior speaks of a refreshing cultural freedom, vitality, and tolerance for variation and divergence. These traits distinguish South Asia from many other regions of the world where multilingualism leads to conflicts, creating intolerance and blind devotion to a single language linked with wealth and power.

The languages spoken by the bilinguals naturally interfere with each other, producing deviation from their norm. Consequently, the bilinguals become a permanent source of linguistic interference and the clash of languages in the same individual becomes linguistically intriguing. The result is an automatic modification and rearrangement in the patterns of phonology, morphology, syntax, and the lexicon of the many languages they speak. A speaker's personality, too, becomes altered when he or she switches from one language to another and thus speaks two or more languages. Thus bilingualism reshapes not only one's languages but also one's culture and personality. Consequently, a monolingual society may have difficulty in comprehending the subtleties of a bilingual society and vice versa.

There have been some studies measuring the intelligence of monolinguals and bilinguals. Some of them have forced a correlation between intellectual inferiority and bilingualism, and thus have concluded bilingualism to be harmful (Eichorn and Jones 1952; Darcy 1953). According to the defenders of this view, given a choice, one should avoid being a bilingual. In the case of the South Asian bilinguals, however, there is no such choice. They have to be bilinguals and the controversy is pointless. It is like saying that given a choice one should avoid being a South Asian. The fact is that in South Asia bilingualism is a cultural necessity, and in light of the overwhelming linguistic diversity, it will continue to be so. Moreover, since the researchers ignored the varying sociocultural contexts of their monolingual and the bilingual subjects, the studies showing correlation between bilingualism and intelligence were considered invalid (Weinreich 1953; Haugen 1956).

I am a bilingual, native Bhojpuri speaker. Before the age of any formal instruction I acquired Hindi from my bilingual parents and from other sources. Once in school, the use of Hindi increased. I use both languages now; however, the use is context sensitive, and in any given situation one or the other language tends to dominate. Consequently, a certain amount of specialization has taken place. For example, within my family and close relatives and with many people of my village and surrounding villages and towns, I always use Bhojpuri, with others I use Hindi. Am I able to translate freely and perfectly between Bhojpuri and Hindi? The answer is "not completely." If I work on it I can, but it does not follow automatically from the possession of Hindi and Bhojpuri. This follows from the fact that I have specialized my two languages into different usages, and these languages are associated with different groups of participants. It also suggests that language is an integral part of its cultural context, and in an altered context its communicative value may remain the same. The reality appears unequally real when expressed in Hindi and Bhojpuri. Thus, neither of these languages can completely replace the other as a way of living, nor are they intended to do so. I cannot disturb the part played by Bhojpuri, even though when I move as an individual away from my immediate environment, Hindi often replaces Bhojpuri in all situations of living.

In the Bhojpuri area, will Bhojpuri ever be abandoned in favor of Hindi with a prolonged transitional period of bilingualism? Will a mixed language develop that will incorporate some features of both? Or will the language distance between Bhojpuri and Hindi decrease? Only time can tell, but I believe that there will be always some compelling reason, some compelling need that only Bhojpuri can fulfill.

What determines the choice of Hindi or Bhojpuri when either language could serve as a medium of conversation? In some cases it is just the desire to acquire a better mastery of Hindi that forces the choice. In other cases the use of Hindi may simply represent a desire to show off. The ease that one feels for Hindi or Bhojpuri may decide the choice for some. When the norm of the group forces one to choose Hindi or Bhojpuri when either language could serve as a medium of conversation, a conflict between personal choice and group demands may arise. (For a similar situation in other bilingual communities, see Herman 1968). As they come into the city, many bilinguals find themselves speaking more and more Hindi, and as stated earlier, their Hindi shows the influence of their native Bhojpuri and also of their class and caste.

In the area of northeast India where I come from, the Bhojpuri-speaking community is larger, and many Bhojpuri speakers are bilingual. There, very few bilinguals have a native-like control in both languages. A majority of them have such control only in Bhojpuri, although they speak and understand Hindi fairly well. These Bhojpuri-Hindi bilinguals do not try to adopt the phonetic pattern of Hindi while speaking Hindi beyond the point where they become comprehensible to Hindi speakers. Thus, they fail to achieve the standard performance in Hindi, and in doing so, what they speak is referred to here as Bhojpuri-Hindi.

Because I acquired both languages very early in my life, I am able to understand them equally well and speak them with equal facility. But there are many, as mentioned earlier, who are unable to comprehend and speak them with equal ease. Moreover, this mastery of skill is often not the same on all linguistic levels. I know several elementary school teachers who have vast Hindi vocabulary, perfect Hindi grammar, but poor Hindi pronunciation. There are others who posses vast Hindi vocabulary but have imperfect grammar and poor pronunciation. In many other cases the Bhojpuri phonology, grammar, vocabulary, semantics, and stylistics not merely influence their Hindi but assault it. The following are a few examples of such Hindi utterances:

> *kupit ke tarah* for the expected *kupit kii tarah* >like an angry (person).

> *ke gardan par* for the expected *kii gardan par* >on his/her neck.

> *dopahar hogayaa* for the expected *dopahar hogayii* >it was midday.

> *laRkii ne aakaash dekh lii* for the expected *laRkii ne aakaash dekh liyaa* >the girl saw the sky.

> *paraakramvaalaa arjun ne* for the expected *paraakramvaale arjun ne* >the mighty Arjuna.

As mentioned earlier, on phonological and grammatical levels many bilinguals understand Hindi well but are unable to show the same care when they speak Hindi. The problem concerning the grammar, however, tends to be progressively eliminated. But those of the phonetics—the pattern of muscular actions—are difficult to eliminate. At a lexical level it is common to find bilinguals who have reading vocabulary that extends far beyond their speaking vocabulary. On a semantic level, depending on their life experiences and professions, Bhojpuri-Hindi bilinguals are able to express their thoughts in some areas better in one language than they could in the other. Likewise, the stylistic range of Hindi and Bhojpuri varies with the subject of the discourse.

The degree of proficiency in Bhojpuri or Hindi depends on its function and the conditions under which it is used. Hindi is the language of schools, the media, and the printed word. In these situations, for many bilinguals the emphasis is mainly on comprehension. For some the emphasis is on both comprehension and expression. In most homes the language spoken is solely Bhojpuri. In few affluent families where there are tutors, Hindi is also used between the tutor and the members of the family. Hindi is also often spoken with the members of a government agency, on the bus and railway stations while traveling, and for the religious talks and explanation in the places of worship. In the work places the work always obliges a Bhojpuri-Hindi bilingual to speak Hindi. Sport activities, musical events, and any other social pastime always favors the use of Hindi. In the schools the language of instruction is Hindi, never Bhojpuri.

However, in the Bengali schools, where the immigrant Bengalis want their children to do their schooling in Bengali, the language of instruction is Bengali. In the universities and colleges both Hindi and English are used as media of instruction. Here subjects such as arithmetic, biology, and physics are taught in English while others in Hindi. Regular correspondence for business is always done in Hindi. Thus, there are economic, administrative, cultural, and political pressures that force the Bhojpuri-Hindi bilingual to use Hindi rather than Bhojpuri.

In the Bhojpuri area and in many other areas of India, the use of Hindi is an economic necessity that leads to many bilinguals practicing Hindi in their home. They believe that this strengthens the chances of economic success for them and their children. The practice of Hindi is not the same as communicating in Hindi. Administrative workers in these areas are required to master Hindi and be fluent in it. And printed matter is all in Hindi. The pressure of groups that want to see Hindi as a national language also favors the use of Hindi. When self-communicating, such as diary writing and note taking, most bilinguals prefer Hindi, but they prefer Bhojpuri for thinking, counting, and for all sorts of inner expression. Bhojpuri words are freely used in Hindi when equivalent words are not known or do not exist. As a result of this bilingualism, the following features distinguish Bhojpuri-Hindi from other varieties of Hindi spoken elsewhere in India.

Phonemic features of Bhojpuri-Hindi
1. Standard Hindi has two voiceless sibilants, a palatal [sh] and a dental [s] occurring in [pa:sh] >snare' and [pa:s] >near.' Since Bhojpuri has only one sibilant, [s], both of these words in Bhojpuri-Hindi are pronounced as [pa:s].
2. In Bhojpuri-Hindi the standard Hindi voiced fricative [z] is replaced by the voiced palatal affricate [j], e.g., Hindi [zami:n] >land' Bhojpuri-Hindi [jami:n].
3. Standard Hindi voiceless labio-dental and velar fricatives [f] and [x] are reproduced as voiceless aspirated [ph] and [kh] in Bhojpuri-Hindi, e.g., Hindi [faki:r] >a Muslim ascetic' and [xush] >happy' are pronounced as [phaki:r] and [khus] in Bhojpuri Hindi.

4. Since Bhojpuri does not have a monophthongal pronunciation of the vowels [ai] and [au] of standard Hindi, these speakers speaking Bhojpuri-Hindi pronounced them as diphthongs, e.g., Hindi [bhaiya:] >brother' and [kauva:] >crow.'

5. Since Bhojpuri does not normally allow onset and coda clusters, Hindi words such as [bhram] >illusion' and [karm] >order' occur as [bharam] and [karam] in Bhojpuri-Hindi.

6. Both Bhojpuri and Hindi have similar stress patterns; however, in Bhojpuri there is tendency to shorten a long vowel before a stressed syllable. Thus, standard Hindi [ra:ji:v] >a proper name' and [na:ra:z] >displeased' are usually pronounced as [raji:v] and [nara:j] in Bhojpuri-Hindi.

Thus, Bhojpuri speakers speaking Hindi with a systemic regularity of incorrectness under-differentiate many sounds that are distinguished in Hindi. As a result, there are many homophonous words in Bhojpuri-Hindi in which the ideal of having one meaning for one form is ignored. The speakers believe, however, that they are articulating two different words, one Hindi and the other Bhojpuri, even though they sound alike. But because many Bhojpuri-Hindi speakers render phonemes of the two languages in the same way, they achieve an economy with a natural ease. They do not have to change their phonetic system. It requires a relatively high degree of sophistication in both languages for a speaker to afford the structural luxury for maintaining separate phonemic systems of each. Thus, in this fashion these Bhojpuri-Hindi speakers are continually creating a variety of Hindi different from the standard Hindi. Of course, there are many Bhojpuri speakers of Hindi who, aware of the high sociocultural status of standard pronunciation, do exert effort to reproduce the sounds of Standard Hindi and in many instances succeed.

Grammatical features of Bhojpuri-Hindi. Because Hindi and Bhojpuri have the same type of word order, the problem of grammatical interference between them mainly involves the use of Bhojpuri grammatical morphemes and bound forms in Hindi. Often Bhojpuri speakers feel a need to express some category of Bhojpuri while speaking Hindi, in which either it is covert or absent. One such example is the marking of definitive nouns. In other cases a Hindi grammatical morpheme is simply replaced by a more familiar Bhojpuri one:

1. Words for tangible objects (tools, utensils, or ornaments) and some basic emotions (affection, anger, and greed) have been transferred in Bhojpuri-Hindi.

2. In the usual list of Bhojpuri morphemes in Hindi, nouns figure predominantly.

3. Unlike Hindi, which had no overt way of marking definite nouns, Bhojpuri marks its definite nouns by the suffix [-wa:], e.g., [laika:] >a boy': [laikwa:] >the boy.' Often Bhojpuri speakers in their Hindi use this suffix after Hindi noun stems as in [laRkwa:] >the boy,' occurring in the sentence: *lagta: hai laRkwa: bhag gaya:* >It looks like the boy had run away.' The standard Hindi form is *lagta: hai laRka: bhag gaya:.*

4. For standard Hindi adverbs and interrogative [pa:s] >near,' [ni:ce] >below' and [kya:] >what?' Bhojpuri-Hindi often substitutes the Bhojpuri forms [lage:], [tare:], and [ka:].

Transfers

1. Transfer of morphemes from one language into another is a means of correcting the inadequacies of a lexiconCor filling the lexical gaps, e.g., Bhojpuri [u:khaR kha:bhaR] >high-low-and-rough land' is used by Bhojpuri speakers of Hindi. The Hindi: [u:nc-ni:c] >high-low' does not carry the same connotations.

2. Transfer of bound morphemes is rare; however, free Bhojpuri forms with and without suffixes when transferred are automatically analyzed by the bilinguals, and thus bound morphemes are detached and then attached to Hindi words. Thus, for example, the Bhojpuri words [bhut-ha:] >haunted,' [balu-ha:] >sandy,' [maTi-ha:] >earthen,' and [laThi-ha:] >carrying a stick,' are normally used by Bhojpuri speakers when speaking Bhojpuri-Hindi. These words have the adjectival derivational suffix [Bha:], which then is detached and then attached to the Hindi word, such as [shabd-ha:] >wordy.'

3. Thinking often involves association between ideas and words. A direct association between an idea and a word from a second language is possible, but often the word from the first language intervenes or appears and may be integrated in the second language discourse. For example, Bhojpuri has two words for the two stages of many fruits, whereas in many cases Hindi has only one. Thus, for the Bhojpuri words [le:Rha:] >a baby jack-fruit' and [kaTahar] >a mature jack-fruit' Hindi has only [kaTahal]. Now it is not uncommon for Bhojpuri speakers when speaking Hindi to use the word [leRha:] when referring to a baby jack-fruit. In this way the Hindi word [kaTahal] acquires a narrower meaning for the speakers of Hindi.

These are just few of the features of Bhojpuri-Hindi that distinguish it from the other varieties of Hindi. As a result of the different kinds of bilingualism, Hindi is no longer a single idiom. It must be regarded as a combination of several idioms, in that it is usually a language accepted as a shared language by the speakers of several different languages such as Punjabi, Gujarati, Bhojpuri, and many others.

Since a majority of the Bhojpuri-Hindi speakers have a greater proficiency in Bhojpuri, it remains the dominant language of the two. In the area of understanding, expression, and inner speech (counting, the names of the day, calculating time, etc.), Bhojpuri is stronger than Hindi at a given moment in a bilingual's life. Of course, the ratio can change in the course of time. As has been mentioned, Bhojpuri-Hindi speakers switch from Hindi to Bhojpuri or Bhojpuri to Hindi according to appropriate changes in the speech situation, but not in an unchanged speech situation, and certainly not within a single sentence, unless they are quotations marked with proper voice and intonation. However, for the city dwellers and their children born in the city, as their fluency in Bhojpuri decreases, so does their switching faculty. They find themselves awkwardly continuing in Hindi even when there is a change in the speech situation. When persons who once used Bhojpuri most of the time in most of the situations cease to speak it as much as they did, for them the memory of things mediated through Bhojpuri may become more distant, and a certain discontinuity in the inner growth of personality may occur. In Bengal, where Bengali is spoken, and in the Dravidian south, where Tamil, Telugu, Kannada, and Malayalam are spoken, at times an evident dislike for the political influence of Hindi replaces the earlier give-and-take view of the period following the Indian independence in 1947. In these places there may appear a visible turning away from the idea of Hindi being the natural unity language of all of India, but the paradox is that there hasn't been any reduction in the number of bilinguals. On the contrary, the numbers of Bengali-Hindi, Tamil-Hindi, Telugu-Hindi, Kannada-Hindi, and Malayalam-Hindi bilinguals have increased remarkably. In the Bhojpuri and other northern areas of India, the desire to embrace Hindi and accept it as the national language has always been strong, and with the passage of time has become stronger. In this sense the Bhojpuri speakers and the speakers of many other northern Indian languages mark themselves off more sharply from other bilinguals by embracing Hindi, which they all speak with ease and pride. The only agitation against Hindi that occurred in the early 1960s in the Bhojpuri speaking area was the *ne-haTaao-aandolan* >*ne-* remove moment' in Patna, in the heart of the Bhojpuri land. It had more humor than anger. Hindi uses the particle [ne] after the subject of a preterit transitive verb. In this position Bhojpuri has no such particle. Many Bhojpuri speakers of Hindi found this use of [ne] unnecessary and revolted against its use in Hindi. In the Bhojpuri-speaking city of Patna in the early 1960s there were many organized and well-publicized demonstrations with colorful banners and loudspeakers shouting in Hindi, "Hindi se *ne-haTaao!*" >remove the particle *ne* from Hindi. However, as soon as the leaders of the remove *ne*-movement realized that their demonstrations had become a nationwide object of ridicule and laughter, many of them abandoned their hope of removing this intrusive particle from Hindi. But some stayed with their "remove *ne*" inspiration and carrying their Bhojpuri ease spoke Hindi without ever using the particle *ne*. Thus new linguistic situations by act of the political will have been and are being continually created in India and other parts of South Asia. This has led to the sporadic nationalistic separations as in the Dravidian south and in Bengal and the strong nationalistic unification as in the rest of the Indo-Aryan north.

Now and then one may encounter an isolated group in a city where they speak only Bhojpuri, while its entire environment uses a language other than Bhojpuri or Hindi, such as Bengali in Calcutta. Here, unless the Bhojpuri community becomes bilingual, there remains a serious barrier to communication between the Bhojpuri immigrants who are laborers and merchants and the natives of Calcutta who proudly speak Bengali. These Calcutta Bhojpuri speakers and their children are compelled by the situation to learn Bengali for use in occupation and school. Here Bhojpuri is limited to the speakers of one ethnic community, while Bengali is used for interethnic communication. A unification of distinct ethnic groups or an understanding between distinct groups is thus accomplished by the growth of bilingualism. Similarly, many other bilingual groups, such as Tamil-Hindi, Bengali-Hindi, Nepali-Hindi, Tamil-Sinhalese, Panjabi-Hindi, Urdu-Panjabi, Sindhi-Urdu, Sindhi-Hindi, Tamil-Bengali, Punjabi-Bengali, Nepali-Bengali, and so on, have come into existence in South Asia. In all these cases, the immigrant community is usually numerous enough to maintain its linguistic and ethnic identity. For the immigrant community the maintenance of its language helps them keep their ethnic identity. It also offers the newcomers a way to undergo the linguistic transformation gradually and, along with the bilingualism, it serves as a safety valve that prevents the South Asian machine with its unforgiving ethnic and regional diversity from breaking down.

REFERENCES

Darcy, Natalie T. 1953. A review of the literature on the effects of bilingualism upon the measurement of intelligence. *Journal of General Psychology* 82: 21–57.
Eichorn, D. M., and H. E. Jones. 1952. Bilingualism. *Review of Educational Research* 22: 425.
Haugen, Einar. 1956. *Bilingualism in the Americas: A bibliography and research guide*. Publication of American Dialect Society No. 26. Montgomery: University of Alabama Press.
Herman, Simon R. 1968. Explorations in the social psychology of language choice. In Joshua A. Fishman (ed.), *Readings in the sociology of language*. The Hague: Mouton.
Weinreich, Uriel. 1953. *Language in contact: Findings and problems*. Publication of the Linguistic Circle of New York, No. 1.

Gods, demi-gods, heroes, anti-heroes, fallen angels, and fallen arches

John A. Rassias
Dartmouth College

*La mythologie est une conque sonore au fond de laquelle on peut entendre re-
muer toute la civilisation.* (Mythology is a sonorous seashell at the bottom of
which all of civilization can be heard stirring.)

Richard Wagner et Téodor de Wyzéwa. 1885.
Revue Wagnérienne, Paris, 14 (*mars*)

I come not to hear your discourse, but to see how my teacher ties his shoes.

Sanskrit proverb

Introduction. In this paper I should like to concentrate on two inclusive
themes: (a) mythology as mirror of who we are, and (b) a definition of teacher. In
doing so, I will provide a cursory view of mythological figures among us, as well
as a discussion of the role of theater and drama, acting and teaching as one and
the same, texts, oral communication, and a personal answer to a dilemma.[1]

I. Figures from mythology adapt themselves to universal values and may
serve as models of behavior. Consider the following possibilities: archetypes of
some of us in the academy. Now never mind the cause of the punishment inflicted
by the gods on those who fell into disfavor, though, curiously, a great number of
those in hell happened to be teachers. In Greek mythology to be born is sinful
enough: it is *amartia.* It is the stuff of tragedies. Let's look for a moment into
blackest Tartarus, located at the fathomless bottom of the imagination, and con-
template the plights of some of those condemned to live there through eternity.

I see Tantalus, terrified by the prospect of a huge rock suspended precari-
ously above his head posing a constant threat of crushing him, being unable to
quench his thirst while immersed up to his throat in water, and trying to satisfy a
ravenous hunger by reaching for fruit that forever eludes his grasp. And that, dear
friends, has to be the mother of all punishments.

Now put Tantalus in a tweed suit or a skirt in a classroom, and he and she is as
consumed by pain and unfulfilled desire as their brother in Tartarus. The classroom

is the pool in which he is mired, and the fruit he seeks to capture is tenure. Before he was immersed up to his neck, he was told in graduate school that all that matters is publication. His sin was to have listened to this ill-conceived advice. So, he publishes: article, after article, after article, but has no time for teaching. Articles consume his interests: they can never be accumulated fast enough, they become the fruit of personal survival, and more and more publications, and less and less teaching, and fewer and fewer students, until there are none.

I can see Narcissus. Narcissus became so enamored with his image reflected in clear water that he is the personification of self-indulgence and vanity, condemned to gaze at his image through time unending. Other versions of the Narcissus legend include his being turned by the gods into a flower that bears his name and which, appropriately when the fullest consequences of his behavior are analyzed, means death. His narcissism renders him impervious to others: he is incapable of being touched or of touching others. He has withdrawn from the world, retreated in his undeviating rectitude, content in his isolation, inwardness, non-intervention, and abdication of the rights and privileges of responsible citizenship in the department.

I see Sisyphus, who according to Homer was the wisest and most prudent of mortals. On a pretenure class visitation, the chair of the department, Professor Odysseus, described the teaching style of Sisyphus: "I saw Sisyphus. He was suffering strong pains and with both arms embracing the monstrous stone, struggling with hands and feet alike, he would try to push the stone upward to the crest of the hill, but when it was on the point of going over the top, the force of gravity turned it backward, and the pitiless stone rolled back down to the level. He then tried once more to push it up, straining hard, and sweat ran all down his body, and over his head a cloud of dust rose" (Lattimore 1967: xi, lines 593–600).

The gods seem to underscore the fact that boredom, fulfilling chores in a robotic, mindless routine, is every bit as excruciating as the punishment Tantalus has to endure. The eternal rock is the yellowed, frayed, outdated notes delivered in a monotonous, bored drone. The end to the ordeal may be early retirement, when he realizes that his students wish more strenuously as the years pass that the rock will crush him.

This Sisysphus is a far cry from Camus's version of a Sisyphus who realizes that in this unreasonable world of deceit, the irrational, the absurd, one must struggle to create through action *une noblesse humaine*. He concludes that all is well. *"Chacun des grains de cette pierre, chaque éclat minéral de cette montagne pleine de nuit, à lui seul, forme un monde. La lutte elle-même vers les sommets suffit à remplir un cœur d'homme. Il faut imaginer Sisyphe heureux."* ("Each particle of that rock, each mineral shard of that mountain-shaped darkness, in itself forms a world. The struggle itself toward the summit is enough to fill a man's heart. One must imagine Sisyphus as happy") (Camus 1942: 162).

And there is bold Prometheus—Shelley's Prometheus—"in addition to courage and majesty, and firm and patient opposition to omnipotent force, he is susceptible of being; described as exempt from the taints of ambition, envy, revenge, and a desire for personal aggrandizement . . . the type of the highest perfection of moral and intellectual nature, impelled by the purest and truest motives to the best and noblest ends" (Zillman 1968: 37). Earth herself proclaims: "Subtle thou art and good; and though the Gods/ Hear not this voice, yet thou art more than God/ Being wise and kind" (Zillman 1968: 57). In a word, a colleague we would kill to have in our ranks. But, in his CV, Prometheus listed a brief but telling account of himself, admitting that he took the side of mankind, devoting his career to their cause. He gave them the forbidden fire, fueling their creativity and empowering them to lead productive lives. The tenuring committee took into consideration this contribution by this young Turk who dared oppose his senior colleagues and particularly Professor Zeus, chair of the department, and his achievement was downgraded to the status of being "morally acceptable, but academically questionable." Tenure denied.

Today, because vultures do not hover over concrete jungles, Prometheus and his ilk suffer from bleeding ulcers, their guts eaten away by obstructionists among colleagues and administrators. And finally, there is Caligula. In his play *Caligula*, Albert Camus transforms the murderous third-century Roman emperor into a superior person, besieged on all sides by the forces of mediocrity, symbolized in turn by the closed ranks of the patricians. A confrontation ensues after Caligula assumes the role of Venus to further the awakening of his patricians. He explains his actions to Scipio, whom he favors.

> *Caligula:* They do not understand destiny and that is why I made myself destiny. I assumed that stupid and incomprehensible face of the gods. . . .

> *Scipio, his interlocutor, responds:* And that is what is called blasphemy.

> *Caligula:* No, Scipio, it is dramatic art! The error of all these men consists in not believing enough in the theater. They would otherwise know that it is permitted to every man to play celestial tragedies and to become god. . . .

> *Scipio:* Indeed, Caius. But if that were true, I believe that you have done what is necessary so that one day, around you, legions of human gods will rise up, implacable in their turn and drown in blood your ephemeral divinity.

> *Caligula, with a precise and hard voice:* I imagine with difficulty the day of which you speak. But I dream of it sometimes. (Camus 1958: 97)

Caligula knows and states that "These people need a teacher who knows what he is doing." And he has a mission, a responsibility to teach. Caligula's quest for "the moon, happiness, or immortality" is all on one plane. To possess the moon, and he means "to possess" in the physical sense, is to attain happiness and immortality; to be happy is to possess the moon; to be immortal is to possess the moon. None of the three is likely of attainment. His sanity lies in the more difficult task, not of attaining the moon but of showing men of what they are capable. What a marvelous teacher! What a goal to uphold! When reason and logic fail, the theater allows one to assume any role and to perform any deed imaginable.

II. Now, to use the classroom as theater requires drama. But let's make a crucial distinction: Classroom as "theater" is counterproductive. Etymologically, theater in Greek means, a place to sit, a place to see. We want classroom as drama, that is, drama from the Greek means, action, participatory action.

The preparation involved in teaching and acting should be long and arduous. Each craft requires mastering rigorous disciplines. Both professions communicate and inform. If the actor's performance is to be compelling, he has to make a thorough search of his past and analyze his relationship to his role, his relationship to the roles played by others, his relationship to his environment, to the techniques of acting, and, most significantly, his relationship to his audience. The relationship to his audience is his first obligation because it nurtures all he does. He is in tune with the audience; he causes the emotional and intellectual reactions they experience; he paces himself according to the pitch of their involvement and intensifies it according to the direction of the drama. He draws his audience into his confidence by his virtuosity, and they rely on him to clarify the purpose of the meaning of the work. The work becomes a living entity, forcing its reality on their consciousness. To heighten his effectiveness, he fills his presentation with new insights and strives constantly to exert the greatest impact on the audience's sensibilities. And thus, in many ways, the teacher is actor, and the actor is teacher.

The first step is to shake loose the chains of fear and inhibitions that keep us ensnared. Most mediocre men, as Madame de Staël states, are slaves to the event and do not have "the force to think higher than the fact." Man justifies his fate in an attempt to live "in peace with it." In a moment of rare humanity, he accuses the mirror, forgetting—as a Spanish proverb would have it—that we, not the mirror make the grimaces.

Rigorous training will permit the teacher to elaborate a technique that will ultimately release his or her own personality and give body to the uniqueness of the individual. What applies in acting also holds for teaching. Stanislavski waited until he was sixty years old before he would commit to paper his methods. *"J'ai besoin d'une théorie, renforcée d'une méthode pratique, bien vérifiée par l'expérience. La théorie pure, sans application, n'est pas mon affaire."*("I need a theory, reinforced by a practical method, truly verified by experience. Pure theory, without application, is of no concern to me") (Meyer 1975: 13).

III. But let's hear advice that we may choose to ignore at our peril. In my travels and lectures and workshops throughout the world, three basic truths were constantly confirmed by thousands of students. At the conclusion of each session, I ask one question: *What do you seek in a good teacher?* The students were of different ages, political bent, socioeconomic status, religions, and philosophies, but their answers are essentially identical. Although the responses were not in the same hierarchical order, all agreed on three basic qualities:

- A teacher should be enthusiastic, totally committed to his or her task, and thoroughly convinced of its worth.
- A teacher should be the same person in and out of the classroom, an identity—a lucid, identifiable personality fashioned not by rhetoric but by action.
- A teacher should respect his or her students by treating them as equals, by sharing knowledge, by appreciating their humanity, by demonstrating a sincere conviction that they possess an intrinsic worth and that they are capable of achievement.

The classroom, like the theater, is not a natural setting in itself. For it to function and for the teacher to be free of the restraints of his or her past and free of the restraints imposed by the artificiality of the classroom, *the teacher has to learn to create virtual reality.* In that sense, language study is a route to maturity. Obviously, gymnastics alone will not produce learning, in the same way that a frenetic conductor cannot always evoke the best performance from his orchestra. A combination of vitality and virtuosity enables maximum achievement. The teacher must be supple. Suppleness is a symbol of life itself.

IV. It is often difficult for a teacher to put a script to work, say, as an actor would the text of a play. Even good actors may suffer from bad material. The damage is lessened significantly in the theater, since actors' audiences are not obliged to study or remember scripts that bomb. The script assumes a different value in the classroom: it is the *point de départ* for the teacher and the *point de repère* for the student.

Here too we encounter problems: I was criticized for featuring an irritable railroad clerk, an impatient chauffeur de taxi, and the mugging of an old man in a grammar as anti-French propaganda (Rassias 1992). Clearly, one would never visit a country in which such aberrant behavior is described in a textbook. We need a reality check here! No muggings in Paris? No muggings in New York?

If these are typical reactions by teachers to life itself and to realism in the classroom, it is of small wonder that we cannot hold onto our students. Above all, students want to relate to real situations, to the truth. They have been raised on instant truth: television brings natural and man-made disasters directly into the living room. Students have seen the world in living color, and we often portray it in black, white, or depressing gray. They know that the world is not neat and pretty, and any attempt to portray it otherwise reduces our credibility and, indeed, makes language texts collections of anodyne cultural anecdotes–almost a return to featuring quaint provincial costumes.

Language texts are most often inhabited by flat, cut-along-the-edges personages who come unglued the minute you try to stand them up. Textbook families are usually happy and clueless natives who inhabit an idyllic desert isle marooned forever where, finally, no one really cares a damn if they are ever heard from again.

It is important that students know as much about themselves as possible. They should have the opportunity not only to fill their minds with knowledge, but also to be allowed to express their prejudices, sentiments, and other emotions. They should be at ease with themselves and be encouraged to articulate their innermost thoughts, to read and *understand their own book within.*

Oral communication is the key: at all costs our students must speak. Speaking is an integral part of our nature and it is through speaking that we learn a language, rather than learning a language in order to speak it. There is nothing new or unprecedented here.

Active use is the key to learning vocabulary. A word atrophies quickly not only when it is not used, but also if it hasn't been incorporated into the body of one's experience or needs. "Hearing words does not result in learning," St. Augustine pointed out in 389 A.D.: "We do not learn words we know; but we can not hope to learn words we do not know unless we have grasped their meaning. This is not achieved by listening to the words, but by getting to know the things signified" (Kelly 1969: 35). Comenius wrote in 1648 that "[a]ll things are taught and learned through examples, precepts, and exercises. . . . The exemplar should always come first, the precept should always follow, and imitation should always be insisted on"(Kelly 1969: 38–39). And in 1819, Lemare wrote: "When for the first time a child hears the sentence: 'Shut the door,' if he does not see a gesture accompanying the order, if he does not see it carried out immediately, he will not know what it means. . . . But if a voice from somewhere shouts, 'Shut the door,' and someone rushes up to close it . . . he perceives the sense of the expression he has heard" (Kelly 1969: 11).

V. I'd never taken a course in methodology and hadn't the foggiest idea of how to conduct a class. I asked him what the first thing was that I should do. After some deliberation, his answer was, "Make sure your fly is zipped." It was curious and cautious advice I soon discovered that I could not in truth follow. As I taught, I learned from experience. I found that I was denying my emotions: I had straightjacketed myself into the preconceived world of who and what a teacher was supposed to be. I needed a battle plan: a way out of the mire of irresolution, of inaction, of conformity. Self-examination was mandatory. In the process, I would establish a five-step framework to guide me. The five-step framework is the underpinning of a pedagogy, and is also a philosophy.

Know thyself. Examine the formation of crusts, containing the influences we experience through the years. The first crust envelops all family input: We are susceptible to all we see, hear, breathe, smell, and touch. We form our ideas on politics, religion, and general outlook. An innocent remark can be heard within our reach and it settles into the crust, then festers, then becomes cancerous and colors our outlook in a detrimental fashion. It may well be the source of most prejudices.

The second crust may be the most dangerous of the lot, for it is forged by peer pressure and sometimes determines behavior for a lifetime. We absorb all we can from our friends primarily and often principally to belong. Thus we dress like our peers, walk, talk, and even smell like them.

Then comes the career crust: That's where no chances are allowed, no risks, only safe ground thinking. We follow the established paradigm of success according to our jobs. Spontaneity, creative risk-taking—anything that threatens the security and predictability of performance is systematically discouraged.

Ultimately, our goal is to have students read their inner book, to teach them to read that inner book, wherein all is writ—the bad, the good—so that they won't be too quick in judging others by their covers.

Connect. We must provide appropriate materials to help the student connect linguistically, culturally, and philosophically with those with whom he would communicate. We have to connect with the environment, the materials we use, the purpose and focus of what we are doing, and *why* we are doing it. We seek authenticity and sincerity.

Special delivery system. A well-defined system will enable one to function as a whole person. It is an all-out assault on students' sensibilities. It is the classroom as arena for involvement, for empowerment, for action. The essential fact here is that, like good theater, the classroom experience must be *shared.* Above any other consideration, our first obligation must be the students. Similarly, truth and honesty must also frame the lesson and be taught with commitment to those principles.

Stage presence. The focus of all communication is the person with whom one is communicating. Here we shift our center of gravity so that the person being addressed is the center of all our attention. The goal is to make our audience feel their own "presence" and become the better for the experience. We prepare them for their presence on the stage of the world.

Senses and the emotions. The senses are the main source, if not the only source, of acquiring knowledge, and the emotions are the site where learning takes place. Nothing is real unless it touches me and I become aware of it. Reality exists for us through feeling. We communicate what we have absorbed though our senses, but the world has to be grasped by emotions. I am defined by my emotions: I must know them, I must learn from them and through them. We remember best those things that touch us. Reality is in touch, in feeling, in being touched, in being moved. The mind alone is not capable of grasping the full nuances of a word or an act. The mind can only entertain what strikes it vicariously. The emotions provide the glue that contains thought. The emotions fuel the imagination, sustain its effort, exploit the potentialities of thought. The emotions are a powerful source for good. We strap its power and ride it headlong to our goal.

The emotions come from the heart, and their power may best be appreciated when we realize that the heart is the only part of the human anatomy that can experience the infinite: qualities such as love, respect, are not bound by time or space. The emotions and the senses together are the basic ingredient of *"la sensibilité"* ("sensitivity").

We find the word throughout the eighteenth century, and particularly in the thought of the French eighteenth-century encyclopedist Denis Diderot. Diderot extolled naturalness in man, the destruction of sham, and the obliteration of the mask man consciously hides behind. He preaches relativism, freedom, and openness, and the salubrious nature of the emotions: *"Les passions sobres font les hommes communs"* ("Sober passions make for ordinary men") (Diderot 1950: 4). And again, *"Les passions amorties dégradent les hommes extraordinaires. La contrainte anéantit la grandeur et l'énergie de la nature. Voyez cet arbre; c'est au luxe de ses branches que vous devez la fraîcheur et l'étendue de ses ombres."* ("Dampened passions diminish extraordinary men. Constraint annihilates the grandeur and energy of nature. Look at this tree, it is to the luxuriant wealth of its branches that you owe the coolness and expanse of its shade") (Diderot 1950: 5). Diderot would finally maintain *"une juste harmonie"* between passion and reason, but the place of passion is firmly established: *"Ce sont les passions qui mettent tout en mouvment, qui animent le tableau de cet univers, qui donnent pour ainsi dire l'âme et la vie a ses diverses parties."* ("Passions set everything into motion which animates our representation of the universe, which, so to speak, gives a soul and life to its various parts") (Diderot in Assézat 1876a: 217).

Diderot speaks of the sensations and how they determine mood and participate in the learning process. *La sensibilité* is an amalgam of physical, emotional, and intellectual states that releases full responses to stimuli (Assézat 1876b: 117–119). The net effect of this expression is the knowledge of our right to be who we are. The concomitant effect is the recognition of that right in others. Self-awareness precedes awareness of others and communication is possible. There are no longer any barriers between people, inhibitions are stripped away, and real learning takes place. One might say that the best learning is anti-intellectual!

VI. So, why do we teach? We teach in order to bring to life through language the tools God gave us to live, to connect, to share, to help. It is through the senses and the emotions that we must proceed to give to language learning a humanistic focus. I think of Kazantzakis (1958: 476) who writes, "Look, listen, smell, taste, and touch all things with all your heart." Taken at face value, the sentence endorses a go-for-broke, all-out assault on life and all that it has to offer. It is rank carpe deism. But Kazantzakis would have us look deeper than the passive state suggests. It doesn't suffice to merely look: we must see, see who we are and how we relate to others, see the strengths and weaknesses we have and how others share them. We must not just listen but hear; hear all that is going on within ourselves and others, hear what the world is telling us while we listen intently; smell the pollution and stench of death where there should be life; taste and go beyond our appetite to confront the tragedy of our time—children the world over dying at an appalling rate daily for lack of food—and finally touch; touch by understanding, by sharing, and, most important, touch in order to be touched to attain the full status as caring, sensitive people. The classroom should be the arena where constant proof of our humanity, the fact that we are all human becomes the sum and substance of all our efforts.

REFERENCES

Assézat, J. 1876a. *Œuvres complètes de Diderot, Etude sur Diderot,* vol. 16. Paris: Garnier Frères.
Assézat, J. 1876b. *Œuvres complètes de Diderot, Etude sur Diderot,* vol. 17. Paris: Garnier Frères.
Camus, Albert. 1942. *Le Mythe de Sisyphe.* Paris: Gallimard. (translation mine).
Camus, Albert. 1958. *Caligula.* Paris: Gallimard. (translation mine).
Diderot, Denis. 1950. *Pensées philosophiques.* Geneva: Textes Littéraires, Français.
Kazantzakis, Nikos. 1958. *The Odyssey, A Modern Sequel,* bk 15, 1. 1105. Kimon Friar, trans. New York: Simon and Schuster.
Kelly, Louis G. 1969. *Twenty-five centuries of language teaching,* Rowley, MA: Newbury House.
Lattimore, Richard. 1967. *The Odyssey of Homer.* New York: Harper & Row.
Meyer, Jean. 1975. *La Formation de l'Acteur au Conservatoire.* Paris: Atac Informations (Juin).
Rassias, John A. 1992. *Le français: départ-arrivee,* 3rd edition. Boston: Heinle & Heinle.
Zillman, Lawrence John (ed.). 1968. *Prometheus unbound: The text and the drafts (toward a modern definitive edition).* New Haven: Yale University Press.

NOTE

1. This paper is based on a lecture given at the TESOL convention in New York in 1998, in honor of Professor James Alatis.

A global perspective on bilingualism and bilingual education

G. Richard Tucker
Carnegie Mellon University

Introduction. The number of languages spoken throughout the world is estimated to be approximately 6,000 (Grimes 1992). Although people frequently observe that a small number of languages such as Arabic, Bengali, English, French, Hindi, Malay, Mandarin, Portuguese, Russian, and Spanish serve as important link languages or languages of wider communication around the world, these are very often spoken as second, third, fourth or later-acquired languages by their speakers (see, for example, Cheshire 1991; Comrie 1987; Edwards 1994). The available evidence seems to indicate that governments in many countries deliberately present a somewhat skewed picture of monolingualism as normative by the explicit or implicit language policies that they adopt and promulgate (Crystal 1987). Thus, fewer than 25% of the world's approximately 200 countries recognize two or more official languages—with a mere handful recognizing *more than two* (e.g., India, Luxembourg, Nigeria, etc.). Despite these conservative government policies, however, available data indicate that there are many more bilingual or multilingual individuals in the world than there are monolingual. In addition, many more children throughout the world have been, and continue to be, educated via a second or a later-acquired language—at least for some portion of their formal education—than the number of children educated exclusively via first language. In many parts of the world, bilingualism or multilingualism and innovative approaches to education that involve the use of two or more languages constitute the normal everyday experience (see, for example Dutcher 1994; World Bank 1995).

Multiple languages in education. The use of multiple languages in education may be attributed to, or be a reflection of, numerous factors such as the linguistic heterogeneity of a country or region (e.g., Luxembourg or Singapore); specific social or religious attitudes (e.g., the addition of Sanskrit to mark Hinduism or Pali to mark Buddhism); or the desire to promote national identity (e.g., in India, Nigeria, the Philippines). In addition, innovative language education programs are often implemented to promote proficiency in international language(s) of wider communication, together with proficiency in national and regional languages. The composite portrait of language education policies and practices throughout the world is exceedingly complex—and simultaneously fascinating. In Eritrea, for instance, an educated person will likely have attended some portion of schooling taught via Tigrigna *and* Arabic *and* English—and developed proficiency in reading these languages, which are written using three different scripts (Geez, Arabic, and Roman)! In Oceania, to take a different example, linguists estimate that a mere 4% of the world's population speaks approximately 20% of the world's 6,000 languages. In Papua New Guinea, a country that has a population of approximately 3,000,000, linguists have described more than 870 languages (Summer Institute of Linguistics 1995). There, it is common for a child to grow up speaking one local indigenous language at home, another in the market place, adding Tok Pisin to her repertoire as a lingua franca, and English if she continues her schooling. Analogous situations recur in many parts of the world such as India, which has declared 15 of its approximately 1,650 indigenous languages to be "official"; or Guatemala, or Nigeria, or South Africa—to name but a few countries in which multilingualism predominates, and in which children are frequently exposed to numerous languages as they move from their homes into their communities and eventually through the formal educational system.

Prevalent educational myths. Despite the prevalence of innovative language education programs around the world, the number of sound, critical, longitudinal, and published evaluations remains relatively small, and there are a plethora of *prevalent educational myths* that continually circulate:

- Creoles are not real languages; therefore, they cannot be used as media of instruction.
- If the major goal is to develop the highest degree of proficiency and subject-matter mastery via English (or French or *XYZ*), the more time spent educating the child via English (or French or *XYZ*), the better.
- Anyone who can speak a language can teach successfully via that language.
- In multilingual countries, it is too "expensive" to develop materials and to train teachers in a number of different languages.
- There is one, and only one, "correct solution" to the choice and sequencing of language(s) for purposes of initial literacy training and content instruction for all multilingual countries.

Against this backdrop, Nadine Dutcher (1994) and I carried out a comprehensive review for the World Bank of the use of first and second languages in education in which we examined, in some detail, the literature from research conducted in three different types of countries: (1) those with no (or few) mother-tongue speakers of the language of wider communication (e.g., Haiti, Nigeria, the Philippines); (2)

those with some mother-tongue speakers of the language of wider communication (e.g., Guatemala); and (3) those with many mother-tongue speakers of the language of wider communication (e.g., Canada, New Zealand, the United States).

I will now describe what I hope will be a few of the familiar highlights of this review—findings that are also consonant with those contained in "Section 3: Case Studies in Multilingual Education" in the splendid recent volume edited by Cenoz and Genesee (1998) as well as with the papers in the special issue of the *Journal of Multilingual Multicultural Education* (1996, vol. 17) and selected papers in two of the volumes of the *Encyclopedia of Language and Education* (Cummins and Corson 1997; Tucker and Corson 1997). Interested readers may also wish to review the excellent case study by Gonzalez and Sibayan (1988) as well as the recent volume by Baker and Jones (1998).

Conclusions from extant research. My reading of the available literature, together with the personal research that I have conducted over the past three decades in varied language-education settings throughout the world leads me to a number of relatively straightforward conclusions.

- The language of school is *very* different from the language of home.
- The development of cognitive-academic language requires *time* (four to seven years of formal instruction).
- Individuals most easily develop literacy skills in a familiar language.
- Individuals most easily develop cognitive skills and master content material that is taught in a familiar language.
- Cognitive-academic language skills, once developed, and content-subject material, once acquired, *transfer* readily.
- The *best* predictor of cognitive-academic language development in a second language is the level of development of cognitive–academic language proficiency in the first language.
- Children learn a second language in different ways depending upon their culture, their group, and their individual personality.

Therefore, if the goal is to help the student ultimately develop the highest possible degree of content mastery and second-language proficiency, time spent instructing the child in a familiar language is a wise investment—that is, Lambert's notion (1980) of "additive" bilingualism.

Common programmatic threads. Furthermore, Dutcher and I noted that the following common threads cut across *all* of the successful programs that we reviewed when the goal is to provide students with multiple-language proficiency and with access to academic content material (even though, we noted, there is a wide range of models available for implementation):

- Development of the mother tongue is encouraged for cognitive development and as a basis for learning the second language.
- Parental and community support and involvement are essential to all successful programs.
- Teachers are able to understand, speak, and use with a high level of proficiency the language of instruction, whether it is their first or second language.
- Teachers are well trained; they have cultural competence and subject-matter knowledge, and they continually upgrade their training.
- Recurrent costs for innovative programs are about the same as they are for "traditional" programs (although there may be additional one-time start-up costs).
- Cost-benefit calculations can typically be estimated in terms of the cost savings to the education system, improvements in years of schooling, and enhanced earning potential for students with multiple language proficiency.

The results from published, longitudinal, and critical research undertaken in varied settings throughout the world indicate clearly that the development of multiple-language proficiency is possible, and indeed that it is viewed as desirable by educators, policy makers, and parents in many countries. Ironically, that which is viewed as desirable in Eritrea, Luxembourg, the Netherlands, Nigeria, the Philippines, or South Africa, to name but a few countries, is not similarly viewed in the United States. Although the focus of this paper is specifically on bilingual education internationally, the findings summarized above are clearly consistent with those reported by researchers in the United States and Canada (e.g., Brisk 1998; Christian 1996; Thomas and Collier 1996).

Cross-cutting themes. I next wish to comment briefly on two cross-cutting themes that seem to me to be critical linchpins for moving forward policy or planning discussions within the domain of language education reform. The first is the critical role of the child's mother tongue in initial literacy attainment and content-subject mastery and the subsequent transfer of skills across languages. Second is the natural tension between importing a model versus importing a "cycle of discovery."

Nurturing the first language. Despite decades of sound educational research, there still remains a belief in many quarters that somehow, when an additional language is introduced into a curriculum, the child must go back and relearn all over again concepts already mastered. Although there remains much to be learned about the contexts and strategies that facilitate transfer across languages, the fact that such transfer occurs should not be a topic for debate. The work of Hakuta

(1986) and his colleagues provides clear evidence that a child who acquires basic literacy or numeracy concepts in one language can transfer these concepts and knowledge easily to a second or third or other later-acquired languages. The literature, and our practical experience, are replete with examples that confirm the importance of nurturing the child's mother tongue. Gonzalez (1998), in particular, writes and speaks especially compellingly about the need to develop basic functions of literacy, numeracy, and scientific discourse in the L1 to the fullest extent possible while facilitating transfer to the L2. We have an imperfect understanding of the constructs of so-called basic interpersonal communication skills (or contextualized language abilities), cognitive academic language proficiency (or decontextualized language abilities), and cognitive processes that facilitate or impede cross-language transfer of skills. This underscores the need for additional basic research on this important topic but should not detract from the utility and the practical importance of the underlying concept.

Importation of models versus importation of "cycles of discovery." At this stage, one is tempted to call for the widespread implementation of new programs based on the results of documented experiences from settings such as Canada, the Philippines, or some of the other countries mentioned previously. I think, however, that it may be instructive to underscore the observations made by Swain (1996) at an international conference on bilingualism held in Brunei Darussalam (see also Tucker 1996). There, she described some of the critical attributes of Canadian immersion programs and shared with participants the ways in which she and colleagues have continued to reflect upon the products of their earlier research in order to better understand and clarify some of the basic processes underlying successful and nonsuccessful language education. She described the need to "transfer" the stages and processes of evaluation, theory building, generation of hypotheses, experimentation, and further evaluation that will help to ensure the implementation of programs appropriate for the unique sociocultural contexts in which they will operate. That is, she cautioned that it is not a particular model of innovative language education (and, in particular, a Western model) that should be transferred, for example, to Brunei Darussalam, Namibia, or Peru; but rather a "cycle of discovery" that should be transferred.

Swain reminded us that the so-called threshold levels of L2 skills required for successful participation in formal education may differ quite dramatically across content areas, and that a majority of children face a language "gap" that must be bridged when they move from learning the target language to using the target language as a medium of instruction. Many policy makers have characterized bilingual education as a "high risk" undertaking by which they mean that it is necessary to attend to a complex set of interacting educational, sociolinguistic, economic, and political factors.

Key issues warranting further attention. Based upon a review of available literature, it is possible to identify four areas that deserve additional attention:

- sociolinguistic research throughout the world,
- a more thorough examination of the concept and parameters of transfer,
- materials development, reproduction, and distribution in the so-called truly less commonly spoken languages (e.g., the majority of the African languages spoken in Namibia; the majority of the languages in Papua New Guinea, etc.), and
- development of a cadre of trained teachers who are proficient speakers of these languages.

Despite several decades of rather extensive sociolinguistic fieldwork in many areas, there remains much to be done to describe the language situation in many parts of the world. For example, personnel from the World Bank were recently engaged in a preliminary educational mission to Guinea Bissau but discovered that they knew relatively little about the distribution and status of languages and their speakers throughout the country, which makes sound educational planning problematic. Many of the world's languages have yet to be written, codified, or elaborated. Furthermore, there are no materials available for initial literacy training or for advanced education; nor are there teachers who have been trained to teach via many of the world's languages. These are all issues that have been identified as crucial by the World Bank in a recent report of priorities and strategies for enhancing educational development in the twenty-first century (World Bank 1995). And they are issues that must be dealt with effectively before systemic reform that will encourage multilingual proficiency can be widely implemented.

Conclusions. By way of summary, let me identify a number of important questions that I think must be addressed whenever parents, educators, and administrators discuss the prospects of multilingual education for their communities:

- What are the explicit or implicit goals for formal education in the region?
- Is there general satisfaction throughout the region with the level of educational attainment by all participants (both those who terminate their education relatively early and those who wish to go on to tertiary studies)?
- Is the region relatively homogeneous or is it heterogeneous linguistically and culturally and how would bilingual education complement the linguistic and cultural characteristics of the community?
- Does the region have an explicit or implicit policy with respect to the role of language in education, and how would bilingual education fit or

not fit with this existing policy? Is this policy based upon tradition or the result of language (education) planning?

- What priorities are accorded to goals such as the development of broadly based permanent functional literacy, the value of education for those who may permanently interrupt their schooling at an early age, and the power of language to foster national identity and cohesiveness?
- Are the language(s) selected for instruction written, codified, standardized, and elaborated?
- Is there a well-developed curriculum for the various levels and stages of formal education (i.e., a framework that specifies fairly explicitly a set of language, content, cognitive, and affective objectives that are then tied to or illustrated by exemplary techniques, activities, and supported by written materials)?
- Are sufficient core *and* reference materials available for teachers and for students in the language(s) of instruction? If not, are there trained individuals available who can prepare such materials?
- Is there a sufficient number of trained and experienced teachers who are fluent speakers of the language(s) of instruction *and* who are trained to teach via that language(s)?

Questions such as these (see Tucker 1991, 1998) must be considered by community leaders as they consider the implementation of any innovative language education program.

As Courtney Cazden, Catherine E. Snow, and Cornelia Heise-Baigorria (1990: 48) noted in their report for UNICEF, "despite the centrality of language achievements in the developmental agenda of the [child], language issues are rarely in the forefront of thinking about how to plan environments for young children. . . . The prevalence of multilingualism in the world adds a particular urgency to the recommendation to attend" to the quality of language instruction available to the child.

The cumulative evidence from research conducted over the last three decades at sites around the world demonstrates conclusively that cognitive, social, personal, and economic benefits accrue to the individual who has an opportunity to develop a high degree of bilingual proficiency when compared with a monolingual counterpart. The message for educators is clear (see also Tucker 1990): Draw upon community resources and involve diverse stakeholders in all phases of program planning and implementation, implement carefully planned and well articulated sequences of study, utilize trained, committed teachers, and begin innovative language education programs that will lead to bilingual or multilingual proficiency for participants as early as possible. The graduates of such programs should be culturally rich, linguistically competent, and socially sensitive individuals prepared to participate actively in our increasingly global economy.

References

Baker, Colin, and Sylvia Prys Jones. 1998. *Encyclopedia of bilingualism and bilingual education.* Clevedon, England: Multilingual Matters.

Brisk, María Estela. 1998. *Bilingual education: From compensatory to quality schooling.* Mahwah, NJ: Lawrence Erlbaum.

Cazden, Courtney, Catherine E. Snow, and Cornelia Heise-Baigorria. 1990. Language planning in preschool education with "annotated bibliography." Report prepared for the Consultative Group on Early Childhood Care and Development, UNICEF.

Christian, Donna. 1996. Language development in two-way immersion: Trends and prospects. In James. E. Alatis (ed.), *Georgetown university roundtable on languages and linguistics 1996.* Washington, DC: Georgetown University Press. 30–42.

Cenoz, Jasone, and Fred Genesee (eds.), England: 1998. *Beyond bilingualism: multilingualism and multilingual education.* Clevedon, England: Multilingual Matters.

Cheshire, Jenny. (ed.). 1991. *English around the world: Sociolinguistic perspectives.* Cambridge: Cambridge University Press.

Comrie, Bernard (ed.). 1987. *The world's major languages.* New York: Oxford University Press.

Crystal, David. 1987. *The Cambridge encyclopedia of language.* Cambridge: Cambridge University Press.

Cummins, Jim, and David Corson (eds.). 1997. *Second language education. Encyclopedia of language & education,* vol. 5. Dordrecht, Netherlands: Kluwer Academic.

Dutcher, Nadine, in collaboration with G. Richard Tucker. 1994. *The use of first and second languages in education: A review of educational experience.* Washington, DC: World Bank, East Asia and the Pacific Region, Country Department III.

Edwards, John. 1994. *Multilingualism.* London: Routledge.

Gonzalez, Andrew. 1998. Teaching in two or more languages in the Philippine context. In Jasone Cenoz and Fred Genesee (eds.), *Beyond bilingualism: Multilingualism and multilingual education.* Clevedon, England: Multilingual Matters. 192–205.

Gonzalez, Andrew, and Bonifacio P. Sibayan. 1988. *Evaluating bilingual education in the Philippines (1974–1985).* Manila: Linguistic Society of the Philippines.

Grimes, Barbara. F. 1992. *Ethnologue: Languages of the world.* Dallas: Summer Institute of Linguistics.

Hakuta, Kenji. 1986. *Mirror of language: The debate on bilingualism.* New York: Basic Books.

Lambert, Wallace E. 1980. The two faces of bilingual education. *NCBE Forum* 3.

Summer Institute of Linguistics. 1995. *A survey of vernacular education programming at the provincial level within Papua New Guinea.* Ukarumpa, Papua New Guinea: Summer Institute of Linguistics.

Swain, Merrill. 1996. Discovering successful second language teaching strategies and practices: From program evaluation to classroom experimentation. *Journal of Multilingual and Multicultural Development* 17(1&2): 89–104.

Thomas, Wayne P., and Virginia Collier. 1996. Language-minority student achievement and program effectiveness. *NABE News* 19(6): 33–35.

Tucker, G. Richard. 1990. Cognitive and social correlates of additive bilinguality. In James E. Alatis (ed.), *Georgetown University round table on languages and linguistics: 1990.* Washington, DC: Georgetown University Press. 90–101.

Tucker, G. Richard. 1991. Developing a language-competent American society: The role of language planning. In Allan G. Reynolds (ed.), *Bilingualism, multiculturalism, and second language learning.* Hillsdale, NJ: Lawrence Erlbaum. 65–79.

Tucker, G. Richard. 1996. Some thoughts concerning innovative language education programs. *Journal of Multilingual and Multicultural Development.* 17(1&2).

Tucker, G. Richard. 1998. A global perspective on multilingualism and multilingual education. In Jasone Cenoz and Fred Genesee (eds.), *Beyond bilingualism: Multilingualism and multilingual education.* Clevedon, England: Multilingual Matters. 3–15.
Tucker, G. Richard, and David Corson (eds.) 1997. *Second language education. Encyclopedia of language & education,* vol. 4. Dordrecht, Netherlands: Kluwer Academic.
World Bank. 1995. *Priorities and strategies for education.* Washington, DC: International Bank for Reconstruction and Development.

Bilingual education with English as an official language: Sociocultural implications

Anne Pakir
National University of Singapore

Introduction. This paper examines the sociocultural implications of a bilingual education with English as an official language in the small city-state and Southeast Asian nation called Singapore. Since its founding in 1819, Singapura, or the Lion City, has been a multilingual society, prompting the country's leaders to adopt a proactive policy of multilingualism when independence was achieved in 1965. Four official languages (English, Malay, Mandarin, and Tamil) were constitutionally enshrined. Today, Singapore's three million people live in a largely metropolitan setting on 680 square kilometers of land. Owing to the high degree of daily interaction in an urban multilingual context, Singaporeans are generally bilingual if not multilingual. Most of the people are what I call English-knowing bilinguals, that is, they are exposed to English to a large extent and use it as a working language in most public spheres of life.

This paper examines two issues that have arisen as a result of Singapore's successful bilingual language management, with English as a cornerstone of the bilingual policy. Two questions are posed: As its global and local importance increases, can English serve as a language of national identity for Singaporeans? What is the sociocultural price to be paid for placing English as the premier co-official language?

A sociolinguistic profile of Singapore and the education system. To contextualize language policy in Singapore, a sociolinguistic profile of the republic and a thumbnail sketch of the education system need to be given. The languages of Singapore represent a hodgepodge drawn from the three identifiable ethnic groups, Chinese (77%), Malay (15%), and Indian (7%), and from other groups such as the Eurasians, Armenians, Jews, and Parsees (1%). The four official languages are English, Malay (also the de jure national language), Mandarin, and Tamil, all belonging to different language families and having different literary traditions. In addition to Tamil (which is an official language), Malayalam and Telegu are the two other Dravidian languages spoken in Singapore. Five other South Asian ethnic languages are represented in the school system: Hindi, Urdu,

Bengali, Punjabi, and Gujerati, all belonging to the Indo-Aryan family of languages. The main Chinese dialects spoken by older Singaporeans are Hokkien, Teochew, Cantonese, Hakka, and Hainanese.

The language policy in Singapore has had to serve multiple purposes:

(a) provide for rapid economic development for a small country that has no hinterland and no natural resources except its people;
(b) promote a common mode of communication among its heterogeneous ethnic groups;
(c) promote a common mode of communication within its largest ethnic group, the Chinese, with five main dialects (not mutually intelligible) represented in the population;
(d) give official recognition to the linguistic and cultural pluralism within the nation;
(e) cultivate a Singaporean identity and loyalty, one drawing from its Asian and Southeast Asian heritage;
(f) integrate into a region that is predominantly Malay speaking; and
(g) expedite strong international links and regional exchange.

English was chosen as the working language for the country, being "neutral" in the sense that it did not belong to any of the three major ethnic groups (Chinese, Malay, and Indian). The bilingual policy, as it evolved, afforded every child in school the opportunity to become bilingual and biliterate in two official languages (English and one other, usually the child's proscribed "mother tongue"). The bilingual policy placed English as the official language that the whole population should know.

In the words of the then minister for education, Tony Tan Keng Yam: "Our policy of bilingualism that each child should learn English and his mother tongue, I regard as a fundamental feature of our education system. Children must learn English so that they will have a window to the knowledge, technology and expertise of the modern world. They must know their mother tongues to enable them to know what makes us what we are" (Tan 1986. Parliamentary Speech, March 1986). With such a directional thrust, language education in the Singapore schools has been taken seriously (see Ang 1998 for the teaching of the Chinese language; Ho 1998 on the English language curriculum; Saravanan 1998 on Tamil bilinguals; and Kamsiah and Bibi 1998 on Malay bilingual schooling).

Education in Singapore is built on the five pillars of literacy, numeracy, bilingualism, physical education, and moral education. Although education is not compulsory, there is near universal acceptance of its importance, with less than 0.01% not enrolling for primary education at the age of six.

Three foci have remained constant throughout the evolution towards excellence in education (see Yip and Sim 1990). First is the aspiration to provide the best form of education in the different phases of Singapore's development, and the second is to ensure that education served the purpose of national cohesion. A third constant has been to ensure that the schooling population is given the opportunity to become bilingual in English and a mother tongue.

Language education beliefs and practices are often taken for granted in a schooling system that emphasizes a national bilingual policy. However, Singapore's policy of bilingualism does not translate into what is normally accepted in academic discussions under the label "bilingual education," which is traditionally defined as education in two languages, with instruction given in both. Instead, since 1987 Singapore has offered a national stream of education in the English medium. Second language learning in the child's mother tongue is available at specially allotted hours in the curriculum. Only in the ten Special Assistance Programme schools are two languages (English and Chinese) offered at first language level.

Over the twelve years of formal schooling, an average of instructional time for language in the Singapore primary classroom amounts to ten periods of half an hour each (=five hours) per week for the mother tongue and twelve periods (= six hours) per week for English. At the secondary school and junior college levels, six periods of forty minutes each (= four hours) per week are devoted to the mother tongue and another four hours to English. The concern for primary school children weak in English compared to their other subjects grew as case studies provided data that English language instruction did not bear the desired results in the 1980s (Ho and Seet 1992; Ng 1984). Ng's (1984) study involving some 4,000 students culminated in the development of a Reading and English Acquisition Programme (REAP) for primary school children in Singapore (Ng 1988). There is a constant desire to upgrade English skills and mother tongue proficiency, and the desire is translated into gate-keeping procedures in terms of student admission to higher levels of education, for example, secondary school to junior college and from junior college to university entrance.

The case of English. Given importance as the premier official language of Singapore and its main medium of education, English has become imbued with status and power and has gained speakers who use it as a first language. This development has been aided by the fact that English is now a global language, with over one billion speakers worldwide (375 million L1 speakers, 375 L2 speakers, and another estimated 750 million FL speakers.) In Singapore, at the last census of population taken (1990), it was clear that one-fifth of the population (20%) used English as a predominant home language. English was also the second most frequently used home language in households that had another predominant home language. What is of greater interest is that the average for six-year-olds is a reported 26% rate for English as a predominant home language, a figure that is higher than the national average. This points to a rapidly developing group of

English-knowing bilinguals whose school languages (English and Mandarin, Malay, or Tamil) are becoming home languages. One trend of bilingualism in Singapore at the turn of the twentieth century is of an increasingly younger population becoming generally biliterate in English (the premier official language) and in one other official language (Mandarin, Malay, or Tamil).

Speakers of English in Singapore usually have English as a second or additional language, but for the 20% who have shifted to English as a predominant household language (including 26% of the six-year-olds), English is becoming something between a first and a second language. New discourses, new discourse strategies, and new canons have emerged, including creative writing and innovative theater, TV, and film productions by, of, and for these English-knowing bilinguals. English-knowing bilinguals govern the country, walk the corridors of power, preside at boardroom meetings, teach in schools, and rule in the courts of law. The overall effect on their offspring and others can be seen in a discernible shift to English speaking and writing practices.

Studies of language policy making and management in Singapore (see Gopinathan et al. 1994/1998; Gupta 1994; Kuo and Jernudd 1994; Kwan-Terry and Kwan-Terry 1993; Pakir 1991a, 1991b, 1992, 1993a, 1993b, 1993c, 1994a, 1994b, 1995a, 1995b, 1997, 1998) show the growing importance attached to English in the country. There has been an increase in the number of users, and English has achieved a range and depth of influence unparalleled in many Asian countries.

The relationship between the English language and an Asian culture. There is, however, the inevitable concern about the relationship between language and culture. The tension and paradox regarding English has been described (Pakir 1992). There is often the fear of what kind of bilinguals or biculturals will ultimately result if English were used as the dominant mode of discourse and negotiation in the international arena. Will the young become bilingual and bicultural, or bilingual while remaining monocultural? Is it important to know?

The language is deemed necessary for access to leading edge technology and world markets. But it is not deemed a worthy vehicle to carry the cultural and social content of the main ethnic groups in the country. In brief, Singapore wants English as a tool rather than a tie; it wants English to serve a utilitarian but not an emotional purpose. This inevitable tension is not easily resolvable, although one of the suggested outcomes is that the language has to "nativize" to carry the identity of its speakers. Here the concept of "functional nativeness" (Kachru 1997: 18) may be useful. When the language shows productive processes that mark its nativization, when it can carry different identities through the specific nativization processes, and when it is a language that is distinct within its new context, English may come to be accepted as one that can represent different national identities. It may yet become a language of national identity in Singaporeans.

Language shift. The cultural implications of the language shifts that have taken place in Singapore have been studied by Hugo Baetens Beardmore (1998). There has been a primary language shift towards English for the general Singapore population, and a secondary shift towards Mandarin among the Chinese (see Xu et al. 1998; Ang 1998). Xu et al. conclude in their study that Mandarin will remain in competition on a bidirectional basis, on the one hand, vis-à-vis English, and on the other, with the other Chinese dialects in increasing private use. Ang (1998) concludes that the opening of its market by the People's Republic of China has made the Chinese language (i.e., Mandarin) an important economic language, taught in many schools in the West as well as the East. This may well have some impact on the Singaporeans' attitudes toward learning Mandarin.

Malay has kept most of its speakers, because it is a school language that is also a home language, although the increasing popularity of English among the Malays has been observed (Kamsiah and Bibi 1998). The only official language to have suffered a loss in numbers is Tamil (see V. Saravanan 1998). In her thesis, Saravanan maintains that the use of Tamil in the home domain is crucial for the continuity of the language. However, her case study indicates that Tamil remains very much a classroom language even among Tamils, who are increasingly English-knowing. The low status accorded to Tamil is also a precipitating factor, since the language is commonly spoken by those occupying the lower rungs of the occupational ladder.

The future of Mandarin, Malay, and Tamil will hinge upon the next fifty years when the ascendancy of English world-wide will surely make its impact on the tiny island republic. The prognosis is that English will take on more roles and functions and spread to more domains of use in Singapore, making it a very competitive language in the multilingual country. The range and depth of English-knowing bilinguals can only increase. The languages-in-competition phenomenon in Singapore has come about partly because of a younger generation brought up to become bilingual in school languages that were not perhaps the home languages of their own parents or grandparents. The bilingual policy of Singapore has tilted the balance in favor of English, even as its policy makers and planners would want to have an even-handed development with the Asian languages given due status as languages for imparting Asian cultural values.

The shift to English made by the younger groups has been analyzed by Kuo and Jernudd (1994) from a wide sociological viewpoint, by Pakir (1995b, 1998) from an educational one, and by Gupta (1994) from an internal linguistic and historical perspective. English has been described as a step tongue in Singapore, although it can be claimed to be more than that. With the increasing numbers of younger bilinguals achieving high proficiency levels in their two school languages, and choosing to read and write mainly in English, the language has become a first or second mother tongue among this group.

The future of English in Singapore is potentially bright because it serves the Republic's purposes. It is the neutral language for the country; it is the official language of the Association for South East Asian Nations (ASEAN); it is the main language represented on the World Wide Web (84% of all the estimated servers have English as the main language of their home pages); and its global future has been assured until 2050 if not later (see Graddol 1997). Singaporeans wanting to plug into the international grid of trade, finance, industry, and scientific advancement will do so in English.

Social class differentiation. With an English-knowing bilingual elite, social class differentiation is also becoming evident. As is the case with many countries, the creation of an upwardly mobile English-knowing elite with high proficiency in the language became inevitable. Membership in the professions, higher income, and higher educational levels are usually found in this group. It is also this group that will have to find innovative solutions to the dilemma of functioning in English predominantly. One suggestion is for the English language in such a context as Singapore to be become "glocal," that is, globally appropriate but culturally relevant.

The case of English as a glocal language. In terms of social reality, English has become the multinational language of the twentieth century. Indeed, it has been both the cause and effect of globalization and of internationalization. We can safely assume that English will remain the global language for big business, the language of e-commerce, and the language of knowledge-based economies for at least the next fifty years. The rapid rate of innovations in information technology has hastened the need to use English. As amply demonstrated by Graddol (1997), the English language is used for 84% of the web-servers in the world at the turn of the century.

English speakers the world over have turned the language into a multifaceted one, serving both global and local needs. Because of globalization, and the role of the English language in it, there is a new direction of "going glocal" in many Asian countries, especially those in Japan and Southeast Asia. Going glocal (that is, going global while maintaining local roots) makes for greater awareness of intercultural and cross-cultural exchanges. The term "glocal," derived from the words "global" and "local," indicates that one has to be open to new ideas and yet be embedded in one's own culture. Today, the clarion call is "think globally, act locally."

The term "Glocal English" can be defined as English that is global and yet rooted in the local contexts of its new users. Glocal English is a language that has international status in its global spread but at the same time expresses local identities. In developing a new role as a global-local language, English supports local users and their uses for it, while serving to connect the world. This phenomenon of Glocal English is most often to be found in the countries where English has an institutionalized role, achieving range and depth in its spread, for example, Singapore. English is needed for international communication, even as it takes root in Singapore. English today cannot avoid becoming subject to the forces of localization in Singapore. Many of the publications in English coming out from Singapore are clearly glocal.

Conclusion. Despite different periods of varying emphases on language policies and language education, Singapore has succeeded in its language management to produce young citizens who are aware of the importance of being or becoming high-level bilinguals. The language policy of Singapore is very much tied to its early modern history as an independent nation, lacking every natural resource except its people, who come from a migrant stock of Chinese and Indians and others coming to the city-port and its indigenous Malay population. The racial, cultural, and linguistic mosaic of Singapore underscores the importance of language management throughout the educational system in the country.

Much of the success of language management in Singapore is the result of a long-standing policy of multiracialism, multiculturalism, and multilingualism. The policy of multilingualism in the early 1960s and 1970s led to a pragmatic response of English-knowing bilingualism in the 1980s and 1990s, as Singapore geared itself to meeting industrial, technological, and information superhighway challenges. Meritocracy, the reward system of giving benefits to those who strive to earn them, pervaded the social consciousness, and it was through education that the system of meritocracy was meted. The latest developments in nation-building in Singapore in the 1990s have begun emphasizing a corporate outlook and regionalism, even while the citizens are reminded to hold shared values.

The younger generation is tied to the pragmatics of English-knowing bilingualism because they are the immediate witnesses of the rise of English as a new global force in the period of the second Diaspora of English (Kachru 1992). The emphasis on the pursuit of excellence in the country has been made possible with a large part of the population, now almost 80%, having some command of English. Moreover, the strong economic growth of the region and the beacon of a China turning to a capitalistic mode, have made many young Singaporeans more aware of the importance of their school languages and the official languages of Singapore.

At the intergroup level, there is the constant use of English among the different ethnic groups. At the intragroup level, the use of Mandarin among the Chinese has increased after almost twenty years of the move to cause a language shift among the Chinese in the Speak Mandarin Campaign. The use of Malay among the Malay ethnic population as the home as well as school language, really meant that different styles (school language versus home language) continue. For the heterogeneous Indian group comprising northern and southern Indians, the use of English and Tamil, Telegu, Hindi, Urdu, Punjabi, or Bengali continues, although there has been a steady decline in the relatively less important languages and the shift to English is clear among them.

The ambivalence vis-à-vis English in Singapore will remain, even as its global importance and local usage increases. Bilingual education with English as the main official language will create some class distinctions. On the linguistic developments, there will emerge eventually a new kind of English for the users of English in Singapore.

REFERENCES

Ang, B. C. 1998. The teaching of the Chinese language in Singapore. In S. Gopinathan et al. (eds.), *Language, society and education in Singapore: Issues and trends.* 2nd edition. Singapore: Times Academic Press. 335–352.

Beardsmore, H. B. 1998. Language shift and cultural implications in Singapore. In S. Gopinathan et al. (eds.), *Language, society and education in Singapore: Issues and trends.* 2nd edition. Singapore: Times Academic Press. 85–98.

Gopinathan, S., A. Pakir, W. K. Ho, and V. Saravanan (eds.). 1994/1998. *Language, society and education in Singapore: Issues and trends.* Singapore: Times Academic Press (2nd edition 1998).

Gopinathan, S. 1994. Language policy changes 1979–1992: Politics and pedagogy. In S. Gopinathan et al. (eds.), *Language, society and education in Singapore: Issues and trends.* Singapore: Times Academic Press.

Graddol, D. 1997. *The future of English? A guide to forecasting the popularity of the English language in the 21st century.* London: British Council.

Gupta, A. F. 1994. *The step-tongue: Children's English in Singapore.* Clevedon: Multilingual Matters.

Gupta, A. F., and P. Y. Siew. 1995. Language shift in a Singapore family. *Journal of Multilingual and Multicultural Development* 16(4): 301–314.

Ho, W. K. 1998. The English language curriculum in perspective: Exogenous influences and indigenisation. In S. Gopinathan et al. (eds.) *Language, society and education in Singapore: Issues and trends.* 2nd edition. Singapore: Times Academic Press. 221–244.

Ho, W. K., and O. B. H. Seet. 1992. Functional objectives in language learning: English language, a report on phase IV of the project. Unpublished. Singapore: National Institute of Education.

Kachru, B. B. 1992. The second diaspora of English. In T. W. Machan and C. T. Scotts (eds.), *English in its social contexts.* Oxford: Oxford University Press. 230–252.

Kachru, B. B. 1997. English as an Asian language. In M.L.S. Bautista (ed.), *English is an Asian language: The Philippine Context.* New South Wales, Australia: Macquarie Library. 1–23.

Kamsiah, A., and J. A. Bibi. 1998. Malay language issues and trends. In S. Gopinathan et al. (eds.) *Language, society and education in Singapore: Issues and trends.* 2nd edition. Singapore: Times Academic Press. 179–190.

Kuo, E. C. Y., and B. H. Jernudd. 1994. Balancing macro- and micro-sociolinguistic perspectives in language management: The case of Singapore. In S. Gopinathan et al. (eds.), *Language, society and education in Singapore: Issues and trends.* 1st edition. Singapore: Times Academic Press. 25–46.

Kwan-Terry, A., and J. Kwan-Terry. 1993. Literacy and the dynamics of language planning: The case of Singapore. In P. Freebody and A. R. Welch (eds.), *Knowledge, culture and power: International perspectives on literacy as policy and practice.* London: Falmer Press. 142–161.

Ng, S. M. 1984. Reading skills project: Progress report. Unpublished.

Ng, S. M. (ed.). 1988. *Research into children's language and reading development.* Singapore: Institute of Education.

Pakir, A. 1991a. The range and depth of English-knowing bilinguals in Singapore. *World Englishes* (10) 2: 167–179.

Pakir, A. 1991b. The status of English and the question of 'standard' in Singapore: A sociolinguistic perspective. In M. L. Tickoo (ed.), *Languages and standards: Issues, attitudes, case studies.* Anthology Series 26. Singapore SEAMEO Regional Language Centre. 109–130.

Pakir, A. 1992. English-knowing bilingualism in Singapore. In K. C. Ban, A. Pakir, and C. K. Tong (eds.), *Imagining Singapore.* Singapore: Times Academic Press. 234–262.

Pakir, A. 1993a. Spoken and written English in Singapore: the differences. In A. Pakir (ed.), *The English language in Singapore: Standards and norms.* Singapore: Singapore Association for Applied Linguistics.

Pakir, A. 1993b. Two tongue tied: bilingualism in Singapore. *Journal of Multilingual and Multicultural Development* 14: 73–90.

Pakir, A. (ed.). 1993c. *The English language in Singapore: Standards and norms.* Singapore: Unipress.

Pakir, A. 1994a. Educational linguistics: looking to the East. In J. Alatis (ed.), *Georgetown University round table on languages and linguistics 1994.* Washington, DC: Georgetown University Press.

Pakir, A. 1994b. Making bilingualism work: Developments in bilingual education in ASEAN. In R. Khoo, U. Kreher, and R. Wong (eds.), *Towards global multilingualism: European models and Asian realities.* Clevedon, England: Multilingual Matters. 13–27.

Pakir, A. 1995a. Beginning at the end: "Bilingual education for all" in Singapore and teacher education. In J. Alatis, C. Straehle, B. Gallenberger, and M. Ronkin (eds.), *Georgetown University round table on languages and linguistics 1995.* Washington, DC: Georgetown University Press.

Pakir, A. 1995b. Expanding triangles of English expression in Singapore: Implications for teaching. In S. C. Teng and M. L. Ho (eds.), *The English language in Singapore: Implications for teaching.* Singapore: Singapore Association for Applied Linguistics.

Pakir, A. 1997. Standards and codification for world Englishes. In L. E. Smith and M. L. Forman (eds.), *World Englishes 2000: Literary studies East and West,* 14. Honolulu: College of Languages, Linguistics, and Literature, University of Hawai'i and East West Center. 169–181.

Pakir, A. 1998. English in Singapore: The codification of competing norms. In S. Gopinathan et al. (eds.), *Language, society and education in Singapore: Issues and trends.* 2nd edition. Singapore: Times Academic Press. 65–84.

Saravanan, V. 1998. Language maintenance and language shift in the Tamil community. In S. Gopinathan et al. (eds.), *Language, society and education in Singapore: Issues and trends.* 2nd edition. Singapore: Times Academic Press.

Xu, D., C. H. Chew, and S. Chen. 1998. Language use and language attitudes in the Singapore Chinese community. In S. Gopinathan et al. (eds.), *Language, society and education in Singapore: Issues and trends.* 2nd edition. Singapore: Times Academic Press. 133–154.

Yip, J. S. K., and W. K. Sim (eds.). 1990. Evolution of educational excellence: 25 years of education in the Republic of Singapore. Singapore: Longman.

Bilingualism, language policy, and the European Union

Reinhold Freudenstein
Philipps-Universität, Marburg

At the beginning of 1999, one of the leading foreign-language journals in the Federal Republic of Germany published an article titled "Der Niedergang der Bilingual Education in den USA," reporting on the decline of bilingual education in the United States. Proposition 227 was mentioned, the 1998 referendum in California that resulted in a ban of bilingual education in that state, as was Theodore Roosevelt, who said at the beginning of this century, "[w]e have room for but one language here, and that is the English language. . . . We must have but one flag. We must also have but one language" (Pilzecker 1999: 83).

The article also mentioned politicians, researchers like Krashen (1996), and ethnic groups, for example, Latinos, who are still in favor of bilingualism. But the overall impression was that English-only gives you better educational and economic chances than bilingual education. This has happened at a time when a growing interest in bilingual education can be observed in Europe, particularly in Germany. The reason for this is obvious. The European Union (EU) is well on its way from being an abstract political concept to becoming a concrete everyday reality. In January 1999 the euro became the official currency for most of the fifteen countries of the EU. Europeans can now pay in the same currency, but they cannot all speak the same language.

The current European language situation. Let me give you a brief introduction to the language situation in the EU. Of its 370 million citizens, about 25 percent speak German as their mother tongue, about 17 percent French or English each, 16 percent Italian, 11 percent Spanish, and 6 percent Dutch. The rest of the languages within the union, for example, Swedish, Finnish, Portuguese, and Danish, are used by less than 3 percent each of the EU's citizens. A closer look at the language-skill abilities of Europeans shows that about half of the entire population can speak English, either as their mother tongue or as a foreign language, 34 percent speak German, 31 percent French, 18 percent Italian, and 14 percent Spanish. In other words, 51 percent of EU citizens cannot speak an official union language other than their mother tongue. This is alarming because communication is a necessary prerequisite for a working political, economic, and social community.

Foreign language teaching and learning is, of course, different in the various countries of the union. While in Germany all children have to learn at least one foreign language at school, other countries offer no compulsory foreign language instruction at all at this level. Of the more than eighty million pupils in the European Union, 89 percent have studied a language; 11 percent have not. But the disturbing fact is that in spite of all instructional efforts, 35 percent of the pupils cannot hold a conversation in the foreign language they have learned and 24 percent are still unable to speak it. This is simply due to the fact that foreign-language teaching in Europe still follows the traditional goals of educational values that no longer exist—those of the nineteenth century. In spite of curricular innovations like "communicative competence" or "language acquisition" (instead of "learning"), grammar instruction, translation, and a focus on literature still dominate the foreign-language classrooms. One hundred years ago Wilhelm Viëtor, a prominent German language educator, became very famous when he challenged his profession by saying that foreign-language teaching must find a new orientation different from the learning of the classical languages Latin and Greek (Viëtor 1882). One hundred years later language instruction in schools still hasn't found that orientation. Textbooks certainly are more colorful, learning materials are available in a greater variety, and teaching strategies have become more flexible. Nevertheless, grammar instruction is still very popular; 40 to 60 percent of the time available in high schools for language instruction is devoted to formal—and not communicative—aspects of language (Zimmermann 1984: 31). This is why many people, after having left school, study the same languages again in adult education classes, private language schools, or industrial in-service courses in order to learn what they really need language-wise for their jobs and leisure time. No wonder, therefore, that another prominent language professor in Germany recently proposed discontinuing language teaching at school level altogether because language teachers were obviously not in a position to teach modern languages for the purpose of everyday communication (Edmondson 1999).

In order to qualify EU citizens linguistically for the world of tomorrow, various proposals have been made, all of which include strategies for a new language policy in Europe. The Commission of the European Union in Brussels has suggested that all young Europeans should learn at least two foreign languages at school. One of its slogans is: "We can all learn to speak three languages." In many countries this is quite normal, and it, therefore, should become a standard language requirement. Only in this way, says the commission, can one take full advantage of European citizenship, move more easily between countries, and more easily find a job in the single market, because linguistic skills are attractive to employers. However, most of the programs sponsored by EU funding—like LINGUA,

SOKRATES, LEONARDO DA VINCI or TEMPUS—are primarily aimed at persons older than sixteen or eighteen, for example, university students, apprentices, or trainees.

Another very popular suggestion is to start foreign-language teaching in primary school. In some European countries, for example, in Austria and some of the German federal states, this is already common practice where qualified teachers and appropriate learning materials are available. So far, language learning at primary level starts in the third year of schooling. It could start much earlier, as has been successfully done in a private German school system since 1919 (Jaffke 1994; Jaffke and Maier 1997). It is, therefore, a welcome decision that, beginning with the school year 1999–2000, Baden-Württemberg was the first state in the Federal Republic of Germany to officially introduce foreign-language instruction when children start school at the age of six.

A further proposal for a new language policy in European schools is to replace long-term language learning of seven to nine years of instruction with short-term intensive or compact courses of no longer than four years, so that a greater number of languages can be offered—not just English, French, and German as in most European Union member states. It was also suggested that multilingual comprehension among people speaking different languages be introduced, although nobody really knows how to teach languages for listening comprehension purposes only.

Last but not least, the idea came up to let native speakers exclusively take over language instruction in European schools (Freudenstein 1996: 53). Among the traditional language-teacher profession this is, as you can imagine, a very unpopular view, but in a future United States of Europe it seems to be a realistic perspective. The entire population of the European Union enjoys freedom of residence and can work in whichever member state they want to. So all it needs is a greater flexibility among language teachers to move from one country to another, similar to someone in the United States who moves from Virginia to Florida or from Ohio to California.

However, none of these initiatives has so far resulted in any basic, comprehensive change of language policy across borders, and language instruction and language methodology have only been marginally affected. In order to prepare Europeans linguistically for their multicultural world of tomorrow, other ways have therefore to be found for the European Union to become a unity in spite of all diversity. A promising one seems to be bilingual education.

A European concept of bilingual education. When we speak of bilingualism in the context of school instruction in Europe, we do not think of persons who master two languages equally well since the time they first learn to speak. Bilingual education in Germany primarily means the learning of other subjects through the use of a foreign language so that the new language becomes a tool rather than an end in itself. Normally this kind of bilingual education starts in the third year of high school, after two years of intensified foreign-language learning when pupils are twelve or thirteen years old. Geography and history are the most popular subjects, but biology and mathematics are also part of the bilingual curriculum. The languages most commonly chosen are English and French. This is in agreement with the results of a public opinion poll conducted among citizens of the European Union. According to this survey, 78 percent said English would be useful to learn and 45 percent voted for French. German was ranked third (34 percent), followed by Spanish (15 percent). The number of schools in Germany offering bilingual options is still very small. Out of more than 63,000 schools, only 200 cover subjects in another language than in German; this is considerably less than half a percent. One hundred twenty of the schools run programs in English, fifty in French, and the rest of the schools have either chosen Dutch, Spanish, Czech, Italian, or Russian. Nevertheless, the popularity of bilingual educational institutions is constantly growing, and so are the number of articles in professional journals that concentrate on the chances and problems of bilingualism in a primarily mother-tongue environment.

The case for bilingual education. Wherever schools offer bilingual schemes, there have been only good reports and positive results about their work. Teachers involved in bilingual instruction find that their pupils are highly motivated and more interested in a foreign language than in traditional, textbook-oriented courses. This is mainly due to the fact that the learning process is concentrated on subject matter that seems to be of greater relevance to those who study it. When using English, pupils are no longer forced to describe the position of pronoun objects, to think about the use of the past perfect in indirect speech, or to distinguish between "can" or "be able." Rather, they learn about the life of people in other countries, are involved in project work, or investigate historical facts that they want to know—not because the linguistic progression of their foreign-language textbook has given the opportunity to deal with them by chance. Subjects taught and learned in another language are part of the regular curriculum. In my view, language policy in Europe should be based on this model. Why should it not be possible in a multicultural and multilingual society to introduce bilingual instruction of the form described as the standard educational scheme? If foreign-language learning starts at primary level, where language learning cannot be based on cognitive insights but is focused on children's interests and is more play-oriented, then there are good chances that after four years of language instruction, various school subjects could be taught in a language other than the mother tongue. This means that each school in Europe could become an institution of bilingual education, not only for highly talented children, but for each and everyone. In this way children would learn to use and accept different languages in a natural way for their general education and not purely for the sake of learning another language for grammatical, literary, or cultural reasons. Being able to communicate equally well in at least two languages is a sound foundation for communication in everyday situations and at the workplace in the European Union.

Problems to be solved. To introduce a bilingual educational system throughout Europe is a difficult task that will certainly take a long time to implement. Let me just mention a few problems that have to be solved in the decades to come. First of all, there must be a political will for an educational reform of this kind. Equally important is public support. If politicians, educationalists, and people in Europe do not believe that bilingual education can better qualify pupils for the challenges of tomorrow, then it will not work. Another issue that has to be discussed and decided upon is the relationship between subject matter and foreign language, particularly in connection with the evaluation process. Are historically relevant insights or language skills to be given priority? A bilingual school system also needs entirely new teaching materials. Here we are in somewhat the same position that Krashen (1996: 67) described for the United States: "The biggest problem, in my view, is the absence of books, both in the first and second language." Whether authentic textbooks in various subjects from other countries serve the purpose is still not known yet. Most probably new media and telecommunication networks will play an increasing role as instructional tools in the future. Finally, teacher training has to be reconsidered and reorganized. Teachers for bilingual schools should be trained to teach their mother tongue as a foreign language, and they should also have studied a school subject that can be taught in a foreign language. This means that in the long run, only native speakers are really qualified for work in a bilingual school.

Conclusion. I know that my views on a future language policy for and in Europe are not very popular at the moment, particularly among foreign-language teachers who fear losing the jobs they have trained for. Teachers who today still have to study philology, historical linguistics (e.g., Old and Middle English), and who speak the language they are supposed to teach as a foreign language themselves are most certainly not the best instructors in an educational system for the twenty-first century. If we really want to establish a multicultural, multiethnic, and multilingual society in Europe, we have to implement reforms that are unpopular. I hope that fifty years from now those reforms will be taken for granted.

References

Edmondson, Willis J. 1999. "Die fremdsprachliche Ausbildung kann nicht den Schulen überlassen werden!" *Praxis des neusprachlichen Unterrichts* 2: 115–123.

Freudenstein, Reinhold. 1996. Foreign-language teaching after the year 2000. In James E. Alatis et al. (eds.), *Georgetown University round table on languages and linguistics 1996.* Washington, DC: Georgetown University Press. 43–54.

Jaffke, Christoph. 1994. *Fremdsprachenunterricht auf der Primärstufe. Seine Begründung und Praxis in der Waldorfpädagogik.* Weinheim: Deutscher Studien Verlag.

Jaffke, Christoph, and Magda Maier. 1997. *Fremdsprachen für alle Kinder. Erfahrungen der Waldorfschulen mit dem Frühbeginn.* Leipzig: Klett.

Krashen, Stephen. 1996. The case against bilingual education. In James E. Alatis et al. (eds.), *Georgetown University round table on languages and linguistics 1996.* Washington, DC: Georgetown University Press. 55–69.

Pilzecker, Burghard. 1999. Der Niedergang der Bilingual Education in den USA. *Praxis des neusprachlichen Unterrichts* 1: 83–86.

Viëtor, Wilhelm. 1882. *Der Sprachunterricht muss umkehren.* Heilbronn: Henninger.

Zimmermann, Günther. 1984. *Erkundungen zur Praxis des Grammatikunterrichts.* Frankfurt: Diesterweg.

Bilingual education and the dialectics of national integration

Wendy D. Bokhorst-Heng[1]
American University

Introduction. My inquiry into bilingual education and national integration focuses on language ideologies and on the connection between these ideologies and broader ideological developments in, using Anderson's (1991) term, the imagining of the nation. Language ideologies emerge in specific historical and material circumstances. As Blommaert writes in his introductory chapter to *Language Ideological Debates* (1999), language ideologies and debates "nearly always develop against a wider socio-political and historical horizon of relationships of power, forms of discrimination, social engineering, nation-building and so forth." This focus on language ideology as it operates within such sociopolitical relations helps illuminate the often peculiar and contradictory effects of bilingual education. In particular, we will be able to see how such language ideologies establish both the possibilities and the constraints of bilingual education, resulting in a story of the *dialectics* of national integration.

The focus of my discussion is Singapore. As one observer writing to Singapore's *Business Times* (November 15, 1991) described it, Singapore is "small in size but big on language." Being a small country with a compact population involving a host of mutually incomprehensible languages and dialects (see Pakir, this volume), Singapore can be compared to a living linguistic laboratory. Unlike in bilingual Switzerland or Belgium where monolingual speakers of different languages are territorially separated, Singapore's small size and urban and dense population ensure that all four official languages involved in the nation's bilingual policy co-exist in very dynamic ways. And so Singapore offers unique insights into the dialectical effects of bilingual education in the imagining of the nation.

Issues and debates concerning language frequently dominate discussions in the mass media, in parliament, and in other venues of public discourse. This gives the ideological construction of language a very visible presence in the nation. In this paper, I will be looking at one instance of these "language ideological debates" in Singapore: the discussion over Chinese Special Assistance Plan (SAP) schools and the creation of a Chinese elite. This debate is important because of its potency in demonstrating both the possibilities and constraints of bilingualism's role in national integration, and in demonstrating how these possibilities and constraints emerge from the particular construction of language ideologies. My paper begins with a discussion of these ideologies, looking at how English and the mother tongue languages in Singapore have been constructed in oppositional relation to each other. I then look briefly at the implementation of bilingual education, particularly as it relates to streaming in the schools. Attention will be given especially to the position of SAP schools within this streaming process. In the last section, I will bring these discussions of language ideology and bilingual education together to consider 'bilingualism and the dialectics of national integration' and how the particular language ideologies involved in Singapore's bilingualism both facilitate and constrain the objectives of national integration.

The discursive-ideological construction of bilingualism. The challenges of national integration in multiethnic, multireligious, multilingual Singapore have always been a primary concern of the Singapore government. National integration has been the focus of housing policy, national service, a mandatory savings policy under the Central Provident Fund, community development programs, and so on (Chua Beng Huat 1995). The most recent endeavor has been an ambitious document called the *Singapore 21 Report,* in which the government outlines the nationalist agenda for the next century. A key issue covered in this report is whether or not Singapore will ever become "one tribe" (*The Straits Times* [*ST*] May 7, 1999).

Historically, the key to becoming "one tribe" has been through Singapore's bilingual language policy. This effort has involved the discursive construction of very particular ideologies about language and about bilingualism, captured in what I call the ideological polarization of language (figure 1).

On the one side of this ideological polarization of language is English. The presence of English has been justified as necessary to meet the instrumental needs

---

Figure 1. The ideological polarization of language.

MOTHER TONGUE	ENGLISH
(Mandarin, Malay, Tamil)	
Mother tongue	Business and economics
Cultural ballast	Science and technology
Cultural identity	Higher education
Intra-ethnic communication and unity	Inter-ethnic communication and national unity

of national integration. In this justification, government leaders hold two key assumptions about the English language: one is that English is the key to economic survival and the second that English is a "neutral" language. To look at these assumptions more closely, consider a speech by Professor Jayakumar, former minister of state (Law and Home Affairs), that was reported in Singapore's main English daily, *The Straits Times* (August 19, 1982). In this speech, Jayakumar outlines three integrative functions for the English language, drawn on these two assumptions.

In terms of economic integration, he argues that "English is the major international language for trade, science, and technology, and proficiency in the language is essential as Singapore becomes a leading financial and banking center," and a leader in the service and high technology industries. This suggests a perceived direct relationship between the direction and possibilities of economic development and English. According to Jayakumar, English is the "key to the productivity concept. With increasing modernization, skilled workers who know English will be in greater demand . . . it is the key to acquisition of skills and training and career advancement." Singapore's leaders frequently point to the fact that the economic advantage Singapore has had over most countries in Southeast and East Asia is this skilled, English-proficient workforce.

These assumptions about the English language also work toward social integration. The argument given by government leaders is that proficiency in English will bring a person and society out of poverty. The English language (and proficiency in English) is thus presented as accessible to all Singaporeans. When this argument is linked to the notion of meritocracy, itself a powerful discourse in the imagining of Singapore, English also puts everyone on an equal playing field. As suggested by then prime minister Lee Kuan Yew, English "is our common working language. . . . It provides a neutral medium, giving no one any advantage in the competition for knowledge and jobs" (*The Mirror* June 19, 1978).

Jayakumar also talks about the relationship between English and cultural integration. Because English is neutral in that it does not belong to any of the major ethnic communities in Singapore, it can be the language for inter-ethnic communication and racial harmony. Jayakumar argues that when English "is the common language here, it will enable all Singaporeans—regardless of race—to communicate with one another." Former education minister Dr. Tony Tan made a similar comment in his speech to parliament (March 16, 1990), arguing that through English "there is a greater understanding among Singaporeans of all races," which has "helped substantially to build the peaceful harmonious Singapore that we have today." Note that these leaders are not suggesting that English can be the language of national identity. They are only saying English can be the language of cultural integration. While it can be argued that English is the de facto national language (Pakir, this volume), Singapore's leaders have never given English the discursive space of national language. To do so would mean English could also occupy the space of culture, which, as I will show in a moment, has also been systematically denied in the ideological polarization of language within bilingualism.

Underlying both these notions of English is the view that it is possible to separate language, culture, and technology—that it is possible to adopt English for its technological advantages without adopting its culture. As Lee Kuan Yew puts it: "I don't think I want to model my life on the Anglo-Saxon. I want to catch up with his material and scientific progress. I want to pick up and emulate some of his methods of organizing society. But I am not accepting as superior his culture or way of life. In fact, I view some of the present day values and practices in [the West] . . . as deplorable, [and] which indeed should be strenuously avoided at all cost" (*ST,* January 8, 1988). This view underscores the notion of the neutrality of the English language.

Opposite English in this polarization of language ideologies are the three mother-tongue languages, Malay, Tamil, and Mandarin. As with the English language, the discursive construction of mother tongue language ideologies focuses on national integration. Already in the 1955 Legislative Assembly, when an independent Singapore outside of the Malayan Federation was not yet even conceived, Lee Kuan Yew raised the complexity of the language issues facing the goals of national integration: "In a free and independent Malay in which every Chinese, every Indian, every Malay, will no longer be Chinese, Malay or Indian but Malayan, what language or languages shall they speak? What language or languages shall the Government use? What language or languages will be acceptable to the people? What are the language or languages of an independent and democratic Malaya? They are thorny delicate problems" (Singapore, *LAD* 1955/1956).

The following year, on the basis of the findings of an All-party Education Committee (of which he was a member) set up to look into these questions, Lee Kuan Yew proposed some answers. While the ideal scenario for national integration would be one dominant language and one dominant culture, he argued, "when one gropes, however consciously, for the language, one comes up against all the primordial prejudices of the other groups." Thus, the recommendation was "bilingualism in the primary stage and trilingualism in the secondary stage" (Singapore: *LAD,* April 12, 1956).

A bilingual policy based on multilingualism thus offers tangible evidence of the government's commitment to Singapore's various races, and to a "Singaporean Singapore"—playing on Lee Kuan Yew's (1998) notion of a Malaysian Malaysia—rather than a nation based on one dominant ethnic group. No one could mistake the People's Action Party's (PAP) commitment to multilingualism as documented in their tenth anniversary book: "We repudiate [the Malaysian Tunku's and the Alliance Party's] position that suppression of the mother tongue or their relegation to positions of minor importance is a prerequisite for national unity. Linguistic diversity is in no way incompatible with the interests of a united

Malayan nation" (PAP 1964: 286). With such a proclamation it would have been very difficult politically for the PAP to abandon its commitment to multilingualism upon independence. As such, the guarantees of multilingualism and multiculturalism have been enshrined in the nation's constitution.

But the ideological construction of mother-tongue languages goes well beyond the state consolidating its own power. For even the term "mother tongue" suggests deeper ideological issues may be at play. As Pakir has also mentioned in this volume, the "mother tongue" status of these languages is not to be understood in the traditional sociolinguistic sense of the word. Crystal's use of "mother tongue" represents this more traditional view: "A person's 'mother tongue' or 'first language' (L1) is distinguished from any further languages that may be acquired (L2, L3, etc.)" (Crystal 1987: 368). In Singapore, a person's "mother tongue" may well be the language acquired later in life, such as in school, and may not even be used in the home at all. The mother tongue is an ascribed language, assigned on the basis of one's father's ethnicity, and ideologically framed in the "a race = a culture = a language" equation.

The focused construction of this equation began in the late 1970s. With consecutive years of rapid economic development, Singaporean society began to change—and in ways that were not particularly welcomed by the leadership. These changes, coupled with a devastating evaluation of the bilingual policy in the 1978 Goh Report indicating an alarming failure of the policy, led to an aggressive "*Speak Mandarin Campaign*" aimed at consolidating the Chinese community around Mandarin (and eliminating their use of other Chinese dialects). With this effort came a very particular discursive construction of the mother-tongue languages.

Mother-tongue languages, the leaders have argued, are essential to countering the negative effects that have come with Singaporeans' exposure to the English language. Because English is a neutral language, it has no cultural value for Singaporeans. Any cultural values it does have are ones seen to be inappropriate for Singapore. As such, if Singaporeans were to learn only English and not their mother tongue languages, they would be in danger of becoming "deculturalized." Lee Kuan Yew referred to the Caribbean society to portray what Singapore might well become. He described it as being "deculturalized" and as being a "calypso-type society . . . speaking pidgin English, mindlessly aping the Americans or British with no basic values or cultures" of their own, and leading a "steel-beating and rum-brewing-and-drinking, happy go lucky life" (November 5, 1972). Frankly, he declared, "I do not believe this [kind of society] is worth the building . . . worth the [*sic*] preserving." In recent years, particularly with the publication of Lodge and Vogel's work in 1987 on the relationship between ideology and national competitiveness, the link between good Asian values and economic development has given the mother tongue–values link even greater importance and urgency.

The mother-tongue languages have thus been presented as insulating Singaporeans from this kind of deculturalization. Unlike English, which supposedly can be separated from culture, the mother-tongue languages are embedded in the logic of multiracialism, captured in the equation "a race = a language = a culture." The analogy of computer programming is often used: through mother-tongue education, children would be "inculcated with good Eastern values and cultures. . . . These values will thus be programmed like a computer in the children and form their basic principles in dealing with society and with problems" (MP Choo Wee Khiang, *PDS,* January 17, 1989).

Therefore, the argument goes, each person must have an ethnicity as prescribed by the government, which means he or she has a mother tongue as determined by her or his ethnicity, and which means that she or he then has a culture transmitted by that mother tongue. And with each of the different communities firmly rooted in their cultures, when pulled together, a common Singaporean culture will emerge. In a recent speech in Parliament, Prime Minister Goh Chok Tong used the imagery of overlapping circles (think of the Olympic logo) to capture his vision of the nation (May 5, 1999):

> Our society is made up of four overlapping circles, like the People's Association logo. Each circle represents one community. The four circles overlap each other. What we can do is maximize the overlapping area. This is the area where all Singaporeans, whatever their race, work and play together. It is an open playing field with English as the common language and equal opportunities for all.
>
> Outside this common area, where the circles do not overlap, each community has his [*sic*] own playing field. In this separate area, each community can retain and speak its own language and practice its own culture and customs. This practical approach of nation building whereby every community has two playing fields has given us multi-racial harmony. This approach helps us to build a harmonious nation of diversity.

As we look at the implementation and effects of bilingualism, we will see that the language ideologies embedded in the bilingual policy both provide the possibilities of what language can do in the government's efforts of national integration, and at the same time, result in tension, paradox, and limitations.

The implementation of bilingual education in Singapore. Perhaps one of the most important features of bilingual education in Singapore as it relates to national integration is the development of language-based streaming. The first stage in the streaming process comes at the end of primary four. On the basis of their final examination results, students are streamed into EM1/EM2, EM2, or EM3. In the EM1/EM2 stream, English is taught at the first-language level and the mother tongue at the first-language or second-language level. In the EM2 stream, English is taught at the first-language level and mother tongue at the second-language level, with remedial lessons in either English or mother tongue. And in the EM3 stream, academically weak students learn either oral English or mother tongue (which is weaker).

The second stage in the streaming process comes at the end of primary six. On the basis of their Primary School Leaving Exam (PSLE) results, students are streamed into special, express, or normal secondary courses. Once again, each level is characterized by a particular level and mix of bilingualism.

The special stream is for "those pupils who are ablest" (only the top 10%) to do two first languages, and possibly a third (such as German or French). Students must score A* in their mother tongue language and A in English before they are allowed to take higher mother tongue. This stream is only offered in the ten SAP schools—schools that have been selected by the government to be elite, "effectively bilingual institutions," responsible to protect the Chinese heritage and to produce the next generation of "social brokers." Given the construction of language ideologies discussed earlier, two issues stand out with respect to these Chinese SAP schools. Although all three mother-tongue languages are placed on equal footing within the ideological polarization of language, there are no similar SAP schools for Malay or Tamil. The lack of a critical student mass at this level has been the most common reason given. Furthermore, because these schools, at least initially, were the only ones to offer both English and mother tongue at the higher language level, there is also the perception that these are elite schools, and with it a government-led agenda to produce a Chinese elite. In fact, the recent debate concerning SAP schools in Singapore has been couched in terms of "fostering a Chinese elite."

Since the implementation of SAP schools, two other developments have occurred that have essentially diffused the uniqueness of the SAP schools as it pertains to language and curriculum, and at the same time reinforced the language-intelligence link. In 1987 the government introduced the status of "independent schools" (with a separate board of directors). Two of the eight independent schools are also SAP schools. These schools accept only the top 3 to 5% of students. Historically, these have always been the top schools in Singapore, producing the nation's leaders. And in 1994, the status of "autonomous schools" (schools that are either government or government-aided) was introduced—seven of the eighteen autonomous schools are SAP. Although they cannot offer the "special stream," the non-SAP independent and autonomous schools also offer classes in Higher Mandarin.

In addition to the special stream, secondary students may also be streamed into the express stream, which is for above-average students and offers English at the first language level and mother tongue at the second language level. The normal stream (academic and technical) is for average students. The academic stream offers English and mother tongue at the second language level; the technical stream offers English and basic mother tongue.

Finally, university entrance has a language requirement; students must obtain a certain level in their English and second language proficiency in order to be accepted. If they are borderline in their language subjects but show promise in all other areas, they are allowed to take remedial lessons during their university program; however, they must pass in order to graduate.

Thus at all levels, streaming in the schools is very much based on language. Because of this link between language and streaming and language, and hence language and intelligence, bilingualism is also intricately tied to the structuring of society in terms of social class and status. Census statistics for 1991 show a strong linkage between proficiency in the English language and high levels of social status and class (see also Pakir in this volume). The relationship between language and social class is also very pertinent to the discussion of the dialectics of national integration, but for lack of space I will focus specifically on the complex challenges that English-knowing bilingualism presents to the cultural component of national integration. The challenge is very real. As Prime Minister Goh Chok Tong put it recently in Parliament, even with the emphasis on unity in diversity, the "divide between the races is always there." As such, "the national heartbeat may become separate heartbeats over time." This tension lies at the center of the 'dialectics of national integration'.

The dialectics of national integration. To guide this discussion of bilingual education and the dialectics of national integration, I will focus on the recent debate in Singapore concerning SAP schools and the creation of a Chinese elite. As with most language ideological debates, this debate is very much part of wider sociopolitical processes and linked to a complex story of power relations, competing views in the imagining of the nation, of discourses and counter discourses, and so forth. In this small space, I unravel some of these complexly interwoven narratives to see how the ideological construction of language both facilitates and limits the possibilities of the bilingual education policy in bringing about national integration.

This particular discursive moment in Singapore's on-going debate about SAP schools was ignited in Parliament after the announcement of a tenth SAP school. Member of Parliament (MP) K Shanmugam set the tone when he posed this question: Are the students of SAP schools able to mix harmoniously with non-Chinese Singaporeans? Will this pose a threat to the pluralistic spirit of Singaporean society? In the months that followed, active debate on the topic dominated discussions in Parliament, government speeches, and in the press.

Essentially, the debate has gone something like this: Singapore's bilingual education policy based on multilingualism embodies the government's commitment to imagining Singapore as a multiracial, multicultural nation. However, to concentrate on developing the language and culture of the various communities separately and in isolation of the others could potentially work against this multicultural ideal. There is a tension between ethnic identity and national identity, which is seen as a threat to Singapore's social cohesion. When it appears that particular attention is given to just one of the ethnic communities, and when that community is the dominant group, the threat to social cohesion goes beyond the maintenance of separate identities to one of social equity. In the rest of this paper, I will unpack these various aspects of the debate. What we will find is that much of the debate emerges from the constraints of the ideological construction of bilingualism, leading to a story of the dialectics of national integration.

The SAP school debate and the question of social cohesion. To introduce us to this first aspect of the SAP school debate, let me isolate a number of excerpts from *The Straits Times.* An editorial (March 24,1999) summarized the debate as follows: "The question is what the fostering of cultural elites, especially through SAP schools, means for inter-racial understanding, tolerance and harmony within Singapore. . . . The question is whether different cultural elites separately help to preserve one national identity for Singapore, or whether that single identity can be weakened by pulls from different cultural directions within."

Earlier in March, similar questions were raised at a seminar held at Hwa Chong Junior College where academics and community leaders discussed the role of Chinese intellectuals in the next century (*ST,* March 1, 1999): "Should Singapore develop a pool of Chinese intellectuals or just an intelligentsia spanning the various races? Would the segregation of the intelligentsia by race or language ultimately divide Singapore along racial lines?"

These questions indicate a conflict between the development of an "ethnic identity" and that of a "national identity." Because the system of English-knowing bilingual education is structured such that it would be very difficult for a student to learn a language not associated with her or his ethnicity, the instruction of the mother-tongue languages along racial lines also maintains a sense of difference among the various communities. This is particularly so in SAP schools where the only mother tongue language offered is Mandarin, thereby excluding the majority of non-Chinese students from enrollment. English is presented as the way out of ethnic distinction; yet one can see the constant tension this brings to the policy.

What makes this issue so potent is that SAP schools are, in theory anyway, designed to produce the next generation of leaders. As noted by MP Dr. Tan Cheng Bock, "It is a well-known fact that a sizeable number of able Chinese students attend such schools and some are going to be leaders of this country" (*ST,* March 2, 1999). At the center of the debate then is not so much that these schools exist, or that there is an effort to produce a Chinese elite, but that these efforts operate in exclusion to the other ethnic communities. Because SAP school students have little interaction with non-Chinese students, the fear is that they will be less sensitive to the fears and hopes of other communities. In Parliament, MP Zulkifli Baharudin presented the issue this way: "What hope can we have if a section of our community grows up into adulthood in an entirely different ethnic-based education? What hope have we got if we allow them to erect walls between us and making it less possible to reach out, embrace and understand other communities in our society?" (*ST,* March 18, 1999).

The racial exclusiveness of the SAP schools emerges here as a principal concern of the non-Chinese communities. Yet Brigade-General George Yeo's (minister for information and the arts) response to the debate completely missed this fundamental issue (*ST,* April 2, 1999). Closing SAP schools, he argued, would be akin to closing schools run by Muslims, Catholics, and Buddhists. Yet, unlike the Chinese SAP schools, enrollment in these schools is not exclusive, based neither on ethnicity or religion.

As is typical of the PAP leadership, the government's response has been comprehensive. One strategy has been to merely reiterate the ideal model of multiculturalism in the imagining of the nation. In this model, the complex nexus of national and ethnic identities are presented as complementary, rather than in competition with one another. *The Straits Times* (March 22, 1999) reported Prime Minister Goh Chok Tong's response to the debate as follows:

> He said Singapore, being a multiracial country, faces the challenge of channeling ethnic pride towards the building of a national identity. This means allowing the different communities to retain their separate identities instead of forcing their different cultures and customs into a common mould. "Our approach is like weaving a beautiful piece of tapestry out of different colored strands of silk," he said.
>
> "Each community needs to nurture a core group of people adept at its own language and culture to preserve the community's uniqueness," he said. So SAP schools should be seen in this context.

The image is one of "unity in diversity," whereby the encouragement of cultural distinction will somehow lead to a national identity. While this argument is somewhat ambiguous in that it remains unclear how exactly this unified national identity will emerge, it nonetheless represents the government's continued commitment to the ideals of multiracialism. The various ethnic communities are seen as equal partners in the imagining of the nation, co-existing in harmonious relation with one another. However, as will be discussed in a moment, if indeed this were the case, there would be no debate.

Another strategy in the government's response has been to demonstrate its awareness of and responsiveness to the potential negative effects of exclusive Chinese elite schools. For a number of months and in various forums, government leaders (including Prime Minister Goh Chok Tong and Deputy Prime Minister Lee Hsien Loong) stated in detail the various efforts taken to help SAP school students keep in contact with other races *(ST,* March 18, 22, 23, 1999). Cluster schools, extracurricular activities involving non-SAP schools, cultural awareness activities (fashion parades, food festivals, etc.), and so forth, were among the efforts mentioned. However, as columnist Cherian George put it, rather than furthering the possibility of transforming SAP schools from exclusive to inclusive, these efforts suggest that interaction with minorities in the SAP schools remains "literally an extra-curricular experience" *(ST,* March 24, 1999), undermining and minimizing the true nature of inter-ethnic interaction.

The particular construction of language ideologies within the bilingual policy also has played a key role in this debate. Given the perceived inherent link between language and culture, one possible avenue for cultural integration would be encouraging SAP school students to learn another local language as their third language. However, this possibility has been limited by the ways in which the mother tongue language has been embedded in the "a race = a culture = a language" equation. The equation suggests a rather limited utility for these languages, particularly in contrast to such languages as French or Japanese that offer more pragmatic possibilities. This is illustrated by the fact that while the non-Chinese communities have frequently requested that their children be allowed to learn Mandarin as their second language, no similar requests have been made by the Chinese community to learn Malay or Tamil. As I have argued elsewhere (Bokhorst-Heng 1999a), this is undoubtedly because, with the recent opening up of China's markets, Mandarin has taken on "value-added" status; it has crossed the polarized divide between English and mother tongue to take on economic value as well as culture. Because the other mother tongue languages have not been able to cross the barrier in the same way, there is no perceived pragmatic value to learn these languages, and they remain locked in the "a race = a culture = a language" equation.

The possibilities and constraints posed by the ideological construction of bilingualism are seen also in one other response given by government leaders to the SAP school debate. In response to the concerns raised by MP Baharudin, Education Minister Teo Chee Hean pointed out that all races are unified through the use of English as a common language. The bilingual policy "has served Singapore well," he argued. "It has enabled us to unify the country while at the same time allowed each community to feel that it has the room and space to develop itself and to retain its own unique identity and characteristics" *(ST,* March 18, 1999). At a very basic level, although this argument may work in ethnically mixed schools, it holds little merit in the SAP schools, where the mother tongue has physically isolated the Chinese students from the others.

Furthermore, the ideological polarization of language meanings presents English as devoid of any culture value. Once again the possibilities of language for cultural integration are limited. For at what level can this communication occur, if English is for functional purposes alone? At what level can this communication occur if English cannot be seen as a "mother tongue"? Furthermore, English continues to be portrayed by the leaders as playing a vital role in exposing Singaporeans to the decadent values of Western societies, threatening the very viability of the nation. Thus, the limited discursive space given to English ultimately hinders the development of true cultural exchange. These limitations have been the subject of considerable debate in Singapore. Letters to the "Forum Page" often express the desire for English to be given the status of mother tongue. National authors struggle with the contradiction between the ideological construction of English and the use of English as a means of cultural expression and national literature (Talib 1998). And academics explore conceptual paradigms that would expand and broaden the role of the English language in Singapore (Ho and Alsagoff 1998).

Thus far the debate concerning SAP schools and about the creation of cultural elites seems to assume equilibrium among the three major ethnic communities—that there is an equal effort to develop an elite in all three communities. Yet, as I mentioned earlier, the voices of some in the debate suggest an even deeper concern than the threat to social cohesion is the perceived threat to social equity.

The SAP school debate and the question of social equity. The comments of one person writing to the "Forum Page" in *The Straits Times* capture the tone of this debate: "What is important is the need to maintain the sacredness of the commitment towards multiracialism and its ideals. To the minorities, the SAP schools represent a tiny breach." (April 2, 1999). His voice was not alone, as is evident in the frequent speeches given by government leaders specifically addressing this concern. One such speech was that of Deputy Prime Minister Lee Hsien Loong given to members of the Sikh community *(ST,* March 21, 1999):

> Minority communities have no cause to worry about moves to develop a Chinese cultural elite and SAP schools, said DPM Lee Hsien Loong last night. He said he was aware that non-Chinese were concerned that these moves might reflect a shift away from the ideal of multiracialism. But they need not worry, he said. The Government remains committed to multiracialism and meritocracy with English remaining as the common working language. He also produced figures to allay fears that SAP students would form a communal elite, swipe top positions, and squeeze out other talented Singaporeans. The reality was that non-SAP students form the majority among the top Chinese

> students at school, among Government scholarship holders and in the premier Administrative service. . . . This makes it impossible for SAP school students to form a communal elite, and squeeze out the other Singaporeans.

A column in *The Straits Times* by Assistant Professor (NIE) Goh Yeng Seng *(ST,* April 13, 1999) reiterated the same argument. When "comparing the source of students, future career opportunities, and the curricula of the SAP and non-SAP schools," he argued, we find that in 1998, SAP schools comprised less than half of the top ten secondary schools. My analysis of President Scholarships recipients (1998) leads to the same conclusion: schools that have historically been the best schools in Singapore (and which today are non-SAP independent schools) continue to produce the mainstream elite leadership in Singapore.

This actually points to yet another issue embedded in this debate, namely that within the Chinese community, it is the English-speaking elites that dominate the center, while the Chinese-speaking intellectuals remain on the periphery. For these "minorities," SAP schools represent a "need to assert political muscle in a milieu in which English-speakers seem to form the majority in circles of influence" *(ST,* March 2, 1999). It is important to note that the implementation of the SAP school program was initially very much a way to appease the growing dissatisfaction of the Chinese-educated members of the Chinese community who saw themselves increasingly as a marginalized underclass. And so in some ways, the SAP schools and the debate are a smoke screen for the continued dominance of English in Singapore, and for the socioeconomic and political benefits that proficiency in English brings.

However, this is not to suggest that then the non-Chinese communities have no cause for concern. The SAP schools do not exist in isolation. Significantly, their inception was also part of a larger effort by the Singaporean government to consolidate the Chinese community around Mandarin, and thereby strengthen the dominant position of the Chinese (Bokhorst-Heng 1999b). It is the context of this larger effort that has produced such unease within the minority communities. In her analysis of language policies as they relate to the South Asian community in Singapore, Tan Su Hwi notes that "although Singapore is a multi-ethnic nation, the real power base . . . must be retained at the ethnic center" (1998: 98). She quotes Deputy Prime Minister Lee Hsien Loong as saying: "The government's overall policies are to ensure that there is succession of and mass support for the English-knowing bilingual Chinese elite in the important spheres of power and privilege" *(ST,* September 4, 1997). In his 1997 National Day rally speech, the Prime Minister said, "We need Chinese scholars for the Government and business, the media and the arts." Thus, while they might not produce the nation's top elite, the SAP schools nonetheless continue to be part of this story, existing as visible evidence to the minorities of the government's breach in its commitment to multiculturalism.

Conclusion. In this paper, I examined the relationship between bilingual education and national integration in Singapore as it has been played out in one instance: the controversy over Chinese SAP schools. The debate is embedded in two contested areas: the cultural and national nexus, where the demands of two sets of identities pose a threat to social cohesion, and the struggle to maintain social equity within an ethnically disproportioned population. While Singapore's bilingual policy has eased the tensions in some areas, it has paradoxically increased the tension in others. I argued that these paradoxes could only be understood when the various language ideologies and their relation to the imagining of the nation are taken into account. This focus on ideology reveals how, as Heller (1999) says of the Canadian context, language is the "terrain on which [such] tensions are neutralized, ambiguities constructed, contradictions masked." And so it is only when we see the ideological construction of the mother tongue languages in the "a race = a culture = a language" equation that we can understand how the bilingual policy can reinforce ethnic walls rather than open doors of cultural exchange. It is only when we consider the ideological construction of the English language that we can understand its dominant yet limited role in bringing about true cultural exchange and social equity. The relationship between bilingual education and national integration therefore is ultimately a dialectical one, played out against the wider sociopolitical horizon of imagining the Singapore nation.

REFERENCES

Anderson, B. 1991. *Imagined Communities: Reflections of the Origins and Spread of Nationalism.* London: Verso.

Blommaert, J. (ed.). 1999. *Language ideological debates.* Berlin: Walter de Gruyter.

Bokhorst-Heng, Wendy D. 1999a. *Language is more than a language.* CAS Research Paper Series No. 6. Singapore: Center for Advanced Studies (CAS), National University of Singapore.

Bokhorst-Heng, Wendy D. 1999b. Singapore's *Speak Mandarin Campaign:* Language Ideological Debates in the Imagining of the Nation. In J. Blommaert (ed.), *Language ideological debates.* Berlin: Walter de Gruyter. 235–265.

Business Times (Singapore), various.

Chua Beng Huat. 1995. *Communitarian ideology and democracy in Singapore.* London and New York: Routledge.

Crystal, D. 1987. *The Cambridge encyclopedia of language.* Cambridge: Cambridge University Press.

Goh Keng Swee and the Education Team. 1979. *Report on the Ministry of Education 1978 (Goh report).* Singapore: Ministry of Education.

Heller, M. 1999. "Heated Language in a Cold Climate." In J. Blommaert (ed.), *Language ideological debates.* Berlin: Walter de Gruyter. 143 170.

Ho C. L., and L. Alsagoff. 1998. English as the common language in multicultural Singapore. In J. A. Foley et al. (eds.), *English in new cultural contexts: Reflections from Singapore.* Singapore: Oxford University Press and SIM. 201–217.

Lee Kuan Yew. 1998. *The Singapore story: Memoirs of Lee Kuan Yew.* Singapore: Singapore Press Holdings and Times Editions.

Lodge, G. C., and E. F. Vogel. (1987). *Ideology and national competitiveness: An analysis of nine countries.* Boston: Harvard Business School Press.

People's Action Party (PAP). (1964). *Our first ten years: PAP tenth anniversary souvenir, 1964.* Singapore: Tiger Press.

Singapore. Legislative Assembly. (1955/1956). *Singapore legislative assembly debates. Official report* (LAD). Singapore: Government Printing Office.

Singapore. *Parliamentary debates. Republic of Singapore. Official report* (PDS). Various.

The Straits Times (Singapore), various.

Talib, I. S. 1998. Singaporean Literature in English. In J. A. Foley et al. (eds.), *English in new cultural contexts: Reflections from Singapore.* Singapore: Oxford University Press and SIM. 270–286.

Tan Su Hwi. 1998. Language planning in multilingual Singapore: Lessons from the ethnic periphery. Ph.D. dissertation, National University of Singapore, Singapore.

NOTE

1. My thanks to Chris Clubine-Ito for his extremely helpful comments and suggestions on earlier drafts of this paper.

The sweet breath of words: Language as nuance in Diaspora creativity

Edwin Thumboo
National University of Singapore

I. In K. S. Maniam's *In a Far Country,* which depicts the challenges facing different ethnic groups seeking a place in the sun, the tiger is the central symbol used to establish and network a number of basic themes. These include the historical position of the Malays, their identity, and their relationship with the land. In political and cultural terms, it sums up what the other races must recognize and negotiate with at various levels. This search for a balance between ethnic and national identities, to accommodate their traditions in a form satisfactory to all, is still ongoing in the continuum of experience from which the novel is drawn. Once introduced, the tiger remains a continuing presence, a silent but potent part of the narrative. Reasonably attentive readers will see that it stands for the land's immemorial spirit, making it a near permanent guardian. It is both a presence and a force that must be sought out and understood. The tiger's symbolic status allows Maniam to locate it at strategic points of the narrative to provide tactful, less overt, but nonetheless powerful comment on deeply sensitive issues. Time for a Tiger, in more ways than one. For the Malays it is a necessary part of their inheritance and identity; for the others—Chinese, Indians, and others—to be understood as part of the accommodations of living in a Malay-dominated society. The fundamental question is whether to integrate or to retain one's Chinese or Indian identity. That is Ravi's, the main protagonist's, dilemma. With his friend Zulkifli, who has inherited the promise and the demands of tradition as his guide, he makes a second attempt to discover the tiger:

> Is it a miracle when after I dump my gun in a cachement of leaves my movements become more fluid? Some of the resistance to our advance seems to withdraw itself. As we go deeper and deeper some of my fatigue falls away. But I can't escape the vigilant eye. It is there on my head or back or legs. It is there in front, ahead of us, besides us but all the time disconcertingly near.

"Any time now," Zulkifli says at my side. "But we've to take on the character of the tiger first. We must see through its eyes. Feel through its body. We must become the tiger."

"I'll kill it first," I say.

"With what?" he says.

"By surprising it," I say.

"Nothing can surprise it," he says. "We don't have the intelligence."

"You seem to know everything about it," I say.

"Through the instinct that has traveled to me through the blood of my ancestors," he says.

"Are you saying I can't have such an instinct?"

"You don't have ancestors here," he says.

"You must be without purpose to come into its presence," Zulkifli says as if reading my thoughts.

"Then I won't." I say.

"You have come this far," he says. "You must surrender your self to be the other self."

He went into a ritual on my behalf. All I remember of it is the incessant chanting that came from his lips. Though words poured from him, I only remember their sounds. . . . All the time the chant poured from Zulkifli's throat like an ageless invitation to disown whatever I was and to merge with the tiger. I didn't wait for that to happen. (Maniam, 1993: 100–101)

This passage raises a number of issues that frame my presentation. These include the distance that most of the new literatures have traveled since their beginnings about five decades ago; the ground they have had to cover, including the changing relationship with the major centres of the ex-colonial language; and the gradual emergence of an essential internal confidence in the new literatures.

As they write themselves into the language, the language is being written into them, turning into their idiolect. That is a process of domesticating, nativizing English, giving it a local habitation and a name.

Making of the writer. Writers and readers approach literature differently. This is especially the case with poets. For instance, Robert Graves had occasion to remark that "I write poems for poets, and satires or grotesques for wits. For people in general I write prose, and am content that they should be unaware that I do anything else. To write poems for other than poets is wasteful" (Graves 1946: Foreword). This helps me make the point I want to with a useful, tangential vigour. And it is this. While the element of pleasure is there, the poet-reader's exegetical, comparative, and judgmental interests are framed and hedged by his own practice. There is a special relationship with meaning. Unlike the reader who is not a poet, he constructs and re-constructs. Few other readers will engage in both processes of construction and re-construction as the poet would. He is in dialogue with the poem, comparing notes. The constant search to strengthen his idiolect, to refine and augment its power to incarnate experience, directs his attention to matters of creative energies, resources of imagery, metaphors, syntax, rhythmic strategies, and so on. Unlike the poet who lifts the paraphrase of what is read by tinkering with it to produce his version of the poem as poem, the reader-reader expands the paraphrase to put the poem into the language of a broader understanding. It is a matter of intention that distinguishes the critic reader who may try to enter the poem as fully as the poet-reader, one for explication, and the other for making.

Writers are generally serious, selective if not avid readers, especially of works in their chosen genre. They serve an apprenticeship, learning from predecessors and contemporaries, constantly seeking out and trying ways of broadening, deepening, and refining their discourse to articulate their subjects, themes, and vision. Such is a broadening that levels up, not down. That compound of thought-emotion-language, which searches out at random, free of apparent sequence, and with remarkable simultaneity, still remains a mystery. It is a supreme inventiveness. We recognize its best results, assign them names, seek them, and revise constantly, until, occasionally, there is the gift of some further magic. Occasionally, again, a slip as we type brings or suggests the metaphor, the adjective, the necessary rhythmic break, or variation that we know is needed, know after and not before. To learn from the strongest masters without being subjugated to their style, the whisper in their voice, that is the consummation devoutly to be wished. For a considerable period of his life, especially during its most active, creative part, his experience is likely to prove more subtle and larger than his language. Not the language at large, but what of it is actively at his disposal.

The works read, studied, re-read, and returned to while writing and re-writing a poem are what shapes a poet as he pursues his calling and its art. He is, no doubt, the product of some sector of the available, centrally planned, or independently constructed primary, secondary, and tertiary education that provides the linguistic tools, which are then developed and directed by the demands of his or her vocation. And behind them is their literature, which educates, bestows—all freely—as inclination and talent lead. Writers do not chose their language; the language chooses them. Exceptions to this rule are rare: Vladimir Nabokov,

Samuel Beckett, and the early Mohd. Hj. Salleh. Most of us find it hard enough to handle one language. But we choose the same genre, which in turn makes its own special, characteristic demands. Generally, do poetry, fiction, and drama use images, rhythm, or punctuation in the same way, and to the same degree?

Starting point. But we need to know that place of broad beginnings, at least its general whereabouts, and for cogent reasons. It involves beginnings in time, in place, in literary province, that is, genre, are viewed within the focus of literatures in English. *Time:* the contemporary. *Place:* post-independent "nations" of the Commonwealth, consisting of former British colonies. This immediately raises the question of whether they are 'nations' in the accepted sense or a collection of peoples occupying ex-colonial, at times externally imposed boundaries, or variations thereof. And more often than not, the new polity is multiracial and multilingual, thus challenged by the usual slew of problems in varying degrees of intensity.

Realities, diversities. These are among realities that bear directly on literary production through the history of peoples: the politics, economics, and languages and their literary, critical, and aesthetic traditions, ethnicities, style of government, and so on, all of which shape current societal experience and expectations. The human impact and variety of that experience, the calculus of fictional possibilities it allows, for instance, is suggested in novels as varied as Bessie Head's *A Question of Power* (1974), C. J. Koch's *The Year of Living Dangerously* (1978), Ngugi wa Thiongo's *Devil on the Cross* (1982), Raja Rao's *The Chessmaster and His Moves* (1988), Brian Castro's *After China* (1992), Lloyd Fernando's *Green is the Colour* (1993), and K. S. Maniam's *In a Far Country* (1993). Genre: poetry, fiction, and drama. While they share features of language ranging from image to length of sentence, each has its own space, management of subject/theme, voice, structure, disjunctions and continuities, and so on, and so on. These overlap, but notwithstanding, the writer prepares himself differently according to the genre he chooses, according to his history, place, and time. You cannot post-colonial the lot without overlooking their "national," their individual creative contexts, occupations, and preoccupations.

Despite its obviousness, we tend to overlook the fact that every writer has a starting point that is, in practice, more the time from which he or she begins to release his or her work. For there is little, if ever, of anything abrupt in the way he is formed as a person, is apprenticed to the art, the 'who' who then begins to produce what is, on self-judgment, satisfactory literature. There are many reasons why we overlook beginnings. First and foremost is interest in the writer's mature works. His development would engage those with a special or specialist interest. Second, we are familiar, at times overly so, with the language, its literary tradition, and the "age" in which the writer belongs. "Point of time" would be more accurate and recognizing, because in newly independent countries or nations that are successful, the changes are fundamental and far-reaching. The most cursory acquaintance with the growth of Singapore in the last forty years, even when unsympathetic, cannot miss the range and depth of transformations, a significant number of which would normally take many generations. Third, with as massively widespread an international language as English, there will be those who are likely to approach the literatures in it from the perspective of its more established traditions—the British and the American— and current critical practices. They are not always aware that crucial differences exist that require if not insist on modifications in habitual critical stances, or that the methods of comparative literature are decidedly useful (see Thumboo 1985, 1996).

As GURT 99 reminds us, we cannot think of language in our time without being deeply aware of bilingualism spreading nationally and regionally. The facts vary; they have both a historical and contemporary force. Bilingualism involves the local and the regional—in both senses of the word, that is, within a nation, and a nation with its neighbors—and international languages. My concern is with English and bilingual creativity, with English forming one-half of the hyphen.

II. Three considerations form the frame of what I have to say. The first is that international languages are also national languages and ex-colonial languages. Herein lie problems and challenges, particularly in the case of English, whose strength derives from a diachronically powerful British literature, a synchronically powerful American literature, and an even more powerful and—in a sense— an overdeveloped mass media and the linguistic network left by the former British Empire. This leads to the second consideration, which is the retention of English as a main, auxiliary, bridge, official, national language, language of modernization, law, administration, education, and so on, in circumstances of such enormous practicality that it has flourished. The majority of non-Angelo-Saxon colonies have been independent for some four decades. During this time the attitude toward English changed significantly. The sense that it was a colonial language has receded. The third is the degree to which young writers and critics are unaware, and unconcerned if not ignorant, of its colonial history. They use it with little inhibition, and in some instances, with less care for the elements such as image, rhythm, the discipline of line and phrase, and organic form, that structure a poem.

The journey begins. The starting points for the writer, then, are different from what they are today. Changes range from matters of technique to matters that are nonliterary. The themes that engaged the first generation of post-independence writers have in some ways receded, according to the politics and history of the nation. But this is the gift of certain essential journeys, certain acts of recovery and self-definition, which had to be first undertaken.

The writing in English that grew after the political independence of nations of the British Commonwealth had its own distinct starting point. That point depended upon a number of factors. The British Empire consisted of nations such as India, with classical literatures at least as old as that in Greek, older than that in Latin, and far older than that in English. There were other new nations, especially in Africa, with equally immemorial oral literatures. In the West Indies, English must be the mother tongue as it is the only language. Finally, we have a place like Singapore where there are four official languages, namely Bahasa Melayu, Chinese (with at least a dozen languages of which four are dominant), Tamil (the main Indian language), and English, the language of administration, commerce, and industry, in addition to serving as a bridge between the various ethnic groups. The unique role English plays in Singapore is perhaps revealed when once I had to remind an audience in Hangzhou, China, that to concentrate on Singapore Chinese literature alone would neglect a considerable and significant amount of the Chinese experience to be discovered only in Singapore fiction, drama, and poetry in English. The starting point for the writer has to vary as his history varies. What then, are the political, economic, and social conditions of his nation? What cultural and specific literary traditions are there as resources to tap into and influence his creativity?

The second concerns the challenges the nation and the individual face; and what are the themes writers find significant? For Derek Walcott (1972: 9), the journey was long: "My generation had looked at life with black skins and blue eyes, but only our own painful, strenuous looking, the learning of looking, could find meaning in the life around us, only our own strenuous hearing, the hearing of our hearing, could make sense of the sounds we made." Activate the senses. Let what they perceive, and perceive steadily and whole, of a necessary beginning. First the individuals, with each contributing to the accumulating perceptions of the state, the condition, of their society. Then the search for answers. "What would deliver him from servitude was the forging of a language that went beyond mimicry, a dialect which had the force of revelation as it invented names for things, one which finally settled on its own mode of inflection, and which began to create an oral culture of chants, jokes, folk-songs and fables; this, not merely the debt of history was his proper claim to the New World" (Walcott 1972: 17).

Making poetic selves. This power of the imagination is something mysterious. We do not know its mode of operation except that it is unpredictable, its aptness validated by what it produces through a certain esemplastic power. In this process, where language stretches itself across the arc of thought and emotion, the judgment comes in as a different kind of laboring. It must not supersede the imagination. It does not generate; it decides. In an established literary tradition, the tutelage, while challenging, does not have the additional dimension of a series of acts toward self-definition. To belong to a multicultural society, to have two cultures, one of which is acquired in another language, raises a number of sharp challenges. Here is Gabriel Okara (1963: 15): "In order to capture the vivid images of African speech, I had to eschew the habit of expressing my thoughts first in English. It was difficult at first but I had to learn. I had to study each jaw expression I used and to discover the probable situation in which it was used in order to bring out the nearest meaning in English. I found it a fascinating exercise."

And there is the question of space, new space, defined by the facts and energies of a bipolar culture, the indigenous and the imported, reflecting a new combination of experience entering the English language. Among the complexities are those associated with the individual assertion for a personal identity defined by the two cultures, undertaken at a time, and in a context, of a society that is itself evolving. On the one hand, there is a search for fresh traditions that incorporate the indigenous and the imported as well as the development of individual talent. It is the equivalent, in spirit at least, of what T. S. Eliot wanted in "Tradition and the Individual Talent" (Eliot 1975). But with a difference: that tradition assumed a high degree of homogeneity, connectedness, and literary lineage and descent. The dynamics of the framework he sketches are universal, but the content needs the addition of indigenous elements. For instance, the actual literary inheritance in terms of forms could involve the Pantun as well as Akam and Puram poetry, whose use of objects as correlatives is both instructive and revealing vis-à-vis Eliot's formulation of the notion in his essay on *Hamlet*. A. K. Ramanujan's *The Interior Landscape* offers examples of the poetry and an instructive afterword that comprehensively sets out details of the convention.

For Raja Rao, creativity in English meant certain re-orientations and adaptations:

> The telling has not been easy. One has to convey in a language that is not one's own the spirit that is one's own. One has to convey the various shades and omissions of a certain thought-movement that looks maltreated in an alien language . . . yet English is not really an alien language to us. It is the language of our intellectual make-up . . . but not of our emotional make-up. We are all instinctively bilingual, many of us writing in our own language and in English. We cannot write like the English. We should not. We cannot write only as Indians. We have grown to look at the large world as part of us. Our method of expression therefore has to be a dialect that will some day prove to be as distinctive and colorful as the Irish or the American. (Rao 1938: Foreword)

Rao's was the challenge of fully locating a sensibility formed by and in one tradition in another with its life uncompromised to function at the highest possible creative level. While the ambition is the same for Walcott and Okara, writing some thirty years later, the processes forming each of them as writers differ, each from the other, and from Rao. Put briefly, Walcott's colonially created society is moving in search of identity, definition, and articulation, through the instruments of social, linguistic, cultural, and other institutions. For Okara, it is chiefly of sensibility moving, but one out of an oral tradition. It is broadly the same language, English, orchestrated to each his own.

Here is the key point. You use English. You are hyphenated, bicultural, and bilingual. As a writer, one half of the creative-technical enterprise is taken from British or American and its or their literature(s), instruction in usage, and lessons on how to process thought and experience. The other half concerns the grammar of interests, the challenging uniqueness of your situation, that is, what the Walcotts, Okaras, and Raos do. While you have to map out new, national routes, there is the great tradition, from Geoffrey Chaucer down to W. B. Yeats and T. S. Eliot. Therein lies the authority of your language. You need its sustenance, yet have to move away. Not to do either, while simultaneously discarding and acquiring, is to wither or grow crippled from failure to move from under the banyan tree, which is the great tradition, into the soil and sunlight of your own.

The earlier pioneering writers had a great quantity of ground to cover. Those who are familiar with Chinua Achebe's and Ngugi wa Thiong'o's essays, for instance, would recall that part of the writer's function was to re-construct his society, retrieving as much as possible of the rhythms and the icons of life before the coming of colonizers. Achebe's *Things Fall Apart* and *Arrow of God* or Ngugi's pre-occupations with the effects of neocolonialism, the systematic abuse and the corruption that destroyed the high hopes of freedom, are both instructive and revealing. So the writing, the fiction especially, has a sociopolitical dimension as well as an artistic one. I have put it this way for emphasis. Although the former remains a theme, there has been a noticeable shift in the focus, which is now increasingly on the individual rather than the group. The 'we' has been converted into an 'I'. It is no longer a case of constructing or re-constructing the past and the immediate present. It is the present that now provides impulse and context. In such circumstances, a considerable part of the communal experience overlaps the individual's, and in a combination that is mutually strengthening, while reaching out with iconic power. There has been a period of national experience. Whatever the successes and failures of that experience, it contributes to and represents a unity of interests that is concurrently national and personal.

Tradition as hegemony. Up to the mid-1950s, the sense and practice of poetry had to take into account the presence of W. B. Yeats and T. S. Eliot, with Ezra Pound, their éminence grise at various removes. Directly and indirectly, that Trinitarian presence was defined by an authority that held for at least thirty years after the publication of *The Waste Land* (1922) and *The Tower* (1928), both of which were more influential than *Hugh Selwyn Mauberley* (1920). Like other writers, poets discover and develop their interests and themes out of life around them. It is an ongoing discovery, a calculus that draws in, shifts, and rearranges. It is the same mind and sensibility that create the poems, that write the reviews and essays. There is an intimate linkage between the poetry and the criticism. We recall Ben Jonson, John Dryden, Samuel Johnson, S. T. Coleridge and Matthew Arnold, Ezra Pound, and T. S. Eliot, perhaps the last of them all.

No poetry can be said to be intellectual or emotional or whatever else. But it is possible for poetry to be classified as such on the basis of the thinking and the conceptualization that lies behind it. When we refer to metaphysical poetry we are encouraged to think of wit, a strong intellectual presence and toughness, the use of irony even in the most lyrical pieces, a boldness of phrase, rhythm as in Donne's "Batter my heart, three-person'd God," and the use of conceits. There is the courage to extract whatever possibilities metaphor can yield, a fact subtly demonstrated in George Herbert's "The Pulley." That is the kind of poetry that influenced Eliot. It accords in its technique, thrust, general atmosphere and sense of detail of how the human mind works in and through language that we find in the sixteenth and seventeenth century dramatists and prose writers whose work engaged Eliot in the 1920s. His essay on Philip Messenger appeared in 1920, that on Marvell in 1921; that on Lancelot Andrews in 1926, and on Thomas Middleton in 1927. The poetry arising from the dynamics of interaction with the writing of this historical period became orthodoxy. That orthodoxy exerted a considerable force both on the production of poetry and the criticism of poetry. Eliot's own criticism, first collected in *The Sacred Wood,* proved influential. F. R. Leavis, who would emerge as the major critic of the 1950s and 1960s, took *The Sacred Wood* as his critical bible.

While Pound was the early schoolmaster to both Yeats and Eliot, it was the latter who emerged as the most influential on the authority of his poetry, and his criticism. A substantial part of this was asserted through the work of those— chiefly critics—they attracted. For the first time in the history of English poetry, the dominant figures were not home grown. Pound was American with European longings, Eliot an American enlarging his English self, and Yeats remade himself with a mix of Irish history, myth, and nationalism.

What is interesting is that all three poets are, in a sense, outsiders, either inspecting that condition as a function of England-as-center or, for the two Americans at least, how they were to work from their position in the fringe back to England-as-center as in the case of Eliot. It is not a question of the empire writing back but the first and largest ex-colony, namely America, some of whose major literati were returning to the mother through a cultural umbilical cord. The point here is that they saw themselves as belonging to the same immediate tradition, a fully English one, behind which lay the sponsoring European tradition with its antecedents in a Greco-Hebraic civilization. Both Pound and Eliot could refer to, and tap into, the whole literature of Europe. It is there in Pound's criticisms and his Cantos; it is there in Eliot's *The Wasteland* and his 1919 essay, "Tradition and the Individual Talent," and in his interest in Dante, on whom he wrote in 1929.

Against hegemony. It is not the case that where the language goes the criticism follows in toto. That is something we are familiar with. It comes as a form of authority, built into both the creative and critical traditions, as Raymond Williams reminds us:

> What is often being defended, it seems, is not just a body of writing but a major projection from this, in which the actually very diverse works of writers in English are composed into a national identity B the more potent because it is largely from the past B in which a mood, a temper, a style, or a set of immediate 'principles' (which can be contrasted not only with "theory" but with all other forms of reasoning) are being celebrated, taught and B where possible "administratively imposed." But among what can be called, with precision, traditional English literary intellectuals, it is not just a profession; it is and has sounded like a calling and a campaign. (Williams n.d.: 195)

This self-confident, deep-rooted hegemony is what T. S. Eliot asserts with uncharacteristic ardour in a 1924 letter to Ford Madox Ford: "I am all for empires, especially the Austro-Hungarian Empire, and I deplore the outburst of artificial nationalities . . . all over the world. . . . There can only be one English literature . . . there cannot be British literature, or American literature" (quoted in Kermode, 1975: 15).

That Eliot subsequently changed his mind merely confirms the irreversible force of history. Given the obvious power of its language and literature, he felt able to talk on "American Literature and the American Language" (Eliot 1965). Furthermore, the artificial nationalities he objected to were legion when the majority of colonies received independence. That force of history should be recognized and constantly kept in mind. It is a force that the New Literatures share increasingly, as they gain their singular authority.

Eliot's desire for unity and oneness—it often hides hegemonic impulses— was central to his thinking. It was the locus of his great tradition. At the time of his assertion about empires, he had no hint that the British Empire would come to an end after World War II, and fairly rapidly at that, with India the first, on August 15, 1947. The British Empire was the greatest creator of artificial nationalities in all history. In the non-Anglo-Saxon parts especially, it compacted various races and their cultures in a single geography, creating a relatively peaceful, plural society under the control of British colonial masters. Malaysia and Singapore are cases in point. At times colonial boundaries could have bizarre post-independent consequences. There was East Pakistan and West Pakistan, forming a polity whose artificiality was exposed when the former became Bangladesh. People do not create artificialities on this scale for themselves. They are constructs that cause nothing but trouble. There is Cameroon, divided between the British and the French, with the consequence that its post-independence literary journal, *Abbia,* had articles in both English and French. These artificial nationalities had to work out their own political, economic, ethnic, psychological, and literary salvation, at times under considerable racial and other tensions.

III.

The new authority. The poet is both critic and creator but the critic in him aids the creator, refining what he produces, strengthening it by expansion and contraction. By achieving a density, one that is simultaneously a further clarity, it reaches out for cadence and rhythm; taking images into a pattern where they support each other, proceeding almost unconsciously; and free, for the moment, from the conscious critical faculty that will be exercised at a later stage when it stands further from the imagination's work. As Auden pointed out, the poetic faculty consists of knowing, making, and judging. The point here of course is that the making arises from the knowing, and the making owes much of its strengths to the judging. The act of revision is paradoxically an act of condensation, an intensification that is simultaneously a release.

The diminution of English. There is a considerable irony that as the pioneers of the new literatures sought and achieved the taught articulation of literary statement and discourse with a considerable measure of success, thus laying foundations, there are developments in the world of English usage that diminish that creativity. The English language has about 700,000 to 800,000 words. They include the archaic, the slangy, and the undesirable, judged on religious, social, and other grounds. That reduces the number actively used in any given epoch, especially if specialized vocabularies are excluded. The number of words used to define the limits and depth of feeling and intellection is somewhat diminished. The reasons for this impoverishment are doubtless familiar to you: the impatient pace of modern life, lowered expectations that become self-fulfilling as regards the quality of conversation, the various journalisms and other components of the mass media, and English for special purposes, administered even before there is English for ordinary purposes. Not that you cannot find the best words B at times provocatively configured B in the best order. And not merely in poetry. You can. The general level has declined. We read more, but far less of quality; with haste, with far less meditation.

The capacity to digest a complex diet is seriously diminished. This leads to a leveling down of subtlety and a consequent loss in sophisticated language management. The syntax of our personalities is the syntax of our language, or languages. The vocabulary of our personalities is the vocabulary of our language or languages. And vice versa. Traditionally, high conversation, good literature, and the Bible, in the authorized version, were the main sources of developing and maintaining sophistications. The decline of its use on account of its difficult, unfamiliar language was met in part by various translations to make it more accessible and, in part again, to recover lost religious ground. But these translations have removed precisely those cruxes in the authorized version that were a constant learning experience. There could be something especially instructive when discussing in current English the fine points of basic theological doctrines formulated in Elizabethan English in the act of translating out of Alexandrine Greek. Two other points to seal this disquiet: the stress on openness, on transparency, especially when taken with accessibility, leads to the neglect, if not loss, of tact and tonal range; and the extent to—and speed at —which more of life and contacts are coming under the gross efficiency of formulaic language. This flattening of language is propelled by a dynamic that is virtually irresistible. It challenges even literary creativity, that bastion of what was often thought but never so well expressed. Language becomes literature when its life is intensified, expressive, heightened, develops direction and indirection, shifts perspectives, agitates, multifarious, cunning, innocent, striped, loaded, silent, tapping and re-arranging the meaning-potential, and meaning of the half-word, the word, phrase, sentence and paragraph, using all available means—image, metaphor, simile, symbol, punctuation—to articulate and construct. These are gestures of release, of multiplication, of unpacking, of generating that substance and spirit that synonyms gather within their boundaries, the calculus of potential which dictionaries hold between their covers. New permutations, new meanings. It is the immemorial promise of a language to its poets at any given moment, and those yet unborn.

Here is the escalating challenge. There was first the great tradition, British; then there emerged a second big tradition, the American, out of that great tradition, then about the middle of this century, the beginnings of an Indian tradition in English laid down by the fiction of Mulk Raj Anand, Raja Rao, and R. K. Narayan. And the yeast grew, re-colonizing the alphabet. The New Literatures, Contact Literatures, Post-Colonial Literature. One language with many literatures. One language? Yes, but only in their early, imitative phase, when the periphery studied English literature and their poetic spirit was moved to write pseudo Rupert Brooke, Eliottish lines and paragraphs. Literature is usually judged on grounds of style—of the particular work—and significance—such as the power and reach of the underlying vision. Bad style is relatively straightforward to judge. Imitative literature, especially when done well, can only be dismissed on the grounds of style. But what happens when each style, and the style of each poet from Antigua to Zimbabwe, is based on a distinct idiolect, when English has been reshaped and negotiated into the rhythms, the colors, the dictates of their lives? This is a central question to which there are many answers, each of them unique for two main reasons. First, they will reflect particular colonial histories, religious, linguistic, philosophical, social differences we find from country to country, nation to nation. And there are other specific factors that set limits, hedge or energize a writer's vision and work. These include cultural disparities, nationalist sentiments, and linguistic chauvinism, the reach and implications of language planning, the number of languages that move culture and environment.

IV. One of the challenges of adapting English to the flux and curve of an experience generated, in part, by a culture not directly associated with it, is the opportunity we have to test and refine as well as shape the experience. In a sense, bending English to meet our experience is equally the sifting of that experience through English and to achieve a fresh statement both of language and of the experience. A fair example of this is the following image from Gabriel Okara's "One Night At Victoria Beach":

> The wind comes rushing from the sea,
>
> the waves curling like mambas strike
>
> the sands and recoiling hiss in rage
>
> washing the Aladuras' feet pressing hard
>
> on the sand and with eyes fixed hard
>
> on what only hearts can see, they shouting
>
> pray, the Aladuras pray. (Okara, 1978: 28)

The image of the mamba striking is vivid because of both the sound of the waves and the hissing of the snake and the way the snake curls back like waves striking the shore. The image encodes a gesture that propels the language. The strength of poetry depends on the line, especially in the case of free verse, in which the bulk of current poetry is written. In what is perhaps the most extensive study of free verse, Hartman has suggested that verse is "language in lines." This distinguishes it from prose. It is through the line that a poet is able "to create and control attention," but perhaps the most important statement he makes concerns rhythm, which for him "in poetry generally, *seems* more highly organized than in other uses of language . . . *it is the system of rhythmic organization that governs the construction and reading of a poem*" (Hartman 1980: 14). Perhaps Pound and his friends formulated the most famous statement regarding the centrality of the image early this century: "In the spring or early summer of 1912, 'H. D.,' Richard Aldington and myself decided that we were agreed upon the three principles following: 1. Direct treatment of the thing whether subjective or objective. 2. To use absolutely no word that does not contribute to the presentation. 3. As regarding rhythm: to compose in the sequence of the musical phrase, not in sequence of a metronome" (Pound 1960: 3).

Where Raja Rao, Derek Walcott, Gabriel Okara, and others felt the need, or compulsion even, to shape a discourse, the younger writers, the poets especially, do not feel the same necessity. This is chiefly because a significant percentage of the population in most Commonwealth countries no longer see English as a foreign language. They use it freely, without inhibitions.

The finding of an idiolect is something every poet undertakes. For the younger writers, the passing of three to four decades makes this search a more direct one because the tasks that Rao and the others prescribed for themselves have either been successful and/or are no longer matters of any urgency. There is more space for writing. One area is the Internet, which enables anyone who wishes to create a site to post his or her poetry. In Singapore, we have a number of websites. There are those who feel that this freedom has affected the management of words. The rapidity with which poetry is made and released suggests that the computer tends to encourage the easy formulation of language. Poetry becomes more instant. The moving finger types and then moves on. Here are lines from "Outcast":

> Entertainment,
>
> The way people treat you,
>
> Causes you to react in different ways.
>
> You go around people who are nice,
>
> Smile, laugh, and have a good time,
>
> But is there a group that,
>
> Makes you cringe,
>
> To go around and work with.
>
> They are mean.
> CyberPagesPoems poetry post:
> http://www.cyberpages.com/dopoem/newones

There is a certain ease in the reading, a high degree of relaxation that could be taken to suggest a similar ease in the act of composition. What we miss is the intensity, which is one of the marks of poetry. There is insufficient drive in the language, of rhetorical push and energy, of layering. One of the tests of poetry is that it should go beyond the reader's expectations, whether it surprises by 'fine excess,' a 'tough inventiveness,' or 'a powerful and passionate syntax'. There are a limited number of linguistic agencies at work. The language is free of that pressure and tensing which usually marks a search for accuracy and precision. The bulk of contemporary poetry is in free verse. As Eliot reminds us, no verse is free: "*Vers libre* has not even the excuse of a polemic; it is a battle-cry of freedom, and there is no freedom in art. And as the so-called *vers libre* which is good is anything but 'free,' it can be better be defended under some other label"(Eliot 1975: 32).

Eliot makes a distinction between what he sees as free verse and what he sees as images, which from one point of view can be described as free verse subjected to special requirements based on a set of principles that can be found most conveniently in Michael Roberts' *Faber Book of Modern Verse*. A section of a recent poem I wrote refers to the trial of Anwar Ibrahim, the former deputy prime minister of Malaysia. Irrespective of the justness or otherwise of the various legal maneuvers, both the television and the press left viewers and readers uncertain as to where the truth possibly lay.

> The dishes come and go.
>
> We do not talk of Michael Angelo.
>
> As light slips into the sunset, as stars compete.
>
> Conversation
>
> Drifts, casting its loose net, drawing in the insects in the hedge.
>
> Singing the sagas of the land, unfolding Hikkayats,
>
> Some bitterly gripping in their own way.
>
> The Anwar trial;
>
> Silat in the Court;
>
> Tuah and Jebat locked in combat, moving
>
> Through intricate legalities, wanting truth and cleansing.

There are sides and retractions in the sorry business of a trial that has political overtones, particularly in a relatively conservative culture. There is the setting of nature in which we think of such events. And Nature must surely have a capital "N." There are sounds and images that condense the events, that link them on account of their import to any sense of the movements of history. For me, the problem here was how to employ a pair of terms that would resonate powerfully within the discourse of Malaysian history, especially that which deals with those in high places. I struck on two words, *sejara* and *hikayat*, which refer to history and story or legend respectively, for an essential working distinction. To call the proceedings *sejara* would be to suggest the uncertainty mentioned earlier. In a sense, it is time that writes history. The observer of events does not have the advantage of distance, of the facts sorting themselves out as calculated discourse breaks up to break open, and settles to reveal its true character.

All these are part of the act of writing ourselves into the language, English, coloring it with the content, the referential range of our history and experience, and so, possess it. And write our-*selves* out of the British Empire. And write ourselves into a defining profile, an identity that is simultaneously a sense of being restored as a sovereign people, through a constructing liberating literature in English. A literature that draws from the other half of the hyphen, the one rooted in our various cultures, which is a whole dimension I have not considered.

Conclusion. There is none. The imagination is open-ended. So, too, the permutations of our interests, our experiences, and, consequently, the occasions for poetry. We lack external means to sort out the good from the bad, the good from the indifferent. Instead, we exercise judgment or, as some may prefer, preference. And when we exercise either judgment or preference, we do so out of that sense of poetry constructed by our reading, by those poems that are central to how we consider, and receive, new poems; how we visit old ones. There is no central point from which to assess. Or a set of generally accepted—or potentially acceptable—principles and procedures that reader and critic of new literatures in older, ex-colonial languages, to help define a critical, exegetical discourse. The means are there, in much of the theory and theorizing, and in the practice despite its decline. They make for different, potent approaches, but where is the power to secure broad acceptance, a functional authority, and even one that is provisional? Language has been democratized, its installation on a web page quick, inexpensive. In one sense, the virtual banishment of grammar has affected ethnic, psychological and literary salvation, at times under considerable racial and other tensions. We have ceased to fear it, ceased to feel uncertain about its hidden power, which demands time and energy, caution and abandonment, conformity and rebellion, for its release, if not deeper revelation.

This sense of fragmentation and loss is not new. It is implicit in every literary movement; part of the built-in dialects that mark and make up the literary collective of nations. As William Blake reminds us, there is no progression without contraries. He himself judged that in the poetry of his time:

> The languid strings do scarcely move!
>
> The sound is forc'd, the notes are few!

To which I add a longish footnote:

> Muse
>
> You ceased to
>
> Celebrate the incumbent rose;

Or gently spur an evening's twist

Of colors, articulate in repose

Above patches of ritual mist.

You neglect

The power of fevers, inherited dreams;

The layered cunning of a splendid phrase;

Or moonbeams entering iridescent streams

For fishes to brighten their liquid gaze.

You shed deep, continental fires

For a grouchy, chemical sun.

Does every poet who aspires

Let computer programmes run

The anxious syllables of discourse?

Where is up-to-date imagination,

Unbidden, restless, sans remorse?

By ardour, treason, occasional verse,

Its leaping, sudden-wild migration

Takes and manages a universe.

Great singularities fall and split:

You have yielded . . . bit by bit.

Nature is untoward, much ravished;

Re-arranged as symptomatic words.

Environment, esp. when tarnished;

Or endangered, esp. elephant herds;

Threatened whales cruising with unshut eye

As Arnold's *Greenpeace* mermaid weeps

Below our broken, gaping Antarctic sky,

Whose destiny she keeps.

Even full-bodied rhyme is separation,

Not the gathering of meaning . . . clan.

Nor must you think it preparation

Of the child as father of the man.

For trade-and-politics are now the hymns.

We lose mysterious richness, marvelous awe

As GATT, MFN . . . our multiplying acronyms,

Replace redemptive image, metaphor.

Accept, knowing such change is death;

A clear betrayal.

Or passionately burn

To help your tribe recover breath,

And yet another compass, to return.

REFERENCES

Blake, William. 1967. *The portable Blake.* New York: Viking.
Eliot, T. S. 1951. *Selected essays.* London: Faber.
Eliot, T. S. 1965. *To criticize the critic.* London: Faber.
Eliot, T. S. 1975. *Selected prose of T. S. Eliot,* Frank Kermode (ed.). London: Faber.
Graves, Robert. 1946. *Poems: 1938–1945.* London: Cassel.
Hartman, Charles O. 1980. *Free verse.* Princeton, NJ: Princeton University Press.
Kermode, Frank. 1975. *The classic.* London: Faber and Faber.
Maniam, K. S. 1993. *In a far country.* London: Skoob.
Okara, Gabriel. 1963. African Speech . . . English Words, *Transition* 10(3): 15.
Okara, Gabriel. 1978. *The fisherman's invocation.* London: Heinemann.
"Outcast" in *CyberPagesPoems* poetry post: http://www.cyberpages.com/dopoem/newones.
Pound, Ezra. 1960. *Literary essays of Ezra Pound.* T. S. Eliot (ed.). London: Faber.
Ramanujan, A. K. (trans.). 1967. *The interior landscape: Love poems from a classic Tamil anthology.* Bloomington: Indiana University Press.
Rao, Raja. 1938. *Kanthapura.* London: George Allen and Unwin.
Thumboo, E. 1985. Twin perspectives and multi-ecosystems: Tradition for a Commonwealth writer. *World Englishes* 4(2): 213–222.
Thumboo, E. 1996. Notions of National/International: Background Implications for Writer and Critic. *Nationalism vs Internationalism: (Inter)National Dimensions of Literatures in English* 10: 3–14.
Williams, Raymond. n.d. *Writing in society.* London: Verso Editions.
Walcott, Derek. 1972. *Dream on Monkey Mountain and other plays.* London: Jonathan Cape.
Yeats, W. B. 1984. *The poems.* Richard J. Finneran (ed.). London: Macmillan.

What in the world is the World of Language?

Roger Bowers
The World of Language, London

Introduction. This is a talk and a demonstration.[1] I begin by listing a few straightforward questions about language in layman's terms. I will be considering what "public awareness of language" means, and why it matters. Finally, I will briefly describe to you the past, present, and future of the World of Language project.

Some questions about language. For a project in Paris that I will mention again later, and with the inestimable help of David Crystal, we drew up a set of questions that the younger inquirer about language might ask. Here they are. As we go through their deceptive simplicity, I hope you will feel that they touch upon one or other of the many academic and research interests represented here today and with which our fields of theoretical, descriptive, and applied linguistics are concerned.

Language in me
1. How did I learn to talk, and what happens when I talk?
2. How did I learn to write, and what happens when I write?
3. How did I learn to use words, and what words are there to learn?
4. How did I learn to use grammar, and what more is there to learn?
5. Which regional accent/dialect do I speak, and what others are there?
6. Which varieties of language do I know, and what others are there?
7. How can I use language in exciting and enjoyable ways?

Language in my society
8. How did human beings learn to speak?
9. How did human beings learn to write?
10. Where did my language (French, English) come from?
11. How did people sound in olden days?
12. Where has my language travelled in the world?
13. Why can't some people speak or write?
14. How can we teach and learn language?

Language in the world
15. What other languages will I hear in France and the United Kingdom?
16. What other languages will I hear in the European Union?
17. How many languages are there, and where will I find them?
18. How many languages can I learn, and can I try now?
19. Why will I hear so much English around the world?
20. Why are some languages dying, and how can I help?
21. Can I put my speech/writing/sign into the World of Language bank?

With the exception of the last question, which might require a little explanation, I hope the others are patent. I call them deceptively simple because I suspect few members of the general public would be able to answer them satisfactorily. And I suspect we as experts would ourselves argue over the most appropriate means of answering them and probably, as academics, over the phrasing of the questions.

Of course, they are, as a curriculum of enquiry, a simplified version of a much more detailed curriculum that we do not have the time to explore today. But if afterwards you would like to investigate that richer curriculum of language awareness, again drawn up with the assistance of David Crystal and incorporating in its encyclopedic compass five subworlds of language and many paths of individual enquiry, you will find it on the World of Language website at http://www.worldoflanguage.com.

Public awareness of language. Those of you who work in ESP and particularly in English for Science and Technology will have no difficulty in interpreting this phrase by analogy with the considerable effort that has gone into the public understanding of science. We can look at two statements available on the web that demonstrate this. First, a policy statement by the Association for Science Education in the United Kingdom:

> Rationale
>
> Science and technology affect many aspects of daily life. Most industrial and public policies and many private decisions involve science and require informed public debate. The promotion of an improved public understanding of science should, therefore, form a significant part in the teaching of science. Now that Science is a significant part of the curriculum, there is the opportunity to provide all learners with a broad and balanced science curriculum which will lay the foundation of a greater public awareness of science.
>
> Policy
>
> The Association believes in the need to increase the public understanding of science. The world in which we live is highly

technological and scientific. Citizens will increasingly need a knowledge of science if well informed judgments are to be made. The work of the Association in formal and non-formal education can help to make a difference to the overall level of Public Understanding of Science in the community.

http://www.ase.org.uk/policy/puspolf.html

They also present some action points:

taking opportunities to promote Science to parents and others (through activities such as institutional open evenings);

fostering links between science educators and the scientific and industrial communities;

supporting the work of organisations whose primary aim is the public understanding of science;

encouraging members to keep abreast of developments in science;

contributing directly to informal education by, for example, providing a high quality science lecture programme open to the public at the Association's Annual Meeting.

http://www.ase.org.uk/policy/puspolf.html

We find, then, in the case of science, that policy flows into communications and activities and the media across the scientific board. So, for example, the United Kingdom's Biotechnology and Biological Sciences Research Council states on its web site as follows (highly relevant in the present debate concerning GM foods): "Our aim is to promote public awareness, appreciation and understanding of biotechnology and biological sciences; and to address the priority identified by the Technology Foresight exercise to engender widespread understanding of scientific achievements and dispel unwarranted fear of leading-edge possibilities" (http://www.bbsrc.ac.uk/opennet/pus/pus.html). Obviously, there are commercial and political issues here that would need some unpacking, but there are social, commercial, and political issues surrounding language too, though we tend to give little prominence to them.

The "PUS" message comes across well in the aerospace sector, as the example of carefully organized links information from the Sussex Space Science Centre site demonstrates (it goes on for pages; see (http://www/susx.ac.uk/engg/research/space/links.html).

I have to say that we, the communication specialists, still have something to learn from the scientists about how to organize information to an agreed industry standard in a comprehensive, attractive, and accessible way. We are still definitely better at talking to each other than we are at talking to the world outside, including our potential customers.

OK. So we know by analogy what the "public understanding of language" is. But does it matter? Obviously, I am going to say "Yes." And I would add, "particularly in the United Kingdom." There are many reasons but I will cite four: the poor take-up of foreign languages in the curriculum in England and Wales; the centrality of language in the school curriculum; the political role of language; and finally the curiosity factor.

FL take-up. I need not labor the point nor explain the reasons for the poor record of the United Kingdom as a language learning society. The Centre for Information in Language Teaching and Research in London has figures that demonstrate this forcefully (see http://www.cilt.org.uk/). We need to change public and pedagogic attitudes toward modern foreign languages and toward Britain's minority languages if we want to provide a foundation for extending increasingly essential language skills.

Language in the curriculum. Again an area that needs little examination here. Language is ubiquitous in the school curriculum, as it is critical to success at higher levels of education, training, and research. Ted Wragg's "cubic curriculum" sets this out visually, and Wragg (1997: 3) writes, "In this second ('cross-curricular') dimension of the cubic curriculum, language is one of the most vibrant channels. It seeps into every cranny of the other dimensions, the subject curriculum and teaching and learning strategies." He continues:

> Since language lies so close to the heart of learning, it is vital that teachers are not only aware of the issues and principles involved, but that there is deliberate scrutiny of the extent to which children are acquiring, or being confused by, the language they need in particular circumstances. It is also an issue for schools to consider on both an individual and group basis, in that the school's "language climate"—that is, the extent to which all teachers encourage language development—is important, but so is the experience of individual students. (Wragg 1997: 63)

I cannot say to what extent this is reflected here in the United States.

The politics of language. The politics of language have a national and an international dimension, both poorly understood by the general public. There is, of course, the constant issue of multilingualism and respect for language rights within the United Kingdom. For example, there is the plaintive comment by speakers of minority languages that they may speak at least two languages including English fluently but get no credit for it, whereas an exam pass in rudimentary French is seen as really "learning a language."

More potent at present is the poorly recorded role of language in major political events elsewhere. Take Kosovo, for example, where the Balkan predicament is reflected in the linguistic fragmentation of the region, itself a potent marker of social division and antagonism. I have seen nothing in the papers that talks about the languages of the region, either as part of the problem or as part of the means of explaining the distribution of and relationship between communities. Yet it is all there on the web: on Ethnologue, for example, and on a general interest site, which you can get to via the Linguist List on the UCL site, that simply shows us how to count up to 10 in 3000 languages. An amazingly personal experience.

Personal curiosity and press coverage. Language and language issues get very little coverage at all in the newspapers, of course, except in the sense of crosswords and word games. You need only look at the Sunday papers to find technology everywhere in the news items, the business pages, the lifestyle supplements, and the ads. Not so language.

Yet language does interest people, and it is newsworthy. Look at the success of word games on the television, and of *Reader's Digest* over the decades, or highly popular joke cards like this one:

I know you believe you understand

what you think I said, but what you

don't realize is that what you heard

is not what I meant.

So there is curiosity about language —enough to build on—provided, unlike the builders of the Tower of Babel, we speak the same language ourselves. So much then for the need to work for a greater visibility and a better public understanding of what language is and what language does. Where does technology come into this agenda? Well, it comes, of course, as an important element in both the medium and the message.

In terms of public awareness, inevitably, technology is streets ahead of language. It has the websites. It has the press coverage. It has the physical presence. And it has the investment. For websites, for instance, we need only look again at the Sussex Science site earlier and follow it into its tour of the nine planets—let us say, to Jupiter. What would our analogy be in language for that voyage of discovery?

However, by the physical presence of technology I don't mean just that technology has, by definition, to do with hardware as well as software and is therefore tangible in a way that language (by and large, and apart from the book) is not. It is that science and technology have also created their shrines here in Washington and in many centers all over the world. But for language we have no single physical presence, unless we interpret every library as a shrine of language.

This is where I want to introduce the World of Language project, at what for the project is a decisive point. First some history, then some impressions, then some content.

The World of Language. The World of Language emerged as a bright idea in 1996. Looking for a focus for a British Council Millennium project, we came up with the notion of a "museum of language." We discussed whether this should be English or language per se and opted to avoid triumphalism. We considered funding and went for a millennium grant from the government, to be matched by sponsorship funding. We considered location and identified a site in Southwark, on the banks of the Thames adjacent to Shakespeare's Globe, redolent with symbolism and in a richly multicultural and multilingual environment. We held workshops and we developed a concept and a curriculum. David Crystal created our language curriculum. We looked at technology and design and educational mission. We investigated markets and other aspects.

We did not get through the millennium grant process, although we had a website, promotional literature in place, and an idea with miles to run. In 1998 we responded to a request from Paris—the wonderful Cité des Sciences et de l'Industrie at Parc de la Villette—for a reduced version of our concept as part of their millennium display. We revised our curriculum and brought our space requirement down from 4,000 to 650 m^2. Again with the support of the British Council, we ran a design competition and came up with revised concepts. The winning design was not The World of Language but Language City. Again, lots of ideas, a guaranteed location and audience—but still no money!

Which brings us to where we are now. We have a mission. We have a curriculum, writ large and small (with options). We have a website (which needs some TLC). We have a mailing list—in sixty-seven countries. We have no money. And we wonder if this is the point where we stop lusting after the concrete and espouse the virtual. Perhaps we should aim for product rather than presence. Go for a virtual, not a concrete, site. And our product would be "PUL"—assisting the public understanding of language internationally, and within the United Kingdom, by providing a rational and attractive environment for a range of language-related resources. The process would be online technology. The audience would be whoever wants to visit.

I have deliberately not associated our initiative with U.S. concerns. I do not know enough about them. I do know that many of our mailing list members live and work in the United States and ask us the same kinds of questions and find the same kinds of things interesting as our United Kingdom and international members.

A similar initiative is under discussion in the United States. We must wait to see who gets there first!

REFERENCES

Wragg E C. 1997. *The cubic curriculum.* London: Routledge.
Websites, in order of presentation
http://www.ase.org.uk/policy/puspolf.html
http://www.bbrsc.ac.uk/opennet/pus/pus.html
http://www.susx.ac.uk/engg/research/space/links.html
http://gillett.connect-2.co.uk/eap/
http://gillett.connect-2.co.uk/eap/linksfram.htm
http://www.sil.org/ethnologue/
http://www.sil.org/ethnologue/countries/
http://www.zompist.com/numbers.shtm/euro.htm#ie
http://seds.lpl.arizona/edu/nineplanets/noneplanets/jupiter.html
http://www.mda.org.uk/vlmp
http://www.liv.ac.uk/~ms2928/ala/
http://www.languagelearn.co.uk/
http://www.baal.org.uk/
http://www.baleap.org.uk/
http://www.cilt.org.uk/www/projects/projects.htm
http://www.cilt.org.uk/www/projects/lingunet.htm
http://www.iatefl.org/
http://clwww.essex.ac.uk/LAGB
http://www.britcoun.org
http://www.tesol.edu
http://www.us-english.org/index.html
http://www.indigo.ie/egt/udhr/udlr-en.htm
http://www.worldoflanguage.com
http://www.rdg.ac.uk/globe/Globe.html
htp://www.worldoflanguage.com/links.cfm

NOTE.

1.   This talk was illustrated with visuals of website pages. The addresses are listed at the end.

World or International or Global English—and what is it anyway?

Tom McArthur
English Today, Cambridge University Press

At the end of the twentieth century, there has been growing worldwide discussion, especially among academics, educationists, and journalists, about the use and nature of English—or, more specifically, about "English as a world language"—or "English as an international language" (often abbreviated as EIL)—or "English as a global language"—or more simply "World English" (with or without a capital W)—or "International English" (with or without a capital I and sometimes abbreviated as IE)—or "Global English" (with or without a capital G)—or indeed simply "Global." Or, again, I could pluralize everything and talk as Braj Kachru and others have done since the late 1970s about such entities as "the Englishes," "the New Englishes," and most importantly "World Englishes" (abbreviated as WE, so as to carry also the implication "we," all of us together as equals, no one excluded). Or, again, I could propose "the English languages," treating the whole of this vast language complex as a family, like the Romance languages or the Turkic languages, whose members are sometimes mutually intelligible and sometimes not (McArthur 1998).

Not that the matter stops there. Because of the need to be ever more specific and explicit, a range of additional terms are currently widely used, such as "World Standard English" (or "Standard World English") and "International Standard English" (or Standard International English"), which perhaps label the same entity, or perhaps don't. In addition, as a result of further efforts to be clear and precise, such terms have been coined as "World Spoken Standard English," "World Written Standard English," "World Standard Printed English," "International Spoken Standard English," "International Written Standard English," and an "international print standard" (for English). All of these in turn contrast with a wider range of lesser territorial terms such as "African English," "West African English," "African American Vernacular English," "West African Pidgin English," "British Standard Written English," "Canadian Standard Spoken English," "South East Asian English," and "Singapore Colloquial English." Dozens of such terms are now in use, as can be seen in any issue of the journals *English World-Wide* (formerly edited by Manfred Görlach, currently by Edgar Schneider, and published by John Benjamins, Amsterdam and Philadelphia), *World Englishes* (edited by Braj Kachru and Larry Smith, and published by Basil Blackwell, Oxford), and my own *English Today* (published by Cambridge University Press).

"World English" appears to be the oldest of the more general terms. It appears to date from just before the Second World War (to use the name favored in Britain) or World War II (as Americans usually call it). A brief aside at this point: In world or international or global English, these two terms—*Second World War* and *World War II*—may well be equal but are unevenly, indeed uncertainly, distributed. This is no small point, because differences between the two main world varieties, American and British, can be tricky matters, and one of the issues attending the idea of an international or a world English is just how the many American and British variants do, or can, or should operate side by side in global terms: Are all such sets of words and phrases currently commensurate beyond the United States and the United Kingdom—as in this instance where both phrases are transparent and pretty well known to everybody? Or are they not at all commensurate beyond the United Kingdom and United States, but marked as socioculturally distinct—for example, all the *curbs/kerbs, pavements, highways, motorways, freeways, interstates, turnpikes, toll roads,* and the like? Could all the easily exchangeable terms become free variants for non-Americans and non-Brits while the Brits and Yanks remain more or less constrained to stick to their own words? Or are Americanisms simply winning out internationally—the phrasal verb "winning out" being, as far as I can tell, itself an Americanism that has already won (out)? American English is, after all, the immense primary engine of English today.

The aim of this paper is to look at two linked issues. My key concern is the emergence for the first time ever of an authentically universal language that is also natural and historical and beset by all kinds of sociocultural pluses and minuses, in contrast, for example, to Esperanto, which is artificial, was deliberately designed for just this role, and is generally considered neutral among all the world's contending languages and cultures (although this may not in fact be so). My second concern is the names we are currently giving to this natural historical universal language in all its diversity or to the subset that we think of as "standard." I have taken these names first, however, because their very abundance and range can tell us a great deal about the phenomenon at large and about the sociocultural positions of the people who create and use them, because all such names are psycholinguistically charged. They are not innocent.

The primary name, *World English,* has been with us long enough to get into some dictionaries, but only in the last decade, and only —as far as I know—in Oxford. In the second edition of the *Oxford English Dictionary* (1989), under the entry *world,* the phrase *world English* [with a lowercase *w*] is glossed simply as "Standard English" (full stop, or period). However, in the *New Shorter Oxford Dictionary* (1993), also under *world,* the subentry runs: *"World English* [now with a capital *W*] a variety of, or the fundamental features of, English regarded as standard or acceptable wherever English is spoken." Most recently, the *New Oxford Dictionary of English* (1998) gives the phrase an entry to itself, which runs: *"world English* [lowercase *w*] the English language including all of its regional varieties, such as North American, Australian, New Zealand, and South African English; a basic form of English, consisting of features common to all regional varieties." In these successive senses we see, as it were, the slow-motion opening of a verbal flower with two intertwined senses: the term *World English* has been used both for all English everywhere and for a common-core or nuclear English that is found within all Englishes everywhere: two very different things indeed.

Just over thirty years ago, in 1967, an article of mine titled "World English" was published in *Opinion* magazine, Bombay, India. In it, I used the term to mean all English everywhere, whatever its form (i.e., Oxford Sense 1), and I did not think for a moment then that it could refer to common-core English (Oxford Sense 2), and I don't recall ever meeting it in this sense. Much later, about ten years ago, I described *world English* in the *Oxford Companion to the English Language* (1992) as "an increasingly common term for English as a world language," adding the comment: "Some scholars use the term cautiously or avoid it, because for them it suggests a global dominance by English and English-speaking countries, with an attendant down-grading of other languages." That seems to me still to be, by and large, the terminological truth about the phrase *world English,* but I would be glad to hear from others on this subject, because I may have to define it again in due course.

The term *international English* appears to date from around 1980. In the *Companion,* my definition was: "The English language, usually in its standard form, either when used, taught, and studied as a lingua franca throughout the world, or when taken as a whole and used in contrast with *American English, British English, South African English,* etc., as in *International English: A Guide to Varieties of Standard English,* title of a work by Peter Trudgill and Jean Hannah (1982) that reviews both standard and non-standard varieties worldwide."

However, this implication of "standardness" in the phrase *international English*—which seems to me to be lacking in the phrase *world English*—can be usefully checked against the following extract from Lise Winer's paper "Intelligibility of Reggae Lyrics in North America" (1990). She says there, discussing a local and a wider English: "The relationship . . . is very complex, owing to the perception that Jamaican and standard international English are not really that different." Winer makes the standardness of a certain global kind of English explicit here, a kind of English which for her is as real as Jamaican English, and not something that might (or might not) some day be real. Here, her *standard international English* seems to me to be strictly synonymous with the other fairly common expression *standard world English,* both terms referring to one and the same contemporary reality.

The buzz term of the later 1990s has, however, been "global English," which belongs in a cluster of usages that relate fairly clearly to *globalization,* a term associated with both a new borderless economic world order and Marshall McLuhan's phrase "the global village": We are all global villagers now and English is the medium of that village: no argument. One of the most prominent works to adopt this and comparable phrases has been David Crystal's *English as a Global Language* (1997), which makes liberal use of all three words (*global, world,* and *international*), as in:

- I have thus tried to tell the story of World English [capital *W*] objectively and without adopting the kind of triumphalist tone which is unfortunately all too common when people write on English in English. (p. viii)
- Even if the New Englishes did become increasingly different, as years went by, the consequences for world English [lowercase *w*] would not necessarily be fatal. (p. 136)
- How far back do we have to go in order to find the origins of global English? [lowercase *g*]. (p. 25)
- English has long been recognized as the international language of the sea." (p. 97)
- English—with all its failings—remains the recommended language of international air travel. (p. 101)

Although Crystal uses "global" in the title and the body of this book, he seems not to be sold on it as a basic technical term: rather, he uses "international" as a handy general term but opts in the end for the following: "A likely scenario is that our current ability to use more than one dialect [of English] would simply extend to meet the fresh demands of the international situation. A new form of English—let us think of it as "World Standard Spoken English" (WSSE)—would almost certainly arise. Indeed, the foundation for such a development is already being laid around us" (pp. 136–137). So we can note that for Winer something like WSSE has been here for some time; for Crystal it is still in the process of establishing itself.

Michael Toolan, another British Anglicist, has taken a rather different tack in his article "Recentering English: New English and Global" (1997). Here he offers us not one but two distinct terms: *New English,* to cover "the English used in mainstream public discourse in countries where English is a major native language," and *Global,* to cover "the public international English used by globetrotting professionals, the only kind of English which is beginning to be truly globally dispersed."

Toolan's primary point is that "with the spread of Global, and as a result of changed attitudes to New English, these two standard Englishes are increasingly treated not as Anglo-Saxon and metropolitan properties, found by or shared with others, but as resources owned by larger constituencies of users. . . . In the case of Global, its non-English majority of users are increasingly claiming ownership of it." An important second point for Toolan is that the mainstream usage of the traditional Anglophone countries has changed in at least one marked respect: it is "more democratized, and is conceptualized as a joint stock enterprise in which we are all invested stakeholders" (a description that uses an economic metaphor popular with the New Labour party of the British Prime Minister Tony Blair rather than the unfettered free-marketeering and globalizing style of the Reagan-Thatcher heritage).

At the end of the day, however, while stressing the enormous role of technological change in the spread and consolidation of some kind of worldwide English, Toolan considers that the phenomenal spread of English is "a kind of linguistic counterpart of the global spread of Microsoft" and therefore "is simply a banal fact": it's there—live with it. It is also for him a banal fact that non-native users of the language now greatly outnumber its native users. For Toolan, as an Englishman of Irish descent (as indeed for me as a Scot), names matter, and "Global" without "English" has a certain appeal; yet it seeks an inclusiveness that would, if adopted (even with the best of intentions in the world) consign the proud and ancient name of this vast linguistic phenomenon to an Orwellian memory hole. Toolan's is a challenging and intriguing approach, and I know others who with similar excellent intentions have wished to re-name English, but this is probably the least likely of all the options open to us.

I am currently engaged in writing a book for Oxford University Press, the fourth in a series that began with the *Oxford Companion to the English Language,* which was followed by an abridged edition in 1996 and a concise updating edition in 1998. This fourth book will describe the current condition of the English language (or languages) continent by continent. It will be a guide this time rather than a companion, and I would have liked to call it *The Oxford Guide to International English,* following in the tradition of Trudgill and Hannah's *International English* (above). Oxford, however, already knew what they wanted: it would be *The Oxford Guide to World English*: no further discussion. For them this was a snappier, more comprehensive term, because the book does indeed deal with every conceivable kind of English. So I conceded the point as gracefully as I could, since I had no choice anyway: the marketeers knew what they wanted.

In the meantime, Oxford has brought out its *New Oxford Dictionary of English* (*NODE,* which they cheerfully pronounce as "Noddy"). Their publicists notably describe Noddy as both "the first dictionary of English as a world language" and "the first genuinely international dictionary of English," and only just fail to call it a dictionary of *World English.* However, an even newer but very non-Oxford dictionary was published in August 1999, masterminded in London by the publishers Bloomsbury (in Soho Square), who marketed the British version while St Martin's Press in New York brought out the American version, each edition putting its own variants first wherever appropriate. I'm told that half a million copies of the first edition have been printed, a truly formidable print run, but more significant than this (and something that is entirely missing from "Noddy") is the parallel electronic version, which is entirely controlled by Microsoft. As a result, both the paper and the electronic versions are entitled (British), titled (American) *The Encarta World English Dictionary* to match Microsoft's *Encarta Encyclopedia.* I am credited in this work as its adviser for *World* English, and my approach in it has been traditional: that is, to treat "World English" as meaning all English everywhere, standard and nonstandard.

So, it would appear that if one is aiming at the general, the familiar, the established, and the comprehensive, then *World English* is the choice. If a loftier term with an egalitarian pedigree, good social intentions, and a suggestion of standardness is desired, then *International English* is the choice. And if one has climbed on board the free-market bandwagon or wants to focus on McLuhan's universal village or wants to get away from the mild authoritarianism of *world* and the receding socialist echoes of *international,* then it will be *global.* Yet, although the general tendency favors *World English,* there is a curious idiosyncrasy about the phrase. American publishers of English-language materials, it seems, tend to contrast the *American editions* with the *World English* editions of some of their products; in this, the United States is perceived as not only not part of the world, but the "global" edition is likely to be given British conventions, because that is apparently what the publishers think the rest of the world expects. This seems odd and out of step, because (as I noted earlier) the engine that powers World English is American. (This rather puzzles me, and I would be glad to have some hard information on this practice.)

As regards the entity or entities that these competing terms refer to, three factors seem to be crucial: the relationship of English to other languages worldwide; the difference between Standard English and other Englishes; and the question of whether there is or can be a universal standard, and how such an entity might relate to the territorial standards we already know.

The ecological concept of the *pecking order* seems to me to be useful in considering the hard realities of language wherever we go. There is and probably always has been a pecking order of languages and within languages a pecking order of dialects. So-called "world languages" such as Arabic, Babylonian, French, Greek, Latin, Mandarin Chinese, Russian, Sanskrit, and Spanish have at various times and in various places headed distinctive regional and even continental pecking orders, and for at least three centuries English has occupied such a position, steadily spreading and consolidating to the exclusion at this time of all other languages on a planet-wide basis. The potential for love-hate relationships, for triumphalism and resentment, and for adulation and rejection is vast.

Such terms as *standard, non-standard,* and *substandard, acrolect, mesolect,* and *basilect,* and even *language of wider communication, world language,* and *international language* relate and refer to matters like these, and while they are useful, they should not be used as ways of palliating or ignoring reality. There are imbalances, inequities, and downright injustices in matters of language and communication, whether they are perceived as hegemonist or imperialist or racist or classist or sexist or linguicist or all of the above. A case can easily be made for, if not worldwide language planning, then certainly an accredited public dialogue regarding language and communication worldwide, so that a consensus can be found for handling everything from the languages that are too powerful to the languages that are so weak that they will cease to exist next year or a decade from now or maybe stagger on into the middle of the next century.

One of the curious features of language contact, past and present, is the degree of hybridization that takes place in multilingual settings. This was true for English in the British Isles, when it ran up against the Celtic languages in Scotland, Ireland, Wales, Cornwall, and the Isle of Man—unfortunately, to the great detriment of those languages. That initial process is now planet wide, as world or international or global English interacts with innumerable other tongues, producing what I call the *Anglo-hybrids,* with such suspect, humorous yet picturesque and accurate names as Frenglish or *français,* Spanglish or *englañol,* Gerlish or *Engleutsch,* Italglish or *itangliano,* and Japlish or *wasei-eigo* ("Made-in-Japan English"). It is far more natural or normal in the world to be multilingual than to be monolingual, and part of that naturalness is and has always been the creation of fertile and fluid hybrids. Indeed, present-day English is the outcome of just such massive disruption in the past, and within it the disruption continues as strongly as ever. Our sense of what "World English" is and what it might become, I suggest, will—and should—be colored as much by its interplay with other languages as by the application of norms from within which might seek to make its most prestigious international standard variety less flexible and absorptive, and less able in its turn to pass words and concepts on to other tongues. I confess though that I don't lose much sleep over that prospect.

Not that clarity and consistency aren't virtues in appropriate situations, as for example in an international airport or on the Internet; yet even here we find chaos as often as we find order. In this regard I would like to mention in closing the observations of Marko Modiano of Gävle University in Sweden, in his appropriately (en)titled article "International English in the Global Village" (1999). The term he uses throughout this piece is "English as an international language" (*EIL* for short), and his main assertion is that the native users of English (including especially its multitudes of non-standard speakers) can no longer be regarded as the owners and arbiters of the world's key language: "I would argue," he says, "that the proficient non-native speakers of EIL, rather than the native speakers who are not proficient in EIL, are better equipped to define and develop English as a tool in cross-cultural communication. . . . A variety is defined by speakers of the variety. A *lingua franca* by definition is not geographically restricted."

One notes here immediately that Modiano's EIL is separated out from the larger mass (presumably of world English in all its diversity), which makes it pretty much like Toolan's "Global": a standard-driven variety with a specific high-level globetrotting role. In Modiano's argument I sense the frustration of a competent non-native language professional who is finally saying what he feels must be said—and said *now*. There is a certain elitism behind what he says, but we should accept—gladly or grimly, but accept—that there has always been an inherent elitism (even a necessary and perhaps a humane elitism) in the idea of a standard language, and what Modiano is talking about is certainly Standard World English (or whatever other name we may elect to give it). I invited a number of established commentators on English worldwide to reply to Modiano's paper, and their thoughtful, varied, and cogent responses appear after his article in the same issue of *ET*. Also in that issue, David Crystal has an article, "The future of Englishes," which he begins with a deceptively simple sentence: "The pace is hotting up." It is indeed.

REFERENCES

Crystal, David. 1997. *English as a global language.* Cambridge: Cambridge University Press.
Crystal, David. 1999. The future of Englishes. *English Today* 58 (April).
McArthur, Tom. 1998. *The English languages.* Cambridge: Cambridge University Press.
Modiano, Marko. 1999. International English in the global village. *English Today* 58 (April).
Toolan, Michael. 1997. Recentering English: New English and global. *English Today* 52 (October).
Trudgill, Peter, and Jean Hannah. 1982. *International English: A guide to varieties of Standard English.* London: Edward Arnold.
Winer, Lise. 1990. Intelligibility of Reggae Lyrics in North America. *English World-Wide* 2: 1.

Multilingualism and intellectual property: Visual holophrastic discourse and the commodity/sign

Ronald Scollon[1]
Georgetown University

Signs of the times. Rosemary Coombe (1998) has pointed out recently that our lives and therefore our day-to-day ordinary discourses are penetrated through and through with the use of what she calls the "commodity/sign." I write this on a Dell®, which is running on a Pentium® II processor using Windows® 98. Dell® is a legal trademark and both Pentium® and Windows® are registered words but oddly enough not II or 98, or at least not just yet. The February 1999 issue of *Harper's* tells us that the numerical sequence 01-01-00® has been registered as a trade name and cannot be used in commercial products without permission of, and no doubt payment of licensing fees to, the owner. The joke went around on the Internet a couple of years ago that Bill Gates had registered the digits '0' and '1' as that was the semiotic basis for the codes on which his—and our—computers run.

As Coombe has noted, our discourses are saturated with the logos, brand names, shop signs, and other registered properties of the worldwide commercial and commodified economy. "Pass me a Kleenex®"; "Is your computer IBM® or Apple® format?" What I am interested in here is not the question of how these commodity/signs bring with them into our daily discourses the formative legal structures of our society, though that is an issue I think of central significance. Rather, I am interested in the way in which these commodity/signs are restructuring our very notion of what language is and how it works.

In the short space I have here I can only hope to illustrate my point, not argue it with very solid evidence. I start with a variety of photos of shop signs taken here and there around the world. With nothing but the photos to work with it might be rather difficult to locate most of the signs within a national/linguistic/cultural space. While the English "Apollo Electronics" is found in Los Angeles and Spanish "Iberia" is found in Barcelona, the English "ABC" labels a building in Tokyo, the French "Collage" is a business in Stockholm, and the mixed code "LIQUOR SHOP Marumata" is a business in Japan.

One cannot very easily associate the national languages, English, French, Italian, and the like with the country of display. In my study I found that the English "Trend Corner" is in Zürich, the mixed French/English "La Ferme Fondue

Room" (without accent markers) is in Montreux, and I don't really know what language to say "Alaska" is in. While it has lost its Aleut heritage for all but a few linguists, it appears in a sign displayed in Liège.

In still other cases "Underwood" is where it belongs, in London, and "dal Marinaio" might be acceptable in Rome—I don't actually know. "Question" is in Yokohama, "Sport" is in Germany, "deco d'or" is also in Germany. Perhaps the truly transnational "Mobby" could not be any place but Shinjuku, Tokyo, and "SEARS" is okay in Honolulu. "Douglas" and "Chorizo," however, do not signal either an English-speaking country or a Spanish-speaking one, as they are both in Germany.

These examples are themselves found in an interesting transnational and multilingual space. They appear in a book titled *Marks—Logos,* first published by Graphic-sha Publishing Company in Tokyo (1993) and republished in China in 1995. The book describes itself in the only extended text it gives on page 4 where it says,

> This book is a collection of photos of marks and logos found in different streets in the world, and is intended to serve as a design source to refer to by those who wish to make a successful sign or facade of a shop or office in an area or street whose environment is becoming increasingly comfortable.

> The book covers about 1,200 cuts of cubic and plane signboards which mainly use letters and marks, facades of buildings having such signboards, and also road or public facility signs which may be applied to shops or offices, by classifying them according to style, theme, and so on. Types of business and name of location where photos were taken are also added as data.

> It is recommended to refer to the book when planning or designing a sign or shop.

> It is requested that you inform us of any interesting sign found in the street. We would like to refer to it when editing the next book. Either a sign recommended by yourself or any other is acceptable.

While the book consists, as it says, of 1,200 glossy photos of logos and signs, many or perhaps most of which are protected by copyright in their home legal jurisdictions, the book itself shows no indication of having secured permission for glossy reproduction. In fact, as the text above suggests, the entire purpose of the book is to facilitate possibly illegal reproduction of these signs for those who would like to make their streets "increasingly comfortable."

We would probably all agree that these are examples of contemporary multi-lingualism. But naming these signs by such national languages this way deeply obscures the problem. I would argue that "Collage" is no longer a French word, at least not when it is displayed as the name of a fashion boutique in Stockholm. Likewise "Douglas," "chorizo," "deco d'or," "Sears," and "Mobby" have been wrenched free of their linguistic and cultural history and recontextualized within a transnational discourse of the commercial enterprise. I have purified my examples here a good bit as well, but perhaps I should not have done that, because in many cases in this same book and in the world around us we have simultaneous multilingualism. That is, we have French simultaneously together with Japanese, English with German, Chinese with Italian.

The argument I want to develop here, then, is that there is a deep prejudice that runs through our understanding of multilingualism. The prejudice is toward taking "language" to mean one of the world's mostly national (at least originally) named languages—English, German, French, Chinese, Japanese, Italian. I will argue that instances of multilingualism such as the signs and logos just mentioned make the idea of national languages difficult to maintain, at least in the transnational discourses of the production and sale of commodities.

I also want to argue that it is probably more important to think about the corporate ownership of these utterances than it is to try to identify their national or historical provenience. And that will lead to the corollary argument that in such highly commodified discourses there are very important new players—the corporations who own these commodity signs (Coombe 1998) and the nation states that authorize their use through copyright and patent protection. In other words, I want to argue that it is probably more important that SONY® belongs to the Sony Corporation than it is to identify which language SONY® is a word in.

That, of course, will lead to my conclusion: that there is a certain kind of discourse that I have termed *"visual holophrastic discourse,"* which amounts to company signs, logos, slogans, trademarks, and all the rest of the commodity/sign apparatus of our contemporary globalized world. This visual holophrastic discourse seems to be setting up shop by defining new language uses, new concepts of what language is, and ultimately what it means to be multilingual as the world makes the turn into the third millennium.

What is multilingualism these days? Is "SONY" a word in English, Japanese, Dutch, or whatever other language is the home language of the product user? What about "NOKIA?" For some years the Finnish company was quite happy to have people believe that their Finnish name was really Japanese as the company thought that might give them a bit of technological edge over their clearly Scandinavian rival "Ericcson."

In a way the sort of question I am raising here is a relatively "new" problem, a problem caused by the nationalizing of language and political life—one might say the nationalizing of political life through language—during this "modern" period of the nation state. Some years ago Ivan Illich (1981) pointed out that not only did Spain expel the Moors in the prototype ethnic cleansing in 1492, and not only did they push Columbus off from European shores to go discover what he would label the "redskins" that same year, but Queen Isabella entertained a proposal from Ilio Antonio de Nebrija to accept his dictionary and grammar of what he called "Castillano" as the official language of Spain as the way to consolidate the political purity of the nation.

Anderson (1991) attributes the development of the nation state to the forces of print capitalism during this same period and, like Billig (1995), argues that an essential aspect of the control and consolidation of the nation state has been the production of the idea of matching up particular languages and particular nation states, preferably in a way that the name of the state and the name of the language are the same or similar: England/English, Spain/Spanish, Italy/Italian, Germany/German, France/French, Japan/Japanese, and China/Chinese. Of course, America or the United States have had trouble in this regard in having to make do with a language named after the old colonial nation that seems to be an embarrassment to this day.

The sort of multilingualism we have come to talk about in not only our general public discourses but also in linguistics, applied linguistics, education, and a number of other academic discourses is largely this modernist, nationalist sort of multilingualism that is continually being mixed together with national politics and even very rough notions of national cultures. I follow both Anderson and Billig in taking it that this equation is not the natural state of language in the world; it is relatively new—even in the oldest of the modern nations it does not date back more than five centuries, and in some such as Italy it is really quite recent, and that it is an idea that directly or indirectly is implicated in the production of political entities and power relationships.

If we do take that point of view, however, what might "multilingualism" mean if we challenge the essentially modernist/nationalist ideology embedded in contemporary notions of language? I would think the most productive reimagining of language we are undertaking in the present period was stimulated by the writings of Bakhtin, but I would also like to remember that there is much in Bakhtin for which Sapir would have found much empathy (Mannheim and Tedlock 1995). Gee, Fairclough, and many others of our contemporaries who are engaged in the reimagining of language point to polyvocality, intertextuality, and interdiscursivity of practice as the key organizing themes (Gee 1999; Fairclough 1992; Chouliaraki and Fairclough 1999). Rather than seeing *a language* as a count noun indicating a large, structured semiotic system with relatively clear boundaries between it and other such systems, these scholars see *language* as a mass noun like mud, air, or whisky for that matter, which freely flows through spaces.

From this point of view the phenomenon of interest is what Bakhtin called "social languages" rather than national languages as the relevant category of interest. These social languages, or what Gee has called "discourses," Foucault and Fairclough have called "orders of discourse" or "discursive formations" might be thought of as the containers that have scooped up mixtures, bits, and pieces of *language* to accomplish particular agendas, to produce particular group memberships and identities, and to do the work of producing social practice in communities of practice. What is crucial in talking about the social language or discourse of medicine, for example, is not whether the doctor is speaking in English, German, or Japanese so much as that he or she is speaking within a framing social language of medicine.

Following this out, then, I would argue that if there is a problem of multilingualism, it is not that people speak or fail to speak multiple national languages. It is that the discourses and social practices of a particular social language—medicine, law, heavy equipment operation, sports training, vegetable selling—are interdiscursively interpenetrated with other social languages. The social languages of medicine, for example, become interpenetrated with the social languages of business. As medical professionals shift from trying to develop the "most effective treatment" to the "most cost-effective treatment," we observe the interpenetration of social practices of the treatment of illness by the social practices of cost effectiveness (Musson and Cohen 1996). I would argue that this sort of interdiscursivity among the social languages of our life worlds is of more central theoretical and more crucial social urgency than identifying whether the relevant diagnoses are conducted in English or German, French, or Japanese. I would also want to push this a bit further and say that, in fact, to address the question of the commodification of our life worlds by globalizing business and governmental enterprises, the reification of languages as national, countable entities serves the function of distraction from these more crucial contemporary social issues.

What is intellectual property? For my purposes there are two areas of intellectual property that are of interest to us as people who study language, the ownership of texts, about which I will only say a little, and the ownership of commodity/signs. There is much more to intellectual property than this, of course. When the United States engages in negotiations with China on questions of intellectual property, the primary concern is not with whether Chinese scholars are giving proper citations in their academic papers. Their concerns tend to focus on computer software, Hollywood movies, and brand-named commercial products, although the list of categories can be quite long and usually includes such items as television and video, film, music, software, CD-ROMs, books, trademarks, new plant species, and integrated circuits.

I am interested, first of all, in ownership of text—citation and attribution. This is because much of our concept of intellectual property was formed around the problem of protecting literary works and so continues to bear the stamp of what might well be outmoded concerns. But also I am concerned with ownership of text in the form of practices for citation and attribution, or to use Fairclough's (1992) term, which I prefer, "discourse representation," because other research I have done shows that the practices for discourse representation vary across social languages as the domain of their operation, not from language to language. I will return to this issue shortly.

I am also interested in commodity/signs (Coombe 1998), both because the rapidly strengthening centrality of commodity/signs in our day-to-day discourses is bringing about major changes in the ways we understand language and because we can see in the use of commodity/signs the intrusion into our daily discourses the power of the corporate owner to shape these discourses far beyond the expected realms of retail sales of consumer products.

Polyvocality, intertextuality, interdiscursivity, and ownership of text. To take up the first point for a moment, the first development of copyright law in the form of the Statute of Anne in 1710 was aimed not at protecting authors against the theft of their works so much as it was aimed at protecting publishers in London against authors the likes of John Milton. It was feared that he and others might take their *Paradise Lost*s up to Scotland, where the feared pirate printers were, and have competing versions printed that were similar enough to the original to undercut the sales of the London publishers (Patterson 1968).

My point here is not to focus on the history of copyright and patent law, but to call attention to the fact that among academics there is a certain kind of contemporary historical reconstruction going on that assumes that the point of copyright is to protect the wordings of individual authors from uncited use by others. This tends to be what we teach our students and what we are so concerned about if they don't seem to be getting it. Elsewhere we have argued that we tend to confound several essentially separable issues. We tend to use the legal issue of copyright to give rhetorical force to what are really ethical or moral issues of plagiarism (Scollon in press). And these issues, both legal and moral, are to a considerable extent covers for what amounts to power positioning. We use moral injunctions against plagiarism and legal threats to position "ourselves" on a moral high ground, particularly in respect to non-academics and to academics who are located outside some inner circle of correct behavior.

At this juncture in talking about plagiarism it is always amusing to point out that there are serious inconsistencies in our academic behavior. Stanford University, like most of our universities, has a booklet for students on the evils of plagiarism. This booklet was itself plagiarized lock, stock, and barrel by the University of Oregon according to Mallon (1989).

In a post-Bakhtinian world we have become acutely aware of the high degrees of intertextuality, polyvocality, and interdiscursivity among, within, and across texts. What is most surprising about the Oregon plagiarism is the genuine lack of surprise. Of course, handbooks, memos, university documents—both internal and external—will be shot through with boilerplate text taken from whatever source is handy. In this we begin to see the relatively narrow scope of our outrage over plagiarism.

In another research project I found that if we compare academic writing, writing in journalism, and writing in advertisements, we find that these three quite distinct communities of practice are distinguished from each other among other ways by their practices for discourse representation (Scollon forthcoming). Academic citation practices use a relatively wide variety of means of discourse representation from direct and indirect quotation to paraphrase, presupposition, and negation. Although there is much variation across academic disciplines, with historians using the highest levels of direct quotation and psychologists almost never directly quoting, throughout the broad community of practice there is a stance taken by the writing author or authors that they are placing themselves within an ongoing discourse as one of a group of conversationalists. Key issues for the academic are the personal integrity and believability of his or her utterances, which are indicated to a great extent through careful acknowledgment of the sources of borrowed texts.

This positioning of the academic within a dialogic or conversational discourse through discourse representation I found to be very different from the positioning of the journalist in relationship to the texts he or she represents. Journalistic discourse uses a very limited number of means of discourse representation by comparison with academic writing. Direct and indirect quotation are the most frequent means of bringing the utterances of others into the journalistic text. More important to my concern here is the positioning of the journalist outside of the discourses he or she represents. Journalists position themselves outside of and behind the public discourses of newsmakers, politicians, accident victims, and entertainers about whom they write and whom they cite. They position themselves as orchestrators and commentators, not as central participants in the discourse.

Perhaps it is this positioning that leads journalists to take what would in academic circles be considered cavalier approaches to the citation of others. As Bell (1991) has pointed out, most journalistic texts are highly complex weavings of voices of others which are authored, edited, and re-authored normally so many times that it would be virtually impossible to identify the author of the text which appears in print. Nevertheless, a very large number of these texts appear under the single byline of an authoring journalist. Academic students who produced texts using journalistic practices of multiple appropriation of sources with minimal citation on the one hand and with rewriting of "direct quotations" on the other would be dismissed for unethical conduct.

Advertisers form yet a third community of practice in which the author of the texts we see stands entirely out of the picture. We virtually never see the author of advertising copy, nor could we guess who he or she might be. The voices in advertisements may often be attributed to known or at least knowable real persons, and yet the texts attributed to them are clearly written as copy by the advertiser who remains, like the Wizard, behind a curtain animating the whole show. More often, of course, the texts of advertising are fictions, little dramas, and narratives mixed together with slogans, brand names, and logos in a weave in which it is virtually impossible to make any connection at all between the authorial work of real persons and the fictional entities presented to us in the advertisements.

Taken from this point of view, I argue that these three communities of practice—academics, journalists, and advertisers—speak among each other and to us as audiences in three highly distinctive ways. These three discourses or social languages (Gee 1999) differ from each other in significant linguistic practices as greatly as do the historically named languages English, Chinese, and Japanese. Or to put it conversely, academics writing in English, Chinese, and Japanese are more *like* each other in their social language or academic discourse; journalists in England, Japan, and Italy are more *like* each other in their positioning of themselves in respect to newsmakers; and advertisers in Canada, France, and Malaysia are more *like* each other in their cavalier use of text and their characteristic obscuring of the ownership of those texts than are all the people who speak and write English, or Japanese, or Chinese, or German.

Perhaps not only from the point of view of intellectual property but certainly from that point of view, the relevant domain for the analysis of linguistic practice is the social language of a community of practice—academics, journalists, advertisers, lawyers, doctors, and so forth—not the historically grounded language of the nation state or of the cultural or ethnic group.

The ownership of the commodity/sign brings national and corporate power into common discourses. My second interest in intellectual property is in the commodity/sign. As I have indicated above, the commodity/sign has come to be a central form of intellectual property in the global commodified economy of fast food restaurants, electronics goods, and fashion. Recently in England I was told of a restaurant which is being enjoined by Kentucky Fried Chicken against the use of their name: "Ken's Tuck-in Fried Chicken." I am personally on the side of Ken.

When legal jurisdictions give ownership rights to corporate or individual owners to the control of commodity/signs—logos, brand names, and slogans, but also styles, appearances, and images—they produce a systematic distortion of normal processes of discourse within which one appropriates words and ideas to shape them anew. As Coombe (1998: 26) puts it, "[t]he law legitimizes new sources of cultural authority by giving the owners of intellectual property priority in struggles to fix social meaning."

The crucial issue here is that the tools of our common discourses are the words, phrases, ideas, and images of our linguistic and discursive commons.

While they may be historically charged with meanings and negotiated in social interactions, we use the semiotic means available to us—the language, the words, the gestures, and styles—to create our own being within our life worlds as well as to contest or struggle against disadvantageous positionings. What happens when the semiotic means of our day-to-day communication are protected by intellectual property is that new forces come into play that go far beyond the Gricean maxims of being relevant and meaningful in our social interactions. Again, as Coombe (1998: 51) puts it, "Intellectual property laws, by prohibiting the reproduction of vital cultural texts, disenable us from subjecting those texts to critical scrutiny and transformative appropriation. Because these texts are constitutive of the cultural milieu in which we live, constructing many of the social salient realities we recognize, their status as exclusive properties that cannot be reproduced without consent and compensation operates to constrain communication within, through, and about the media that surround us."

In sum, my interests in intellectual property and multilingualism stem from two areas of concern. In the first place, I argue that the ownership of text and the indication of the ownership of these texts through citation and attribution is not governed by any universal legal or moral principles. Instead, I argue that practices for citation and attribution vary across communities of practices, even within what must be called the same language group if we take "language" to mean the modernist concept of named, national language—English, Japanese, German. In the second place, I argue that a particularly postmodern form of semiotics—the commodity/sign—is rapidly moving to occupy center stage in contemporary discourse, and because these commodity/signs are owned intellectual properties, this development amounts to a significant reconstitution of at least one important field of discourse. Taken together, these two issues force us to reconsider what "multilingualism" might mean in the globalized, transnational semiotic spaces within which many of us move.

From infant holophrasis to postmodernist corporate holophrasis. I have played with a lot of terms to try to characterize the sort of discourse in which I have an interest here. Kress and Van Leeuwen (1996) are interested in multimodal discourses as part of their critical social semiotics, and there is much of what I am interested in that is multimodal—involving text, image, and sound. But for my interest in brand names, logos, shop signs, and the like, there is something almost nondiscursive about the ways in which meanings are coded. I thought for a while I might call it nonsyntactic discourse, as that would capture the observation that, on the whole, the signs with which I began and in which I am interested appear largely as single words or short phrases.

That thought recalled for me the interest in children's language for which the term "holophrastic" language was coined some decades ago. What is captured with the term holophrastic is the notion that a single utterance carries a full pragmatic load without the complex syntactic niceties of the language that develops later. "Share" can be read as holophrastic for saying "Give some of that to me," in contrast to "some," which is read by the caregivers as the child saying "I will give some of that to you" (Scollon 1976). Central to the idea of holophrastic language in children's discourse is the necessity for caregivers and others to engage in sometimes rather imaginative acts of interpretation. Very little is specified in the holophrase; much depends on the goodwill, interest, and engaged personal involvement of the interpreter, normally the mother or other caregiver in the data most commonly reported.

A crucial difference, however, between the "share" and "some" of the one-year-old child and the "Collage," "chorizo," "trend corner," and "Mobby" signs with which I began is that the child's utterances are oral—literacy is not yet a possibility—and strongly contextualized in the ongoing social interactions between the child and caregivers. But the signs in which I have an interest are visual semiotic displays in which shape, color, fonts, and design are as important as the words used and the contextualization is that of the "increasingly comfortable streets" of commercial discourse.

To capture what I would like to talk about, I will use the term "visual holophrastic discourse." That is, it is the many moments in contemporary commodified social life when utterances in the form of signs, logos, brand names, and the like are displayed as holophrasitic utterances given to be engaged in interpretatively by the personal interest of the consumer. Visual holophrastic discourse is, I would argue, one of the central forms of contemporary multilingualism. What language, after all, is "SONY®" in?

Visual holophrastic discourse is a complex matter, so for the moment I only want to suggest a few quite salient properties that I would hope would not be taken as anything like a definitive or exhaustive analysis. Visual holophrastic discourse is:

Multimoda—the linguistic elements from words to slogan phrases appear in distinctive and invariable fonts, colors, semiotic orientations to other texts and images. Often they also carry a superordinate symbol such as ® or ™ to indicate their legal status.

Disarticulated from national language of origin—one finds French signs in Japan, Italian signs in Hong Kong, English in Norway, or Spanish in Germany. In many cases it seems that it is *distance from* a national origin that gives power to visual holophrastic discourse, not *location within* a national environment.

Made-up orthographies—the word "clean" in *Kleenex®*, like many other examples of visual holophrastic discourses, stands out by its distortion of standard phonologies or at least spelling practices.

Nonsyntactic—it is impossible to argue that a holophrase represents any unique syntactic process of deletion. SONY® cannot be asserted to be derived from "Buy a SONY® product" or "This is a SONY®.

Nonpragmatic—in like manner, it is impossible to argue that a holophrase represents any unique pragmatic function such as an imperative to buy.

Minimally discursive—consequently, such commercial holophrases are minimally discursive in that there are only tenuous contextualization cues or indicators of cohesion within the broader texts of "comfortable streets" or labeled products. This is not to say that there is no semiotic structure of interpretation, only that the processes of interpretation are as yet very little understood through traditional formal analysis.

Simultaneously multilingua—in many cases the multilingualism that occurs within visual holophrastic discourse is simultaneous. We see French and Japanese, German and English, Chinese and Italian within the same sign, not as a code-switched sequence as has been studied within other forms of linear discourse.

Owned property—finally, these holophrases are to a great extent owned properties. Everything in the holophrase including its characteristic coloration, font, and design are protected.

Contemporary multilingualism stands largely outside of contemporary linguistic analysis. I conclude by saying that when we consider the implications of intellectual property for discourse analysis, at least two themes need to be understood. First, the main domains of linguistic analysis must be discourses or social languages—those of academics, journalism, advertising, law, medicine, education, and so on—not the language derived from the historical modern nation states. Second, visual holophrastic discourse is a domain of language use that is rapidly growing and yet remains largely outside of our common theories, methodologies, and domains of interest in both the study of language and the teaching of language.

To bring this to ground a bit, I can't prove it, but my own first experiences outside the sphere of my native language would suggest that the ability to work out which of the signs shows the way to the toilet in a foreign city is a more urgent need for the traveling would-be multilingual than the correct translation of "culture" into Chinese or even than the most idiomatic way to respond to "Good morning, how are you?"

On a somewhat more elevated plane, if we come to the issue with a concern for linguistic analysis, even if that interest is in real world applications, we find that many of the issues raised here tend to be sidestepped in contemporary linguistic and discursive analysis. On the question of citation and attribution, we tend to excessively simplify the matter by trying to say things like, "[i]n English we use a verb of saying such as 'said,' followed by a comma, a quotation mark and then the cited bit of text exactly as it was originally written or spoken followed by a closing quotation mark." My data show that this hardly ever happens in this way in English, and if we just look across the way into other social languages, we see that journalists are doing very different things—as are advertisers within their domain. Worse, of course, is that our students are likely to have read a great deal more advertising copy and journalistic text than they ever will read academic text.

If we look at the visual holophrastic discourse that surrounds our every trip to the supermarket or to a restaurant or, for that matter, decorates our homes and the objects we use from moment to moment to live our lives, we find ourselves somewhat theoretically bankrupt in trying to talk about it. What *do* we do with a form of language that is multimodal, disarticulated from the nation of origin, which appears in made-up orthographies, with language that is both nonsyntactic and nonpragmatic, that is minimally discursive and cohesive, simultaneously multilingual (if I can borrow back that term for a moment), and which is owned by corporate interests who can bring legal action against us for misusing it?

What does it mean to a sociolinguist with an interest in visual holophrastic discourse that much of this discourse consists of owned intellectual properties? Perhaps ultimately for me the most important issue is that the study of this highly significant discursive phenomenon remains an analytical backwater. This is quite simply an outcome of the difficulty of making reference to these properties within our own academic discourses. I have written about visual holophrastic discourse in this paper. In the oral version given at the Georgetown Round Table I somewhat cavalierly used scanned images of pages of a book that on the copyright pages says:

I have made printed overhead transparencies from the images residing electronically in my computer. All of this is in violation of the law. The guidelines for submission for publication say that nothing can appear for which permission has not been secured. This means that in the printed version of this paper I had to do one of two things: (1) secure permission to use the images and pay the licensing fees or (2) substitute textual descriptions for the images. From a rhetorical point of view, my argument is most likely substantially limited by the pallid textual descriptions of vivid color images used herein.

The analysis of visual holophrastic discourse requires work with visual images recorded in photographs and in some cases scanned into electronic format. The presentation of this sort of analysis is sapped by the complexity of securing permissions for use, and barred in most cases by the prohibitive cost of licensed use. Yet once again linguistic and discursive analysis retreats into the alphabetic textual production of alphabetic textual analyses couched in monolingual strings of national languages. My own problem in this text exemplifies the tremendous significance in contemporary of the ownership of the commodity/signs of contemporary discourse.

References

Anderson, Benedict. 1991. *Imagined communities*. London: Verso.
Bell, Allan. 1991. *The language of the news media*. Oxford: Basil Blackwell.
Billig, Michael. 1995. *Banal nationalism*. London: Sage.
Chouliaraki, Lilie, and Norman Fairclough. 1999. *Discourse and late modernity*. Edinburgh: Edinburgh University Press.
Coombe, Rosemary J. 1998. *The cultural life of intellectual properties: Authorship, appropriation, and the law*. Durham: Duke University Press.
Fairclough, Norman. 1992. *Discourse and social change*. Cambridge: Polity Press.
Gee, James Paul. 1999. *An introduction to discourse analysis*. London: Routledge.
Graphic-sha. 1993. *Marks-logos*. Tokyo: Graphic-sha.
Harper's Index. *Harper's,* February 1999, 298 (1785): 13.
Illich, Ivan. 1981. *Shadow work*. Boston: Boyard.
Kress, Gunther, and Theo van Leeuwen. 1996. *Reading images: The grammar of visual design*. London: Routledge.
Mallon, Thomas. 1989. *Stolen words: Forays into the origins and ravages of plagiarism*. New York: Ticknor and Fields.
Mannheim, Bruce, and Dennis Tedlock. 1995. *The dialogic emergence of culture*. Urbana: University of Illinois Press.
Musson, Gill, and Laurie Cohen. 1996. The enterprise discourse: An empirical analysis of its effects. Paper presented at "Communication and Culture: China in the 21st Century," Beijing University, August.
Patterson, Lyman Ray. 1968. *Copyright in historical perspective*. Nashville: Vanderbilt University Press.
Scollon, Ron. 1976. *Conversations with a one year old: A case study of the developmental foundation of syntax*. Honolulu: University Press of Hawaii.
Scollon, Ron. In press. Plagiarism. Special issue, Lexicon for the new millennium. *Journal of Linguistic Anthropology* 9(1): 184-186.
Scollon, Ron. Forthcoming. Intertextuality across communities of practice: Academics, journalism, and advertising. In Carol Lynn Moder and Aida Martinovic-Zic (eds.), *Discourse across languages and cultures*. Philadelphia: John Benjamins.

Note

1. The research on which this study is based was supported in part by a grant from the Hong Kong University Grants Council "Plagiarization as Social Practice: Discourse Representation in Contemporary Hong Kong Chinese and English Public Discourse." Ron Scollon, PI, Suzanne Scol-

lon, AI, and Vicki Yung, AI, and from the Research Committee, City University of Hong Kong "Literate Design and the Implied Reader: Hong Kong, Guangzhou, and Kunming," Ron Scollon, PI, Suzanne Scollon, AI, Yuling Pan, AI, and Rachel Scollon, AI. I would like to thank my colleagues and research assistants on these projects for many fruitful discussions of the ideas I present here. None should be thought responsible for the infelicities of statement and conceptualization that remain.

The removal of Arturo: An immigration case nightmare

Roger W. Shuy
Georgetown University

Many scholars have argued that linguists ought to be missionaries, taking linguistic knowledge to other areas of daily life such as medical communication, criminal and civil law, diplomacy, advertising, negotiation, and therapy. The case described here, an immigration hearing, should make it clear that there is much work to be done by linguists in the real world of immigration procedures.

Recent research has made a strong case for the problems facing non-experts in administrative hearings and trials. For example, Garcia (1995) concludes that women are disadvantaged in the mediation process, because cooperation is the highest normative value in this process, and women, who are innately more cooperative than men and whose role is to facilitate communication, build consensus, and actively listen, are bound to bear the bias of the system. Likewise, Conley and O'Barr (1998), studying small claims courts, show how the demanded format of these courts exerts its power by transforming the claimants' disputes into new and unfamiliar thought processes, concepts, and words. Matoesian's recent work (1993) focuses on language features used by attorneys in rape trials to control witnesses, such as question forms, topic management, evaluative commentary, and challenges to the witness's capacity for knowledge.

The immigration case described here is a classic in the unfairness and bias that the court system can produce when it is not kept in check by linguistic analysis of the procedures followed by the courts. It is a real case, still active, and one that is an embarrassment to the legal system.

Background. In 1979, like many others from Mexico, a man we will call Arturo entered the United States illegally, or, as Immigration calls it, EWI (entered without inspection). Again like many others, he began to do agricultural work. He eventually married, began to raise a family, and lived a better life than he would have had in Mexico.

In 1988 he benefited from a special amnesty program that allowed undocumented persons like him, who could prove that they were in the country for a certain number of years and were doing agricultural work, to apply for green cards.

Arturo did so and was approved. Things seemed to be going very well for him and his young family.

Then, one night in 1991, Arturo got drunk and broke a plate-glass store window in a small town in the state of Washington. He was arrested, spent the night in jail, and paid a fine. A few months later, in Medford, Oregon, Arturo applied for the second stage of the amnesty program, called "adjustment of status." This involved filling out an application form, which included many questions such as, "Were you a member of the Nazi party in Germany between 1939 and 1945?" and "Are you a sexual deviant?" Among the questions was the following: "Have you ever been arrested or convicted of a crime?" This form was filled out for Arturo by what he later described as "an overworked person" in a Medford social services office. Possibly in an effort to be clear and to save time, this social services worker simplified the questions for Arturo. However it was read to him, he took the question to mean, "Are you in trouble with the police?" Since he'd already paid his fine, he assumed that he was not, so he answered "no."

In 1995, for reasons that are still not clear, the Immigration and Naturalization Service (INS) discovered this crime of fraud and decided to rescind Arturo's residency. He did not understand what had occurred. He had the right to appeal the recission, but did not since he did not understand it. He still had his green card, so he continued to work.

By 1997, Arturo really had his life together. By then he had three children, all born in the United States and, therefore, U.S. citizens. He had been working for a chain of Mexican restaurants and had been promoted several times. He was earning pretty good money. But then, disaster struck.

Arturo's wife, Isabel, had a brother who was allegedly a drug dealer. The police, along with the INS, came looking for this brother at Arturo's house. In a terrifying raid, they did not find the brother but violently arrested Arturo and Isabel while the children looked on. The oldest boy, about five at the time, soon began to have nightmares stemming from the raid and continues to have them to this day. Isabel, who was undocumented, was wrenched from her children and deported immediately to Mexico. Arturo was allowed out on bond but placed into deportation proceedings on the ground that he was unlawfully present in the United States.

Arturo went to see an advisor at his church, who told him that his wife should not try to come back from Mexico, and that Arturo should seek a procedure called "cancellation of removal." This is a "remedy," as INS calls it, available to certain undocumented people who can prove that they have been in the United States for at least ten years and have family members who will be harmed if the person is deported ("removed").

Arturo qualified for this remedy because his children are U.S. citizens. Cancellation of removal is normally difficult to win because the 1996 law by which it operates places a very high standard on "hardship to a U.S. citizen." For example, if the deportee's child is seriously ill with a disease that cannot be treated in a developing country, the applicant sometimes has a chance of succeeding. The issue at court is normally just how bad the hardship is. In addition to having to prove "hardship to a U.S. citizen," the applicant must be deemed to be of good moral character.

Normally a hearing is set to investigate whether or not such hardships exist and whether or not the applicant is of good moral character. Immigration cases usually involve only the immigration judge, a lawyer for the INS who serves as prosecutor, and the person facing deportation, sometimes with a lawyer. Arturo was represented by a lawyer for his hearing on December 1, 1998, but there is little evidence from the hearing that this lawyer had done any research into the well-being of Arturo's children. There is little evidence, in fact, that he did any preparation at all.

It is common for the INS lawyer to ask hard questions and to assume guilt, much as prosecutors do in criminal cases. In Arturo's hearing, however, the INS lawyer said very little. Instead, almost all of the questioning was done by the judge, who focused almost entirely on one issue: whether Arturo had helped his wife return illegally from Mexico. Arturo denied this charge over and over again. There was no evidence that he had even encouraged Isabel to re-enter the country, much less that he had assisted her to do so. Nevertheless, the judge concluded that Arturo was lying, which enabled the judge to conclude that Arturo was not of good moral character. He was therefore determined to be not eligible for cancellation.

It should also be noted that often when persons face deportation/removal, they are first offered something called "voluntary departure." If the applicant agrees to this, it saves the INS the expense of sending them home, and such persons must leave within a specified number of days. Arturo was offered voluntary departure three times during the hearing. He rejected it the first two times it was suggested, but by the end of the hearing, broken and confused, he finally not only accepted it but also unknowingly waived his right to appeal.

In April 1999 I was asked by the law firm now representing Arturo to examine and analyze the tape-recorded deportation hearing in order to determine issues of clarity and fairness. This law firm has sent in a request to "reopen" the matter. The following reports some of the analysis I submitted in this case.

Overview of the analysis. I began by addressing the major question, asked repeatedly by the judge: whether or not Arturo had aided his wife to return to the U.S. illegally after her deportation. I also analyzed the judge's conversational strategies with Arturo during the hearing. In my declaration, I noted that the judge refused to accept Arturo's repeated statements that he did not assist his wife to reenter the United States, that the judge attacked Isabel's character, that he asked confusing questions, that he reframed Arturo's responses to mean something other than what Arturo said, and that he frequently interrupted Arturo while he attempted to frame his answers. The judge demonstrated his intolerance with Arturo's unfamiliarity with the mechanics of the hearing itself as well as with Arturo's cultural and linguistic difficulties in negotiating the judicial system. The judge also evinced inappropriate emotion, in this case anger, apparently provoked by Arturo's unwillingness to accept voluntary departure at the outset of the hearing.

I further noted that the contents of the hearing indicate that the judge had prejudged the outcome. He had decided in advance to determine that Arturo was not of good moral character and he refused to consider any testimony to the contrary. In the process, the judge refused to hear any evidence of extreme hardship that would be suffered by Arturo's children.

Did Arturo aid in his wife's illegal reentry into the United States? Taking passages from the tape-recorded hearing, I isolated the following exchanges that show how the judge never gets Arturo to admit that he assisted, encouraged, or even knew that Isabel was returning to the United States illegally:

> Judge: Did you tell her to come back to the United States?
>
> Arturo: No, I don't tell her. I tell her to wait so I can see what I do here to bring back legally. I tried to do something you know.
>
> Judge: So when you talked to your wife (by phone), you knew that your wife and that baby needed to be together?
>
> Arturo: Yes, but I don't want to my kids go to Mexico 'cause there's too hard for them to be together.
>
> Judge: What you're telling me is a bit contradictory. If you told your wife to wait in Mexico while you tried to figure it out, but you don't want your kids in Mexico.

As it turns out, Isabel's sudden deportation came at a time when she was breast feeding her baby. Arturo then sent all three children to his sister-in-law in San Francisco. The sister tried to feed the baby from a bottle but the baby would not take it. The judge, ignoring this hardship and realizing that he could not deport a child born in the United States, played on this issue to build what he called "circumstantial evidence" that Arturo was lying.

> Judge: The babies need to be with their mother but you're saying you just told your wife, wait, I'll just try to figure something out.
>
> Arturo: I was talking to my lawyer here.

Judge: You knew it could take a month, a week, six months, a long time to straighten out a deportation.

Arturo: Well I had no idea.

Judge: Well you had no idea but you had an idea that the baby needed to go with your wife, right?

Arturo: Well I tried to send it with my brother's wife.

Judge: But your brother's wife is not going to breast feed.

Arturo: I know, but they can give a bottle or something. I know there are other ways to survive, but the baby when they give it the bottle, her body doesn't take it.

Judge: So you knew that your wife and the baby had to be reunited, correct?

Arturo: Yeah.

The fact that it was in the best interest of the baby to be with her mother is indisputable here. But the judge disassociates this dilemma from any time frame. Arturo agrees that he knew that at some time they needed to be reunited. Since the judge does not specify the time, it could appear that Arturo admitted that he had encouraged his wife to reenter. The judge continues:

Judge: So you're telling me you didn't tell your wife that she should get together with the baby? You just told her to wait in Mexico?

Arturo: I tell her to wait a little bit so I can see what can I do myself here, like I told you.

Judge: That doesn't sound realistic. You'd been arrested and been placed in jail.

Arturo: Yeah, for nothing, that I didn't do nothing.

Judge: Well if you didn't do anything, how do you think you could get that straightened out in a few days or a few weeks even?

Arturo: I have not in mind but to get together in a few weeks here.

Judge: Okay then, the two things don't match up. What you're telling me doesn't match up. You told me you told your wife to wait because you're trying to take care of it. But you got two things. You don't want the children to go to Mexico, but you know that your wife and the children need to be together. Your plan to get your wife back into the U.S. you're saying was going to be legal but there was no time frame. You didn't know when that would happen, right?

Arturo: Yes, I don't know how to take it but I was with some lawyer and I tell everything, how it happened. They give me a phone number from a lawyer here that maybe can try to help me.

Judge: You're getting off the point because you're not getting anywhere closer to getting your wife back in.

Here the judge appears to be telling Arturo that his experience of being thrown in jail for doing nothing should tell him that his case is hopeless. Unfortunately, this may be true. The judge is building his case that there is conflict between the fact that Arturo told his wife to wait and that she needed to be with her children. It is a dilemma, but hardly a reason to accuse Arturo of influencing his wife's decision.

The oddest part of the judge's argument, however, is his statement that Arturo had "no time frame," meaning that Arturo did not know that immigration was a bureaucratic mess and would take much longer than Arturo might imagine. How this can be an argument that Arturo told his wife to reenter is seriously problematic. Finally, the judge accuses Arturo of wandering off topic, which is difficult to prove from what was actually said. One begins to suspect that "off topic" means only that Arturo did not say what the judge wanted him to say.

Finally, the judge changed his strategy somewhat, moving from what Arturo may have told his wife to what Arturo thought Isabel might do:

Judge: You say that she told you she crossed at Tijuana. Now you still maintain you didn't want her to cross, right?

Arturo: Yes.

Judge: She could just cross and say she's a citizen and get back? You didn't think that she could do that?

Arturo: I don't know that she can do that or not.

Judge: Did you think she might be able to?

Arturo: I don't know. I never know that she's going to Tijuana.

Judge: Okay, well would you want her to enter illegally in Tecate? Did you think that she might try to cross, since the children were in Tehachape?

Arturo: Well—

Judge: (interrupting) Didn't you think that she would try to cross to get together with her child who was about 150 to 180 miles away from Tecate? Don't you think that she was going to try to get there?

Arturo: Well I—

Judge: (interrupting) You did, didn't you?

Arturo: I never think she would do it.

Judge: A sick little child and that your family desired to be together. You didn't think that she was going to try that?

Arturo: Yeah, well uh—

Judge: (interrupting) So it wasn't important enough to her then. The mother wouldn't try to get together with her children. I'm starting not to believe you.

The judge here manages to ignore the fact that Arturo's not knowing whether or not his wife planned to reenter is actually consistent with his earlier statements that he did not tell her to reenter. If Arturo had told her this, he might also have told her how and where to do it. And if he had told her this, he would also think that she might do it.

Whether or not Arturo thought or believed Isabel might try to reenter, of course, is not an issue that bears on his good moral character. The judge does not accept Arturo's answers about what he thought any more that he accepted Arturo's answers about what he did. He stopped at this point, pointing out that he now had enough "circumstantial evidence" that Arturo "arranged for her to come in at Tehachape."

The judge's interviewing strategies. The judge's interviewing strategies framed the second prong of my analysis. It is understood that the requirement of a judge's discourse is that it be fair and impartial. Five of the judge's discourse strategies formed a stark contrast to this understanding:

- his insulting and shaming of both Arturo and the absent Isabel,
- his frequent interruptions of Arturo as he tried to respond,
- his attacking Arturo's responses as off-point,
- his taking advantage of Arturo's lack of skill in the legal register, and
- his venting anger at Arturo.

Some of the earlier quotes have shown how the judge shamed Arturo when he accused him of neglecting his wife by letting her stay in Mexico while her babies badly needed her. The judge took this shaming even a step further, however, as follows:

Insulting and shaming Arturo and his wife.
Judge: Now you think Tijuana is a dangerous place for a young woman to be?

Arturo: Yes.

Judge: Were you worried about your wife, sir?

Arturo: Of course.

Judge: But you didn't make any arrangements for her. You just let her go on her own. Whoever wanted to take advantage of her. You're the kind of husband that, she can take care of herself. Would you be worried about your wife, whether these kind of people might do something to her?

Arturo: Yes.

Judge: But you never discussed trying to help her then. The mother wouldn't try to get together with her children.

To this point, Arturo has denied encouraging, helping, or even believing that his wife would reenter. The judge's next ploy was to get Arturo to say that he *thought* she might try to reenter. This failed also. Now the judge resorts to shaming Arturo for not being man enough to care about his wife's well being and he shames Isabel by insinuating that by going through Tijuana, she is now a fallen or tarnished woman. Curiously enough, the judge's argument seems to be that Arturo was wrong *not* to tell Isabel to reenter the country.

Interrupting Arturo. In the passages cited above it has already been shown how the judge interrupts Arturo when he tries to respond to questions. The following example illustrates how the judge has no patience with Arturo's effort to answer, interrupting him constantly:

> Judge: So did you talk to your wife about taking the baby down to Mexico with her?
>
> Arturo: When she was in Mexico, I tell her I'm going to try to do something here to see because I never have idea—
>
> Judge: (interrupting) You're not answering my question. You told me that already. My question is, you have a six-month-old baby who is breast feeding.

The judge was quite aware that Isabel had been deported immediately after the raid on Arturo's house, while Arturo was taken to jail. Since there was no time for the couple to have discussed anything, his question to Arturo was confusing at best. Arturo appears to have taken "did you talk to your wife" to mean on the telephone, so he starts to give the judge his answer once again. The judge will have none of this and then, amazingly enough, interrupts and restates his question in a form that is not only different from his original question but grammatically meaningless, not a question at all.

Attacking Arturo's answers as off-point. As noted in the previous exchange, a common theme of the judge's questions included the accusation that Arturo was off point in his answers. Such a strategy is likely to confuse anyone, but especially a person unfamiliar with the rigid format of the judicial process and whose culture and language are different from it. The judge continues this practice, as the following examples show:

> Judge: On the other hand, your plan to get your wife back into the U.S., you're saying was going to be legal. There was no time frame. You didn't know when that would happen, right?
>
> Arturo: Yes, I don't know how to take it but I was with some lawyer and I tell everything, how it happened. And they give me a phone number from a lawyer here that maybe can help me.

> Judge: You're getting off the point because you're not getting anywhere closer to getting your wife back in.

Again the judge accuses Arturo of being ignorant about the slow nature of immigration procedures. In this, he is probably quite right. But when Arturo tries to explain what he tried to do about his ignorance of this process (getting a lawyer to help him), the judge claims that he is "off the point." One can speculate that this impatient judge was not happy that Arturo went to a lawyer and would prefer that immigrants simply obey his suggestion to accept voluntary departure and not to take up valuable court time and expense. There is no need to even speculate, however, about the judge's impatience in the following example:

> Judge: But you didn't make any arrangements for her. You just let her go on her own. Whoever wanted to take advantage of her, you're the kind of husband that, she can take care of herself, is that what you did?

> Arturo: We never discussed—

> Judge: (interrupting) I asked you a question. I didn't ask what you discussed.

Apparently the only acceptable answer to the judge's question is for Arturo to admit that he is "that kind of husband." But this was not clear to Arturo, who attempted to begin an answer, which from his previous responses was heading in the direction of explaining that he and his wife never made any arrangements at all about her return to the United States. This interrupted, three-word effort receives the insulting response, "I asked you a question," as though Arturo was not aware of what a question actually is.

Taking advantage of Arturo's lack of skill in the legal register. Like many people, immigrant or not, Arturo does not have the skill required by the courts involving reporting exact time issues. Not surprisingly, he had spoken to his wife by telephone several times while she was in Mexico. Now, months later, he found it difficult to recall exactly how many times they spoke and what they said to each other in each call. Most of us, including the judge, would have the same problem.

> Judge: So they were in Tehachape four days and then your wife got there, correct?

> Arturo: Well, something like that. I don't have—

> Judge: (interrupting) Not something like that. It was that. You de-
> cided this way, sir. You rejected my advice and we're going this
> way. Don't talk while I'm talking. We may go on a long time.

Throughout the hearing, Arturo evidences difficulty recalling exact details, especially concerning time. He often punctuates his answers with hedges, such as "I think," "I wanted to do something," "I don't know how," "I believe it was. . . ," and "I was thinking to." Such hedging is to be expected of non-experts in the face of hostile questioning such as is often found in immigration hearings. It is only natural to protect oneself against the accusation of mis-speaking by hedging in this way. Although Arturo may speak this way normally, when the stakes are as high as they were here, the need to hedge was amplified considerably.

Venting his anger at Arturo. The judge is obviously angry at this point. Arturo had rejected the judge's advice to take voluntary departure, causing this whole hearing to take place. Arturo is not precise on his reporting of times. This infuriates the judge while providing him, at the same time, with small bits that he can eventually reassemble as evidence of Arturo's alleged lying. The judge continues this approach, as follows:

> Judge: And the second discussion, what did you talk about
> then?
>
> Arturo: I tell her the kids were in San Francisco with her
> cousins.
>
> Judge: The second time you told me that you told her they were
> already in Tehachape.
>
> Arturo: Sir, I tell you that they arrive in San Francisco.
>
> Judge: That was the first time. You said previously, that you
> told her they were in Tehachape. Now maybe it was the third
> time.
>
> Arturo: When I tell the kids were in San Francisco, it was on
> the second time we called each other.
>
> Judge: You're changing your testimony.
>
> Arturo: We talk to each other a few times. I don't remember ex-
> actly how many times. But I never tell her to come back be-
> cause I know, do you imagine, I know—

Judge: (interrupting) This is not your show. It's mine. You're going to answer my questions the way that I ask them. Now you didn't answer that question. You wanted to go on to something else. I find you're evasive of my questions. Now when did you tell your wife that your children were in Tehachape? That's the question. You remember that you didn't tell her to come back. You remember that she was in Tecate. You remember quite a bit when it serves you to remember it.

It is difficult to describe the judge's meandering thoughts at this point. Again he claims that the question was really one thing while it was clearly something else. He interrupts Arturo's attempts to answer. He accuses Arturo of being deliberately evasive and changing his testimony when Arturo was desperately trying to recall exact times and conversations. Meanwhile, it had become obvious to Arturo that the central issue was whether or not he had assisted or encouraged his wife to re-enter the country illegally, or had even imagined that she might. So he tries to direct his answers along this line. This is considered evasive by the judge, who becomes furious again:

Judge: Okay, I've had enough. I'm going to find circumstantially. One, circumstances don't lie; people lie. We can't always draw conclusions from circumstances but I'm going to draw the conclusion that you sent your children to Tehachape and you arranged for your wife, and that's the end of this case. And you decided to blow off your opportunity to keep your record clean enough so that you could get a visa in the future. So you'll have to fight with this now.

Arturo: Like I told you, your honor—

Judge: (interrupting) I didn't ask you to speak.

Arturo: I will not speak.

Judge: I find that you're eligible based on the children, but not eligible because you don't possess good moral character.

Conclusions. As noted earlier, the two issues that might mitigate a deportation of this type are (1) the hardship such a removal might place on U.S. citizens, in this case Arturo's children, and (2) the good moral character of the applicant. The judge could not find reason to reject the matter of hardship to the children so he constructed, by his confusing questions, his insulting and shaming remarks, and his reframing Arturo's words to appear to mean something else, a scenario by which he could follow his prejudged conclusion that Arturo was lying. Then, if it is true that Arturo was lying, he must have assisted, encouraged, or believed that his wife would reenter the United States illegally, leading to the inevitable conclusion that he obviously was not of good moral character.

In his book *The Language of Judges,* Solan (1993) describes the teachings of the late U.S. Supreme Court justice Benjamin Cardozo. Solan points out that it is rare, indeed, for judges to write about the problems of judging, at least not while they are still on the bench. Solan reports that Cardozo described the tension between the need for the law to be both sufficiently flexible to accommodate new cases as they arise and sufficiently rigid to maintain its predictive power: "If the law is not flexible enough, then it is doomed to irrelevance and to becoming the source of injustice. If the law is too flexible, then it becomes so unstable that it fails to define with any reliability people's rights and obligations"(Solan 1993: 12).

The judge in this case seems to illustrate neither of these tensions. For this judge, there is no flexibility in the courtroom exchange. Nor is there any flexibility in terms of bending the rigid register and format of proceedings involving a non-native speaker of English. Likewise, there is no flexibility in judging, with no outward evidence, the falsehood of the statements made by Arturo at this hearing. There is no flexibility of letting Arturo, unfamiliar with the rigid question-answer format of a hearing, to tell his story in his own way. Conley and O'Barr (1998) point out the inequalities of courtroom procedures caused by the asymmetries of power and patriarchy of judges. Although their research focused on the language of women in the courtroom, the failure to be assertive and rational rather than uncertain, deferential, and relational obtain in the immigration hearing, regardless of the gender of the applicant.

The judge's handling of this immigration hearing is not simply unfair and partial; it is truly outrageous. There is no reasonable excuse for the judge to vent is anger at Arturo for not accepting his earlier advice to him to take voluntary departure. There is no reasonable excuse for the judge to accuse Arturo of not caring about the welfare of his children and his wife. There is no reasonable excuse for the judge to have suggested that since Isabel was allegedly in Tijuana by herself, she must now be a tarnished woman. Finally, there is no reasonable excuse for the judge to reject Arturo's many consistent statements that he did not encourage his wife to reenter the United States illegally. That the judge could conclude that a man is lying based on the content of this hearing is an embarrassment to the judicial system. This case also should be instructive to linguists as a way for us to become involved in the uses and misuses of language in immigration cases.

REFERENCES

Conley, John, and William O'Barr. 1998. *Just words.* Chicago: University of Chicago Press.
Garcia, Angela. 1995. The problematices of representation in community mediation hearings: Implications for mediation practice. *Journal of Sociology and Social Welfare* 56: 818–835.
Matoesian, Gregory. 1993. *Reproducing rape.* Chicago: University of Chicago Press.
Solan, Lawrence. 1993. *The language of judges.* Chicago: University of Chicago Press.